WHEN IN DOUBT...

CHOOSE FREEDOM

— A Pursuit of Liberty and Steak —

Fitz Conrad

For Mama,

Who taught me to read
one snowy afternoon...

Table of Contents

Acknowledgements

It is understated to note that I have had more than my fair share of fun in this life, and a great many have contributed to that ride to this point. Whether through good advice, inspirations dignified or zany, keeping me out of trouble, or just keeping in touch, I have been blessed in friends and family. Some have passed away, and some have passed beyond continued contact, but you yet have my heartfelt thanks, and best wishes.

To The Summerset Fish Club for their steadfast friendship over the miles and years, and to the brothers of El Cid '83.

To the Diamondcutters of squadron VS-30, and Skipper Phil Voss, with whom it was a true honor to fly.

To Walton Sun editor Gwen Break, for the opportunity to write, for which I am particularly grateful.
To the Belles of Cape Coral, with my abiding affection.
To my sister Kathryn, and her guy Chip, for all the laughs, fun, and inspiration.

To Baja, for her love and support.

To Jeff and Jay, and their wonderful families.

To my grandmother Jessie, for her wisdom, and for her enduring curiosity.

To my grandmother Mabel, for her grace and boundless love.

To my aunt Deedle, for always keeping an eye on me.

To Lou and Wes, my dear friends of long years, and practitioners of the best in medicine.

To my pal Lisa, one damn funny gal.

To Jerry, a great guy and dependable hand in all weather fair or foul.

To Paul, whose politically incorrect humor, is exceeded only by his big heart.

To Carlos, coach and friend, who is still trying to teach me patience.

Special thanks to Todd West, friend, advisor, colleague, and co-conspirator, in an undisclosed location, and to Tammy, Cassidy, and Chloe, my adopted family. When the zombies come, set an extra place and save the couch for me.

Most special gratitude and love to the Old Man, from whom continues to flow more challenges, inspirations, insights, eccentricity, and surprises than I can reliably catalogue or match. Whether as a surgeon, pilot, farmer, sailor, writer, counselor, or thinker, my dad continues to cultivate a love of living that astounds and confounds those lucky enough to share in it. That will always remain my greatest inheritance.

To those who live in, and love the South, my homeland, which I in turn love more than I will ever be able to express.

And to my late-night editor. She knows who she is.

Forward

"We must be free not because we claim freedom,
but because we practice it."

William Faulkner

December 26, 2007

Boxing Day throughout the old empire and common-
wealths, a day otherwise nondescript and bereft of any
higher purpose than to take up space between Christmas
and the New Year, the annual nod to servants having transformed somewhere along the post-modern way into the
day to hit the malls for gift returns and great deals on next
year's decorations. A day of activity without too much serious business, of work for some but not many, and as good a
day as any other for reflection. On the day after Christmas
in a Florida panhandle emergency room, in rural mode a
world away from the swelling celebrations rising in South
Beach, and the thronging Yankee crowds washing like
mocking waves into Orlando, the day has a feel of contented
isolation, a big pleasant bowl of don't-give-a-damn. It's a
good day and we are all in a good humor, talking about
travels to come or just completed, who showed their ass at

the latest Christmas party, the funny episodes and mishaps with which small emergency rooms are replete, the latest round of who's seeing who, and the individual fears of the lurking menace, a viral gastroenteritis just now making the rounds, which shall lay your vulnerable correspondent low just three days hence.

Boxing Day, as good as any day to take aim, which is better than taking stock. Sitting and counting the little boxes of time and memory we have packed our lives into can be a lot of fun, in a rainy day, remember when, sort of way. But sometimes you need to slide a round into the chamber, adjust your sight, feel the sun on your back, and look for something to shoot. It is more fun to draw a bead than merely to count, and it makes the projected task one hell of a lot more interesting. Be he convenience store clerk or millionaire, though she be unhappy housewife or self-satisfied chat show tsarina, anyone may succumb to the weakness of spirit that transforms into a low-level aisle clerk or cubicle rat trying to hang on to finish his or her twenty. The goal becomes just to exist, and in doing so, being, which is to say joyful, deliberate existence, is dissipated for lack of interest. A real goal is what one wants, and must have before the shadows grow too long and the ghosts of dependency begin clanging their bedpans together. Brrr. The New Year is scant days away and will be great fun to celebrate but we pause, to give not too short a shrift to the page nearly turned. Does this past year merit such special attention, a redhead among the other kids that deserves a special attaboy from the podium? Or was it just the luck of this time that made this particular year the one that I will remember more than most and will celebrate long after the last cork pops in a few days? I suspect the latter, that this year was not so

much different as was the observer's perspective. Sometimes you just wake up and the air smells better, a fact you
notice above and beyond the debris strewn through the
yard from the big storm last night. In any case the damp,
unnaturally warm north Florida air our there in the scrub
darkness swirling around the Christmas lights and convenience stores seems more of a challenge, a big grin from
an old friend I could not yet have met, telling me it's time
for a new trip, a new story, and a fresh aim.

A lot has been said and written about mid life crises
as an acknowledged psychological phenomenon, and
snickered-over pageant of futile male juvenility. And really, who does not deep down believe that the antics of a
new sports car, secretary-mistress, and surprise stud ear-
ring under a balding head represents little but the insecu-
rities of a weaker mind? Do we however damn all course
changes, cataclysms, and revelations that just happen to
fall halfway around the track as similarly pitiable failings?
Can sometimes the great stretch-and-smile of fresh perspective healthily and happily coincide with the midway
mark?

The idea was flirted with a couple of months before
the holidays, chuckled about in half-seriousness and forgotten in the climactic crash of the football season and
gluttonous rush of the holidays. But here on Boxing Day
the challenge is one that will not depart the mind's eye,
but grins ever larger from the fog swirling past the garish
sign lighting up the parking lot. It is intimidating, ridiculous, uproarious, and just a bit scary. There is no point to
it whatsoever, making it paradoxically THE POINT. Or as
described sagely by the philosophers in the film *Animal
House*, 2007 demanded something really futile and stupid

be done on someone's part in 2008. And I might be just the guy to do it.

❖ ❖ ❖

Embarking into the nascent days of 2008 is among other things, boring. Oh not in a bad way, quite the contrary, in a utilitarian, rejuvenating, hibernating sort of languid contemplation. New Year's Day and college football has gone, and apart from the national championship game in the Superdome where LSU will blot out Ohio State, my sports interest has dialed back down to minimal. Politics usually get entertaining in the winter, especially in election years, and so the primary season is just weeks away, but not quite here. Work is work, with a few more coughs, colds, arthritis flares, and cases of cold weather malaise wandering through the doors at the several ER's where I hang out, but that is just a little more of the usual, nothing new, nothing interesting. Deep winter is the time of slow, where the cold sludges the mind and dulls the initiative, and so, I'm bored. One night at work, I sit and absent-mindedly kill a moment or two in the ER while waiting for lab results to return, and surf some of my favorite old sites. I love the style, feel, over-the-top splashy contrast and drama of the Lounge Era, the Cold War bongo aesthetic, the Space Age Populuxe hot dog, finger snapping cool of the late Fifties/ early Sixties, and one great place to immerse oneself in this is Greg Knight's Patio Culture web site, with all sorts of nifty and keen art work, locales, and collectibles to browse. One of the links there offered under the category "Route 66" is for the Big Texan Steak House in Amarillo, Texas. Opened in 1906, the tourist stop has become famous for the 72-ounce challenge, whereby the brave aspirant will be offered a 4-1/2 pound steak, to be eaten in front of the restaurant crowd, for free IF one completes it in an hour. Hmm. That got me to thinking in a big strategic way. To start with, I like steak. A born carnivore, it has become increasingly clear to me over the years and occasional PETA eruptions that the protest group is a knot of mind-controlled lackeys dealt by sinister forces that wish us ill, and that the explosive overgrowth from potentially uneaten farm animals could threaten the human hegemony on earth. It has been my longstanding personal policy to consume as many chickens, pigs, and cows as possible if for no other reason, that they will threaten humanity if allowed to breed unchecked. That, and they taste good. I had heard of these roadside, tourist trap kinds of places out West over the years, and never thought much on them, but now... in the boring part of the year, with the impetus of wanting to do something new and different, the possibility of this endeavor jumped into my brain and would not be dislodged. What if I could pull this off? Why would I even want to?

The answer to the first was easy, because I'm a dedicated carnivore and can eat a ridiculous amount of dead animal flesh without even thinking. The second question required more thought. The competition is an obvious stunt, inviting mere mortals into a bad odds gamble that their stomachs are as big as their eyes, that they won't be stuck with the $72 bill that comes with failure. It is a tourist gimmick for the greenhorns and tenderfoots back east, more precisely, the NORTH-east and Midwest. A southerner such as myself, who knows his way around mounds of pulled pork and tubs of cheese grits, would not arrive a layperson to such a challenge. In my professional capacity as physician, I have been heckled and bedeviled by colleagues and family for years about the evils of cholesterol, and the need to live a somber and austere culinary existence for decades so that I could achieve the reward of spending my dying years atop an endless succession of bedpans in the nursing home. Exciting as that has always sounded, I have nonetheless always tended toward the 'quality-of-life' side of the longevity debate. Working in American medicine as a physician for over a decade, I had heard countless lectures about seemingly innumerable pills that would peak and tweak the body's products and processes in such a way that patients may reach the afore-mentioned goal. Yes all the peer-reviewed, double-blinded literature (a great deal if not all of it funded by private corporations or the government, all with their own sales agendas) shows that taking the proper pills and altering one's diet to the point of twitching fits will afford one a few more sentient years with which to contemplate one's golf swing. But the by-product of this has been a furtherance of the erosion of American stoicism, and a generalized nervousness fueled by advertising ("You COULD die!") and doctors' aversion to helpful lawyers and their flaming cannonball lawsuits trying to win a nice cash prize for the poor widder woman whose chain-smoking, obese husband with a history of heart disease just could not... quite... reach...his cholesterol targets. No I never said that cholesterol and its effect were not real, just that the effect that had on society was at least as bad if not worse.

We are in such a politically correct age, where English lords and MTV have made public pronouncements that eschewing a tasty meat diet would help save the planet, and nervous, mousy women, wimpy men, and government drones all scurry to and fro to make dinner less fun. Maybe that was it, that pulling this off would be fun. But would there be no other serious motive here? The cattle industry is iconically American, with the legacy of the cowboy and wide-open spaces, a big, dripping, medium rare, charbroiled explosion of flavor as the reward for a hard-ridden, long and dusty trail. The cowboy deserved a good steak before blowing his earnings on redeye whiskey, poker, and dance hall girls, and doggone it, so do we all. The raising, transporting, preparing, and eating of cows still raised on this good earth of North America hearken us back to simpler days, and often to more valid standards, where the expected ideal was one of greater individual courage and achievement. And yet with our victory in World War II, the recognition of the so-called "American Century" put us in the cross-hairs for the rest of the world and made our grand existence the object of whining and nitpicking for the multitude of malcontents so happy to sponge off of the system that makes their chronic fussing possible.

In the dawning years of the 21st century, the heralded *and successful* American values of free will, capitalism, individual achievement, and downright pleasure have been under assault both here at home, and from abroad. From afar we were assailed by Islamofascist bombers and the cries and obfuscations of greedy and envious nations, or those frankly hostile to us. At home the nannies, do-gooders, and the deeply concerned have served as covers and fronts for wealth-redistributionists, liberals, progressives, and plain old corrupt government thieves. The enemies of capitalism both overseas and around the corner have shared a need to control and restrict behavior, and a disdain for happiness dressed in the sheep's' skins of compassion and fairness.

In contrast stands, for one example, a long-time tourist stop that weathered world wars, a depression, and the Carter years to still deliver an obscene, gaudy offer of a free brontosaurus-sized steak for anyone up to the gamble. Cattle are raised, with grain, vet bills, water for grazing, fuel, coffee, and snacks for four-wheelers, money for hands, and a significant expense to ship and process, not to mention the hope that the rancher make a buck along the way. After a quick tour of the slaughter house, also with myriad overhead items including quality controls, safety inspections, workers' comp and liability bills for all those missing digits, and floor scrubbing chemicals, our happy cows will ride dreamy wholesale clouds to waiting restaurants, where other layers of processing, labor, quality control, gradations of quality selection (real or perceived) will obtain. At each step along the way, from the calf being pulled from the womb, to the splendid grill-marked result next to the baked potato, work is done and profit is expected. There would be no ranch hand, cattle auctioneer, butcher, or restaurateur without the expectation of profit, and these and sundry associates would disappear without the repeated tribute of cash money for their efforts. The same may be said of their customers at each step along the way, until we come to see Adam Smith's magical hand shimmering through the land like a rumor of free money, laying down millions upon millions of relationships large and tiny, all shifting, yet growing stronger in their participation in the larger enterprise known as the free market. These relationships, founded as they are on hopes for personal gain, have a long and indisputable record of salutary effect upon those involved whether directly or by osmosis, or fallout. This phenomenon, the functional manifestation of the human spirit, is the greatest beauty ever to spring forth from man's nature, if we are not to be too theological about it. Our soldiers overseas defend our freedom, and that means our free will to participate or not as we choose with our fellows. At home, our governing institutions and their source documents protect – well, they are supposed to – these abilities, the very basis for the unique American self-governance.

The ability to produce a steak and serve it voluntarily to another who chooses to pay the requested price, and then publicly brag about the serving and the eating is a microcosm of America. Our nation's legacy at its best has been big, gregarious, and fun, sometimes gaudy, with a swagger and grin that has been the envy of human history. What better symbol apart from the green broad in the harbor, that cracked bell, or the Super Bowl could there be to represent such a heroic tradition than to scarf a gigantic steak simply because it's there?

With a moment of excited, joyous clarity, it became clear to me, above and through the piddling daily pressures of work and personal obligations that nibble away at the spirited long-view, that it was my duty as an unapologetic defender of freedom and proud American, to journey to the heartland and assail this mountain, knife and fork in hand. I would eat the steak in the service of liberty and in tribute to this land and ideals that I love. Damn, this was going to be fun.

❖ ❖ ❖

Beginning in 2003, I began publishing a regular op-ed column as a lark for our local paper in the western Florida panhandle. For our journey together, I have selected my favorite columns over nearly seven years of shooting my mouth off in print. The columns are grouped broadly into witty insights and rhetorical flourishes on our schizophrenic politics, our confused foreign policy, the dysfunctional U.S. health care system, our amusing culture, and life during the early Obama years. For several years I also published a now-defunct website, www.DoctorsForFreedom.com, from which I have borrowed several relevant pieces to enliven the health care chapter.

My purpose is to present a thematic tour in service of my governing principle, that freedom is the highest secular value to which we can aspire (I leave spiritual values to those better trained to enunciate them). The book is not a "how to" for every little problem some collectivist critic may devise. Albert Schweitzer famously promoted his doctrine of reverence for life, and said, "If a man loses his reverence for any part of life, he will lose his reverence for all of life." His aim was not a step-by-step daily cookbook that would be dragged down by its adherence to minutiae. Likewise, I suspect that any willingness to forgo a little freedom here or there, allows one to eventually reject all freedoms if the rationale fits. What I propose to share, and hope you will enjoy, is an embrace of freedom as an attitude and an instinct. Winston Churchill observed, "All great things are simple, and many can be expressed in single words: freedom, justice, honor, duty, mercy, hope." To which I must add, not one of those is possible without the first.

Whether the topic is a terrorist threat, or the threat of some idiot mayor banning trans-fats, I believe the best way to approach the topic is to ask how best to protect, and advance the liberty of the individual. That I truly believe, is the essence of America, and it soars beautifully over sclerotic government and mean ambitions.

A note of explanation: This book is neither a travelogue per se, nor is it strictly a manifesto. The columns herein are mostly, but not strictly, in chronological sequence, within their larger chapters. I have used a road trip out west in September 2008 as scaffolding for these broader topics, and as a way for me to make sense such as it was, of the whole circus. As I think back on that trip, I reflect upon the broader elements of our American freedom that pertained to, or even permitted the joys and excesses of aspiring to gastronomic immortality. I had fun writing, and living it. May you have fun within these pages, and in whatever journey you choose to undertake in this wonderful land.

Patrick "Fitz" Conrad
Port Saint Joe, Florida
June, 2011

Part 1

"To those who have been accustomed to the possession, or even to the hope of public admiration, all other pleasures sicken and decay."

Adam Smith

"The fact that I have no remedy for all the sorrows of the world is no reason for my accepting yours. It simply supports the strong probability that yours is a fake."

H.L. Mencken

Politics: From "Da Bushes" to "The Big O"

When in Doubt * When Disaster Strikes * How Bush Actually Screwed Up After Katrina * Les Bon Temps Toujours * The Real Lesson of Katrina * Post-Election Blues: Cheering Up the Libs * The GOP Blowing It Again * Election '06: Race to the Bottom * Bush, Bears, and Hypocrisy * Romney and the Pinup * Is It Okay to Be Gouged? * Passing the Plate * 2007 Primaries: Going or God's Endorsement / Is the GOP Serious? / Seriously, is the GOP Serious? / A Mule Staple / Letters to Santa / The Year That Probably Was * The Two Towers * McCain Sputters * Where Will the Wind Fall? * The Hole Truth * What Is Patriotic, Really? * A Fourth of July Pause *

1

*An American Princess * Fear the Night * A Last Chance at St. Paul * Only Gov't is Never Discredited * A Whale of an Electoral's Eve * Bushes Were Expensive Landscaping * RIP Rosa Parks * It's A Black Thing Apparently * Just Another Racist * Same Old Dems, Same Old Racism **

Beginning the second week of September, 2008 I was ready for a little breather from politics. The mass adulation from the Obama faux Greek columns rally was long gone; it already looked like the fix was in, and that all the really cool kids were going to vote "O" before heading over to Timmy's lake house while his parents were out of town. The week before John Mc-Cain had been nominated, and apart from a sparky VP pick, his utter lack of philosophy did not auger well for the majority of us that did not want to return to high school. In the early fall of '08, while stock prices fell disastrously and portfolio managers and traders wondered how far a drop it would be from the top of the nearest skyscraper, the Bush '43 administration fell into (worse) shambles as it's would-be First Defender of capitalism fell on his rhetorical plastic sword. Pleasantly oblivious, I was enjoying a trip with a buddy across a goodly portion of the vast American west. The day that the media recognized the impending crash and first announced that there might be a teensy little problem with the entire economy, we were in Los Vegas having a big time. Flying in the night before, it was exciting and jolting to look at the vast and desolate Nevada deserts, where nothing could ever grow, land forever useless for want of water, and there in the middle of it all off our left wing as we descended, an explosion of bubbling, boiling flashing color as though some disco volcano had suddenly erupted showering the surrounding landscape with polyester and forgettable rhythms. The airport was bustling, thronging if you like, under huge banners announcing a plethora of new shows, new casinos, new restaurants, new…you get the picture. The city which would be damned and castigated by a screaming tantrum of an administration not six *months hence was open for business in a big way. We rushed to the car rental window, lucked into a bigger size vehicle than originally contracted, zipped off to a monstrous, over-the-top, gaudy hotel complete with enormous indoor gardens to suck up all the cigarette smoke from the armies of slot players, and ran upstairs to change before the show. I thought about flipping the TV on for just a moment, just to check the news and the latest poll numbers, and then decided nah, it will all be there tomorrow and still a damn bloody mess.*

Like many in the days before Phil Donahue began performing public self-emasculations and "My Little Pony" infantilized Saturday morning cartoons, many of us were raised with some pretty basic ideas: freedom was good, the Russkies, Nazis, and Klingons were bad, and large guns or anything that carried them, such as tanks, jets and battleships, were cool. Simplistic to be sure, but it kept the young mind on the right track when other distractions like babes and motorcycles, and beer, and babes, and college, and babes...well, a young guy can get distracted. In those dark days awash with post-Watergate angst and Jimmy Carter malaise, my view of politics was simplistic at best. I knew that low taxes and a strong military were good, and that Democrats were always in favor of more welfare. Apart from the gloomy, seemingly permanent cloud cover of the Cold War, my concept of politics and underlying philosophy were pretty limited. I was a huge fan of military history, which led to my interest in eventually joining the United States Navy in which I served as a naval flight officer.

And what a blast that was! If ever there was a time to enter active service it was during the early Reagan years when it was again cool to be pro-American, and a newly reinvigorated military was a great place to start. Through no particular skill on my part, a short two years after college found me shot halfway around the world, banging off the decks of an aircraft carrier,

and having adventures I could not have imagined before join-
ing. During my very first week in the fleet I was smack in the
middle of a major international incident, followed by port visits
in Italy, Israel, a midnight ride through the Suez Canal, and
Thanksgiving off the Arabian Peninsula. Later I got to spend a
week loafing on a coral atoll in the Indian Ocean, spent Christ-
mas in Singapore, and then a mounting terrorist conflagration
had us roaring back to the Mediterranean, which included visits
to more fun ports, skiing in the Alps, and one scary night during
the opening shots of our slap-down of Libya. Two years later my
squadron was back in the Mediterranean, where we had even
more fun than the last visit. By the time the ship headed back
home after this second cruise, I was in a real moment of indirec-
tion. To stay in the navy means one works hard at climbing the
ladder, arranging the next job assignment to remain competitive
in the tightening race to achieve higher rank and command. It is
not that I was not driven, but I simply had no ambition for these
things. I had joined the navy out of a desire for adventure and
fun, and also a plan to avoid what we might consider a "real
job." Realizing that my thinking had been too shortsighted got
me to considering what my longer-range goals should be. I had
no marketable skill apart from some basic mid-level management
experience, and some experience in hunting Commie submarines,
which is all really cool, but not what they are looking for in the
greater part of the executive job market.

So I took a deep breath, took a dead-end desk job while I
planned on night school, and in so doing pulled the plug on any
real subsequent advancement. While passing the mornings over
pots of coffee in my windowless office, I got into the habit of pick-
ing up the daily paper, and scrupulously reading every op-ed col-
umn I could get my hands on. Though possessed of a somewhat
liberal bent, the major paper in the area carried both conservative
and liberal syndicated columns, which I read like mad. For the

first time I was not merely watching CNN or listening to NPR on the drive in (yes I used to listen to them) but digesting the issues of the day. This happened as I read opinions from both the right and left, and compared their take whichever topic had popped up. As the months passed it became apparent that as a general approach, the more liberal writers spent more time discussing their feelings and so in turn, the way they thought the world should be with respect to whatever issue or event was presented. The columnists on the right, if occasionally bombastic, nonetheless seemed to spend more time citing actual facts around which they structured their arguments. Yes one could say that, having been raised to be at least friendly toward that side, I might have been expected or predisposed to view the conservative op-eds more favorably. Maybe, but it does not change the, well, fact, that I was learning more by reading what the right had to say, even − and this is a crucial distinction − when I disagreed. And in so doing I was developing a more cogent political philosophy, organized above and beyond simple party partisanship.

Almost a full decade in the military, a generally conservative environment, followed by a career in medicine which boasts a strong liberal component, has also given me a broad comparative experience with many specific examples to support a particular outlook. This outlook has only been reinforced by the political, cultural, and societal battles that have been waged throughout my adult life and particularly in the past twenty or so years. Somewhere along the way I gave a mentor in residency gray hair as he lamented my linear thinking, and it is to his great credit that he was able to somehow train me to at least minimal competency. Maybe we cannot all be cause-and-effect thinkers, and maybe that is not always the absolute standard. But when it comes to understanding politics and its underlying ideologies, one must continue to refine and question basic premises and assumptions, and it is in this that I came to understand a simple, vital truth:

it is ALL about freedom. Reject out of hand the maxim from that Kristofferson classic, that "freedom's just another word for nothing left to lose." It is when we lose freedom that we will shortly lose it all, if we have not already done so. After starting to write my own op-ed columns, I kept returning to a simple slogan, "When in doubt, choose freedom." We being imperfect creatures in an imperfect world, cannot devise perfection in any endeavor. What we can do however is to set a standard to always pursue that will afford in us and our neighbors the greatest possible degree of happiness, accomplishment, prosperity, security, and fun. If we cannot devise the guaranteed contingency plan for every situation, when in doubt, we may at least use as our civic polar star a desire to be free and a similar hope for our neighbors.

Being free is actually hard work as the history of this nation has shown, and it requires a conscious periodic renewal of the actual choice to be free. By choosing freedom we place all the responsibility, blame, and reward upon ourselves, and we knowingly chart our own course. That simple notion often referred to with dismay and horror in academia as "rugged individualism" lies at the heart of America.

Fair Warnings

In 2004 I hoped to see the Bush Campaign build on some of the things they got right in the first term. There should have been no hesitance in defending the tax cuts that were shown to work, and the "for the rich" adjective should have been aggressively fought from the top down. No such luck. It was obvious that Pres. Bush had shown himself to be otherwise mostly a bust on domestic issues, co-opting the Democrats to placate the Great Whining Society. The fun old W. was having to gain votes with the Latinos, seniors, single moms et al would present one hell of a bill to the rest of us when he left office. The school bus full of Democrat imbeciles trying to catch up to the Bush limo was merely sputtering and comical, whose inhabitants fell roughly into two camps: idiots and liars (granted, they all attempt to venture into both camps with great frequency). The likes of Dean, Gephardt, Kerry, and Edwards offered no serious ideological or intellectual competition to Bush, and in so failing did not push him to be a better candidate with better ideas. But W. and the Dems were able to find common ground in their convergent paths toward fashioning a better world, namely their proclivity for telling other people what to do. Apart from national security, the differences between the major parties are more blurred than ever before, and the voters of 2004 had only a choice between (R) Big Government and an aggressive war on terror, or; (D) Big Government and hoping the French would like us again. It was and remains, sad and disgusting to see so much of the electorate apparently eager to be told what to do, but there was another, better way. In the spirit of selfless sacrifice, with the ambition to serve to improve the lives of others (as all the other candidates claim) I offered then and now my plan to fix the country. For the children.

After a couple years of submitting columns on this or that topical issue, my editor suggested I describe what my philosophy, what my agenda might entail. A fun yet daunting idea for so small a space as a column, until thinking on it, I began to understand that a truly important idea like this, while expressible and applicable in myriad ways, could be succinctly put. And so I set to work...

When in Doubt Choose Freedom

"Unlike the average moderate Republican, I think that one should have an animating philosophy around which could be shaped policies and agendas. The point of my column has been its motto: "When in doubt, choose freedom." The motto is neither a set of stone tablets nor extensive writ designed to unravel every contingency, and therein avoids the trap of arrogance by recognizing that there is no perfect, one-size-fits-all prescription. Whatever spin flows from elected leaders or Hollywood glitterati, life will go on being imperfect and messy, and no amount of good feeling or mislabeling will make entitlement programs or the War on Drugs workable. Before you read further and get angry in the process, understand that what I have proposed makes sense. It makes sense because we have decades if not centuries of history showing us what works between people and their government, and what does not. Irrational, emotion-based collective solutions are great for making politicians and ostentatiously compassionate celebrities feel really good about themselves, and are effective in making downcast men and "Oprah" viewers feel as though they matter. But they do not work, never have, and never will. The most rational, optimistic, and productive, philosophical approach to pursue is one that values freedom as far and away the highest of secular values. American freedom is humanist and compassionate. It frees people to be their best and help those around them; it does not engage in the lie of forced "charity." America is a state of mind irrespective of geography, and will always bloom somewhere as the logical aspiration of the human desire for freedom. With that as the goal, one seeks to fashion policies and goals.

How does freedom translate to policy? A society that values freedom above all else will recognize two imperatives: the primacy of the individual, and the subordination of all other good intentions to that standard. If all individuals are of equal worth before the law, then no individual should be favored by public policy over another; and therefore all should contribute each an equal share for whatever common provision is deemed *constitutional* (therein the source of a great many problems – the national defense is constitutional, Medicare and agricultural subsidies are not). To love freedom one must comprehend that Money=Time=Property= Life. If you take any of the first three, you confiscate the life that was traded for it. Consider taxes. Punishing the wealthy simply because they produce the wealth reduces their real value below that of those who live off of them, making the rich a commodity for all the rest. This is cannibalism. There is no nobility in poverty, nor is there in parasitism.

Institute a true Flat Tax- if one actually believes in the equal protection mentioned in some document whose name escapes me, then this is a no-brainer, and would be the domestic equivalent of winning the Cold War. Abolish all Capital Gains and Inheritance Taxes-If double and triple taxation is as moral as it is presently legal, why don't we tax even more? Punishing younger generations simply because their seniors want to live longer, and be retired more securely than they themselves could have earned is un-American. What about essentials like housing, or food? Making either a right only enslaves their producers. Abolish Medicare and Medicaid- the central state has no constitutional role in keeping you healthy. These are dehumanizing programs that cause far more harm than good, have already put us on the path to socialized medicine, and allowed far too many politicians to be compassionate with other peoples' money. And the same goes for Social Security. Excluding those who enjoy ill-gotten gains, real Americans don't waste time roiling in envy of others' success: they seek to emulate, and surpass it. And while we are at it, why not suspend the voting rights of any citizen on Federal assistance on the grounds of an obvious conflict of interest? While I have no idea how many on welfare actually vote, I damn sure do not want the able-bodied being able to promote their own livelihood and slothfulness on my nickel. Not only a worthy principle, it would irritate the daylights out of the apologists for the lazy and over-procreative.

It would be proper and heroic to eliminate the Department of Education, as most states are perfectly capable of screwing up young people without any help from Washington. And speaking of screwed up people, we should end the War on Drugs. Preventing you from making cheese fondue out of your brain should NEVER infringe on my civil rights. If a little Darwinism is necessary to preserve freedom, then it's worth the trade. (And hammer any evildoer giving the junk to children).

In terms of foreign policy, nations who are true friends, and seek to trade peacefully and imitate, or even improve on our success should enjoy our unqualified friendship. Those who seek to undermine us should not be treated with the respect due an equal, and those who contemplate harming us should feel very deterred from so. The timidity recent administrations have felt regarding the ruthless use of overwhelming military power belies their philosophical discomfort with the idea of American exceptionalism, and with real freedom. The American love of freedom does not want to conquer the world, but it should threaten the hell out of anyone who seeks to violently usurp ours. Further improve the lethality of our military, and increase the pay for combat troops. Sharply reduce the hoards of paper-pushers in uniform by giving them guns and use them to move the Mexican border from the theoretical to reality. And that would be something useful to do with some of the females who seem to want to play at combat. This way we could forcibly seal the border with Mexico where needed and have our unemployed picked up the slack.

Additional fun and useful steps would include putting as many strict constructionists as possible into the Supreme Court. Why is it pejoratively "ideological" to insist that those who enforce a document actually believe in that document? (For those who see the Constitution as a "living" document, well, so was "Pravda"). This would allow us to declare as unconstitutional the EEOC and eminent domain, two peas in a pod of government corrupted against private interests by other private interests. If you ever see the city block of prime D.C. real estate the EPA hogs up, you will wonder if there actually is enough environment to justify such a huge bureaucracy. Give them a 50% haircut, and while we are it to hell with the rabid snow foxes and over-multiplying caribou, and drill OUR oil out of ANWAR!

"Did you hear that Martha? Why that guy is a warmonger who wants to steal from poor people! You know I think he's just a Naz..." Whoa, stop right there. Before some of you melt down in a seething rage, realize that every single proposal of mine either increases individual liberty, increases our national security, or both. I believe in compassion for one's neighbor, but it is vile for me to acquiesce to my neighbor's demands for unearned money or power. The instinct should be for our freedom. Wasn't that the whole point of this great nation? It would be a hoot to run for public office on this platform, but presently election rules seem to discourage having campaign contributions sent to conradscaribbeanvacation-slushfund.com (I'll keep you posted). For those incensed at my glib treatment of serious national questions, please realize that there are substantive arguments to support each position. And I really would work for the forcible deportation of Sean Penn and Barbara Streisand."

❖ ❖ ❖

Adam Smith once noted: "It is not from the benevolence of the butcher, the brewer, or the baker, that we expect our dinner, but from the regard to their own interest. We address ourselves not to their humanity, but their self-love." Politics in the United States has and we may suppose, always will revolve around competing versions of which party can demonstrate the most ostentatious love for the common voter, and this has become a hobby for ineffectual Republicans and central policy for government-loving Democrats. But is not freedom the love to choose for one's self rather than for one's fellows? On the other hand John Tolland said "Then we prefer the quiet, good-natured hypocrite to the implacable, turbulent zealot of any kind. In plain terms, we are not so fond of any set of notions, as to think them more important than the peace of society." Call me a troublemaker, but Adam Smith's view supercedes Tolland's every time if only because the former reflects human nature while the latter accurately describes the potential for fecklessness in each of us. Do not Americans yet have a willingness to stand up, holler, bitch, threaten, cry out, cheer, and fight to preserve indivisible liberties? There are unquestionably some silly elements in the Tea Party, and their as-yet intransigence to push for entitlement reform may be their undoing; but witness how their central message of smaller government as been the target of elitist media invective, not directed at the merits of the arguments, but at their anger. It is as though only one side in American politics has the right to be angry, which demonstrates that for all their free-speech piety, the media and the Left insists that fans of small government sit down, and shut up. Mr. Jefferson had that great line about refreshing the tree of liberty with the blood of patriots, and Alexander Ball said, "Courage is the natural product of familiarity with danger." Both would be castigated by the media and addle-brained Beltway suburbanites as being divisive, and inflammatory. Both men are right, and the chin-tucking cocktail partygoers and effete mainstream media types expressing such revulsion over citizens demanding to protect their freedoms is a byproduct of a great many years of relative peace and plenty. None of us want to be fearful, but we should have at least the good graces not to take our freedoms for granted.

❖ ❖ ❖

On Hurricane Katrina...

To say Hurricane Katrina was a big deal to those of us on the Gulf Coast does not quite get it. In the summer of 2005, a major disaster hit the region in the form of a hurricane, or more precisely, the aftermath of a hurricane. The worst of the storm flattened coastal Mississippi, devastating townships and homes, and wrecking the lives of the residents. While lesser storm forces hit Louisiana, a perfect storm was unleashed: the combination of a city built below sea-level, inadequate protections for an admittedly unfortunate geographical choice, and bureaucratic ineptitude at multiple levels of government, all visited on a population featuring a large portion of state dependents whose instincts toward self-sufficiency had too lately been discovered to be sadly diminished. One will make no friends defending the George W. Bush administration's handling of the backwash in human suffering, hyped, amplified, and celebrated by a partisan media; the same "journalism" that was unable to comprehend the utter incompetence of the Democrat governor who pointlessly delayed federal intervention, or the apathy and dithering of a Democrat mayor unwilling to deploy available public transportation before the streets were flooded. It seems necessary to constantly remind the reader that I am NOT a George W. Bush fan, but it is contemptible to reflexively blame a figure you dislike for mishaps in which he played no part. Yep there was plenty of blame to go around, too complicated for muddled heads whose agenda was only to solely blame Bush for any bad occurrence rather than do an honest post-mortem on the sorry episode. It was a mess that touched the nation, especially those of us on the gulf who love the Crescent City as our own. And like most disasters, it gave us all a great opportunity for reevaluating our state and our direction...

When Disaster Strikes:
The Proper Role of the Federal Government

"Hurricane Katrina has blown away a lot of property, dreams, and lives. And it should have also blown away a lot of stupidity. The horror of such an aftermath is not the setting in which to score easy debating points, but nor is it the time to avoid serious analysis and reflection. Following the 9/11 terrorist attacks, the federal government moved to aggrandize its power, and its sclerotic hold on the American psyche. Now in Katrina's aftermath, the federal government has a good and proper role to fill and is in motion to do just that. But what must not be lost is the opportunity to learn from the missteps and dangerously wrongheaded ideas laid bare by the devastation along the Gulf Coast, the effects of which are surely reaching northward to touch us all, like so many reverse tributaries of the swollen Mississippi.

We are faced with a rising energy crisis, largely of our own making, in the wake of Katrina's impact on the rigs in the Gulf and the maze of pipelines and fuel terminals in coastal areas that serve so much of our region and the Midwest. This will have a domino effect on gas prices, airline ticket prices, transport and shipping costs, and every single transaction cost in our incredibly interdependent economic web. W.'s (Pres. Bush) releasing of the Strategic Oil Reserve is really a penny-ante political move which will have no more than a temporary cosmetic effect. The president should truly have the courage he has summoned in other crises and deal with the public and our cynical masters in D.C. honestly, and with the firepower of his expertise in the

15

industry. Reflexive squawking critics of W. will scream as the gas pump prices climb and the economy slows. But these were the same well-informed idiots who stymied his work four years ago to open up Alaska for drilling. As Jonah Goldberg described in National Review back in Jan. 2001, the area in question equaled one-tenth of a dime sitting on an average tabletop (where the tabletop equaled the whole of Alaska). Strict environmental controls were guaranteed and yet still angst-ridden moderates and liberal 'environmentalists" were swayed by images of fuzzy bears and happy salmon in an area hundreds of miles from the oil deposits. Had we begun drilling, we might be within a year or two of accessing those oil assets to alleviate our present mess. Instead we must deal with Saudi's who despise us, a wholly untrustworthy Mexican government, and a Venezuelan socialist dictator whose recent dealings with us have laughably involved the preacher-huckster Pat Robertson and shakedown expert Jesse Jackson. And what of the oil we CAN obtain? As usual, the Feds won't be able to do with a single penny less and will use this disaster as justification to clutch every tax revenue tighter still. But we pay enormous federal fuel taxes at present, confiscations that could and should be immediately suspended to dampen the coming economic constriction and stimulate renewed commerce and new jobs.

To blazes with the boondoggle transportation bill recently enacted by weasely Republicans! Americans should be allowed to simply deal with the potholes and get those trucks and cars of the nation rolling. The oil we have can be used far more effectively, and the urgent need for expanding our own sources has been so clearly demonstrated one would think Jimmy Carter had snuck back into the White House.

For years we have been told by earnest-faced mothers, Sarah Brady, spineless physicians' groups, and liberal autocrats everywhere that the Founding Fathers got it wrong, that guns are bad, and that we should leave our self-defense concerns to those trained to correctly enact them. Well here we are. The canals and islands of New Orleans have become the free-fire turf of gangs, the police have temporarily pulled back for their own safety, and the National Guard has begun advancing at a less than satisfactory pace, using less than adequate force, in protecting the lives and property of trapped citizens. Can anyone watch the violence and carnage in the powerless night streets of the Crescent City and seriously argue against the Second Amendment protection of the right to self-defense? The stories of rape and murder in the Superdome and throughout the city strip away the veneer of polite discussion regarding what ought to be, in a fluffy, kid-friendly, liberal world. Sober people should pause at this opportunity to consider what really happens when the fabric of society is rent and the predators are turned loose in the streets. Decades of government dependence now only threaten the lives of those whom the National Guard has not yet reached, for whom N.Y. Sen. Schumer's cries for gun sale restrictions will be scant comfort.

Since the Twin Towers fell, we have openly fretted over a terrorist WMD set off in a major U.S. city. Well now we have a perfect demonstration of what such an aftermath will look like. Substitute radiation for flooding and New Orleans becomes Cleveland after an Al Queda visit. Mass panic, evacuations, and disease, thousands of deaths, an un-usable region, and a national economic ripple that will last for years are what we have in store. Our other problems have not gone away with this natural tragedy, yet not learning the lessons here will not only compound but may make possible a comparable man-made disaster in the near future. Let Cindy Sheehan thoughtlessly martyr herself, using no more logical insight than an oyster that only takes in and spews out what others feed to it. If you doubt the need to find, pursue, and kill anti-American terrorists, look to New Orleans. If you think the U.S. death toll in Iraq and Afghanistan is too high, consider that there will be many more deaths in a bombed city/aftermath than there have been fighting terrorists overseas. It may not be a perfect plan or approach. But isn't trying to preemptively smoke out our enemies preferable to simply waiting for another major city to be devastated, when the Weather Channel will not be able to give us a 24-hour forecast probability on which city will likely contain the hidden dirty bomb waiting to explode?

There will be plenty of blame to go around if we cannot logically absorb the lessons of this horrible blow to our region and nation. The final conclusion is that we cannot altogether escape disaster. But the federal government focused on its appropriate roles, with a consistent appreciation for and expansion of our economic and personal freedoms will make the next blow easier to take."

Certainly then-Pres. Bush did not take my pointed and excellent advice, which is surprising. He had every opportunity. Inept as ever, the Bush White House staged a national address in front of the St. Louis Cathedral in Jackson Square, New Orleans just weeks after the storm and her tearing aftermath. Louisiana and indeed the entire nation had taken an emotional, not to mention economic hit from the images on the screen and the disruption from that important transportation grid. The Compassionate-in-Chief rolled out some typical platitudes and talked about more federal money rolling in. What he missed was a great opportunity, not to score cheap political points, but to make a serious case for the proper role of government in making our society and its individuals more resilient and sustainable in such times...

How Bush Really Actually Screwed Up after Katrina

"Conservative voters from '04 wanted the following: "Good evening my fellow Americans...I am speaking to you from New Orleans. Tonight our nation faces a challenge we have never before faced – re-populating a major U.S. city, and ensuring hope and prosperity during her rebuilding. And yes, the work will be hard, and our endurance will be tested. But this is our city, and the Gulf Coast is a region that deserves the compassion of our national family in the hard, but hopeful years ahead. And as a family our nation must face hard questions, and remember that while it is the task of the government to promote fairness and opportunity, only people can be compassionate. When a family is faced with a crisis, an illness, house fire, or car wreck, it must prioritize and make the tough choices. And tonight as our American family joins together to help one of our own, so we too must make these tough choices. Those with certain expectations may feel disappointed, and many Americans will have to adapt to new circumstances as our nation adapts to absorb the devastation wrought on our citizens on the Gulf Coast. These choices will not be popular, nor will they be easy. But your leadership was not elected to take the easy way out, but to advance the interests of all Americans equally and without preference. To that end I have directed my administration to prepare for the following initiatives, which shall be accomplished via Executive Order where legally feasible, and presented to Congress for ratification.

We shall freeze Medicare spending, allowing increases only at the rate of inflation. The Medicare Part D program to purchase prescription medications for our seniors (enacted in 2004) is not affordable, and must be revoked. Federal Medicaid expenditures will be cut 10%, and all restrictions on eligibility or benefits will be lifted and left to the individual states. We have suffered a significant economic blow and must quickly move to ensure our economic vitality. To that end, we must immediately abolish the estate tax, and reduce capitol gains tax rates 10% for every bracket. In this time of crisis I will have no patience for those who claim that only the rich will benefit. These moves will create jobs and opportunity and must be enacted swiftly. I will move to immediately suspend the Davis-Bacon Act and allow the federal government to accept unrestricted bids from all contractors in all of the Gulf Coast states. Preserving the clout of union bureaucracy in the devastated regions is less important than putting people back to work and rebuilding this wonderful region. Reducing government expenditures must and will be a priority. I will move to rescind ALL discretionary spending in the recently passed highway bill. All domestic discretionary spending including the 2005 Farm Bill subsidies will be held at 2004 levels, and only increased annually equal to the rate of inflation. And as our family must tighten its belts, so we cannot be as generous to our neighbors. I will seek to suspend all foreign aid, pending re-approval by the Congress, on a nation-by-nation basis. Any nation not meeting strict cost-benefit goals that are in American interests or any allotments submitted in multi-national bundles, or with attached amendments, will be automatically vetoed. Any surviving foreign aid will not exceed year-2000 levels. Illegal immigration must finally be dealt with. I will propose to withhold from each state federal monies equal to those spent on illegal aliens, which amounts will be determined by independent, bi-partisan commission and will go into effect in 6 months.

Some will call these initiatives draconian, or even immoral. Some will decry the economic upheaval these changes will cause by disrupting the status quo. Well let me tell them and all of you something – we have a lot of folks down here who are hurting and need our help, and they have already been through a terrible upheaval. It would be a disservice to the victims of Hurricane Katrina to turn a blind eye to their suffering. But it would be equally wrong to simply give take money from the rest of our hardworking citizens, without also trying to help those from whom the money is taken. As president, I cannot choose between a deserving senior who needs free medicines, and a storm victim who needs a new home, and we cannot afford both without raising taxes and harming our economy. So I must look out for all Americans and call for sacrifices that will advance the cause of personal liberty and prosperity for all."

That's what Pres. Bush should have said. Instead his "Hurri-CARE" program apes another, far less principled Texan and launches another chapter in America's welfare addiction. In what W. said would require "the creative skill and generosity of a united country" he announced the allocation of $60 (B)illion with nary an explanation of what will keep the big money machine in the Treasury basement oiled and humming. True enough, the Stafford Act of 1988 provides for all sorts of federal assistance after a disaster, from housing reimbursement and unemployment compensation, to crisis counseling and legal services. Perhaps you don't agree that Uncle Sam providing such assistance strains the boundaries of federalism. But don't we at least have the obligation to each other and the integrity of our country to decide what will – and what will NOT – be paid for? The welfare state in New Orleans' was shown to be a failure, in which poor neighborhoods became the stalking grounds savagery and blind rage over perceived "racism." Incredibly, Bush accepted the blame and the derision of his critics. He tied the poverty to the history of racial discrimination (partly excusing by implication, the violence), and pledged in his most chilling line: We have a duty to confront this poverty with bold action." Vintage LBJ. As Lincoln used slavery for the moral impetus to invade the South, Bush now rhetorically accepts the blame for historical racism and uses it as the emotional justification to give the Gulf Coast a hug. In doing so he will further enlarged the power of the federal government. He will worsen our deficit and our economic prospects without challenging the nation to live with fewer government services and move back toward self-reliance. As the largest domestic spender in history, W. is wrapping a gift for Pres. Clinton's Wife, waiting in the wings. In '08, Dems will simultaneously screech that Republicans didn't care about the poor they (Dems) created, but still ran up enormous deficits. The Dems will be half right, which is more than usual."

Okay, so Pres. Clinton's Wife did not use this effectively in her failed 2008 campaign. But the Obama supporters pounced on this and so many other examples of how the Bush White House spent like a really drunk sailor even as they castigated Republicans for racism, greed, and general mean-spiritedness.

We will digress to recall that even as W. was setting up the nation for an even bigger hit in 2008, New Orleans got back on her gorgeous drunken feet. Old-timer fans of the city had told me that with too much displacement of the locals, the Crescent City had lost her flavor and would never quite be the same. I remember Charleston, South Carolina after Hurricane Hugo smashed it in 1989, and how it rebuilt and has gotten steadily better. I predicted the same for New Orleans in her first bittersweet Mardi Gras after the storm...

"Les Bon Temps Toujours"

"Finally, Britney Spears is doing something useful. America's latest has-been one-girl jiggle fest will be featured on the Fat Tuesday episode of ABC's "Good Morning America", live from New Orleans to help celebrate the Big Party in the Big Easy. With no sarcasm intended, this is how it should be. When New Orleans was flushed by Katrina, I was surprised at how personally I took the grim news, having only visited the city once just 2 years before. But along with Atlanta and Charleston, New Orleans is one of the three cultural anchor bolts of the South and critical piece of our heritage. After my visit to the Big Easy, all I could think was "Charleston and Key West in a blender..." New Orleans is the capitol city of the primordial birth swamp of jazz and blues, the finest music God in his wisdom ever gave to this land. It boasts foods that ages the eater by leaps and makes them glad for the journey, and hang any fool who even uses the word "cholesterol" within the city limits. It may not seem like an accomplishment, but I am actually proud to have eaten beignets, and if you can listen to Elvis singing "Crawfish" from the movie "Kid Creole" without your mouth watering, then your tongue has died. I did the tourist things on my one visit: saw the aquarium, then enjoyed dinner and a fantastic Jimmy Vaughn concert at the House of Blues; wandered through the cigar shops in the Quarter, and ogled a Marie Laveau voodoo shop. The Storyville Jazz Parlour serves up proper Blue Moon Belgian ale, in a tall glass with an orange slice, and Marva Wright wails some excellent blues there. We wandered Bourbon Street repeatedly, happy to watch the free show, and the rumor was that the balcony girls knew a trick to get free beads. Did I mention the beignets?

One visit as a lousy tourist, and I feel a tiny bit invested. Then along comes a murderous storm, abetted by the thunderous incompetence of the Louisiana state government (controlled by which party?) and a racist, boorish mayor who should be relegated to trash pickup in an Arizona retirement village. Now the news shows are couching their coverage of Mardi Gras with the concerns of those who find it inappropriate or offensive that the scene of so much recent death and destruction should be the site for a party. But this is New Orleans, where the jazz funeral was invented. Britney Spears may not be as important to the big scheme of things as say, a great mind like Sean Penn. But she is frivolity personified, perfect for the occasion, and I say good for her! This city has always understood that Life and Death are two halves of the whole, and they learned to cheer, rather than bemoan, this sweet eventuality. To moan about the future rather than celebrate those who wish to celebrate is to betray the beauty, lunacy, danger, food, music, spirit, and life of the Crescent City. There is a sweetness to fatalism, when you add a little hot sauce. Laissez Les Bon Temps Roullaiez!"

But there are always those who willingly miss the obvious beauty, mean little furtive minds that will try to drag everyone down...

The Real Lesson of Katrina

"It is ridiculous for New Orleans in the wake of Katrina to have been characterized by so many hyperventilating newsies as "Hell." On the other hand, there is great truth here again demonstrated that the path to the nether world is studded and lined with the very best of intentions.

Many of us missed the most significant development in the early wake of the New Orleans catastrophe. Oh we didn't miss much, and certainly not what will drive the fate of the Big Easy and our country now for another generation. The AP reported on 9/12 that "Reporters took off the gloves again", documenting Brian Williams' assertion that Hurricane Katrina marked the "end of an unusual four-year period of deference to people in power." What the hell did that mean? Rather and Jennings are gone, but the stupidity and self-servitude of the U.S. media has been handed down rather smoothly. True, the cable networks have assaulted us with continuous coverage of the most stilted, breathless, and unprofessional journalistic compassion since the Twin Towers fell. The tube has blared the hysterical Geraldo stuffing the displaced into a chopper with one hand while parading his humanitarian goodness with the other. We witnessed the usually nonplussed Shepherd Smith of FOX badgering local policeman to the point of childish absurdity; long gone is the cool detachment of David Brinkley on Sunday morning, replaced with the self-important huffing of Tim Russert doing his utmost to show how smart he is and how much he cares while bullying any government official too spineless to put up a fight.

The hero in the coverage of the New Orleans flood has been whatever company produces the outstanding portable video cameras that have given us fantastic shots of this incredibly complex and wrenching disaster. The villains in Katrina's aftermath have included the egomaniacal members of the media, too intent on taking a hand in the events for their own emotional self-aggrandizement to merely do their damn job. They have gushed so over the victims of the floodwaters that they were unable to muster criticism for those able-bodied that were unable to rouse themselves from their dependency torpor and get out of the danger zone. Quick to blame the government from which all salvation flows, the media were slow to hold accountable those whose descent into barbarism was wholly predictable though no less deplorable. How many times did we have to see reporters dramatically "on the ground" pleading for something to be done to get water and food to those resorting to violence against not only relief efforts, but their own neighbors? These same correspondents then angrily analyzed the strife as somehow a natural, even reasonable response to the immediate lack of federal troops with goody bags and bottled water. This is not a slap at the elderly or infirm who could not get out, nor at those who stayed to help them. And there is a strong case to be argued for those who chose to remain in their own homes – if they accepted the responsibility for their own sustenance.

This is an indictment of an ugly facet of our society, made manifest in a dependency population utterly relieved of the hope of self-sufficiency by good intentions. The need to evince caring got us an earful from a discombobulated and unhinged mayor, too awash in local politics and institutionalized incompetence to be coherent. We got a bag full of anger from the Louisiana governor over the lack of federal response to pick up the enormous slack left by her own local relationships, such as they were. And we got wall-to-wall turbine powered Senate chamber caterwauling from Mary Landrieu exhibiting as fine a display of irrational, whirling, guilt-displacing rage as has ever graced the camera. The need to appear compassionate has again resulted in Republicans seeking blame for themselves, adopting the liberal standard that guilt equals worth and failure means goodness. W. accepting responsibility for the initial FEMA deployment difficulties amidst storm obstacles and local government incompetence is so absolutely needless that I think he deserves the grief he gets.

Beyond the man-made catastrophe New Orleans catastrophe born of "compassion", sloth, and savagery, we have the resumption of another, wider ranging problem. Sometime after World War II, and generally coinciding with the ascendancy of the Baby Boomers, America developed a new and debilitating love. We love to have a pity party. The determined pioneer-capitalist spirit that made us the envy of the world has been replace in the media and in political rhetoric with its antithesis. Where Americans

once strove to build, achieve, and conquer, our public pro-
clivities are now seek to understand, to care, and to hug.
There are millions of real Americans out there who still
produce, improve, and prosper, relishing and vanquish-
ing the challenges thrown at us by nature and bloodthirsty
Islamo-fascists. When our Twin Towers were knocked
down we knocked back with a fury. But now New Yorkers
led by Pataki and Guiliani lend their support to a ground-
zero memorial to the 9/11 victims, which will be in truth,
a monument to our failure. 9/11 is nothing to memorial-
ize, other than to recall as a defeat that sparked us again
to the action to which we are all called: the preservation
and expansion of freedom. Our monument to those
murdered in the Twin Towers should be to build bigger,
better towers with which to prosper and in doing so, scorn
the evil of our enemies. We don't need Oprah and Dr.
Phil hugging their way through New Orleans, nor do we
need reporters padding their ratings by helping us all to
feel a little worse. Evil walks the earth, and disasters will
always happen. The magnitude of these calamities will
be best measured by our response to them. As for New
Orleans, the monument to this horrible flood has already
begun construction, without federal aid, angry politicos,
or weepy reporters. Two weeks to the day after the levees
broke, a bar in the French Quarter re-opened for business,
and had customers. Though scarred, the best of the Big
Easy will be restored for profit, by free men and women,
and it will be just fine."

*I got back to New Orleans in June, 2009. The Storyville
Jazz Parlour has been turned into some other sort of establishment, sadly. The blue-hair "doo-waggers" still gather Fridays at
Galatoire's, where we enjoyed milk punch and the most heavenly
fried softshell crab with which I have ever been blessed. There*

were some blocks of rubble away from the quarter, and there were many, very lively neighborhoods full of kids and walkers and bright new flowers and flags adorning porches that clearly saw most if not all of the last century. Everything you hear about the fried chicken at Willie Mae's Scotch House is true, and I can't wait to go back. New Orleans is doing just fine, and I still have that Marva Wright CD.

The 2008 Campaign

Campaign 2008 was certainly teed up by the 2006 congressional races, wherein the Republicans showed themselves to be so sclerotic that they lost by default. It was truly sad to see the remnants of the 1994 republican revolution waving in a tepid breeze, interested only in holding on to office and nibbling around the edges while their president of the same party collaborated with them in more, and more pointless spending that we could not afford. The nation had the lousy choices of a cheap buffet near closing time, when nothing in the warming trays looked appetizing, but they still had to eat.

Actually we have to go back to the aftermath of the 2004 race, notable only for its mediocrity and ability to turn Republicans into masochists. But the GOP had no monopoly on dolefulness that year, and a little outreach to despondent libs seemed like the charitable approach...

Post-Election Blues: Cheering Up the Libs

"In 1996, the Republicans nominated the most unimaginative of their primary field, and Bob-Dole (one word) went down to predictable, yawning defeat at the hands of a jaded electorate unconcerned over minor questions of national security and equal justice. The prospect of an El Camino as the presidential limo for anther term found a deflated, beaten GOP that morose November. Hurrah for <u>National Review</u>, whose immediate post-election issue was entitled "A Guide to Pleasure", a wonderful tonic to depressed conservatives in need of a little break. Topics covered therein-included hints on fine dining, the joy of elegant cruises, the triumph of a single malt whiskey, the thrill of train travel, and the wisdom of fine cigars as a last vestige of Western refinement. A delightful "Special Cholesterol Dinner" menu insert that doubtless prompted a tax audit courtesy of the U.S. Surgeon General: an appetizer of salamis and pates; a scrumptious-sounding *Aveyron omelette* comprised of potatoes fried in duck fat with eggs and garlic; an ironically-named *Poulet a l'intellectuel* stuffed with calf's brain; steamed chocolate pudding *with cream*; and Stilton cheese for desert, which the author assures has a higher fat content than either gorgonzola or Roquefort, topped off of course with a fine port and a Punch cigar. Sorry, I guess I should have warned all of you mothers to cover your children's' eyes before that last bit. Small government, libertarianism has remained an ally to greater conservatism, bolstering their spirits in times of defeat, and calling, when they will heed, to better things.

But back to 2004: in the wee hours, hours after Fox had called Ohio for W., Dan Rather looked like Baghdad Bob huddled in the bunker, threatening counterattack against the infidels. But such was not to be, and the Wednesday dawn brought a frightful glare to the liberals, trapped in a land more Republican than they could believe. The month before I was in Portland, Oregon, where we saw hordes of union members, aging boomers, and bright blue-haired, lip-pierced, earnest looking youths waiting for a John Edwards rally to focus their angst for the common man. And as a magnanimous, caring sort, I fear for them. Has anyone seen Michael Moore, or Ben Affleck, and are they okay? These are dark days for America's malcontents, slapped with a sharp reversal of their hopes to subjugate their neighbors, and I want to do what I can to help.

Take a deep breath Lefties, unburden yourselves, and write your own guide to pleasure. Given their ostentatious embrace of all the suffering in the world, it will be tough for the libs to adopt an atavistic pursuit of good times separate from their ideology, so we'll have to make allowances. For instance, a movie might help. Though "Fast Times at "Ridgemont High" was Sean Penn's greatest work, it might be a little too upbeat for you this week. So try "Dead Man Walking" to get a double dose of earnest with the foreign policy expert himself and the equally knowledgeable Susan Sarandon. Or you could go for really painful earnestness and remember the good old days, and curse Nixon along with Tom Cruise in "Born on the Fourth of July." If you want to exorcise your anguish over evil corporate-delivered health care, rent "John Q." starring Denzel Washington (a flick so egregious in stereotypes that even Michael Moore's upcoming hit piece on health care will have to stoop mighty low to compete). Those feeling both misunderstood and nostalgic may want to try "The Way We Were", a film about loving Commies starring a couple of them. Another warped right-wing friend of mine recommends that sad liberals needing to re-energize should sacrifice the three hours and watch "Woodstock", to help them remember when being musically savvy freeloaders was celebrated.

And speaking of music, all of you gloomy grumps, throw on some good old, I-feel-rotten-and-the-world-isn't-fair-we-must-organize music to lift your spirits. The Dixie Chicks and Sheryl Crow may be a little too fluffy, and John Mellencamp can grate a bit surly. If you don't mind echoes from the campaign trail, then "The River" by Bruce Springsteen will help you to re-focus on all of those out of work union laborers in Ohio with too much free time to celebrate gun rights and fight gay marriage. On second thought, maybe that's a bad idea. Then pull out some old Joan Baez or Peter, Paul, & Mary – don't deny it, you still listen to them – and hearken back to the golden days of consciousness raising when it was all about the music, man. If you really need to be bucked up, go to the original source of musical proletarian ranting with Pete Seeger singing "If I Had a Hammer", his original COMINTERN fundraiser from the Forties. Why you'll be writing checks to Uncle Joe Stalin in no time.

Fancy a vacation? MSNBC reported a six-fold jump in the hits on Canada's immigration websites after the election, so there may be a bit of a wait if you want an extended stay. Apparently similar circumstances abound in New Zealand, where the immigration officials have purportedly begun to scrutinize skill levels of applicants as a pre-condition for acceptance. A forlorn collectivist might take a sunny jaunt down to Cuba to see how things really should be run, what with all the free health care, free schools, low crime rate, and high official employment figures. One word of advice: take your own toilet paper, just in case.

The concept of comfort food is no stranger to the left, and Ben and Jerry's Ice Cream will fit the bill nicely. Though all of their flavors really are excellent, "Rain Forest Crunch" sends proceeds to help save you know where. Their delicious "One Sweet Whirled" (featuring endorsement and printed message by rock star Dave Matthews) will teach one to "discover how easy it is to make a measurable impact combating climate change personally" while enjoying a tasty treat – presumably raising enough consciousness to offset the energy produced to refrigerate the product. You could arrange a meal of curry powdered tofu-tossed organic seaweed and fair-trade grown herbal tea, to develop passive and peaceful thoughts. Or for a perverse thrill, go get an actual hamburger at McDonald's. The damage you do to the environment and the aggression you develop from eating flesh will be offset by publicly worrying over the plight of the minimum wage flippers in the back whose social security taxes will need to be raised in order to take care of them decades from now. Whatever it takes, American liberals get out and enjoy your day, and put the election thumping you just suffered out of your mind. Leave the heavy lifting on the economy, entitlements, and national security up to the GOP. Given the past decade, they aren't likely to do too much before you return."

And bless 'em, the impotent GOP did not disappoint. If ever there was a party in need of rhetorical Viagra it was the Republicans, whose confidence was already flagging as the summer of 2005 began a long season of opportunities missed. The Bush Administration moved ahead so swiftly in pursuing no positive initiative in its second term that voters could be excused for wondering why they had even bothered...

The GOP Blowing It Again

"Beyond the media hype, this summer's big blockbuster features wrenching plot twists and turns, in a plot which echoes the revenge motive of Moby Dick, the self-destruction parody of Frankenstein, and the incomprehensible charity of the Lord of the Rings. No, no, I don't mean the Star Wars finale. I'm talking about the hapless Republicans. Tell the truth be you deranged right-winger or craven liberal, didn't you just know this was going to happen. Amidst a rising howl of media protest, flipping one news cycle into the next in command of the topic of debate, riding a building wave of momentum, the GOP simply...did it again. As has been famously repeated for forty years plus, Republicans never miss an opportunity to miss an opportunity.

Since World War II Republicans have been oddly apologetic for being Right. They championed the fight against cold war communism, and have been doing their sad duck-and-covers ever since whenever a spineless lib hisses "McCarthyism!" The GOP got the 1964 Civil Rights Act passed and us OUT of Vietnam after the Dems got us in, yet will not forcibly refute their media portrayals of racists and warmongers. Nixon gave away the store on the home front in a big government fiesta complete with price-control punch and an OSHA piñata. Then after the wonder years of foreign and domestic success under the brilliant Jimmy Carter, Reagan's white horse had to step for eight years around piles left by congressional donkeys of less noble purpose.

The first Pres. Bush was so embarrassed by the positions of his former boss that he made the awful phrase "kinder but gentler" manifest in public policy, buying into unsubstantiated global warming foolishness, and the biggest sucker deal offered any U.S. president in thirty years. As a "compromiser" Bush '41 brought us increased taxes, on income, gas, and luxuries; no increase in gross federal revenue, yet higher inflation, and higher unemployment (including Pres. Bush, who forgot to read his own lips). Instead of spending cuts, we got blossoming expenditures in Medicare, highway funds, local pork, and an enlarged constituency for government handouts. In the four years after Reagan, the average voter was given no reason to vote FOR a set of ideals, but rather encouraged to vote for whoever would dispense more government goodies. And donkeys will always outpace the elephants in that race.

In her first term the unelected Mrs. Clinton went a bridge to far (good thing she wasn't riding with Uncle Ted) with her attempted nationalization of health care, and returned the Congress to Republican control in 1994. And though they forced Pres. Clinton into welfare reform, the Republican Congress has presided over uninterrupted government growth for the past 11 years.

And now like Captain Ahab, the Dems chase the great white W., thus far to their electoral peril. The sand upon which John Kerry's electoral demise was built was this simple fault: there was never any reason to vote FOR him. There were plenty of plausible reasons to vote against W., but there were no reasons to vote for Kerry. Domestically the GOP has not been seriously challenged on their ideas, which daily have become more watered down in the public eye due to their spending habits. As with Nixon thirty years ago, the liberals' job is being done for them by cowardly Republicans afraid to advance their own ideas. The GOP should have eliminated the wasteful Dept. of Education, searched for ways to cut or privatize Medicare, eliminate Medicaid, and shrink the size of government. Instead they increased funding across the board and worked to out-bribe the Dems in preparation for the past election. Republicans have saddled the nation with a stupid "homeland security" boondoggle full of brand new union workers (although you can now politely air out your feet while waiting in the airport security line). W. and Senate Majority Leader Frist strong-armed through a grotesque increase in Medicare benefits that guarantees a descent into the system that Hillary promised. The Party of Lincoln continues to feed an unholy monster of growing government in hopes of taming it and giving it kindness, even as the peasants' torches grow dimmer for want of fuel.

In her latest book Anne Coulter eviscerates, noting how "Weak and frightened conservatives crave liberal approval and will do anything to get it", and here is proof: the Republicans control Congress and the White House and accordingly, with the future of the judiciary on the line, they caved again. The Democrats were on the mat with an elephant's foot on their yellow neck, bleeding under the power of party discipline and the force of reasoned argument. And the GOP let them up, let them off, and screwed their red state supporters again. By allowing the Dems to hide behind a completely extra-constitutional filibuster instrument, the Republicans have again shown themselves to be ineffectual leaders of a status quo, made to look competent only in comparison to their retarded competition. Of the filibuster compromise, dastardly architect Sen. John McCain said "I believe that good will prevail." To blazes with that! When if not now when we have the advantage, is it time for a fight? The minority party was promised the right to filibuster judicial nominees or any other competent conservative under "extraordinary circumstances" which means, "Whenever they feel like it."

Frodo spared Gollum's life because he glimpsed some goodness within, as well a Republican might see in the intentions of a Democrat colleague. But the core ideas of the Democrats invite only evil and subjugation, and should be fought and snuffed out whenever the chance arises. Remember also from the Lord of the Rings that the forces of Good could not wield the One Ring without themselves transforming into evil. An elderly friend of mine took great umbrage at my referring to her as a "yellow dog Democrat" until I explained the term, which she then accepted with pride. She and I enjoy a little joust over the conflicts of the day, but we are in complete agreement on a sad point. God-fearing right-wingers such as I will generally vote Republican because we have nowhere else to land. But for the great masses of less informed and undecided, there is at present no effort to convince them of the rightness of conservative ideas and if Republicans do not reverse this, the country will burn for it."

Yep, I got that one right. In the year following, the public face of the GOP became Alaska's corrupt Senator Ted Stevens who built the famous "bridge to nowhere", and Florida's Rep. Mark Foley who never considered that his e-mail come-ons to minors would ever see the light of day. Whoops! By Election Day 2006, any conservative rhetoric had no punch left with the voters, and the GOP got what it richly deserved...

Election Wrap-Up '06:
The Race to the Bottom

"The general election is around the corner, and one wonders which team to back. In 2004 W. faced reelection against a challenger so bad that there was no other sane alternative, and an opposition party so ridiculous that they could not be trusted with important work. As we discussed two years ago, both candidates would increase government and reduce our freedoms; one would try hard to get the French to like us, and the other would blow more enemies up. If not optimal, the choice was at least an easy one.

But two years later, the Republican administration is stalemated on all fronts. Abroad they have not prosecuted the war with the ferocity it deserves, and enemies that should have been broken to dust are growing in strength and number. At home the GOP has not put its back into the fight, and its rhetoric is all that is mildly distinguishable from the Dems. Republicans should have held W.'s feet to the fire and forced him to sell the public on his vision for Iraq. They have not, and so neither has he. Republicans should have eviscerated the Dept. of Education. A lot of "No Child Left Behind" blather later, the education budget continues to rise with no lessening of the power of the teachers' unions. Talk about tax cuts is great, but all new spending is just taxes deferred, and NOTHING has been done to reduce entitlement spending. The GOP had the courage to vote free drugs for Granny, but they didn't have the guts to force drilling in ANWAR to keep gas prices low. The GOP and the Dems have collaborated after two major shocks- 9/11 and Katrina – to increase spending, and increase the intrusion of government into private lives. (Airport security is a perfect demonstration of bipartisanship combining good old Republican authoritarianism with sniveling Democrat unionism, invading privacy, wasting money, and accomplishing nothing in terms of improving security). Everywhere the federal government is overreaching its limits (eminent domain anyone?), yet will not enforce proper constitutional functions. The failure of both major parties to secure our border rivals their failure to secure the budget, with consequences soon to be just a disastrous.

Are post-modern Democrats un-American? It is obvious to all but the willfully self-delusional that 21st Century Democrats routinely vote for figures and policies that deliberately tear down the principles of our founding-you know, things like limited government, private property rights, and national defense. On the national level, a vote for the donkey is a vote against an America founded on freedom. (In response to a detractor of pro-freedom principles, I observed that that a certain set of standards was in play:

All you have to do to be a Democrat today is to believe:

1. We are a society of tolerance and diversity, that accepts Muslims, gay pride parades, Greenie naturists, and pretty much everyone else so long as they do not profess any public pro-Christian sentiment, which is just plain offensive.

2. Saddam should have been stopped when he was gassing the Kurds and Iranians, and when he was known to be acquiring nuclear power technology through France and Germany; and after being warned for several months about U.N. inspections, he would not possibly have moved any WMD evidence to Syria, Jordan, or hidden it

3. When Kim Il-Sung built nuclear weapons it was a clear failure of the Bush administration's refusal to enter in bilateral talks, but when North Korea Trade first ac-

quired their nuclear technology courtesy of bilateral talks with the Clinton administration, that represented good diplomacy.

4. The United States should place the dictates of the United Nations above our own interests, and we should continue to fund them when they criticize us, dictate how to use our military, and seek to redistribute our wealth to other countries.

5. It makes sense that if a woman elects to have an abortion, she is making a rational choice regarding a part of her body not considered to be a separate individual; AND if that same woman is hit by a drunk driver and loses the pregnancy, the driver can be charged with vehicular homicide for killing a baby.

6. The best way to improve military morale is risk our troops in "peacekeeping operations" in areas such as Haiti, Somalia, Darfur, Bosnia, and anywhere else there are human rights abuses and most importantly, no vital U.S. interests.

7. Educating children about sexuality will be best accomplished by the very institutions proven to be unable to teach them basic math or reading skills.

8. The best way to prevent terrorist attacks is to try to understand why they hate us, apologize for being who we are, and hope they won't do it again. (Maybe the U.N. will put in a good word for us). Above all we should look to the French, a culture and government crumbling from within to entitlement and Muslim immigration, for approval and guidance.

9. Providing health care to our deserving seniors and anyone wishing to be defined as needy is the obligation of a compassionate society, even if it prevents those who pay the bills from buying their own medical care and bankrupts the nation. Society has no authority to force contraception on mothers unable to afford more children, but every obligation to pay for further offspring.

10. Global warming is largely the fault of the U.S., which should adhere to the Kyoto Protocols, while nations that produce far more carbon emissions – India, China, Brazil – should still be able to opt out

11. When Pres. Clinton launched major air strikes the day before his grand jury testimony (Sudan) and the day before the start of his impeachment trial (Iraq), he had the best interests of the nation in mind. When W. invaded Iraq on the basis of information agreed upon by the CIA and British intelligence, he did so for personal reasons. In the 1990's Clinton was right when he publicly stated on multiple occasions that Saddam should be gotten rid of; when W. actually did it, he was irresponsible and reckless.

12. The Constitution is a living document, including a "right to privacy" not actually enumerated; the First Amendment is sacred and cannot be infringed upon (except for campaign finance "reform" and when it comes to reviving the Fairness Doctrine to shut up talk radio). The Second Amendment is anachronistic and a threat to our kids. The Equal Protection clause does not apply to the wealthy, however we choose to define them.

13. Having leaders in power who understand an industry is utterly corrupt; having leaders who have no business experience whatsoever is pure and promotes "fair" markets.

14. The fact that the health care system has been collapsing since the inception of government-run health care – Medicare and Medicaid – is clear evidence that the government needs to control more of health care.

15. A person who puts in 40-hour weeks working on an assembly line is a "working" American who should be celebrated and whose family's needs should be guaranteed by government assistance; a self-made millionaire who averaged 60+ hours / week building the company that provided jobs for those on the assembly line and who pays many times the worker's share of taxes is a man of leisure and not doing his fair share.

16. Bill Clinton fudging on his draft notice, first agreeing to serve and then seeking a questionable waiver, was savvy and legitimate. George W. Bush serving in the Air National Guard was dishonorable.

17. Billions spent on the U.S. Dept of Education to keep the teachers' unions in charge of education is good for the nation; billions spent on high tech weaponry that our enemies cannot match is a terrible waste.

18. A hapless senator caught foot-tapping in a men's' room gay sting is good riddance; a crusading anti-business liberal governor caught in a prostitutions ring is a personal tragedy.

(After acclaiming Barak Obama as our Dear Leader, Democrats may be offended by the preceding characterization, to which I respond: good. Here is your opportunity for improvement. And not one word of this thumbnail analysis of the F.D.R. crowd is in any way a defense of the anemic Republicans! Now back to our column in progress)

Voters may be excused if they vote away from the party of Reagan, and sadly, the Bushes. By timidly mentioning, but not fighting for their beliefs (whatever they may be) the GOP has done nothing to inspire voters to reward them with continued power. The two faces representing the parties this past week were dismal: a red-faced, embarrassed former Democrat president, jabbing his finger at a reporter while trying to defend his indefensible record; and a sleazy Republican congressman, playing the traces of power to sexually exploit minors in his charge. American politics as in days of old, is still in a smoky tavern. At one table are seated loud, angry felons, willing to lie, steal, and enslave with abandon for their own ego and perverted sense of goodness. At another table are men who appear sober and strong, cowards in reality who tuck their chins in disdain at the turmoil, yet who will do nothing to stop it. A third table appears less crowded, and with a better view, but is ignored by the waitress. In November it truly matters that we DO vote. But this year on the national level, it may not matter so much for whom we pull the lever."

The following January, 2007, in his last State of the Union address, the George W. Bush's shambling, incoherent philosophy was on grand display in a last formal description of what would become a miserably failed presidency, and (fatal?) lost opportunity...

Bears, Bush, and Hypocrisy

"A former congressman and a lawyer on Fox News were debating the shocking double standard over Chicago Bears defensive tackle Tank Johnson. Badly needed in a bid to win the Super Bowl this week, Johnson has been forbidden to leave his locale of record due to weapons charges, but wait – the ruling judge reversed himself, what with the need to have Johnson in the Big Game in Miami. The debate that followed featured the former congressman asking the lawyer whether Americans are really such hypocrites, as to look the other way and to grant special prerogatives to a big time athlete. The lawyer in an unguarded moment of honesty, answered that yes, Americans anymore really are that hypocritical. Americans prefer to think of themselves as celebrants of the rule of law – providing of course that that it won't interfere with their right to enjoy a championship contest.

Pres. Bush spoke to those same variable standards in his latest State of the (dis)Union, offering through lame rhetoric policy positions that simultaneously give us what we want, while standing at odds with who we claim to be. W. touted a 41st month of uninterrupted job growth and 7.2 million new jobs, and claimed that our vibrant economy will remain so "not with more government, but with more enterprise." He then proceeded to call for a great deal more government. Bush described Social Security and Medicare and Medicaid as "commitments of conscience" which we have a duty to keep permanently sound. He knows this is impossible, and has neither the foresight nor the courage to speak the truth to the nation's self-absorbed seniors and the generations they will bankrupt. Bush

44

called for more -MORE?! – education spending, ignoring utterly that every increase in federal education spending has led to more subsequent spending. The Commander-In-Chief incredibly seeks a "volunteer Civilian Reserve Corps to give people who do not wear the uniform a chance to serve in the defining struggle of our time." He called for more cash to fight African AIDS and malaria, foreign debt relief (hello Bono!), the general elimination of worldwide poverty, and a greater energy reliance on, I am not making this up, grasses and wood chips.

Bush said, "The greatest strength we have is the heroic kindness, courage, and self-sacrifice of the American people." The statement makes sense if one believes our soldiers are properly put at risk in humanitarian nation building amidst murderous adversaries; that our treasure ought to be showered abroad to fight contagion and corruption, while being sapped at home through wildly profligate spending AKA 'compassion"; that our national identity is usefully sacrificed to a southern neighbor who will not put its affairs in order. Self-sacrifice was the defining value of the USSR. To those that believe in the primacy of the individual and the ideal of American Exceptionalism, the president's statement was simply un-American. The very president who has yet to veto a spending bill called for an elimination of the federal spending deficit within five years. He has not allowed the ruthless prosecution of a war that requires it, but now wants us to believe that an additional twenty thousand troops will finish the job absent a truly new tactical or strategic policy. Bush has not faced down his political opponents, who should be privately overjoyed at the capitulation of ideas so meekly laid before them. And can we blame him?

He is responding to voters and a media that call for freedom, and then seek to support their liberties through laws governing every conceivable human activity and aspiration. Bush wants to appeal to an electorate that claims it believes in the sanctity of free enterprise – unless it involves health care, education, retirement planning, government jobs, or corporations that need bailouts. The Dems are gleeful to now stoke the passions of a people who want to be praised as free men, and cared for as entitled wards. We want our lawbreakers off the street, unless they are needed to help the Bears win on Sunday. Play ball.

No, the last belches of stale beer and nachos after the State of the Superbowl did not taste good. And the one shot at conservatism for the GOP started behind the pop-culture eight ball, in one of the dumbest media periods in memory, which was saying something...

Romney and the Pinup

"Mitt Romney, just retired as governor of Massachusetts, may have committed one of the worst blunders in timing in recent political memory. One supposes a splash, a break in tempo, some crease of the public consciousness is needed to validate such a grandiose pronouncement, that one indeed is going to run...for...President of the United States! (applause). Gov. Romney is a photogenic, evenly spoken pol with a somewhat innovative universal health care plan. Some say he will have a tough road in the primaries, due to flip-flopping on abortion as a governor, and due to his being from a liberal state that has fastened on to the neck of the national body politic like a liquored-up bat searching for a mixer. But it's not like Romney is running against any conservative. Giuliani? Cleaned up New York and looked really tough on 9/11, but he will be ripped by the social conservatives less concerned with a broad notion of freedom than with its moral overlay. McCain? Oh please, Mr. Insider has been in the thick of too many deals too many spending increases, and too many episodes of "Hardball" with Chris Matthews to accomplish much more than give the media goo-goo eyes.

No, Gov. Romney's problem is one of horrendous timing. Five days before his big, long planned announcement in his birth state, time stopped. He had it all planned out: go to Dearborn, Michigan to capitalize both on the legacy of his dad – a former Michigan governor, and auto exec – and to dig an early spur into the all-important primary state where he could put paid to McCain. The EMP that no one was prepared for was not the Electromagnetic Pulse of a nuclear warhead; it was Engorging Media Parasites, bursting in all directions away from and toward the detonation of Anna Nicole Smith. Geraldo, Wolff, Larry, Keith, Greta, and all the rest have fallen on the corpse of the pinup princess like hybrid-powered maggots, munching, digesting, and self-composting as they pick the bones clean, soil them, and then scrape them anew. She was a fried doper, a graduate of the Ozzy Ozbourne School of Really Higher Education and (Ad)Diction whose only assets could not purchase the friends or judgment she desperately lacked. Her orphan is a carbon-based lotto ticket in for misery in perpetuity if some compassionate stranger doesn't abduct the kid when the lawyers aren't looking, and take her to live with a kindly pack of wolves. Society consumed this beautiful, vacant creature and let her wander the streets for years in a coma as a

Leno punch line and Trim-spa zombie, and then finally a beaker for chemicals flung by quack doctors willy-nilly at sad, ignorant patients. But we are in danger of being pulled ourselves into the maelstrom.

Kim Jung Il is attempting to hoodwink us again, and the Iraq-Iran storm is gathering strength. Our national budget is a mess, the illegals aren't waiting for a wall to be built, and a BET spokesman called Candidate Obama an "African African-American." Ice caps are melting, killing 40,000 polar bears every hour, and psychologists have now begun to recognize "affluenza", the emotional malady that perpetrates untoward guilt on the well-to-do. There is news out there, but we can't find it. Time and space have ground to a halt, and the laws of physics have warped before the calamity at the core of our society. And Romney announced in the middle of it. Someone should have been ready for a media black hole like this, and delayed the announcement. Excuses be damned, some staffer's head should roll over this major flub-up. Romney's only chance to make back the lost time is to claim that he is the father of Anna Nicole's baby, plan on the attached millions as campaign revenue, hire Danny Bonaduce as his press spokesman, and then sue the McCain camp if the DNA doesn't pan out. *(Well 'ol Mitt did not take my advice either, and decided to run only on record and issues. The candidacy would die on the following Super Tuesday, fatally wounded by a pointless and stupid Guiliani candidacy, a last-second moderate local Florida governor endorsement, and downright lies from the McCain campaign that cost Romney Florida, and Republicans their last chance at winning in '08.)*

By 2007, the Dems were in full cry like starved, retarded hound dogs, bounding to and fro over every issue, whizzing on the linoleum, never caring what they had previously said on this or that topic, but rushing to the next pre-debate debate to exhort and puff and spew over this or that trouble. A lot of class warfare got thrown around in that pre-election year (doesn't it always?) and a big target was EVIL BIG OIL! Unaware of the far worse gas prices six months around the bend, I tried to wrap my poor brain around the concept of unfair profits and "gouging"...

Is It Okay to Be Gouged?

"Sometimes life can be so confusing. The other day while riding around with my father, we stopped at a light in front of a gas station billboard proclaiming the latest prices. I had noticed just the day before that diesel prices have often now exceed regular gasoline prices, and mentioned the observation. Genuinely sage in most matters, the old man growled out that in fact diesel prices had soared now that more consumers are buying diesel vehicles, and that it amounted to "(expletive) gouging." Now in point of fact, gasoline prices according to the federal government reached their pick this year in June and are now slightly lower, whereas diesel prices have risen steadily to their current average high of $3.30/gallon (it must also be repeated that Uncle Sam still makes more profit from each gallon of gas than does anyone who actually provides said product, but we digress). What bewildered me so was the whole concept of "gouging." Not only are more such cars being purchased from diesel market stalwarts Mercedes and Volkswagen, but more manufacturers including GM and Honda are seeking to produce cleaner hybrid diesel cars. Apparently the auto industry as well as consumers sense good mileage value as well as good ecological sense in the future of diesel, thus a greater demand for crude's first fractionated level. Hmm.

With all humility I asked the old man whether the increase in diesel prices was not just a normal, even healthy price response to increased consumer demand. "Well" he huffed, "the government shouldn't let them get away with that!" Oh dear. But why, I meekly suggested, should the government interfere with normal market forces, which increased the demand for a good value and logically led to higher prices? And truly what constitutes gouging? Does a twenty-five cent increase in the price of diesel meet the definition of "gouge?" A buck? When a hurricane slaps our coast the locals cast a jaundiced eye upon the merchant whose prices for chainsaws and plywood go a bit higher than expected. Silly local officials sometimes posture that they will come down hard on gouging, but that is just their own way of exploiting circumstances which makes them no better than the alleged gouger. If the merchant charges more than the community thinks fair as the storm crosses the horizon or in a bad aftermath, will he not pay the price in lost community goodwill and decreased sales? Is he not therefore, by modulating his profits in time of perceived crisis, responding to expected market forces?

The old man was unimpressed. Look, I asked, what about health care? "Same thing" he replied, "look at the (expletive unnamed insurance company). They should be in the business of helping people, yet they were going to cut payments to our hospital last year by the exact percentage of their CEO's bonus (But isn't the company supposed to be in the biz of maximizing its profits?) He continued: "The (plural expletives) were sticking it to us just to pay this guy a big bonus, so we threatened to stop accepting their insurance and hold a press conference explaining why." He described the end result in which the CEO backed down and the payment cuts were abandoned. Was this then not the result of market forces, the customer pressuring the seller by threatening not to purchase further? And should not determinations of CEO bonuses be the concern of his stockholders? What business is it of the customer, whether he buy by fuel or medical care, so long as the buyer gets what he paid for? "Well yeah, but they shouldn't be allowed to get away with that." But they didn't! I pressed the question: "What defines gouging?" Nonplussed, the elder parked the car and declared it was time for coffee, leaving me to wonder what a "fair" price would be for a large cup of java."

❖ ❖ ❖

Another permanent feature in U.S. politics, public requests for and claims of support from the Almighty, lost no verve in the election season that would showcase (racist) Preacher Wright calling for God to damn the nation. I'd like to scrape politics clean of the clergy, but suppose there is the entertainment value as consolation for the bother...

Passing the Plate

"Before Inauguration Day '05, in between dusting off our best shoes and trying to get the mothball smell out of our tuxedoes for the Inaugural Ball, one found a moment or two to reflect on the hapless Democrats. Our blue-state buddies were flopping around on the electoral beach, starving for the influence-rich waters from whence they were heaved by the rube knuckle-draggers of the South and the Midwest. CSPAN, the cable shows, et al. had been replete since Election Day with Democrat operatives, James Carville clones, and concerned-looking talking heads over the effects of faith in turning the race, as exemplified by Bill Clinton's Sec. of Labor, Robert Reich: "My recommendation to Democrats is not to become more religious, [but to] talk more about faith ... and yes, it is a matter of faith that in all these respects, and many more, this nation can become a more just society." Stopping to pause, and listen closely, we heard the teeth grinding and mental gears screaming, as all of the usual suspects on the Left began to tone their rhetoric toward the rhythms, if not the actual substance, of faith. Worse yet, we soon saw a reemphasis on bending the substance of faith toward the purposes of a bigger, more benevolent government.

After his heroic stand against the idiot cruelty of institutionalized racism, Martin Luther King, Jr. turned his energies toward problems that he should have known he could not solve. He once said, "Without love, benevolence becomes egotism." This marvelous quote contrasts usefully with a later one: "The curse of poverty has no justification in our age. It is socially as cruel and blind as the practice of cannibalism at the dawn of civilization, when men ate each other because they had not yet learned to take food from the soil", with which King was making the case for wealth redistribution in his final work, *Where Do We Go From Here?* In this instance he failed to grasp that to love something was to understand it. Wealth redistribution always involves coercion, and limits freedom. How can one love humans without loving their freedom? A pattern of using heartfelt faith to rationalize political ends emerges, though always with the best of intentions.

Washington Post columnist David Broder advised that Democrats must "restore the language of values to the party's rhetoric, and try to reconnect with people of faith." That reconnection has often and will further still, take the form of clergy pushing their flock toward political positions for purposes of faith; and politicians using the faith of their listeners as leverage toward greater power, though of course with the best of intentions. In 2004 Rt. Rev. John Crane, Bishop of the Episcopalian Diocese of Washington, implored his flock to fight against a "draconian program of social welfare", stating that such spending cuts were "not at all what Jesus meant when he said 'suffer the little children.'" The U.S. Catholic Bishops' Conference echoed these sentiments in their policy statements which support "a right to …food, clothing, shelter, education, health care, a safe environment, and economic security…to just wages and benefits, to organize and join unions…" and so on. And lest we need reminding, it was this bunch who came out very publicly against the Republican attempts to reform welfare in 1995, reiterated that same year by the Catholic Bishop's of Florida who decreed that "Solidarity must be promoted in both the public and private sectors to generate jobs at a fair wage." Statements like these distill to the Church having government pass the plate, reinvigorating my enthusiasm for church-state separation.

Now let's consider the comments of a couple of leftist wackos, sorry, concerned activists. Attorney Beth Shulman, co-director of the "Fairness Initiative on Low-Wage Work": "It is a moral issue whether or not a child has healthcare, whether a family has quality childcare, or whether parents have enough to feed their children or send them to college." (So she makes the leap from demanding Frosted Flakes to demanding an undergraduate degree?). And Prof. Dan Carter of the Univ. of South Carolina: [The Democrats' 2008 choice should be] "a physically attractive, white male...able to feel the pain of the American people (or fake it satisfactorily) and talk about Jesus without looking as if he had stumbled fully clothed into a nudist colony...the 'Christian Right' is simply reactionary politics with gospel lip gloss.'" So if we put the faith-based intentions of the clergy and the big-government hug of concerned activists into a blender, what might we get? "We must stop thinking of the individual and start thinking about what is best for society." [Hillary Clinton, 1993] "I don't think people realize how strong your faith is."– Barbara Walters to Hillary Clinton. "Probably my worst quality is that I get very passionate about what I think is right." Said Sen. Clinton, "On the Record" with Bob Costas. Yes indeed, Hillary and challenger Obama had the ideology, religious rhetoric, and proclivity toward coercion to use the passions of the faithful to enlarge government. Unfortunately, W.'s groundless "compassionate conservatism", including the dispensing of federal funds to faith-based organizations, would further condition the nation to such initiatives for the poor, caught in the swirl of a deficit-laden economy 'round about 2007. Back in 1996, Hillary spoke to the Methodist General Conference: "What areas of common agreement do we have that can lead us as individuals, as a church, as community and society to work together on behalf of our children?...we know the biblical admonitions about caring for each other. We continue in this church to answer John Wesley's call to provide for the educational health and spiritual needs of children. We can be proud that our church has been a leader in the fight to improve the quality of education, promote parental responsibility, curb smoking among young people, expand comprehensive health care, strengthen marriages, and help people of all kinds of backgrounds."

Now I'm no biblical scholar, but it seems that the Central Character in the New Testament said that the poor would always be here. His admonitions to the individual to help the poor notwithstanding, I would be grateful if someone could direct me to the passage encouraging the use of government force to take from some to give to others."

Combining charm, snake oil, and a penchant for benevolent force made Bill Clinton America's first TV-preacher president. His ideological successor would take the game to the next level, using his preacher to perform a rhetorical slingshot past reluctant media criticism. But before Barak Obama's preacher would cause the media to lose interest in such topics, we were treated to the usual electioneering religious garbage...

2007 Primaries: Going for God's Endorsement

"With a zany election season gearing up, we increasingly hear candidates ending with "God Bless you all", a cheap tagline that should leave the voter cringing. As the candidates rush to pander, sorry, explain their respective views on religious faith, the role of a modern presidential aspirant is to achieve a workable schizophrenic dissonance: they must be preachers without really preaching (twin Revs Al and Jesse, the dynamic duo of civil rights, are available for counseling – for a fee). We feel better that a candidate both has a faith, and promises not to use it too much. Faith in general for a candidate may reassure as a prescriptive antidote to arrogance, but as demonstrated by Jimmy Carter and both Bushes, this is not a guaranteed preventive.

Why exactly is it so important that we know to whom and for what candidate so-and-so prays, provided there is no advocacy of violent martyrdom or Prohibition? The Founding Fathers were famously men of faith who neither established a state religion nor proscribed the joust of competing faiths. Their civic values that were greatly informed by the Judeo-Christian ethic are logical, and work perfectly well in the context of liberal individualism and free-market capitalism. One need not "believe" to believe that the system works and is the envy of the world.

We are threatened by Muslim extremists with bio-nuclear terrorism, and lazy moderators want to know how Mitt Romney's Mormonism will play in Alabama. We face a serious financial meltdown due to runaway entitlement spending and MSNBC goes all a-lather over whether Guiliani's abortion non-stance can survive Iowa. Country club Republicans a' la Nelson Rockefeller were an anchor dragging down conservative forcefulness in the face of liberal malaise and Communism. As a reaction the Falwell Moral Majority bolstered conservative ranks in the 1980's, but left a lingering hayseed image that has hampered persuasion in more cosmopolitan areas. In the 2000 GOP primaries, candidates were asked to name their biggest philosophical influence. His obvious and sincere faith notwithstanding, W.'s answer of "Jesus Christ" WAS smart politics, adroitly winking to spiritual brethren whose votes he coveted. It was also cheap and calculating, and cheated voters by displaying a lack of intellectual seriousness for that venue.

Democrats have honed their skills for religious marketing to new heights. No longer willing to simply rely on their amen corner in the "independent" black churches, the latest crop seeks to ape the GOP in listing God on their ballot. Pres. Clinton's Wife declared herself "a little too suspicious of people who wear their faith on their sleeves", and then did just that by describing how her faith had gotten her through her marital troubles. But in a political context, why ought that to be any of our business, except that PCW is obviously using her faith to play our emotions in order to accumulate power? From LBJ to Carter to Clinton, Democrats use religion to ironically speak in socialist tongues like the shadiest tent preachers. John Edwards affirmed that he prays daily and that "We are all sinners and we all fall short." That's great senator – now why is a multi-millionaire so interested in raising my taxes?

On the Right Falwell advised the White House on relations with Israel, and Pat Robertson does a verbal "Rambo" on Hugo Chavez in between commercials for his protein shakes. On the Left is the (anti-) U.S. Conference of Catholic Bishops, opposing welfare reform and border enforcement, effectively seeking to pick taxpayer pockets through federal programs to strengthen and sustain families. This brings us full circle to W.s identical rhetoric in pushing faith-based initiatives that are constitutionally inappropriate. Both tracks seek the same goal, wealth redistribution on a planetary scale as propounded by Bono and the new religious environmentalists. In order to protect our religiously founded traditional values, we must protect the equally important secular liberties of property rights and equality before the law, as well as national military and economic security. Ironically voters of faith should wish for a secular society that promotes shared civic virtues across religious lines, and which can reaffirm American values far better than thoughtless leaders parroting "God Bless..." whomever."

It is true that in practically every two-term presidential administration, by the last half of the second term the White House seems to lose steam, whether through loss of focus, frustration, or simple fatigue. That said, the 2008 presidential campaign was certainly shaped by the waning George W. Bush, and it was disastrous. W.'s last year in office was bad enough, with his growing penchant for government's compassionate interference and an unwillingness to restate again and again his reasons for pursuing the war in Iraq. The rhetorical incompetence of this White House was blinding, and its mumbling was aid to it's critics. W. responded ineffectually to $4/gallon gas prices by shelling out an expensive, and pointless refund check to those who had not earned it; when the real economic willies got hold of Wall Street, the Bushies swooped in with a bailout, about which he was later reputed to have said: "I've abandoned free market principles to save the free market system." The following year Pres. Obama used this as a justification to launch a far grander, far more damaging assault on the free market in the guise of assistance, and could always look back to W. with a shrug, saying his predecessor started it. 2008 was a year of ascendancy for mushy-minded, glib-tongued, populist liberalism, and we got what was coming to us. The GOP lost control of the Congress in 2006 by acting like Democrats, and now the same was about to happen to the White House. Bush set us up, but we allowed him *to. And as for the GOP hopefuls frantically elbowing their way to the spotlight...*

2007 Primaries: Is the GOP Serious?

"As the Republican ship languishes in the dog days doldrums before the run up to the most frenetic primary season in recent history, three potential forces are uncertainly hovering. The first is the current crop of primary candidates. Personally I would love to see Ron Paul take the lead, but neither himself, Huckabee, Tancredo, Hunter, nor Brownback can do little more than influence a debate here or there. None can muster any national buzz and none will therefore even be serious VP contenders. John McCain after having supported so many anti-freedom initiatives like the McCain-Feingold campaign reform bill, finally go his comeuppance over supporting W.'s "come-on-in" immigration policy in refutation of an increasingly grumpy base. The nomination is left at present, to either Mitt Romney or Rudy Giuliani. Romney is photogenic and sticking to a reasonable anti-tax message. On the down side he pushed through the Massachusetts universal coverage plan which, for all its market based verbiage, is not too dissimilar from Clinton Care in 1994. Romney's Mormonism should remain firmly in the "So What" bin, so long as his religion doesn't encourage suicide bombing or getting rid of SUV's, but after all these are the primaries. Romney has flipped on gay "rights", abortion, and conveniently joined the NRA only last year. He has started to criticize the administration's handling of the Iraq war, but has not yet slapped the White House for their failure to attempt serious entitlement reform, the latter that undercuts his appeal as the no-nonsense-CEO-candidate. Mayor Rudy still carries the greater name recognition, which continues to translate into first place as a GOP contender. The buzz on the 'net is that Giuliani has revved up his organization and is making strides in Iowa (which he was previously planning to ignore). Rudy also wants to cut some taxes, and he is additionally proposing tax credits to help keep private medical care affordable. His moderate pro-abortion, pro-gun control, pro-gay "rights" positions may survive the primaries, if Rudy can convince the base that they will land him in better stead vs. President Clinton's Wife come the general election. Both front-runner camps have generic, conservative-sounding platforms with nice rhetoric, not too many specifics, and thus far, absolutely no rhetorical fire whatsoever.

What does the GOP want to do? With no autumn winds yet on the horizon, Republicans must ask, then answer the serious question of what it is they really stand for. From the Congress to the individual candidates, the GOP continues to show the now-expected fealty to the Religious Right, yet makes no serious effort to court the libertarian, free economic so-called "South Park" conservatives (there really IS such a demographic). Positions taken by Mitt and Rudy are generally pro-war, yet not critical of Bush enough to peel off any independent votes from the Dems, and neither has laid out a forceful case to beat back the class warfare of the Left. "Hillary is Scary" is true, but as a central campaign theme will be only as effective as the last time the GOP Bob Dole'd itself right back to the bench. If nothing else George W. proved that rhetorical competence and oratory effectiveness are prerequisites for the job. Reagan is gone and the available candidates reflect the middling mediocrity of what passes for current Republican aspirations. The silent ominous question hanging in the sticky August heat for Romney, Giuliani, and the party: what of Fred Thompson? What does he stand for, what will he do, and can the large on-screen persona meld his booming voice with words and ideas effective enough to overcome inflated expectations and reenergize a languishing party?"

Man, had I ever picked a winner there. Not content with this one outing of superior prescience, I persisted with a hopeful Brittney Spears metaphor...

2007 Primaries: Seriously, Is the GOP Serious?

"The media tried to be kind, really they did. But the image that trotted out on stage was still too scantily clad for a frame that sagged in the wrong places. The lip-syncing occasionally was out of sync with the sound track, and the lone figure, revealed under the lights for the first time since (hopefully) leaving rehab, looked confused, diffused, and a little stoned. There was little glint of purpose or vision in the vacant eyes, searching desperately for approval. It was an expected performance from a big name star whose minimal potential talent was put at risk by a premature reentry into the spotlight, pursuing a successful comeback without the benefit of serious rehearsal or the requisite commitment to getting back in shape before baring most of it on a national stage. Thankfully last month's Iowa straw poll passed without inflicting any lasting damage on the GOP, or for that matter, any lasting impression.

Millionaire Mitt gaffed, comparing his sons' work on his campaign to service performed by the troops in Iraq, and then crawfished quick enough to give Paul Prud-homme new recipe ideas. Frontrunner Rudy Giuliani dodged the pageant, as did Senator "Amnesty" McCain, the latter presumably ringing up a good oral-podiatrist to undo his support for W.'s no-fence immigration fiasco. With only one of the top-tier candidates present in Iowa, a starving media regurgitated Gov. Mike Huckabee as the new conservative flavor, puffing him up as a possible alternative whose possibility will be zilch by New Hampshire. Sadly Rep. Ron Paul had long since allowed himself to be caricatured as the Right's Kucinich, an unfair portrayal which nonetheless has overshadowed his many other splendid ideas in the sound bite popularity game.

The biggest no-show in the Iowa non-show was former Tennessee senator Fred Thompson. Last week on Jay Leno Thompson pulled the pin and rolled his hat into the GOP big tent. Now a week later the race between Giuliani and Thompson for #1 among Republicans ranges from a dead heat (CNN/Opinion Research Corp poll) to a 12-point Rudy lead (USA/Gallup). McCain, Huckabee, and the rest can start angling for cabinet posts, or maybe the VP nod, but they are all second-string and all done. In the most compressed primary season ever, Romney must take New Hampshire to develop momentum heading into the South and Midwest where he will have to battle Rudy's national recognition and Fred's regional appeal. Giuliani may have larger "winability" appeal to primary voters desperate to defeat Pres. Clinton's Wife. His attraction will rest on a perceived eagerness to crack terrorist skulls, a reputation for running the trains on time, and the hope that moderation on social issues will quiet the media's froth over the zany evangelicals. The price paid will be an embrace of more of the same, yet another GOP administration cooperating with Democrats in pursuit of the vain goals of enlarging government compassion and a growing stock market. What of Thompson?

The actor/senator's announcement, website, and early appearances have all been relaxed, matter-of-fact, and highly effective in a basic 'aw shucks sort of way, if a bit light on specifics. His website contains a pretty comprehensive essay on the benefits of federalism, but also gives one a mild shiver when reading "It is appropriate for the federal government to provide funding [for education] and set goals for the state to meet in exchange for that funding." Conservatives want to be reassured by the cliché that "one in three Republicans in Hollywood goes on to be president," and will cheer his opposition to new taxes, support of The Fence (with Mexico), and a new firepower-diplomacy combo approach in the Middle East. His commonsense talk about the need for bipartisan entitlement reform is of course just that until we see some action that his predecessors shrank from. All in all a fresh face with the rejuvenated potential to remake the image of the GOP, but will he? Could Brittney Spears ever be remade into a Talbot's model? Not likely, but in this country, never impossible. And neither action would do its respective party any harm." *I know, I know, don't remind me...but whereas I completely overestimated the strategic thinking of the Republican primary voters, there was no question that whichever prizewinner the donkey party boiled up, he/she would be bad news.*

As noted, the Republicans had spent outlandishly in their attempt to be as likable as Democrats, and the latter were, uniformly against wealth creation, for wealth redistribution, and against responsible border control or foreign policy security –

which is to say, Democrats. While the waiter was figuring out the bill for the GOP abdication, the Democrats had already begun their march to the Oval Office. Those of us that had watched them, and had seen their results over the years, were not fooled a bit, and the party of McGovern/Carter/Mondale/Dukakis/ Kerry looked poised to serve up more of the same in late 2007 leading up to the primaries.

2007 Primaries: A Mule Staple

"Democrat presidential hopefuls gathered in South Carolina last week for their first formal debate, and the result was even more vapid and vacuous than the poor showing reasonably expected. Brian Williams of MSNBC was brilliantly lackluster, disguising softballs as "tough" questions, and pursuing nothing resembling edgy follow-up. Most of the talk was devoted to Iraq, a topic in which the candidates tried their best to find slither room around each other in the context of opposition to the war, and anything else the White House favors. Any given candidate was either for the war until realizing they were deceived by Bush-Cheney-CIA-Halliburton-FOX News (Clinton, Edwards, Biden, Richardson); against the war (Obama, Dodd), or they were against any war any time, ever (Kucinich, Gravel). It was shades of gray, and all meaningless. There were chances to explore serious questions, left unasked. Pres. Clinton's wife stated she was against the "sectarian civil war" in Iraq, but had been in favor of our intervention in the sectarian civil strife in the Balkans. What was the difference? She was not asked. Sen. Biden stated it was time to drop preemption as strategic policy to combat terrorism. How then would the senator, given intelligence of an impending attack, propose to deal with rogue states harboring terrorists? Incredibly Gov. Richardson, late of the Clinton administration, praised his own work: "We made the North Korean situation better" (the same terrorist state that has since developed nukes), and then wondered aloud why we don't care enough to get involved militarily in Darfur. Apart from George Clooney's self-esteem, it was left unclear what U.S. interest would be advanced in that post-Blackhawk Down part of the scrub. The most cogent, if loony, response came from perennial punch line Rep. Dennis Kucinich who "oppose(s) war as policy." (That Kucinich was supported in '04 by Willie Nelson proves the country legend has spent too much time in his tour bus smoking doobies). Obama fumbled an answer over how he would respond to another terrorist attack, but Democrats willing to nominate Kerry will forget that mini-gaffe by the weekend.

On the domestic side moderator Williams proved truly incompetent. He asked each hopeful an "800 lb gorilla" question designed to highlight a recent uncomfortable issue or stumble specific to the candidate. We heard references to Joe Biden's famous 1988 plagiarism, and John Edward's $400 hair cuts. We did not hear any serious queries regarding the really heavy primate, the domestic evil axis of Medicare/Social Security, the intergenerational wealth transfer that is devouring the economic future of the nation. John Edwards spun a sob story of his daddy being too poor take the family to Sunday dinner out, and assured viewers that this multi-millionaire remembered his working class roots well enough to want to raise taxes on anyone aspiring to become a millionaire. Clinton's Wife and Biden both agreed that the federal government did not do enough to prevent the Virginia Tech shootings through mental health screenings – the same government that cannot even close its own border to illegals, an idea proffered by none of the candidates. Edwards wants universal coverage provided by employer mandate, enlarging the riches he can loot when he returns to his medical malpractice day job. Obama urgently wants to "control costs", possible only through paying health workers less and denying more services to more patients, while Richardson wants to "focus on prevention." (Forgive the redundancy, but that rings sooo hollow from a man who helped allow Kim Jung-Il nukes and can't support controlling his own New Mexican border. Prevention indeed!)

The pep rally was a big nothing punctuated with a yawn. We already know that Democrats cannot be trusted with foreign policy, and will engage in class warfare for political power at every turn. And herein is the grand strategy. The Dems as currently arrayed are so bad, and so boring, that they will not seem to pose any serious threat on issues to the GOP. Republicans a' la Dole '96 (or Bush '06) may not feel the obligation to forcefully advance real ideas to counter the such a vacuum, and will play into the hands of a party better able to seed its own ignorance and apathy across the electoral plain." *Man oh man, I nailed that one, as the Obama love-plague the following year bore out.*

That 2007 pre-election year holiday season augured little of political improvement for the coming year. Trying to get a handle on things, I used one of my connections with the North Pole, and – after filling out numerous federal privacy guarantee forms – was given access to the letters heading in to Santa from nervous little boys and girls. After surveying and sifting through tens of thousands by subject line, I found letters from two adorable little tykes to Boss Red Suit which, along with his responses, summed it all up...

2007 Primaries: Letters to Santa

"Dear Santa,

I am very upset this Christmas. People don't seem to like me, and make fun of me constantly. They say I never know what I am doing, but then they turn around and ask me to help them with every little problem, and I'm glad to do it. I really think that war is bad all of the time if there is anything to gain. I feel very bad about what happened to New Orleans and I know I could have helped, even though I don't specifically know how. I know I am smarter than all of the others who disagree with me, but they are too stupid to shut up and do as I say, which is really a shame, because they would be so much happier if they would! Even if my plans don't always work out, isn't it more important that I wanted to help and that my intentions are good? I saw an old TV commercial where everyone held hands on a hilltop and had a Coke, and my parents told me that was the way things were supposed to have been. I wanted to ask Mommy and Daddy what I should do to make things that way, but they aren't back from the pharmacy yet – they said they were going to pick up their free prescriptions and might be celebrate with a nice dinner, and I was sad when they said they might not choose my ideas anymore. Since you are a Democrat like me, don't you think people should be nicer and listen to me?

Taylor

Dear Taylor,

Thank you for your letter. You sound like a very sad little girl...or boy, I couldn't tell for sure. I must tell you that no, I am not a Democrat. (As you may recall, my original name was Saint Nicholas, a moniker with religious overtones that would likely offend many in your group.)   Many like you think I am a Democrat, because I am always giving away free stuff. But what I give away is not taken from others through taxes or confiscations, nor are they merely the products of love or goodwill. They also come from hard work, something for which today's Democrats have scant relish. The reason that I keep a list of good little boys and girls is not only to reward good behavior, but to encourage it. There is no better way than by demonstrating cause-and-effect logic to youngsters, so that they can perceive the rewards that might be gained from their personal industry and discipline. Were I to promise children a reward up front, then it would be no reward at all. If children were made to feel entitled by building government candy stores or putting them in Toy Stamps programs, then the joy of receiving gifts would be lost to them and to their children, as generation after generation sat around their subsidized plastic Christmas trees in sullen expectation, waiting for a share they feel to be owed them. If ever they did not receive what they were expecting, they would protest mightily that they were being cheated by the very entity that had been their original benefactor. Eventually I might be hauled before Congress or grilled by Katy Couric to explain myself, even though I had done nothing wrong. And I really haven't the time. The latest OSHA regulations and the EDA (Elves With Disabilities Act) have really increased my overhead, and I have to spend every spare minute I have keeping the production lines going. This year I'm in a real fix – PETA is suing me for "enslaving" reindeer, and with the gas prices the way they are, trucks are out of the question. As for your Christ..., sorry, "holiday" wish, all I can say is that people will only be nicer and more respectful toward you if your ideas make sense. It's really neat I'm sure that you want to teach the world to sing, but you really do have to come up with better ideas than "Bush loves war" and "Republicans hate poor people." Do you have any ideas that don't involve big giveaways or taking from others, that will actually work? I'll be leaving a lump of coal in your stocking this year but don't be offended! After the way you have blocked any improved energy policy, you might need it. I'd like to leave some actual beliefs under the tree, but you will have to develop those on your own, if you can.

Santa

Dear St. Nicholas,

I have been extra good this year. I have been continuing the War on Terror, getting free drugs for old people, talking very seriously about putting up a fence to keep out the illegals, and acting concerned about baseball players taking steroids, all without taking a strong ideological stand on anything. My side controls the House, Senate, and Presidency, but we still can't seem to get much done. The press doesn't ever say nice things about us, nor do our dignified colleagues across the aisle, for whom we have the greatest respect. I really love freedom and limited government, and just to prove it I have increased the size of government and spent more than anyone ever has! I do everything I can to prevent terminal cancer patients from becoming potheads, and I have been very successful in keeping smut off of prime time TV, so parents won't have to actually monitor what their children are watching unless it's on cable. Wouldn't it be great if the Democrats would play fair and let us get back to making America a place where everyone can succeed?

Buddy

Dear Buddy,

Thanks for your letter. I can see that you are very confused. Maybe it's because you let your opposition define you, like when a nut-job, vitamin-pushing carnival bark like Pat Robertson says we ought to be assassinating disagreeable world leaders and CNN refers to him as a "Republican." Or maybe it's because you have developed such poor corporate self-esteem that you are willing to view adulation as accomplishment and can't stop chasing it. Maybe you are just confused because you don't know who you are supposed to be any more. It's okay to believe in Santa, but if you believe in the compassion of big government, or that the Democrats will ever play fair, then you really need to grow up. I would leave some core principles in your stockings this year, but you already have them. They won't work, however, unless you take them out of the box and use them.

Santa

I wish I had been wrong on that last point, but the GOP jumped, no stumbled, right into the trap. As 2007 closed out, it was obvious we were in for a great deal more silliness. I spent New Year's Eve that year with dear friends and, night owl that I am, was still wide awake with a fresh bottle of champagne around 3 AM, all by my lonesome. Searching for a good movie, I settled on one of my favorites, "The Big Chill" and settled back into a dreamy holiday recumbency. I closed out the night, plugging earphones into my swimmy head, and fell fast asleep with George Winston's "December" caressing my synapses on the last night of the year legal so to do. I dreamed, or think I did, and looked out on a new landscape wondering what had happened the year before...

2007: The Year That Probably Was

"No matter how you slice it, 2007 was a year to remember. Of course the big kickoff was in D.C. when the Dem horde regained Congress. Speaker Pelosi forced the White House to sign off on a minimum wage increase to $10.00, and an increased marginal rate on corporate CEO earnings to 90%, hailing these moves as a "triumph for working people everywhere." Following the sharp spike in inflation and unemployment in the third quarter, Pelosi promised, "the government could, and would do more." When stock prices fell in April, the drop in investment earnings soured many in the retired ranks, leading AARP to schedule a "Walkers in Washington" rally on the Mall. Podium speakers railed against the Bush Administration for their drop fixed income, the government's lack of responsiveness to growing lines at emergency departments, and the shrinking number of Medicare providers. In a televised address to the crowd, Pres. Bush assured them that he would press for a "seniors' tax credit refund", to remit 1% per year of life over 65. Shortly thereafter, West Virginia Sen. Byrd bypassed Jay Rockefeller to become the senate's richest member.

In foreign policy, things just got muddier. In exchange for the billions needed to renovate the U.N. building, W.

got the Secretary General to take over in Iraq – which seemed like a good deal until the blue helmets were besieged in the Green Zone, forcing the U.S. to re-deploy two new divisions to bail them out. Hugo Chavez invited the Iranian prez to a "Summit of the Oppressed" in Caracas, prompting Pat Robertson to state that an air strike on the conference would be "the loving thing to do." After another of his missiles blew up during launch, North Korean Beloved Leader Kim Jong Il blamed the U.S., and threatened a missile attack against the West Coast if it happened again.

In popular culture, the surprise movie hit of the year was "The Apologetic Congressman", a retelling of the heroic life struggles of Rep. Patrick Kennedy. Director Mel Gibson was humble in receiving the Best Picture Golden Globe nod, while title role Best Actor Robert Downey, Jr., suffering from "exhaustion", was unable to attend the ceremony. After her latest acquisition of a starving African child was blocked by the British government, Madonna infuriated her adopted countrymen by describing them "as dumb as Americans", whereupon she moved to Paris to "pursue her spiritual side." Faith paid as Brittany Spears described being born again on "Oprah", launching a surprisingly profitable Christian dance album featuring the hit single "Wiggle for Him." The sporting world was rocked by scandal and protest: first news broke that the NBA, in an effort to boost falling ratings, was actually paying players to start fights in the stands; then a PETA protest turned ugly following former heavyweight champ Mike Tyson's unfortunate actions during his first-ever bull ride.

In the run up to the 2008 presidential primaries, Pres. Clinton's wife expressed shock that rival Barak Obama had withdrawn from the race, following the surprising disappearance of his cat. In response to a visibly shaken Obama's statement that he needed to spend more time with his family, Bill's wife said that she was certain he would be available in time to accept the vice presidential nomination. (Campaigning for his wife in Maui during the Miss Hawaiian Tropic finals, Bill was unavailable for comment).

Speaker Pelosi adjourned the Congress in December, and promised that a Democrat return to the White House in 2008 would overcome Republican obstructionism, and allow her side to once and for all deal with entitlements growth, corporate greed, global warming, family dissolution, drug use, homelessness, illegal immigration, and universal health care. Furious, Republicans vowed to continue their fight against gay marriage."

I awoke New Year's Day to a spate of bowl games, hot coffee, and a nary a touch of hangover. And I think my dream mostly came true.

2008 – America Shoots Her Foot Off

The year began with an exciting weekly playoff of primaries, pure chocolate-covered gold for a politics junkie and welcome relief after the loss of football season. The races themselves were overlaid by the directionless final months of the W. Disappointment. By May, the last chance for conservatism, (even) lip service to limited government, and economic sanity had been left in a smoldering heap on the roadside leading out of Super Tuesday. Fred Thompson went back to bed, Guiliani became his own punch line, and Preacher Mike Huckabee strangely abetted eventual nominee McCain as the latter kneecapped Mitt Romney with last minute endorsements and outright lies, clearing the way for a Democrat victory. The die were already miscast by May when gas prices soared, allowing an anti-oil media to convince a populace growing dumber by the minute, that it was the fault of the administration that had actually been prevented from procuring more oil. W. responded with more compassion, sending out $1,500 checks largely to those who had not earned them, and was further castigated – simultaneously – for doing too little, and not enough. This sort of illogic made sense to the swelling herd-for-cool for whom confident pronouncements and good intentions beamed directly into their shrinking intellects formed a warm, *fuzzy sensation that crowded out all unpleasant thoughts and need for substance.*

When Candidate Obama went to Berlin to declare himself "a citizen of the world", it was a race to see which would win: his astounding self-importance, or his explicit anti-Americanism. As he ascended the mount to accept the Democrat nomination, it was clearly a tie which had gone to the loser, in this case, the nation. The following month John McCain as next-in-line threw an ingenious long bomb by nominating an actual conservative (and real looker to boot) in Sarah Palin. Then Gov. Palin was immediately dismantled by the popular media, and undercut by her own running mate. The media that thought nothing of Candidate Obama touring "all 57 states" called Palin dumb because of a folksy reference to the geographical proximity of Russia to her home state of Alaska. Having finally garnered plaudits from his conservative base for selecting Palin, McCain was a boring disaster in the debates. In mid-September the market crashed and the western economy apparently teetered on the brink. The cause was, as usual, government meddling in the economy, this time in the real-estate market. Not content with inflating home prices and coercing lending to the unqualified, Uncle Sam had then started to invest in the very structure he had destabilized. The Bush Administration had attempted to call for reforms in 2003 and was publicly blocked by Rep. Barney Frank (D-Ma). It was Frank and sweetheart loan recipient Senator "Country-wide" Chris Dodd (D-Ct) who had fed the gorging appetites of Fannie Mae and Freddie Mac, and when shown to be terminally corrupt, blamed the whole thing on capitalism. To be sure there were greedy, criminal types like Bernie Madoff who furthered the damage, but lost on an idiot public was that the crooks would have been able to inflict far, far less damage without the enabling hand of government compassion. The Bush Administration in a panic infamously ignored the free market in order to save it; with the Troubled Assets Relief Program, Bush blew a ton of money and gave rhetorical cover for his socialist successor to blow far more. Autumn 2008 was a season of growing fear among actual taxpayers, and unfounded "Hope" among voters gleeful for "Change." America had spent the last several years drunkenly pointing her fiscal pistol at her toes, flirting with something too stupid to contemplate. With the election of Barak Obama, she sited the middle of her foot and with manic, desperate joy, pulled the trigger.

As John McCain tightened his grip on the Republican nomination in Spring, 2008, the developing scenario reminded me of one of my favorite movies...

The Two Towers

"In 2002 the second part of director Peter Jackson's legendary masterpiece, "The Lord of the Rings" was released. "The Two Towers", told the story of the desperate struggle of small fragmented societies caught between two dueling powers each bent on controlling the world to fulfill its own egomania. The story's author J.R.R. Tolkein demonstrated in his tome a highly developed grasp of the spectrum of human psychology from grief to superego to narcissism to addiction, in such a way that would have superbly equipped him to chronicle the '08 presidential election. The Two Towers each represented a rival wizard with his own respective agenda, but sharing in common a desire to bend all others to his own worldview. The twist was that the lesser of the two battling wizards was so corrupted by his own lust for power that he could not comprehend that his own short-term successes were inextricable contributors to the eventual triumph of his greater rival, whose seeds he was unwittingly sewing. In short the lesser tyrant could not triumph, even if he won.

This past week has been substantively remarkable, and highly entertaining in political and historical terms. The fracas over Preacher Wright has shaken the Obama campaign even as it closes in on an historical triumph over President Clinton's Wife. Wright has emerged from his seclusion over the weekend in a racist doubleheader, speaking first to the national NAACP convention, and then to the National Press Club. Preacher Wright strutted and jutted his jaw, swiveled his hips, and pursed his lips has he sought and won cheap laugh after laugh lampooning the speech, manner, and culture of "white folks" in the blandest of Richard Pryor rip offs that left the viewer irritated, sad, and tired. It feels unfair to blame this awful race pimp on Senator Obama; yet it is in fact increasingly clear that the defenses, apologies, and chin tucking over Wright by the mainstream media begin to outline the far greater, oppressive mindset arising to seize the general election, a mindset that will push Obama's election by any and all means, and will accept any confabulation to secure power. The template will be that evil, rich, white Republicans planted Wright and pushed him to say the insane things that now have Obama cringing.

From the perch of its maverick tower, the McCain campaign is too overawed by itself to grasp the danger. Presently the fault lines of identity politics and economic ignorance as presented by two dim-bulb candidates are shaking the very foundations of the Democrat Party such as we have not seen in a more than a generation. The response of McCain's egomania to the Left's racism and class warfare is to accept liberal premises while taking conservatives for granted, insulting them by adopting such Democrat positions as the need for government to prevent climate change, and blaming W. for the Katrina mess. McCain is aiding the media and Democrats in destroying the ability of Republicans to defend themselves, while breathing new life to liberal causes collapsing under their own weaknesses. Not content merely to preside over the damage wrought by his rhetorical and ideological incompetence, W. sits fumbling upon the steward's throne congratulating himself on handing out tax rebates to non-taxpayers, and increased debt to those that carry the rest on their backs. Like his father before him, W. has opened up the belly of the conservative ox and invited the liberal carrion fowl to dine. Bereft of initiative or direction, the GOP looks to McCain whose words and actions are a succession of Democrat triumphs. If the Arizona senator wins in November, it will be a benefit only to those who cannot stand Hillary's shrill nagging or Obama's vapid generalities. There is no magic ring for a freedom-loving Frodo to hurl into the fires of Mt. Doom. The closest we may come is the fun of discovering that Preacher Wright is, as suspected, on Hillary's payroll."

McCain wrapped it up on Super Tuesday that February, 2008, and followed it up with his own prolonged bridge to nowhere the following month...

McCain Sputters

"Republican presidential nominee John McCain's "Service to America" speech in Annapolis was a schizophrenic's joyride. McCain slid from describing his screw-up college years into an appreciation that life is supreme with irony, and then a Kennedy-esque admission, "My accomplishments are more a testament to my country, the land of opportunity, than they are to me. In America, everything is possible." Bravo, Senator! He followed up with a few celebratory lines regarding the virtues of discipline, and praised the Naval Academy's "honor code that simply assumed your fidelity to its principles." Excellent words curiously offered from someone who has heroically defended, and then participated in the undoing of our nation's founding principles, namely national sovereignty and freedom of speech. That is the tough part about dealing with McCain, a genuine hero who sacrificed as a patriot. And then like so many in the generation before him, has subsequently fought to undermine those very structures he sought to defend. What confounds now is a candidate that skips across the philosophical lines and back so quickly that he appears to be standing on both sides at once. In a Democrat that is praised as adroitness, and savvy. In a Republican, well... McCain cited "that dominant individualism" of frontier historian Frederick Turner, and "that buoyancy and exuberance which comes with freedom"; and then - BAM - switched his stance and popped the listener, bemoaning how "many Americans are indifferent to or cynical about the virtues that our country claims ... attributable to the dislocations economic change causes ... to the experience of Americans who have, through no fault of their own, been left behind as others profit as they never have before." What? How does a race of dominant individuals fall into such moroseness? McCain: "In part, it is in reaction to government's mistakes and incompetence, and to the selfishness of some public figures who seek to shine the luster of their public reputations at the expense of the public good." Now who might that describe, Senator?

The internal tennis match continues, volley back to the right: "Self-reliance – not foisting our responsibilities off on others – is the ethic that made America great ... and to some people, the expectations of liberty are reduced to the right to choose among competing brands of designer coffee." Great line and true, followed by the perplexity of McCain's description of citizenship, a subsuming of the very individual that made the country great, into causes "greater than yourself." The senator's definition of citizenship includes "anywhere Americans come together to govern their lives" and is defined "by countless acts of love, kindness and courage that have no witness or heraldry and are especially commendable because they are unrecorded." This is the same sort of Leftist exhortation given us recently by Michelle Obama when she urged listeners not to go into profitable pursuits like "corporate law or hedge-fund management." Why doesn't the senator's definition of citizenship include starting great companies, building great industries, or getting filthy, stinking rich and in doing so, creating new opportunities through thousands of other new jobs? Again, McCain: "Success, wealth and celebrity gained and kept for private interest is a small thing. But sacrifice for a cause greater than yourself, and you invest your life with the eminence of that cause, your self-respect assured. All lives are a struggle against selfishness." That is a heartbreaking. It seems McCain does not comprehend, or has forgotten, that the Pilgrims, the Irish, the Koreans and every other willing traveler to this country did so out of selfishness. A great civil war was waged in part to confirm individual liberties for all Americans, and the frontiersmen, industrialists, the scientists, artists, and common laborers of this nation have all been pursuing their own self-interests since. Whether the candidate blathers on about "Change," spins fanciful yarns about sniper fire, or sanctimoniously admonishes, there will be a core truth attached to who-ever next enters the White House: If a politician can lecture you on self-sacrifice, he or she thinks it makes them immune from having to explain why they keep putting their hand into your pocket."

As the heat from the primaries leveled off, Memorial Day 2008 caught a lot of holiday travelers on the nation's highways scratching their heads, and checking their wallets – enter the Dem-agogues...

Where Will the Wind Fall?

"While battling down the fabled road toward being anointed as our latest savior, the spoiled kids in the back of the Democrat hybrid are each demonstrating a shared lack of anything resembling original thought. In the spring of 2002 drivers were wringing their hands over the potential for permanent $3/gallon gas, even as they bought the nonsense of U.S. climate guilt, propagated by a frankly anti-American liberal party, and abetted by the White House's abdication of leadership on the issue. Now six years later we find ourselves no closer to tapping the Alaskan or Gulf oil reserves, even as we whine more and more about the lack of friendly supply. Harry Reid and Nancy Pelosi have since come into their own, having abdicated their own (previous) statements regarding energy relief, and now paradoxically work to disengage from the Middle East while opposing the best way to accomplish that very goal by procuring our own oil. But surely a new administration will bring a fresh look, and dare we hope for it, even "CHANGE"?

Webster tells us that "windfall" is defined, in a financial context, as "an unexpected, unearned, or sudden gain or advantage." Windfall is a term that has been tossed about with ever-greater fervor as pump prices have risen. While the sad Republican nominee bumbles his way toward cementing his place as Bob-Dole's successor, the two Dem hopefuls have found a new focus word for their shared instinct for class warfare. The Bloomberg News service reports Barak Obama seeks a windfall profits tax on Big Oil that will carve a $15 billion filet from the fatted calf of last year's profits. "The tax would help pay for a $1,000 tax cut for working families, and ...assistance for people who can't afford their energy bills." "The [oil company] profits right now are so remarkable that one could trim them 10 percent or so" said Jason Grumet, Obama's advisor on environmental and energy policy, a man we might reasonably suspect to possess the sort of arrogance that will propel a man to devise all the right solutions – if we will only just listen and do as he says. The smarmy retort: "Oil companies would still have ample reason to continue to pursue production, while at the same time providing relief to consumers." What he says presently is that a company that manufactures and distributes a legal product to the enrichment of its customers may expect, if too successful, to be fleeced by those who have made not even a tiny fraction of a similar economic contribution. The plan features a 20 percent tax on the cost of a barrel of oil above $80, which will function as a price cap, albeit graduated. Those of us who remember the Seventies should remember how well those worked.

Of course Pres. Clinton's Wife and Warrior Queen of the Little Guy plays a similar tune, offering, to seize a $20 billion windfall profits tax on oil companies over the next decade, and repeal $30 billion in tax breaks over 10 years to pay into a strategic energy fund whose lockbox will be picked by Medicare quicker than you can say "Gore."

If a doughnut shop owner suddenly finds his street widened and his business doubled, should his community be allowed to tap him on the shoulder with its hand out? The core question is left unasked by a sycophantic media too lost in their own self-fascination: just because someone suddenly makes an unexpected profit, why does the government automatically have a claim on their "windfall"? If the oil companies get tax breaks then repeal them, along with other corporate welfare - but allow Big Oil to expand their domestic exploration and refining, and give us all the windfall of a little less government theft."

Eventual nominee Obama had learned the craft of Beltway blather well by the time he hit his stride. His lapdog media notwithstanding, his twists and dodges and pirouettes running through questions and issues might have been the envy of many an NFL hopeful, especially in a game where no one seemed to keep score...

The Hole Truth

"What in the world is the fascination with Beltway politicians for doughnuts??? First we had Pres. Bush, Medicare/Medicaid head Mark McClellan, and an assortment of flimsy-minded, bribing congressmen taking the "mature" approach of giving seniors free (sort of) medicines in exchange for their votes. That was in 2003. Since then the GOP has lost the House, the national debt (and drug prices) have soared, W. has disemboweled the conservative movement, and the retirees still think they have a right to free drugs. And all of this rested on a functional logic best described as bizarre, wherein the Medicare beneficiary pays a certain portion of pill costs up to a certain level, all costs beyond that to a certain amount, and then practically nothing when things get really pricey. The middle senior-pays-all portion was called the doughnut.

Inside the Beltway bad ideas have a communicability that would make the Ebola virus blush. Presidential aspirant Obama calls for "establishing such a "doughnut hole" in the amount of income subject to the Social Security tax", according to the AP. Last week the Telegenic One stated his wish that annual earnings above $250,000 be subject to the Social Security payroll tax. "Campaign aides said the additional tax, like the current one, would apply only to wages and salaries and not to other forms of income such as investments." Whoa, stop right there! So a liberal politico-celebrity who criticizes capitol gains tax cuts as breaks for the wealthy would countenance exempting investment income from other forms of income, uh, payroll tax? What sense does that make when the point of this farce is to nail the rich? Obama: "We should exempt anyone making under $250,000 from this increase so that the change doesn't burden middle-class Americans." Is that the Obama definition of the upper limit of "middle class"? Will he be willing to stick to that when it comes time to propose his first round of tax increases, or will he (like the last Dem prez) pull out the "I worked as hard as I could, BUT…" malarkey?

B.O. wants the 6.2 percent payroll tax to stop between $102 K and $250 K, and then kick in again on everything over a quarter million. The very junior Illinois senator said the plan "allows us to extend the life of Social Security" without raising the retirement age or cutting benefits, after which he criticized any notion of privatizing the program, even on a partial basis. Let us see if we have this right: Social Security is a great program that is in such tough shape it must be saved by attacking the rich and forbidding working, future seniors to invest their money as they wish. But if the program is so great then why does it need saving at all?

A few years ago this column caught a little flak from readers who were incensed at the notion that retirees had no right to pick the pockets of those younger to ensure their own comfortable retirement. Seniors in the 1930's bought the snake oil that FDR was selling which promised them security; their replacements bought the LBJ lie that health care was a right that could be forcibly taken from their children. Today's retirees like those that preceded them have been furious at the possibility of not getting all that they paid into the system. The delicious irony they fail to grasp is that they have never actually paid as much as they will spend (the difference being taken from others), which is now leading to insolvency. Means testing will ensue, the usual class warfare where the legitimate contributions of the wealthier will be confiscated to placate the majority. As a preferred group gets ripped off by the same politicians who tell them they deserve more, it will be fun to see who gets the doughnuts and who gets the holes."

All glory is truly fleeting in this life, even for the previous champions of Teflon spin. Amazingly the nation's leading organized crime family, the Clintons, did not have the dirt, muscle, or favors in the end to stop the Obama onslaught and its slavish media. By July the formulaic contest between progressive upstart and crusty war hero had been declared mandatory.

Obama was promising to re-make the country, and McCain was promising not to, sort of, at least not as much. A lot of folks on one side thought the Constitution should suit the moment, and a lot on the other side thought the document should be applied to the moment. A sad feature of the presidential race of 2008 was the absolute paucity, indeed near-absence of ideological struggle. What did it mean to be "American", or did it still even mean anything at all beyond a given election cycle? It was an unasked question that would rise anew a year later when the rise of a new grass roots movement had many in power questioning its members' patriotism…

What Is Patriotic, Really?

"It's worth considering the meaning of patriotism because the question of who is—or is not—a patriot all too often poisons our political debates," quoth Barak Obama, raising an interesting topic. Why should Americans care so much about his disdain for ostentatious flag pins when he is promising to take more of their money? As much as we respect McCain's war service, what did his disastrous immigration stand tell us about his view of the nation?

The air this Fourth of July is filled with a whole bunch of hooey flying back and forth in the gathering presidential campaign between Grandpa Grumpy and Junior Know-Nothing. A lot is being made or implied about the role and importance of patriotism this election season, timely enough for or celebratory weekend. Prior to the '92 Clinton campaign the question of a candidate's patriotism was never raised in post-WWII America. Webster tells us that patriotism "is love and support for one's country", a rather wide-ranging invitation to interpretation.

Are you or I being patriotic this July 4th when we festoon with red, white, and blue, and cheer the fireworks, or does the question need to run a little deeper? Does patriotism apply just to wars and international conflicts or does it apply as well to domestic principles. The worn phrase that "dissent is the highest form of patriotism" has been back in vogue the past couple of years. Is it more patriotic to protest an unpopular war, or to saddle up and head overseas to take the fire? Some corporations have fled offshore to escape our punitive tax structure. Does such a company ultimately show more love of country by providing cheaper goods to Americans, or is the loss of jobs here treasonous? Some think that love of country means sacrificing her interests to the world's agenda; others want to reinvigorate our vitality by tapping our own oil reserves. Are both courses equally patriotic? It will be a wise, or rash soul to seize that answer.

For the past three decades Republicans were able to clamber atop the issue of patriotism as the party more concerned with national security, a position legitimately earned at least by the default of the negligent party opposite. Following Vietnam the Democrats were downright derelict with respect to defense and their invitation to the Soviets to win the Cold War, Scoop Jackson and Sam Nunn notwithstanding. Then the Party of Clinton, encouraged in all fairness by the first Pres. Bush, rushed into every possible foreign entanglement in every scrub-backwater piece of dirt they could find that contained no possible U.S. interest. In 1990 scolding journalists wondered whether it was proper to enter a conflict over oil; several years later they encouraged our involvement where dead bodies were the only potential byproduct (Rwanda) and cheered our meddling when it invited larger, fruitless conflict (the Balkans). Is it patriotic to cheer for your nation as it pursues imperialistic self-determination, or is more pure to support a war where no self-interested gain is possible?

In the War on Terror there has been a lot of healthy criticism of the White House with respect to civil liberties, spying, what constitutes torture, and how we best adhere to the Constitution. Such is the line from those that see the document as "living", malleable by the tides of social fashion. Those who would extend constitutional protections to terrorist prisoners see no similar obligations when attempting to seize the guns and "unfairly" earned wealth from their fellow citizens.

In the heated yell-fests on cable TV, screams greet the suggestion that someone is less than patriotic. But is every citizen equally patriotic, and immune from questioning? Does our patriotism apply to the mountain ranges, plains, and coastlines that the Indians loved before they were taken from them? Or does – should – patriotism mean a love for something other than geography? Are there any core American principles left to which we should all adhere, and why can't we regard those who feel otherwise as unpatriotic?"

To me the topic of patriotism is not an abject, obligatory love of the United States. Criticisms of political commentary often degrade to "Name a better country" or "This is still the best country in the world", the bland equivalent of "America: love it or leave it." This is a simple-minded premise that may be rejected out of hand as a cheap attempt to stifle legitimate disagreement. Sometimes very real concepts of freedom come into painful, even violent contradiction from which there is no easy extrication.

The primary summer of 2008 saw knee-jerk battle lines drawn between fearful Republicans and festival Democrats while the media lauded the sensible middle. A couple years earlier I had written about another, less popular contemplation of Independence Day. That Fourth of July 2008 left me wondering (still) about the high ideals missing from this juvenile campaign, about the great goals to which we should aspire, and about the high and deadly cost when we get it wrong...

A Fourth of July pause...

Mothers are filling the shopping carts with hamburger buns and potato chips, while the dads are eyeing the little roadside stands, or even contemplating a quick trip across state lines for fireworks. The Fourth of July is near, the world's greatest patriotic celebration in truly the greatest nation on the globe. But underlying the fun and celebration, the communal embrace and healthy frivolity, there is a huge contradiction, and a question.

The Fourth of July in 1863 was marked by the surrender of the great fortress on the Mississippi, the city of Vicksburg, to Union forces. The Confederacy was formally cut in two the day after Gettysburg, in a mortal wound from which the Southern cause could not recover. The Union weathered its greatest trial that summer as the Confederate cannon were wheeled out of the trees on Seminary Ridge to begin the bombardment of the Union line in preparation for Lee's gamble, Pickett's Charge. The charge is the great moment of the Lost Cause, emblazoned rhetorically by William Faulkner's wistful statement that every Southern boy may, whenever he wishes, return to a July afternoon when it's not yet two o'clock, and it hasn't happened yet: "*Maybe this time with all this much* to lose and all this much to gain." There was so much to gain, and so much was lost. Beyond the messy inexactitudes of conflicting survivors' accounts and battlefield archeology, there is the romantic legend of Pickett's Charge, to which I proudly subscribe. And it is this legend ironically enough that comes to mind on July 4th. In the Ted Turner-produced film "Gettysburg", Union hero Lawrence Chamberlain gives a riveting, inspiring plea to would-be deserters to take up their arms in defense of a greater ideal, of a Union where all men are brothers with equal protections under a robust and divinely-inspired central government. Later in the movie the Confederate point of view was expressed simply, by rebel prisoners, dismayed that their Yankee captors believe them to be in Pennsylvania fighting to defend the institution of slavery. The prisoners were not slaveholders (as was the case for over 90% of the rebel army), and were there fighting for their rights, to be left alone free of interference and invasion.

Two generations before, Thomas Jefferson had feared that slavery would be a poison to the soul of the nation, and he has been proved right to our present day. Lincoln made war on the South to preserve the Union, but without slavery, there would have been no moral impetus for the North to wage such a fight. Lincoln wished above all to preserve that strong, divinely inspired Union as a great force of good and (secondarily) to end the evil subjugation of slavery. Yet in this preservation and liberation, the balance was forever shifted away from local, limited government and toward an ever-expanding central government without end. It is noteworthy that the Union government that would free the slaves had fewer reservations about corralling the freedom of the western Indians, all in the cause of building a greater nation. And the drive to ensure that all men be treated as equals grew into a government that would preferentially deprive some of their legal property, all for the common good.

The men in blue behind the stone wall, sighting down the barrels of their guns across the gentle slope, were heroes, fighting for the salvation of a great nation and, later, for the liberation of their brothers. And the heroes in gray who stepped out of the trees to form up for the great charge also fought for a noble purpose, to preserve the existence of a life free from foreign interference so destructive to individual freedom. The cannons stopped and the massive gray lines surged forward toward the waiting Union guns, confident and unafraid, both sides aware that it all hung on this very day, on this very charge. Pickett galloped the line, flashing a smile, as his boys stepped off toward immortality.

Under fire from the start, the regiments moved across over a mile of open fields through a howl of shell and shot, but did not falter. Survivors of torn units huddled together, converged, and charged the center of the line, crossing the stone wall and breaking the federal ranks. Union reinforcements surged forward and the High Water Mark became the Lost Cause in an instant. Only a few straggled back from that awful slaughter, and the country was set in a permanent direction. The men in blue that shot their rebel brothers down did so in the name of freedom, to preserve a country that would continue to diminish the simple freedoms upon which it had been founded. The men in gray who charged that wall came from a land that sanctioned slavery – a fatal contradiction to their heartfelt love of the freedoms derived from the revolutionary birthright of their homeland. Both sides fought for freedom that day, and both sides lost it. The South as part of a greater nation benefits to this day, yet is saddled with the slavery of an oppressively big government. The North saved the Union that day, but ensured that all free men would only be free within the confines set by Washington. Among the dead in blue and gray lay the bodies of slavery and of limited government, a grotesque contradiction entwined in sadness.

This July Fourth, there will be picnics, and starlight concerts, too much good food, and a wholly deserved expression of love for nation and home. The neighbors might wonder whether the Confederate battle flag on my porch will remain up for the Fourth, but it never does, out of respect for the day and history's hope for a nation truly dedicated to freedom. For me America is not defined by the geographic boundaries of the United States, but by the idea shared by both sides at Gettysburg, neither of which won. This holiday too many will identify their freedom with a government that looks out for their material concerns, from retirement to health care to wages to hurricane relief, at the cost of taking from our fellow citizens. In the Land of the Free, many are proud to embrace a government that makes King George's rule seem positively laissez-faire by comparison. On this July Fourth it is also proper to remember the patriots in gray who died the day before in a desperate charge for freedom. How shall each of us, on this great holiday, define the liberty we celebrate?

❖ ❖ ❖

No one could accuse me of showering Barak Obama with patriotic laurels, what with his constant apologizing for his country, but even I was caught off guard by the sheer magnitude of his narcissism that election summer when he won the European primary ...

An American Princess

"The pageant of a slobbering pack of newsies galloping and yelping after the Telegenic One at the pep rally in Berlin, recording and spewing over his every joint flexure as significant, reminded one of the shoe vs. gourd debate over the True Messiah in Monty Python's "Life of Brian." What passed for journalists were mere reflections of an accelerating self-importance that spoke "not as a candidate for President, but as a citizen – a proud citizen of the United States, and a fellow citizen of the world." In one sentence Obama released a palpable untruth like a diseased pigeon, and turned his back on the concept of American exceptionalism i.e. "We're No. 1!" The candidate who refused to make his campaign about race did just that in his second paragraph: "I know that I don't look like the Americans who've previously spoken in this great city," and then tried to keep rhetorical company with the two heroic presidents who spoke in Berlin. Obama had fun (I guess) constantly referencing the Cold War, which is disgusting considering how antithetical he would prove to the spirit of freedom that defeated the Soviets. He ignorantly proclaimed that "the Cold War born in this city was not a battle for land or treasure," when it most certainly was, in addition to being an ideological conflict. Were it not a battle for economic power, Regan's snuffing of the technology transfers that devastated the Soviet natural gas exports and the arms buildup that relied on it would have been pointless. On the

subject of gas – the Big O' decried how, despite any conclusive proof whatsoever, "cars in Boston and factories
in Beijing are melting the ice caps in the Arctic, shrinking coastlines in the Atlantic, and bringing drought to
farms from Kansas to Kenya." Regular citizen-motorists
in Barack's America, don't you see, are as complicit as the
worst polluters in communist China in killing the polar
bears! Check out how B.O. continued to play the Blame
America card in some pretty sly language: "In Europe,
the view that America is part of what has gone wrong in
our world, rather than a force to help make it right, has
become all too common" (i.e., "We're sorry for being a
bunch of cowboys"). "In America, there are voices that
deride and deny the importance of Europe's role in our
security and our future" (i.e., "Oh, and we're not too
bright in my country either."). The language: America is
wrong. Obama derided walls in a city that should know,
cheering the progress in Belfast and whatever is going on
in the Balkans. Of course, if the French had been a little
more studious with their immigration "walls," or the Brits
been a bit more stringent in protecting their majestic
liberal traditions, those countries might not be presently
enjoying the fruits of fanatical Islamist diversity. Barack
has given Americans concerned with border security and
illegal immigration a very clear signal regarding his (lack
of) intentions. He addressed nuclear terrorism, stating,
"My country must stand with yours and with Europe in
sending a direct message to Iran that it must abandon its
nuclear ambitions." Or what, senator? He asked "Will we
stand for the human rights of the dissident in Burma, the
blogger in Iran, or the voter in Zimbabwe? Will we give
meaning to the words 'never again' in Darfur?" No mention of the religious persecutions in China or the near-
cannibalism in North Korea. Obama told the Berliners

that we are all united by a set of ideals, and if he has his way we shall be. Some of us don't actually want to become just like Europe if for no other reason than that will leave no one to come rescue us. But as America prepares to choose a class president, Europe seems to have already crowned its replacement for Princess Dianna, all good looks and fluff, and ready to hug the world."

It was a pleasant summer, crazy gas prices and insufferable media bootlicking notwithstanding, and it was nice to cool off that globally warmed July in a cool movie theater...

Fear the Night

"This is the opening weekend for likely the best in a summer of great movies, "The Dark Knight." This brooding play on words and the best-ever description of Batman is also the sequel to the hero's re-introduction in 2005, bringing to a new level a career spanning over six decades. Batman prowled the night under the pen of creator Bob Kane in 1939 as Detective Comics' answer to Action Comics' "Superman" who first flew the year before to heretofore-unseen financial heights. While many of the early pulp action figures, such as cowboys, explorers, and spacemen operated in the light of day, the 1930's saw the rise of darker, masked characters that moved in darkness and began to introduce a duality that disturbed the traditional notion of comic superhero.

Numerous essayists, sociology majors, and comics' connoisseurs have continued to explore how superheroes reflect the culture and times from whence they sprang. Some have noted that America's two most recognizable pre-war comic heroes, Superman and Batman, had respective styles and origins informed by the socialism and fascism, respectively, of the1930's.

Pop-culture historians have described that Superman was just the thing in 1938 for an America struggling out of depression, flexing a square-jawed optimism that make glad the hearts of the plebian farmers who had adopted him. A man of the people, the style of the undocumented worker from Krypton (some say) suggested the sunny can-do feel of propaganda posters depicting happy Ukrainian proletariats baring their broad arms under the sun setting over their bountiful wheat harvests.

Enter wealthy heir Bruce Wayne, certainly not a man of the people, who prowls the night with a grasp of human motivation and frailty far beyond the imagination of the Man of Steel. Batman was always the greatest of the superheroes precisely because he was the smartest, and he was so because he had to be. No alien origins, atomic-powered suits, or gamma-ray mutations for this guy. It was his greatest scar, the murder of his childhood that allowed the brooding billionaire to assume his alter ego and fly into the minds of evildoers. Batman does not always allow for the niceties of politeness, nor of the efficiencies of formal justice. He is a vigilante whose style (some have argued) invoked the fascist black mood at work in the frustrations of those clambering for the ruthlessness of expedient force. Ironic really, that of the two the one who most inspires fear resorts less often to the use of force. Superman looks through walls then knocks them down while Batman looks into the criminal mind and lays a trap.

"The Dark Knight" will re-introduce Batman's greatest foe, The Joker, once a man now twisted into permanent anarchical self-destruction by his own fractured self-esteem. The Joker's murderous mayhem challenges Batman not only to make the hard choices, but also to confront himself as potential accessory to the carnage.

America again faces a poisonous tide of doubt and self-hatred led by increasingly shrill and irrational arguments from leaders unable to articulate their own passions accurately, much less any real solutions. In the light of summer candidate Obama appears more so to be what he always was, a telegenic, aurally pleasing mirage of "change" that is nothing more than a vessel for the vapidity of his followers' hopes. He will not be capable to deal with the leering arrogance of a government eager to bail out foolhardy banks while refusing citizens the opportunity to access our own energy resources. As the maniac prowls the streets of the American political psyche, screaming about global warming, looting more tax dollars, and murdering little freedoms at will, one looks vainly skyward for a rescuing shadow. But all we get is a Commissioner Gordon philosophically well into retirement." *(After Obama was inaugurated as president, comparisons in to form of a now-infamous edited photo began to emerge which compared him to the Joker. Mine was not so famous but so far as I know, it was the first, and all too prophetic).*

The Joker candidate was indeed anointed before faux columns and a weeping, addled mass of sycophants, moochers, and do-gooders-by-proxy in the most frenzied exercise of misplaced self-esteem since the last VH1 Celebrity Rehab reality show. Like all of the speeches before or since, the acclaimed 'Big O' waxed a vacuous platitudinous tapestry in populist tones that fooled eve-

ryone in its pretension to seriousness. In hindsight it may have already been over at that point, but the rituals had to be observed. McCain got his big payoff as GOP nominee, as the delegates held their noses and pretended to have a winner on their hands. And lo and behold, out trots a babe, complete with smile and the rhetoric of limited government, to wow the crowd and give false hope later to be cruelly dashed by the top of the ticket...

A Last Chance in St. Paul

"Though it is often a consolation, at least one good thing that comes out of all Republican victories, which is the chance to see painfully earnest liberal writhe in their own self-importance. Ordinarily I do not applaud women in politics not named Thatcher. The gaining of suffrage by women 88 years ago has led to a good deal of suffering by those who have struggled to pay the bills of the female proclivity toward social spending, those same ladies included, bless their hearts. Years ago I wrote that the most dangerous demographic in America was concerned mothers, who would strip our civil rights and get us into wars if they could rationalize such in favor of their children. The rampant growth of government under feminized men in Washington and their fairer handlers has proven the first point right; Bill Clinton's giddiness for military adventure in the Balkans in 1999 to shore up his sagging poll numbers was at least enabled by the gender gap that could not stand to see such a cuddle bear impeached. The nannying ghost of Eleanor Roosevelt hangs over this nation like an industrial pall.

On the eve of her acceptance speech for a vice presidential nomination Gov. Sarah Palin might well represent another step in this unfortunate progression. Picked by a moderate Republican who himself doesn't mind the occasional tinker with the Constitution, Palin may be a mere continuance in the complete blurring of ideologies in gooey bipartisanship and a plunge toward socialism. Why then has the response from the Left has been so swift and predictably shrill? In a pronouncement that was the logical somersault of a Slick Willy denial performing in Cirque de Soleil, a liberal friend of mine exclaimed that by selecting Palin, John McCain proved that he is a misogynist. So McCain proves he hates women by picking one? Yes my friend continued, adding that her (unprintable) stances prove she is not a real woman. Whew. That thinking is akin to believing that taxing Big Oil will lower gas prices, and it's enough to make your head hurt.

This loony drumbeat is echoing throughout the pro-Obama media, permitting insidious questions regarding not only her competence as a chief executive, but also her fitness as a mother, and the imperfections of her loved ones. Suddenly her husband's distant DUI and her daughter's pregnancy are being seen as legitimate reasons to ask whether she can take Hillary's 3 AM phone call. If we are going to sweat Gov. Palin's foreign policy credentials, then should we not at least ask why Joe Biden opposed Reagan's plan to defeat the Soviets and opposed the 1991 war to liberate Kuwait? (The American Thinker, 8/30/08). Can we not at least ask why Biden's earnest anti-war supporters are not apparently troubled by his vote FOR the 2003 Iraqi invasion? All of a sudden "experience" Beltway-style seems a bit less convincing.

So what is it about Palin that has well-heeled, fashionably guilty suburban moms choking on their pomegranate martinis? The pseudo-intelligentsia that is so rabidly pro-choice also routinely (no doubt to assuage their guilt) supports candidates who use tax dollars to pay ever-larger sums to mothers to have babies on the public dole. And yet they seem incensed at the woman who chose differently then they, to have her children and to pay for them. And by making the "wrong" choice Sarah Palin is shown to not really be a woman in the way that Clarence Thomas was shown by the perpetually aggrieved to not be really "black." McCain may be guilty of tokenism. That does not however excuse the Left, now utterly unmasked as the Party of Misogyny, not promoting women but using them as objects to gain power. The storm is heading Palin's way and who is to say whether she weathers it? Let us hope so and with flying colors, if only to infuriate the sisterhood and their lapdogs."

Palin gave a thrilling, inspiring speech in support of freedom and limited government, ideals immediately attacked by the media and apologized for by her running mate. The same "journalists" who thought it charming that John Edwards got $400 haircuts and Obama had visited "all 57 states" now amplified catcalls about Palin's looks as "slutty" and mocked her claim that she could see Russia from her back yard [in Alaska]. Popular media from Katie Couric (of "South Park" fame), Tina Fey, and Comedy Central let us all know that the fix was in, there was to be no deviation from the script, that this was the moment and they were the change we had all waited for. With the economy in jitters, and despite decades of experience to the contrary, the popular imagination of the herd rushed pell-mell back to the buffet of stupid, to get another helping...

Only the Government Is Never Dis-credited

"As Obama tries to exploit his good fortune by running out the clock on an intellectually wheezy McCain campaign, the real monster behind the credit crisis is left unchallenged, obscured by the phony stage empathy of both candidates and a simpleton's media. The topic is confusing, a spider's web of abstract assumptions and esoteric jargon. Here's hoping my friends in banking, accounting, developing, and investing will forgive a lack of expert insight when it comes to the timeline of this mess, but hey, it never stops the gang at MSNBC. The central, if not the only major culprit, is as usual, Big Government.

We are told that de-regulation of Wall Street is to blame, that greedy, unscrupulous Wall Streeters bilked the system and figuratively left for the Caymans. While it is true that some CEO's knowingly made poor investments while folding a golden parachute, what of the regulations in place? Were they really too few, and insufficiently stringent, and why were we allowed to rely on them? What of those responsible for the failed oversight? (and do stockholders and investors have no responsibility in what is after all a gamble?) The GOP and the Dems alike are to blame. The Left in red-faced outrage blusters about "THE LAST EIGHT YEARS!" yet five years ago the White House was pushing for more regulation of Fannie and Freddie. Democrat Barney Frank of the House Financial Services Committee, who previously squelched the reforms, bleating that such would reduce the availability of "affordable" housing, is now credited with saving the bailout bill, and the economy in turn. Were the pre-2006 GOP congressional majorities and president in agreement with this foolishness, cowed by an unfriendly media for being cruel to the needy, or just asleep? Clearly such housing was affordable neither to its residents, nor now to the taxpayer. While Fannie and Freddie were started and expanded by

Democrats, housing welfare was insufficiently opposed by Republicans. The poor risks upon which rested mortgage-backed securities had their legs knocked out by falling real-estate values. And while that may not be the whole picture, the wobbly credit industry is certainly one just desert for a society that has swiped its card a few too many times, and that adopted (actively or passively) the falsity of a compassionate government under the sainted FDR, whose great-grandchildren now prepare for more of his good works. The generation that hit their formative years under the New Deal heralded a tectonic shift in the psyche of U.S. politics: henceforth they and their progeny would feel and expect the federal government as a presence in their daily lives.

To what result has this led? The poisonous philosophy underlying the entitlement mentality, with its inevitable expansion of government and diminution of personal liberty is again on tiresome display for the electorate. We are told that voters are angry over the $700B bailout bill (really $850B including the pork W. was too timid to veto). Yet the polls indicate that those same voters are moving toward increasing the power of the very machine that landed us in this fix. As elected officials emote the cheap compassion of the unaffected, wailing over their constituents' misfortunes, it is painfully clear: injecting the housing and credit markets with easy government cash poisoned those industries. And now a new generation is being trained to look to Big Government for its every need."

The debates were forgettable in the extreme, with McCain, playing permanently from behind, scored no points, and substance-free

Obama made none. Mercifully it was fall, and the crisp morning temperatures and balmy college football Saturdays were pleasant distractions from the now inevitable civic paroxysm. Never did America more desperately need an informed electorate then when she did not have one, as the Halloween shadows crept longer...

A Whale of an All Electorals' Eve

"You have all seen the video on YouTube, and if not, enter in the search terms "exploding whale." True story: in November 1970 a dead whale washed ashore on the beach near Florence Oregon, giving the locals an odiferous perplexity. They could not effectively bury it, nor could any volunteers be found to chainsaw what was becoming an increasingly swollen carcass. What to do? The decision was made to blow the thing into little bits, and allow the tide and carrion fowl to clean up the rest.

It is always fitting to have a major election on the heels of our national trick-or-treat festival, if only to provide for continuity of thought. While the youngsters are about with open bags trying to score some candy, here come the Lehmans and AIG's and Fannies and Freddies, all threatening to egg Wall Street if we don't dig deep for some grownup treats to placate them. After all, we don't want the poor dears to do without lobbying cash or spa vacations in the cold dreary months ahead. As this vapid campaign stumbles ahead, the rest of the kiddies are getting fistfuls of "Hope & Change", and "Fight with Me My Friends" thrown in their sacks, sugary and utterly non-filling. Mom, better leave the leftovers out for later tonight.

One of the favorite houses to hit this All Electorals' Eve is that whitewashed columned affair on the corner, the one financed on the sub-prime. Ring the bell and out bounces a chortling Barney Frank, smiling in red nose and floppy shoes as his predatory brows clutch over the horn-rims, hiding the killer clown who keeps enticing little capitalists inside with promises and intimidations, both delighting and frightening, until he can chain them in the basement, strangling them and burying them under the house at his leisure. W. is too scared to make a health inspection so there's no one to scold him but cousin Chris Dodd, passed out in front of the TV in his gray granny wig, a half-fifth of Uncle Ted's whiskey and a butcher knife on the table beside him.

Back out in the street, poor old Mr. Magoo shuffles from darkened porch to porch, trying a different slogan at each doorbell and vainly hoping for a candied-poll bump in his lonely sack. Laughing to himself at his good fortune he has not noticed that his trick-or-treat partner has been bound to a stake, her endearing "you betcha's" for limited government lost in the roar of the fire as the girls from The View dance and fan the flames with their broomsticks. Coming down the street a smiling man of serious countenance lurches from curb to curb, directing all the kids in soothing tones to the rich folks' houses where they are sure to find more candy. As they squeal and giggle, these little Children of the Acorn light their torches and make for their first stop, (Joe) the plumber's house. The night chills as the dignified smiling man rips off his mask, revealing the grinning lunatic beneath, laughing the maniacal howl that terrorized the streets of Paris, Caracas, St. Petersburg, and Havana. The last

Republicans bolt their doors and cover their ears against the laughter, praying for the morning.

And morning comes. It finds a stinking whale of deficit, dead of ignorance and unworkable philosophy, cluttering up the beach. The county workers gather and pack dynamite around the problem, settling the fears of the gathering crowd desperately wanting to blow something up without thought to the aftermath. The charge is set, and the plunger drops. Huge chunks of rotting flesh fall from the sky up to a quarter mile away, smashing in car roofs and windows, splattering goo and gore over the crowd as it takes to its heels. The largest part of the carcass still lies on the beach smelling worse than ever, and no one can get their insurance agents on the phone on Election Day."

And boy did it smell. It was a mélange of terminal earnestness, revenge, betrayal, and silliness that when mixed up in a big plastic go-cup left over from the party, smelled worse than stale, cheap whiskey left over from the prohibitive 1930's. As predicted the Republicans woke up in the gutter, aching, stinking of excess and vomit, wondering what the hell had happened. As dawn broke with the Obama Light, 1994 seemed a lost memory and sad, faded fairytale. Hope and Change had come, and all that was left was for George W. Bush to pack up his sorry show...

These Bushes Were Expensive Landscaping

"As we rub our hands gleefully in anticipation of Hope & Change, we have a farewell chance to regard the crumbling edifice of the Bush '43 presidency and ponder what we might have learned. Surely the doddering example of George H.W. Bush should have taught Republicans a thing or two: caving to liberal spending Democrats only earns contempt and invites even more public aggression from those who wish to limit freedom; shoving around a tin-pot dictator is pretty worthless without a support-ing, long-term rationale (anyone remember Noreiga?); when starting a war it is important to actually finish it; a failed conservative pretender sets the nation up for a Left-ward lurch. But no, the Gimpy Old Party just couldn't get enough of the grandfatherly war-hero moderate type, and stumbled from Bob Dole to McCain without learning a thing from the W. Years. Republicans were moderate on immigration and border control, and got spanked in the Hispanic vote. All the cross-hand-holding in churches singing "We Shall Overcome" made not a dent in the Democrat grip on the black vote, and left the self-deluding minority vote on the dependency planta-tion. W. bullied allied congressmen into the largest ever pork fest on the far side of the mega-bailouts, determined to pay for the old folks' medicines with other peoples' money. Result: while Granny and Grandpa tended to vote for McCain, it fared him little and reinforced the notion of federally secured golden years. Bush refused to wield the veto pen on pork until the hog was out of the barn, by which time scandals, corruption, and the famous "Bridge to Nowhere" had deservedly doomed the GOP in Congress. In fairness the Bush Administration tried to blow the whistle on the poison seeping out of Fannie & Freddie, but didn't have the guts to make it stick, and worse, rolled into the slop with the enemy. The last two months of G.H.W. Bush's presidency could be defined in one word: Somalia. Poppy Bush belched a last sigh of compassion with other peoples' blood and treasure, setting us up for short-term failure and ultimately inviting the 9/11 attacks. The last months of the W. Years may be summed up thusly: Bailout. In caving to the likes of Paulson, Frank, and Dodd, the masochistic Republicans are spending a whole lot of other peoples' money while inviting the aggression of resurgent Liberalism, thereby keeping themselves in laughable minority while sacrificing the freedom of the citizenry they were sworn to protect (in fairness a citizenry too dim-witted to know what they are losing). Incredibly the War on Terror was initially decisively prosecuted, then mush-mouthed and ceded to a hostile media capable only of thought within the template of America as a superpower bully. How the Republicans allowed the creation of their own "Vietnam" should be truly an object of shock and awe for any honest student.

Democrats have learned, repeatedly, that a Republican administration weak on PR and vision is the greatest possible vehicle for increasing the size and scope of government. The media has learned nothing whatsoever, but they never intended to. The same "journalists" that moaned over Nixon and W. subverting the Constitution find FDR's packing of the Supreme Court whimsical, and LBJ's enslavements to be homespun. While Keith Olbermann and The View disdain W.'s smirky chuckles, they swoon over the unintelligible "uhs" and "y'knows" of Obama and Princess Kennedy. The newsies will not learn, and must not be courted. What should the dwindling numbers of Americans dedicated to freedom have learned? That there is no, NO substitute for a philosophical core and rhetorical competence, both of which were lacking these last eight years. There is little purpose to defending the nation on the outside while allowing it to be gutted from within. What we should have learned in the early 1990's was put so eloquently by none other than Jesse Jackson with whom I am sadly forced to agree: "America should stay out 'da Bushes."

❖ ❖ ❖

When in Doubt Cry Racism: Ethnicity and the Deferred Dream

When it comes to the subject of "race" I prefer the term "ethnicity." For crying out loud, we are all members of the human race and the misapplication of the term only feeds, well, racism. Which I suppose, is the goal. The object again and again from the race baiters, civil rights industry, and celebrators of "diversity" is to keep race squarely in the public eye lest the cash dry up. Sometimes I wonder, despite their verbiage, whether the twin Rev's Jesse and Al are even racist, or if it is simply the product they sell. Probably the latter. I remember back to the 1960's, and actually seeing "Song of the South" in the theater. It did not imbue me with racism, given that after all, the only wise character in the movie was the black man. But now the flick is banned for stereotyping, we have coerced "MLK" holidays into every state, and a mandatory national "Black History Month", an out of control EEOC, and even a black president inflames an ongoing national presumption of rampant racism. The sad eventuality taking shape is that it will be a problem still when I am trying to grope the nurses while feigning dementia in the home, because the purveyors of this garbage will not leave it alone. In his first year in office, Pres. Obama has taken questionable if not obviously racist positions, most famously concluding in his famous "beer summit", forced because he presumptuously took the side of the black guy over the white guy with no factual basis. The Election 2008 poll-goers in a Philadelphia suburb faced nightstick wielding Black Panthers, a glaring display which would be dismissed by black Attorney General Holder. It is a sad, and sadly lasting legacy of slavery that the Left has co-opted the left-out, furthered and fueled their ignorance, and fostered notions and phantoms of persecution and bigotry where there need be none. Archie Bunker did more to fight racism than Barak Obama will ever accomplish.

In 2005, a truly American woman died, prompting some reflection...

RIP Rosa Parks, American

"Last week an American hero died, and received the tributes that were her due. Rosa Parks performed a courageous act of defiance consistent with the American spirit, and stands properly as a symbol of that spirit of freedom. In refusing her seat to an ill-bred boor, Ms. Parks reminded a nation and a people of the value of the individual mind and soul, born of the same spark as those of our neighbor. Her funeral bier lying in state in the nation's capitol was surely fitting tribute to a moment in history that ranks with other great American acts of courage. Pres. Bush offered the remarks equal to the occasion the day after she died, and in the capitol Secretary of State Condoleeza Rice noted that "Without Mrs. Parks, I would not be standing here today as Secretary of State." In a wonderful tribute, Alabama Governor Bob Riley called Parks one of the people God puts "in different parts of history so great things can happen." Race pimp Jesse Jackson paused to exclaim of Parks: "She was not arrested for sewing. She was a free-dom fighter" before he returned to shaking down honest corporations for cash and patrimony. Speaker J. Dennis Hastert and Minority Leader Nancy Pelosi, issued a joint statement: "The Capitol serves as a beacon of American liberty, freedom and democracy, and Rosa Parks served as the mother of the America we grew to be." This in some respects is sadly true, but I surely don't blame Ms. Parks.

For her part, Parks was tired of the foolishness, tired of stupidity, and fed up with collective insult. But as a symbol, Ms. Parks has been defined not only by her courageous action, but also by those who celebrated it, from Martin Luther King, Jr. to George W. Bush. Over the last fifty years, others white and black, liberal and conservative have portrayed her as someone who fought for a color-blind society and against the routine computation of race in daily affairs. Amen. And yet have those who today mourn her passing truly worked toward the goal of a color-blind society? Dr. King strayed from his heroic declarations of civil rights and justice, toward calls for "economic justice" and euphemistic socialism in the last year of his life. Like the French heroes of the Great War, the old marchers of the civil rights movement have succumbed to the pulls of ego, loot, weariness, and petty self-aggrandizement. Once idealistic and heroic, civil rights icons like Rep. John Lewis, Julian Bond, and Rev. Jackson are now more con-cerned with maintaining a power structure founded on racial preference and white guilt than with ethnic equality. Guilty white liberal thinking propelled LBJ into the great-est power grab in fifty years, establishing an economic plantation from which millions of blacks have still been unable to escape. And when they do, they are met with the insidious racism of condescension, foisting upon them college quotas, preferential contracts, and other governmental assurances that the poor things simply can't make it on their own. But hold on, we have another example fresh off today's headlines.

Recently sports journalists nationwide were outraged by the comments of Air Force Academy head football coach Fisher DeBerry following a loss to the TCU Horned Frogs. DeBerry observed that the winning team "had a lot more Afro-American players than we did and they ran a lot faster than we did ... It just seems to me to be that way, Afro-American kids can run very well. That doesn't mean that Caucasian kids and other descents can't run, but it's very obvious to me that they run extremely well." Apparently the coup de grace was DeBerry stating that the academy needed to recruit faster players and that "you don't see many minority athletes in our program." Oh the shock, the horror! How dare a simple coach state so clearly what every fan, journalist, coach, and player nationwide knows to be true?? Forthwith the coach was called to the principal's office and made to give obeisance. His boss athletic director Hans Mueh, said the academy "has a zero-tolerance policy for any racial or ethnic discrimination," adding "It was a seriously, seriously inappropriate comment. I'd like for us to all just move on from there." Well let's not, not yet. I want to know WHY the comments were inappropriate. The sports media took the coach to task, screaming that at the very least his sentiments were dumb. This left me so confused. You see, every August, just before the start of football season, these same bleating clones from ESPN, CBS, and every major paper all make what are now seasonal, obligatory remarks regarding race in football, marking the calendar as surely as Labor Day. To a person, they all decry the "shame" or "embarrassment" of what they perceive as too few black head football coaches. So while it is good and noble to call for more blacks in one part of the sport, it is horrible and racist to call for more in another position.

Our elected leaders take a cue from the culture, and this sort of idiotic hypocrisy only reinforces their hurtful policies. We cannot, dare not, cut social spending for fear of being branded racists by the same crowd which saw a racial plot against blacks in the wake of Hurricane Katrina. So stumbling over themselves to prove that they are not racists, politicians prove the exact opposite to their critics, and no advance toward true equality is gained from the billions spent. Via their intransigence over social programs, Democrats have become the party of racism preservation, while the cowardice of the GOP leadership has co-opted their compassion in the service of racial division. Dr. King warned against "the tranquilizing drug of gradualism", yet scurrying through the corridors of Washington, our elected leaders of both parties battle over racial spoils and the legacy of the Civil Rights movement like so many rats gnawing over a rind of stale cheese. Every American, be they football coach, politician, seamstress, or even loud-mouthed opinion columnists must refuse to give up their seat. As long as logic and honest discourse without fear are confined to the back of the bus, the dream of a brave lady will remain unrealized."

But of course if you make your living in the race industry, hey, you have to pay the bills. The topic came up a few times over the past several years before the terrible earthquake in Haiti, including the following February on a memorable CSPAN Saturday, when we saw again, some folks' true colors...

115

It's A Black Thing, Apparently

"As a braying virtuoso of ignorance, Rep. Corrine Brown (D) of Jacksonville is matchless: not content with describing the Bush's Haiti policy as racist, she then denounced the Administration as "bunch of white men" who "all look alike to me." Shakespeare would have redefined the theatrical fool had he met this masterpiece. If Rep. Brown and her cohort in the civil rights community have been to Haiti, then they have totally missed its significance. Overpopulated and terminally corrupt, Haiti is what can happen to any country when respect for individual rights and the rule of law is systematically deforested from the civic consciousness.

Late Saturday night, I caught a re-broadcast of the "State of the Black Family" conference in Miami, hosted by race-raconteur Tavist Smiley. A crowd of well-dressed, attentive black Americans watched a roll call of self-important, largely condescending academics more interested in platitudinous theatrics than logical persuasion. The kick-off was a rant from a rabble-rouser dressed as a bishop, railing against Falwell, conformists, and promising to march on Tallahassee (to elect the right guy this time)? A Ms. Vanzant of "Inner Visions Worldwide" assured the crowd that more of us need to be on anti-depressants... [that] we are lonely" in the earnest tones usually emanating from undergrads protesting war during peacetime. How anyone could have been heretofore unfamiliar with the likes of Gwen Godsby Grant, sex columnist and alleged psychologist for Essence magazine, is a mystery. The woman is a stomping, snorting apparition in red, channeling the style of Jesse Jackson, intoning rhyme as fact, and screaming, yes screaming, that every person should adopt a black child "not their own, as their own black project." Desperate for attention, Grant would wag her finger, jump up into a preach/dance stance, and exhort the crowd that "depression is killing black people…you [black people] have enough to be depressed about." Anyone taking emotional advice from this camera hog would doubtless have earned the diagnosis.

The well-heeled Valerie Morris, a CNN financial news anchor, patiently explained that "money is not just green", and that "no one has taken the time to explain it to us." Thomas Dortch of "100 Black Men" cleared up the confusion, pointing out "current rappers re-invest in their communities" (in what, tech stocks?) but that "old school folks have Jewish lawyers and agents." And Mel Gibson catches heat!

An American-accented gentleman named Jawanza Kunjufu, an "educational consultant", described a likely relationship between Ritalin and cocaine, and predicted that the "future of the black race lies in the hands of white female teachers." Too bad none seemed to be in attendance at the conference. J.K. added further that "If we know that boys have a shorter attention span, then teachers need to shorten their lesson plan." Call me a fuddy-dud, but I never remember any of my teachers shortening their attention-getting rulers, and I scraped by. One fellow on the stage who apparently didn't require dumbed-down lesson plans was Dr. Ben Carson, a pediatric neurosurgeon. Dr. Carson made good points about how mass media influences held more sway than history books in reinforcing role models. Then he lost me by claiming that the preponderance of black male incarceration could be alleviated by explaining the technical advancements pioneered by blacks to young black men. This argues that the majority of crime committed by black males stems from our old liberal friend, Poor Self-Esteem! Columnist Stanley Crouch had it right when he answered that "the dreams of young black men and women are so narrow", absorbing the "thug vision" of the rap culture. He aptly described this as intellectual genocide/suicide – and was quickly cut off by the moderator for making far too much sense. In rushed U. Penn Prof. Michael Eric Dyson, proof that ANYONE can get tenure. I'm not making this up: Dyson claimed that "pimping as a metaphor" was fine, but that using the word as a "reality-metaphor is self-using" literalism (I think that speaks for itself). Prof. Dyson began rapping about Socrates, denounced, "black bourgeois capitulation" (otherwise known as "paying the mortgage"), and declared "Janet Jackson was victimized by the hand of white supremacy reaching across the chasm of history." Dyson seemed determined to wrest the camera time away from the sex columnist, and repeatedly launched into streams of rap to explain the symbolism of current sociological trends. He wailed that "crass commercialism has infiltrated the hip-hop game" (it was so pure and unspoiled before), and repeatedly resorted to the "N" word to make his finer points. This learned man of letters also, I swear, used the word "sammich." The audience loved him.

Back in 1997, I went to Haiti as part of a medical team hosted by the pastor of a church in the deforested foothills. Children living literally on mud floors came to the clinic in sparkling white apparel. We drove past the fetid slum of Citie Soleil, observed endless stretches of poorly constructed, crumbling buildings; saw swollen bellies and abscesses; the bright, ominous walls of voodoo temples, the impotent, ridiculous U.N. guard towers; the wide-eyed stares regarding well-fed white Americans with envy, wonder, and anger. We saw what two black despots had done to a black nation, the former wealthiest colony of the French empire, reducing it to primtivism. Accusing white Americans of this disaster has a logical basis strikingly similar to the prescriptions from Tavist Smiley's family circus.

A couple of years later we had the first serious black contender for the presidency, if you don't count that pseudo-preacher back in 1984. Destined to win high office, Barak Obama was praised by fellow Democrat and Senate Majority Leader Harry Reid for being "light-skinned" and not having a "negro" dialect. You can bet the media was despondent on such juicy comments being wasted on a non-conservative. Candidate Obama had a little trouble to deal with, as he had been a parishioner for some twenty years of a colorful, screaming, hate-spewing racist which a sympathetic media tried to simultaneously explain as authentic or crazy, or misunderstood, and sweep him under the rug. The electorate's supposed sensitivity to issues ethnic seemed to diffuse when faced with a black example, after having it all explained to them by then-Candidate Obama…

Just Another Racist

"It was, all in all a good speech. Barak Obama's response to the hateful pronouncements from his preacher Rev. Wright's was instructive, both damage control and a clear reiteration of ideological bent crafted to reassure the masses. He described the U.S. constitution in fungible terms, as something to be "perfected overtime" in our quest to be a society both "more free" and "more caring", as if a benevolent government could accomplish those contradictory goals. In what was a genuinely wonderful line, Obama noted that someone of his mixed ethnic and cultural background could only have risen to such opportunities in America. It was a solid observation that underscored the beauty of our nation and her freedoms.

And then Obama addressed the central issue and threat to his campaign, that of angry black divisiveness, by skillfully blurring the lines and masterfully twisting the tone of the topics toward his own purposes. Just before he condemned Rev. Wright's rants in "unequivocal terms", Obama referenced the state of South Carolina "where the Confederate flag still flies." That it no longer flies over the state capital where it was placed by a *Democrat* does not matter when there is unity to be gained. Obama gave a heartfelt and candid description of his Chicago Trinity Church as a vessel and core sample of Black America that encompassed its hopes, passions, anger, and resentments. The description then expanded to include the Rev. Wright, whose failings Obama illustrated by comparing him to the senator's white grandmother and her own imperfections regarding ethnic attitudes. It was subtly crafted, and crafty to begin defusing the blatant racism of his pastor by signal-averaging it with a white woman born in a different place and pre-Segregation time. And it was a clever set-up shot that allowed Obama to deflect the recent Hillary-launched racial attacks into a national problem that we all must face, leaving the younger candidate looking like the good guy above it all. Ideology roared out as Obama bemoaned the "wealth and income gap between blacks and whites" as though we had progressed no further than sharecropping; when he ended his speech with the story of a poor white girl, he flatly equated income disparity with "injustice." This is a recurring theme of his campaign and at great odds with his assertion that we must move beyond the mindset that one person's gain requires another's loss, but such is the acceleration of Obama's fence-straddling acumen. Rev. Wright denounced America in no uncertain terms, and the rich white people that had caused so much harm; Obama was quick to include racism as a vital component of the Reagan Coalition (which launched an era of wealth creation in minority demographics that Obama will do well to ignore). A talent for understatement was demonstrated when the senator assigned the primary blame for the erosion of the black family to the shame of the breadwinners not being able to provided adequately, a problem "welfare policies may have worsened."

The spiritual advisor to the presidential candidate called upon the Almighty to condemn our nation for its [foreign policy] sins. Whether Obama agrees with this declaration of national guilt with respect to foreign policy remains an open question. Obama said in his speech that Wright's understandable and predictable anger should come as a surprise to no one, equating this to an almost as easily justified anger of working-class whites. The primary in union-heavy Pennsylvania after all, is on the horizon. This empathy for the downtrodden-at-large included criticisms of the corporate culture of short-term greed, whose practitioners move overseas "for nothing more than profit" (gasp!) without an unkind word toward the government or union lobbyists that so drive them. What began as Martin Luther King, Jr. devolved in many ways into John Edward's "Two Americas." If Obama truly seeks justice and unity in this nation, then preferring class warfare over truly denouncing racist preachers may yield disappointing results." When the smoke cleared, we were left where we started. Any supposed war against racism has nothing any longer to do with ethnic bigotry, and everything to do with the redistribution of power and wealth.

Back in 2004 I was fortunate to meet black columnist and policy reformer Star Parker (had my picture made with her too!), after she had just released an excellent book "Uncle Sam's Plantation", an evisceration of the welfare states' effect on black America. More recently Ms. Parker wrote, "Trillions of dollars later, black poverty is the same. But black families are not, with triple the incidence of single parent homes and out of wedlock births. It's not complicated. Americans can accept Barack Obama's invitation to move onto the plantation. Or they can choose personal responsibility and freedom." Just another racist trying to fight against compassion.

Whatever the peasants may have chosen, our elected masters stuck to their traditional race-baiting plantation system under our new black president. By the second year of the Obama Magnificence, a lot of us were numb to further insult and outrage. As a sideshow during the titanic fight over nationalizing health care, the mask slipped once again, reminding us that only the Left may ever fling the accusation of "Racism!" and to deny it is just further proof of, well…

Same Old Dems, Same Old Racism

"Thank you Democrats, for once again making things clear. Thank you for enlightening those of us little people who cannot aspire to your magnanimity, your grace, and your clarity of thought. The latest uproar to afflict

Republicans is that Senate Majority Leader Harry Reid is perhaps, possibly, skirting the edge of propriety in the context of speech regarding accepted ethnic paradigms. No they do not mean to call him a racist, no, nothing so coarse and ugly as that. The Gravely Obtuse Party would not dare label as racist those who over the past decades have called all Republicans warmongers, racists, murderers, robber barons, sexists, homophobes, and Garth Brooks fans. But some braver Republican politicians and the cable neo-cons are feigning shock and offering staid, cocktail hour conniptions over Reid's observation that future-Pres. Obama was ""light skinned" ... with no Negro dialect, unless he wanted to have one" as when the latter wishes to woo the easily skittish audience of the Lifetime Channel. Republicans are outraged, in a polite way, over the apparent double standard showed by those who fried Trent Lott for his praises of ex-segregationist Strom Thurman, comments that did NOT include any praise of segregation. These Ford & Bush Republicans completely miss the irony that Trent Lott died in a pool of his own cordiality, an affect that has served his own fellows so equally well in defending and advancing what passes for their ideas.

Now poetically, a major leader in the greatest modern oppressive force against American blacks vomits up a gaffe bouquet from 1-800-RETIREE, delivered just in time for the Martin Luther King holiday. This has led to some professional strength confusion. Trent Lott was run out of D.C. for saying something that had nothing to do with race, on the grounds of racism, the mere hint of which can never be forgiven under any circumstance. Harry Reid gave an honest assessment with no obvious intent at forbidden thought, but he did use a banned word ("Negro", as in the "The United ____ College Fund"), and seemed to suggest that some black folks speak with an accent that is different from the mainstream, also a concept popularly deserving of condemnations and opprobrium. What exactly did Reid say that was racist? In fairness I have seen candidate, and later President Obama alter the meter and rhythm of his speech to sound, shall we say, more colloquial with respect to the immediate audience. And as far as his hue, is Reid a racist if he admits to gaining these observations while watching a color TV? (Whoa don't blame me, he said it). President Obama said Reid's comments were "in-artful" (no I don't know what dialect he used), and justice merchant Al Sharpton, though aggrieved, assures us that "these comments should not distract America from its continued focus on securing healthcare or creating jobs for its people." Well wishes of support have poured in from Democrats nationwide as they continue to stand heroically against racism, while a backlash of support among the national media has started to cover some of Reid's hardscrabble roots, and his legendary recent work in undoing freedom.

That Reid said nothing racist is beside the point. Comments that would be cause for summary execution in the public apology square for any Republican no matter how ineffectual are no big deal if the speaker is committed to wealth redistribution, socializing health care, and greater government interference in private lives. We learned from the O.J. trial that racism is a worse crime than murder; Democrats have for months inferred that anything obstructing the plans of a black president is racist on its face, and they back it up by giving a pass to one of their own. If you ask me, the real racist is Umar Farouk Abdulmutallab, the Christmas Day "underwear bomber."

Using the Democrat's own logic, by diverting Obama's attention from his socialist agenda, AbdulEtc., who happens to be black, has shown flagrant racism, and should receive the death penalty for this crime. After he apologizes, of course."

In the summer of 2009, in response to the Democrat plan to make health coverage affordable to all, a new grass roots movement took shape in opposition. Declaring the Obama-countenanced Democrat agenda for health care a "government takeover", the new Tea Party formed, without national leadership or central location. Soon congressmen from both parties were assailed in their home districts at town hall meetings, leaving both they and the media shocked at the furor and fear that had been provoked. Beginning that summer and well beyond the eventual, contentious passage of the Democrat health bill, sources from the White House to Congress to the media continued to brand the opposition to an increased government role in health care as racist. The election of a black president had formalized reverse racism, and by slandering non-racist voters as just the opposite, set Martin Luther King's dream back yet another generation. Shall we overcome, anyone?

❖ ❖ ❖

Part 2

"A fleet of British ships of war are the best negotiators in Europe; they always speak to be understood and generally gain their point."

Horatio Nelson

"I remember meeting a mother of a child who was abducted by the North Koreans right here in the Oval Office."

George W. Bush, Washington, D.C., June 26, 2008

A Foreign Affair – Couldn't We Have Just Left the Money on the Nightstand for the Mercenaries?

*Do We Really Want to Win? * Doubt for the American Age * Lesson From the Great War * A Bad Hand * If Only the Terrorists Were Zombies * America's Chosen Yard Dog * Catching Up With Oppenheimer's Kids * AM-241, Nuclear War: The Home Version * One Scary Second * Ordinary Citizens Embarrass the Government * Illegal Immigration Is OUR Fault * Bush Sides with the Free Rangers * Build the Damn Fence! * Time for a Grown Up Foreign Policy * Can Space Be Free?*

The Beatles "Love" show by Cirque de Soleil, was as fantastic, nostalgic, and happy as we had been led to expect. My sister had arrived the day before, exploring various culinary efforts in her capacity as professional chef and food project analyzer, and was there to meet us at the front window. Cold, over-priced beers in hand, we rushed in to grab our seat to watch the Fab Four. In the past decade training first-year medical students, I have made very clear that they will be bothered, badgered, abused, nitpicked, and hassled for years to come, and I would leave such mean pursuits to others. To be sure we had much to learn together, but the only fact that I ever required them to learn, and to never dispute on pain of failure and ridicule, was that The Beatles are simply the greatest musical moment in the whole of human history. This was abundantly reinforced at "The Love Show", and it is to be highly recommended for all ages. Western civilization from Greece to Rome to Chicago has as its linchpin, the British Empire. As the Royal Navy was the deadly expression of the most advanced economic system of its day, so The Beatles were a pinnacle expression of the advances of classical liberal thought through theater, literature, science, marketing, and yes, music. By now the reader, hoping to glean insights on foreign policy and its relation to freedom, will wonder whether I have gone back for another overpriced beer. Stick with me.

After the show we hit the New York Deli for cartoonishly large pastrami sandwiches, and cheesecake, after which my colleague retired, and my sister and I went to Caesar's Palace to tell lies, and win vast fortunes. Sis piddled back and forth a bit on the slots while I rang up a quick $160 on roulette, and bought two of the most lavish, expensive martinis the cute gals in min-togas could serve. We sat amidst gilt faux-finery, bulging aquariums, and the serving routes of flitting and prancing Roman cheerleaders while we told funny stories and yucked it up till bedtime.

Sis caught the early bird the next day, while my buddy and I took a leisurely ride to Hash Browns-A-Go-Go, a brunch I will never remember but with fondness and drool. We walked off our meal in the high-dollar promenades of The Venetian and the Forum Shops, after which I returned to the roulette wheel to graciously donate the previous night's winnings back to Caesar, for his trouble (I kept one $10 chip in my pocket so I could honestly claim I left Vegas a winner). With that we headed out of town for Phoenix, the Rat Pack on the iPod.

The point of American foreign policy (as opposed to the U.S. State Department) is or ought to be, defending that which is America in accordance with the directives and confines of the Constitution. Coming in to land in Las Vegas, there was no doubt in my mind that Adam Smith's celebrants, if they could build this wonder in the desert, could build the same in any desert. To our south we have an unfriendly government seeking to use our good graces, perpetual, self-imposed guilt, and our affinity for cheap labor for their own ends. On the other side of the world we have plenty of deserts full of oil to replace that which we own but dare not drill for ourselves; thieves and madmen aplenty are looking for a chance to take down the Big Dog; and there are tens of millions that don't know, and may not choose to learn, what we have learned and now need to defend: freedom and capitalism work in any desert, jungle, city, or nation it is tried. I don't really suppose that Nelson broke the French line-of-battle and received his mortal wound at Trafalgar just so I could enjoy The Beatles, but that's the way it worked out. If the beloved Brits would ever pull their collective head out of the 20th century (to say nothing of other places) they might again realize the greatness which they inspired and in which they could share. Sparta and Athens fought against a pushy know-it-all-god-for-life Xerxes, and won because of what they defended, which of course had allowed them to be the defenders needed.

Centuries later the Romans gave the same to all challengers, until they themselves became too civically fat and complacent to remember what it was they had valued. The Visigoths and Huns valued it of course, for a while, until the fires burned down and the wine ran out. But on the burial mounds of Charlemagne and various greedy popes, the Renaissance flowered, allowing the Italian city-states of the Holy League to whip up on the Ottoman Empire, again securing a win for the west. The occasional French or Prussian fits cropping up on the continent for the next few centuries notwithstanding, every time the illiberal, economically stilted and stunted East has come up against the West, the individual losses of a Gallipoli or Pearl Harbor have been vastly overshadowed by triumphal culminations on the deck of the USS Missouri, or at Reykjavik. Societies that boast personal liberty at their core have a largely unbroken string of wins over despotism and barbarism for about three thousand years. Capitalism kicks ass, and can grow a bloom in the desert. But will it always win? A championship team cannot win the Super Bowl if they don't actually take the field, or if its top linebacker is benched because the fans are worried he might hurt an opponent. The fight to convince skeptics and apologists is incredibly far from over.

When I started writing columns in 2003, several months after the victorious "Shock and Awe" Iraq offensive, the dramatic toppling of Saddam Hussein's statue served as a starting point to consider exactly where America was heading in the wake of this heady victory. The essay's conclusion was that American freedom would never be won or lost in some foreign desert, but here at home. The stunning blitzkrieg victory was of course, followed up with piddling nation building and muddled messages from the administration and the Pentagon; the complete lack of clarity sure to strengthen anti-American sentiment at home, and aid our enemies abroad. It was numbing, horrifying even, to watch the Republicans in 2004 conjure up their very own quagmire. In

April 2004, U.S. Marines were on the outskirts of Fallujah wait-
ing to take the city. Snipers found refuge among the city build-
ings, most notably, a prominent mosque. In the midst of brutal
street-by-block fighting, the U.S. command decided it was time to
prove once again, that this was not a war on Islam...

Do We Really Want to Win?

"The great P.J. O'Rourke has just released a new book
entitled: <u>Peace Kills: America's Fun New Imperialism</u>, in
which he examines the current state of American foreign
policy. The book is thoroughly hilarious in the typically
sarcastic O'Rourke meter and jab that always makes him
such a welcome antidote toward goofy liberal earnestness. He notes most Americans' antipathy toward foreign
policy results from our inability to have consistent foreign
policy goals, which is painfully correct. Nowhere have
Americans been more conflicted than in regard to their
potential conflicts with others around the globe since the
end of WWII. As O'Rourke does a fine job of cataloging
America's present foreign policy challenges and gaffs, he
pointedly notes the dichotomy of our foreign policy: that
seeking international cooperation and improving trade
in a world where many seek to undersell, or kill us might
prove a trifle contradictory. We can't withdraw from the
world ("Our previous attempts at isolationism were successful...for Hitler...Tojo") and we don't want to rule the
world. Look how much trouble it is to keep Puerto Rico
from becoming a state.

The problem with American foreign policy generally
is our unwillingness to declare our legitimate interests,
and then effectively intimidate those that threaten them.

Korea 1950 was a successful endeavor in that we accomplished our stated goals (preventing the spread of the Red Menace), followed up by perceived indecision based on Truman's firing of Macarthur for the latter's willingness to set the Yalu River on "extra-crispy." Kennedy of course bungled the Bay of Pigs, spun the Missile Crisis into a win, and subsequently put "Edsel" McNamara in charge of the flexible response. The Vietnam conflict actually gets a worse rap than it deserves. Yes it was prosecuted worse than Bill Clinton's impeachment, but there was a good reason for being there: American self-interest demanded fighting Communism. Historians have begun to properly recognize the Vietnam conflict as an important (if lost) battle in the Cold War, though the villainous LBJ continues to evade the popular blame for that mess which he so richly deserved. And how did his successor Nixon re-assert American interests? With bombs, incursions into Cambodia, and the understanding that stomping on Commies was a good way to achieve the peace, albeit a temporary one. It wasn't Santa Claus that got Hanoi back to the peace table, but big fat B-52's spreading a more focused brand of cheer that Christmas, 1972. Nixon knew that we had already lost, and wanted to promote American interests by minimizing that loss.

Dealing with the Soviets head-on was more daunting, and only effective when we had clearly stated interests from which we would not be dissuaded. The limitations of the SALT talks were not in our best interests, which is why the Soviets eagerly signed them. Human rights, non-existent though they were behind the Iron Curtain, were none of our business, which is why the Kremlin let the Peanut Farmer prattle on about them while Brezhnev's chef was researching which vodka went best with Afghanistan. True, Reagan spoke forcefully for the rights of the enslaved citizens in the Eastern Bloc, but that served his (our) larger objective, which was the dissolution of the USSR. Without the military power that the Gipper resurrected, his call for freeing the Polish shipyard workers would have been as pointless as anything coming out of his predecessor's yap. After Reagan won the Big One, Bush '41 discredited himself and us by (1) invading a foreign power on spurious grounds, and then (2) not keeping control of the major strategic asset (Panama Canal) which occasioned the original affair. Later in Gulf War I, after Prime Minister Thatcher lent Bush some testosterone, our leader spun an embarrassing rhetorical fog prior to finally admitting that gee, maybe we might be worried about the black gold rumored to be bubbling up somewhere 'round there. But wait, hadn't he also raised the concern of Saddam's nukes? Our willingness to achieve our first goal resulted in a devastation of the Iraqi Army, followed by our timidity in accomplishing a goal seen in later years to be at least as important. We blinked in pursing the vital interest of finishing the job, guaranteeing a future war. As a consolation, Bush tried to use our military to prove to the world that we are good guys by sending food to starving, and surprisingly belligerent Somalis. Our lack of legitimate American interest not only got good men killed to no purpose, but also set the stage for 9/11. This last Bush '41 blunder was a good harbinger of the Slick Willy World Tour, where our military was only committed if it met the Somali criteria: there was no conceivable benefit to America, and it was perceived by the White House to make the current president look good.

And so we come to Iraq. Over the past several months my eyes have begun to glaze when I hear names like Najaf, Fallujah, or al-Sadr. I have been very supportive of W.'s policy of blowing up jerks in the desert ever since its inception around Kabul, and "Shock-and-Awe" was truly a thing of beauty. But did we do our job too well? The precision with which we minimized collateral damage, a laudable and honorable policy, now seems to have become a self-imposed limitation. If our men are dying, then the physical integrity of a mosque is not consistent with American interests. A lot of intellect and treasure went into developing the MOAB bombs, and we should bloody well use them to "win the peace." (The Massive Ordnance Air Blast Bomb / "Mother Of All Bombs" was a 21,000 pound masterpiece. The day the first one was dropped on the Eglin Air Force test range in the Florida panhandle over fifteen miles away, the windows of my office rattled. The thing was made to flatten insurgent cities, and it would have worked beautifully on Fallujah). There is a looming question: after trying to placate certain spineless European states, after buying chocolates and roses for the overfed streetwalker known as the U.N., and after tiptoeing around murdering mullahs whose trip to Allah should be expedited; after all this, what are we prepared to do about Iran? P.J. O'Rourke on terrorists: "No matter how horrific the terrorist attack, it's conducted by losers. Winners don't need to hijack airplanes. Winners have an air force." But, it must be added, winners have to be willing to use it."

Of course we did not use the MOAB and whatever fruits the famous "Surge" would later bear, the Bush administration dissipated enormous amounts of resources, good will, and blood in an ill-conceived and less explained attempt to democratize opposing tribes cobbled together in an imperial construct by the last great empire to parade through the neighborhood. Liberals and convenient moderates notwithstanding, George W. Bush had the support of the clear majority of his fellow citizens when he launched the invasion of Iraq, intent on removing Saddam Hussein from power. He had the support of Americans – myself included - who believed there to be a threat from weapons of mass destruction, and a national interest in kicking the crap out of an obvious enemy that remained a threat to our access to oil.

As the 2004 presidential campaign moved into the summer, the war in Iraq was the central topic, so much so that lost amidst the talk of tactics and peace it seemed, were greater questions: what is our overall strategy to protect the nation and advance our interests? How can geopolitics and armed might be used in a way truly consistent with our great ideals. What the hell were we fighting for? In the middle of '04, the contrast between the two candidates included a distinction of strategic character...

Doubt for the American Age

"Despite the availability of heroes, we are not living in a Heroic Age. This distinction seemed apparent last week, amid the hubbub of our perplexing Fallujah timidity and the media's glee over discovering a few soldier-bully idiots in our ranks (the Abu Ghraib scandal), ignoring a more interesting and perilous nod given toward recent history. I've been revisiting this recent history, devouring When Character Was King, the 2001 release from that most graceful of commentators, Peggy Noonan. She studies and describes the development of a character from modest beginnings, shaped by ambition as much as privation. This ambition was anchored by faith, from which flowed optimism and good cheer, allowing the developing character to analyze and assimilate those philosophies found to be truthful and good. This developing character became irrepressible even as it rose in purposefulness, and grew into a formidable weapon, which changed the world.

One part of the historical reflection last week was given to the European Union, which increased its membership to 25 nations with the addition of many ex-members of the defunct Warsaw Pact. The Estonian prime minister gleefully cheered joining a "community that shares the same values and visions." It is surely an indictment of the old U.S.S.R. that the bureaucratic torpor of Brussels, cold German cynicism, or traditional French sleaziness seem like a step up to the bedraggled urchins of eastern Europe. CNN reported that the Polish prime minister proclaimed the merger of the modern democratic European states to signal the true end of the Cold War. Reuters reported former German chancellor Helmut Kohl to tearfully bubble "The message is there will never again be war in Europe." Right. Amidst a backdrop of struggling economies, chronic unemployment, and red-tape inertia in the major European players, the EU will continue imposing economic quotas, standards for the new EU currency, wage guarantees/restrictions, and coalesce growing antipathy against a resiliently robust U.S. economy borne of relatively freer circumstances (and we may all be absolutely certain of seeing European leaders foursquare in support of U.S. nationalized healthcare to "level" the playing field). One recalls the British produce merchant a couple of years back criminally charged for selling a banana that exceeded EU weight standards. A different definition of "free" market. On the up side, the EU is a voluntary joining of members with a supposedly common purpose, a decidedly different origin than the brittle, iron-bound birth of the Warsaw Pact whose only purpose was the eventual conquest of the West. Unions begun in common cause for the positive can be fine things. They can negotiate for higher wages, or settle entire continents under the banner of equal treatment for all. Or they may be used to give moral cover to one group that wishes to illegally invade and burn to the ground the homes of another group, freeing individuals while suppressing individuals. Unions are tricky.

Six thousand miles or so to the west, Candidate Kerry went to Fulton, MO. to talk a little foreign policy. While the muddled heads of Europe were celebrating what they saw as the end of the Cold War, Kerry claimed the sight of Churchill's heroic "Iron Curtain" pronouncement to share his vision for foreign policy. Which was definitely less than heroic. Perhaps JFK2 was sleepy from sitting up too late trying to remember what he had really done with which medal or ribbon, but his logic really needed a little work. The transcript from the Kerry website stated that we must "reclaim our country's standing in the world by doing what has kept America safe and secure before." We need to get the "world's major powers invested with us in building Iraq's future", make Iraq "part of NATO's global mission", and invest a High Commissioner authorized by the U.N. to oversee Iraqi sovereignty. With nimble amnesia, Kerry exclaimed, "when NATO members have been treated with respect they have always answered the call of duty." Kerry's efforts to appear statesmanlike and mature are ridiculous, and devoid of real leadership. As with his ribbons/medals, Kerry is afflicted with shifting memory: we DID get the world's major powers invested in Iraq, resulting in the silly oil-for-food program which helped to line Kofi Annan's crooked pockets. We certainly tried to make Iraq part of NATO's mission; we bought off the Turks for back-door strategic pressure, and we all know how helpful NATO signatories France and Germany were. Pre-socialist Spain and Italy, both NATO members, joined our British buddies with us in the invasion. Keeping us "safe and secure" means for Kerry that we must "share responsibility and share authority", further proof that he paddles in an ill-defined pond. We were kept secure by leading the world in rebuilding the West against the Soviet threat, by leading largely as we saw fit through our own economic, political, and military initiatives, for our own interests, which is the part JFK2 doesn't like. NATO's lessened usefulness may be lesser still, with its power subsumed by the EU: the rising European power which may be our next enemy is concurrent with our NATO "allies."

Ms. Noonan's depiction of the development of Ronald Reagan's character as the century's great sword of freedom is useful in these deliberations. Reagan had the imagination to see a better world, free of the threat of nuclear destruction, and he had the strength of purpose to pursue this vision to its success. He understood that the pursuit of truly American interests would work for the betterment of the world, for those who sought freedom worldwide. Whatever declarations may be made from eastern European ministers, the Cold War was won the day Reagan stared down Gorbachev at Reykjavik and said "No." The Cold War became a Heroic Age because of American self-interest and resolve, fired and led by a great hero. We face emboldened socialism at home, and new enemies rising out of opportunities created by the victory we won for them. Our president takes a heroic stand against the terrorists, leading a gallant military in the service of American interests. But whether our belief in American freedom will render this a new heroic age is still an open question."

A lot of us that year went to the polls wary of Bush's expensive compassion, but convinced both that he could handle the terrorists, and that Kerry would be the latest in a long line of Democrat apologist wimps. While we may have improved our ability to influence oil flow in the region, we missed the WMD's. The Washington Post and New York Times were joyful in pouncing when no nukes were dug up out of the desert (interestingly enough, the NY Times several years later finally admitted that yes, there probably were such weapons, which had been moved. Nothing like cutting edge journalism). The disconcertingly large portion of the U.S. electorate that chose to get their news from Dan Rather and <u>People</u> *magazine, that were vaguely certain that Bush had stolen the 2000 election, enjoyed displaced vindication as though the missing weapons were conclusive proof that Bush was a liar and a fool. The worst of those moronic screams were that he invaded Iraq because Hussein had tried to assassinate his daddy. To believe this is to ignore the use of gas attacks by Hussein on the Kurds; his attempted procurement through multiple sources of nuclear weapons and supporting hardware; the months of stalling during which such weapons could have been spirited to Syria (do we have the Mossad on speed dial?); the independent finding of British intelligence that yes, such weapons existed; and the discovery of mobile labs in the desert capable of producing bio-weapons. Maybe in this Muslim tee-totaling nation, it really belonged to home brewers. The lack of serious critique and the never-ending scramble for a political edge, as it had in the last century, was a disservice to our troops and the freedom that they were pledged to defend. 2005-06 showcased a muddled, disgraceful performance on both sides of the political aisle...*

Lesson from the Great War

A partisan congressional faction hurls accusations against the administration over the battlefield conduct of a war whose outcome has been decided. The opposing congressional faction reflexively defends the administration, questions the patriotism of the critics, and attempts to squash debate in the public arena. The media adopts the popular view, in full defiance of the publicly available facts, including sworn congressional testimony from battlefield commanders. The question of whether American lives were wasted by a negligent chain-of-command hangs in the air for a time, and then vanishes into the mist. Sound familiar? These were all circumstances following 11:00 AM, 11/11/18: The Armistice of the Great War.

A delegation from the Imperial German High Command was received by French Marshall Foch on 11/7, and presented with the stern ultimatum in which was sewn the seeds of World War II. The Germans were given 72 hours to reply, and the Armistice was signed at 5:00 AM, 11/11, and the order given to stop firing at 11:00 AM. In the next 5 hours and 59 minutes, Americans suffered over 3,500 casualties – including 320 dead – in pointless assaults against an enemy who thought peace was declared, and who was attempting to withdraw. German descendant and American soldier Pvt. Henry Gunther fell dead from machine gun rounds to the head at 10:59, the official last

Part 2

U.S. casualty of the Great War. Inquiries from soldiers present to their congressmen regarding these curious final hours began in 1919, and led to the official inquests in 1920. In an excerpt from his recent book on the Armistice, author Joseph Persico takes a tense and painful backward glance from the halls of Congress to the muddy doughboys praying for respite from orders that would not be countermanded. A war begun accidentally ended stupidly, with more soldiers from both sides falling after peace was declared than fell on D-Day. The counsel for congressional Republicans eviscerated the officers testifying. The explanations ran from the practical –commanders could not KNOW that the Germans would honor the truce – to the criminally stupid – the commander of the 89th Div. assaulting a defended town to procure "proper bathing facilities" rather than let the enemy reside there after the truce. Sixty-one men died to take that town. Up and down the line the pattern was repeated: it was plainly ridiculous to continue the assaults, and yet none of the officers and men who had braved the horrific trenches would refuse orders. Perceiving the Republicans to seek political tarnish for the White House, the Democrats fought successfully to expunge from the committee report any note of wasted lives, a view adopted by the New York Times, in their proud tradition of aloofness from facts.

The analogy is not a tight one. The grounds are shadowy doorways, not shell-raked murder fields between static lines. Our war goes on, while an end-time was known for theirs. The congressional factions have switched, and uncertainties will always abound in the hindsight of battle, to be exploited by the ambitious. Is our war just? Vietnam is now seen more responsibly as a vital battle that showed our resolve in the Cold War, and the Battle for Iraq may accomplish the same in World War IV. But there is no justification for Republicans who reflexively defend the White House, or for Democrats who daily betray the country with cheap partisanship."

No matter, as a rhetorical leader Bush failed and in so doing, lost the confidence of the nation in his strategic vision for Iraq. A lot of us were pro-American hawks, who wanted to secure our interests through victory. A lot of us wanted to support a president in willing to decisively deal with our enemies. A lot of us wanted to win the damn thing. By 2006 a lot of us were fed up...

A Bad Hand

"At the 1988 Tailhook convention, before such gatherings were unacceptable, one fighter-bomber squadron had some nifty cards printed up with their logo. The wallet-sized guides unfolded to show a graph detailing every possible blackjack combination, useful for aviators too enthusiastic in their celebrations to properly count cards. On the back were listed 5 rules, detailing the fundamentals of the game. The last and most valuable rule was "When the dealer is lucky, leave!" Sage advice.

That Pres. Bush would choose the night of the season's opening Monday Night Football game to address the nation on Iraq is emblematic of the clumsy circumstances through which the administration now treads. I recall several heated debates with some of those very same Tailhookers, veterans of the 1991 Gulf War, over the first Pres. Bush's strategic decision NOT to invade Iraq. My former shipmates argued in favor of the U.N. mandate limiting our actions, as a justification for the ceasefire. I argued that the U.N. was (and is) the cheap streetwalker in the community of nations, and should be ignored at our convenience for our own interests. If the threat voiced by then-Sec. of State Baker of WMD's was real, then it was only common sense to dethrone Saddam on the spot. We knew we would be back.

It has been mantra for the media and Michael Moore contingent that, since no WMD's were found and no link with the 9/11 attacks were proven, our 2003 Iraqi invasion was unjustified, Bush is a scoundrel, and America is the modern progenitor of misery. And despite finding strong evidence of the existence of WMD's, the White House inexplicably allowed the media to ignore the evidence and repeat the lie to a degree that it is now accepted truth. So desperate was the administration to capitalize on the post-9/11 fervor, they allowed the Iraqi invasion to be directly tied in the public imagination to that specific attack. We were right to invade Iraq for to defend our own interests, but we were obligated to do so decisively, once the case for invasion was forcefully made. In the intervening three years, Pres. Bush's strategic vision of Iraq as a metastasis of democracy has been clumsily put to the nation without forcefulness. That lack of forcefulness was previewed in the siege of Fallujah, where high intensity U.S. ordinance went unused in an effort to develop good feelings in a combative native populace. In 2004 America buried its greatest modern president, Ronald Reagan, who wielded rhetoric with more effectiveness than the most powerful smart bombs or armored division. We have been reminded that part of the job description of president is an ability to convey powerful thoughts, calls to action that become the very actions themselves. His hopeful vision notwithstanding, Pres. Bush's rhetoric failed the country and in its failure, gave a de facto victory to her enemies both foreign and domestic. In Vietnam, we had very good reasons to fight against the spread of communism and establish another Asian democracy. We lost that battle and left unaware that we would later win the greater war. Now we are in another fight, once easily winnable, in which we showed insufficient resolve during the crucial window. A leader with better vision would have explained to the nation that we did not need the excuse of 9/11 to attack a very real threat. A leader with that vision would have flattened Fallujah without loss of American life, and utterly destroyed any will to resist our forces. We cannot now establish an effective democracy in Iraq, and though it would be preferable, it is not essential. A far better bastion of democracy resides just to the west, and one far friendlier to our interests. Remaining in Iraq is simply no longer worth the cost. The dealer has a hot hand, and it's time for us to leave the table, conserve our chips, and prepare for the next game. We won't have long to wait."

I love zombie movies, some of which with varying degrees of success have attempted to provide social or topical commentary. In 2007 there was another such offering on that seemed to speak to the ongoing Iraqi muddle …

If Only the Terrorists Were Zombies

"Two points for the reader before proceeding further into this column: the author unapologetically loves zombie movies, and every attempt will be made to avoid plot spoiling. That said, proceed at your own risk.

In 1968 critics praised George Romero's black & white original spooky satire "Night of the Living Dead." It was a fresh look at an old monster (ourselves), dealt with themes of racism, communal cooperation, and Armageddon. Fun stuff, lots of gore, and scared the bejabbers out of yours truly. Over the years we took a trip to the mall with a slam on consumerism (Dawn of the Dead), followed by several years of progressively less scary, dumber knockoffs, remakes, parodies, and low-budget goo. Not all of the lesser children were equally worthless, as exemplified by the low-budget, dreadful "Hood of the Living Dead. If you can watch this tale of a zombie outbreak in a poor Oakland ghetto without laughing…forget it, you can't. Zombie flicks jumped back to the fore with the more recent "28 Days Later" and the remake of "Dawn of the Dead." Both of these movies are absolutely frightening, each resting on the inherent terror within the familiar gone horribly wrong. Unfortunately the genre's father Romero saw the success of these two movies as an invitation to recapture his ghoulish lightning and expand the satirical vehicle. His plodding "Land of the Dead" commentary on the Iraq invasion and corporate America was dumb, predictable – and worse – not frightening in the least. Can zombies still be scary? Yes, because they really do exist. Watching the recent GOP presidential debate, or considering how many Americans would vote for Bill Clinton's wife is proof enough that we live under the constant threat an outbreak of stumbling, lurching, drooling brain munchers.

So it was with baited breath that one rushed to the theater this past weekend to catch the new"28 Weeks Later", a sequel in which post-zombie Britain is rebuilt courtesy of the U.S. Army. Fans of the previous "28 Days Later" will recall that a government engineered bio-weapon – the "Rage Virus" – got loose thanks to some animal rights hippies and turned London residents into millions of homicidal carnivores. The violence has come, ravished the Sceptred Isle, and left a deserted canvas upon which to paint nation building. The metaphor, like the virus, waits just under the soil to spring forth into a larger cycle of mayhem.

Early in the sequel, the seeds for later family conflict are sewn. Have we learned nothing from interfering in Bosnian or Iraqi civil wars? Then witness American troops interject themselves, to their own undoing, into a parent trap Disney never envisioned. As a group of new Londoners arrive to begin repopulation in a "safe zone", U.S. troops inspect them and direct their charges to new homes. Snipers prowl the rooftops and choppers claw the skies waiting to snuff out any unlikely outbreak of terror- ist, sorry, viral violence. An unauthorized foray into non-secure London teaches us an object lesson in the perils of poor border control. Power sharing between our military and local authorities rapidly undoes both. The tough love of effective nation building soon leaves captive Brits quarantined in the dark for their own protection, remi-niscent of both the Blitz and 9/11. Unfortunately they are trapped with infected in their midst, and soon troops ordered to fire cannot discern who are the ter-, zombies and who are the panicky innocents. Spanish director Juan Carlos Fresnadillo is probably pro-European Union, given the story's ending (really trying to be intentionally vague here), a sort of reverse warning to recalcitrant Brits who would rather depend on their American cousins. The bright spot is the military's over-the-top response to a new outbreak, a re-telling of what SHOULD have happened to Fallujah three years ago. Unfortunately, their now oafish escalation is undone by ...well, go see the movie. Like the news, it might all seem a little too familiar."

❧ ❧ ❧

As we walked uncertainly into 2011, dyspeptic at home and uncoordinated abroad, we faced the usual ongoing confrontation with North Korea, a tiger-by-the-tail relationship with Red China, confusion over Russia, impotence (ours) in Latin America, and yet another Muslim street surge, this time in Egypt. On the heels of similar in Tunisia, our usual suspect ally in Egypt, Mubarak, was busy packing his loved ones off on an extended English vacation while mobs began to overrun his security forces in the streets, egged on by a bunch called 'The Muslim Brotherhood.' We can hope that Pres. Obama's "America Loves Islam" speech in Cairo in 2009 will keep any new Islamist regime happy with us, but do any of us actually believe that it will? We are on the brink of another state run by angry, glowering sons of Mohammed, intent on damning our strip-mall, "OMG" culture while exterminating Israel quicker than you can say jihad. This will, for reasons good and ill, force an even tighter U.S.-Israel bond, especially if our current president wants to win electoral rich Florida in 2012. The state of our ally was no less significant in 2006...

America's Chosen Yard Dog

"A reader of this column wrote last week to ask my opinion on the current dust-up over in the Middle East. It's a tough question, spawned by tougher and conflicting facts. What do we know? Beginning in 1917 Israel was born of a chain of bad decisions running the gamut from the dreamy League of Nations to our majestically incompetent U.N. Pres. Truman believed that Nazi persecutions justified a Jewish homeland, and in the 1947 UN Resolution 181, British rule was ended (they were happy to leave, as they had been just as thrilled to leave their protectorate in Iraq a generation earlier. Anyone see a pattern here?), with a permanent division of Palestine approved. Truman quickly supported 181, Jewish reaction was mixed, and the Arab states began moving troops to the Palestinian border. The new State of Israel was born on May 14, 1948; on May 15, Arab armies invaded Israel, and were stomped 4 times in the next 25 years. It was enough to make a guy even suffer through lunch with Jimmy Carter, which Egypt's Sadat did, just so terrorist-turned-prime minister Begin would quit slapping him around. In 1981 Israeli F-16's reminded Saddam Hussein that he had not filed the proper variance requests to build the Osirak reactor in that neighborhood. By 1982 the Israelis had had it with the PLO katyusha rocket attacks (another Communist invention) and Syrian-backed instability oozing out of Lebanon, and invaded. They ripped up the PLO power structure in Lebanon, which allowed the rise of Hezbollah who themselves became katyusha- proficient. We lost some Marines in a civil war in Lebanon and wisely got out. Now the Israelis are back in Lebanon and we are in a civil war in Iraq. JCS Chairman and Marine Corps commandant Gen. Peter Pace said last week: "...Shiia and Sunni are gonna have to love their children more than they hate each other." When our highest ranking military leader – and a Marine for crying out loud – comes off sounding like Maury Povich, it's time to re-think a few things. Now the blue-helmet clowns squatting on valuable Manhattan property are trying to force a peace plan that won't work, while the Middle East antagonists continue to escalate. The plan has the support of France, which by definition will be against our interests. What DO we know?

We know that it was a really dumb idea to forcibly establish the Israeli state, which has worked about as well as other such forced state constructs (Yugoslavia, the U.S.S.R., Southern California). We know we generally like Israel and don't want to see her destroyed. It is clear from this latest conflict that no one in Hezbollah, the U.N. or Paris has seen the movie "Munich." This is not an apologia for Israel, which I have visited twice and for which I have great admiration. We know during the 1967 Six-Day War Israeli jets and ships knowingly attacked a U.S. Navy ship, the U.S.S. Liberty, killing 34 sailors, and were never held to account for it. Later the Israelis used the Pollard spy operation to steal naval intelligence secrets from their friends, U.S., in the 1980's. The Israelis are proficient, and determined killers who to their great credit, side with their nation far more stridently than a large number of Americans side with theirs. Israel is out for herself and we can take a lesson from her example. Ironically we must emulate the Victorians of the 19th century Pax Britannica, playing off our enemies and friends against each other and exploiting every weakness. We know that our oil security and Middle East strategy are linked to the security of Israel. And if our surly stepsister has gotten tired of 35 years of rocket attacks on her northern towns, we should look for ways to play that to our advantage. If the Israeli Defense Force can be used as a power card against terrorist regimes in Iran and Syria, so much the better. And we should ignore the blue helmets of the U.N.. Unless of course, they would like to take over in Iraq."

And now in the wake of the Egyptian turmoil and ouster of Mubarak, tiresomely, Israel may once again have to worry about their Sinai border, along with all the rest.

❖ ❖ ❖

In 2009 we got another round of the bluff and posture from the retarded Kim Jung-Il kingdom in North Korea, always excited to remind us of their new nuclear capability. For all their chest puffing, it's still unlikely that they would invade South Korea. Apart from some economic help from China, the North Korean "big push" Soviet-style military, once overrunning the border and decimating Seoul, would be spent, unable to replace lost armaments, and unable to effectively re-supply their occupying forces. They would face worldwide condemnation, uncertain Chinese support, an inabiliity to operate or emulate South Korea's economy, and would remain easily exposed to attacks from superior U.S. forces. Sure they could launch a nuke at Los Angeles, but even if it hit, what would be our response? Elsewhere the Pakistanis and Indians continue their Mexican standoff; Tehran is near acquiring their own nukes, and the West appears utterly incompetent to control or direct events. All in all, no progress at all since 2005...

Catching Up with Oppenheimer's Kids

"Uh-oh. A recumbent couch-view of cable news last week included some interesting foreign policy items, none of which were surprising, but all of which are beginning to seem a bit more convergent. The news included a look forward at Pres. Bush's upcoming European tour and

visit with Russian head Vlad Putin. Even as W. is beginning to glare in the direction of Iran and their nascent
nukes, Putin is declaring that Iran is not a nuclear threat,
has no interest in making nuclear weapons, and anyway,
the Russians need cash and are going to keep selling
nuclear parts and training to the mullahs. Several thousand miles east, creeping under the wave of post-tsunami
grieving and goodness are the inscrutable Chinese, who
are enlarging their fleet with an eye toward challenging
the U.S. Navy in the Taiwan straits while asserting larger
hegemony interests. In a stunning "victory" for the Clinton foreign policy team, China's retarded little brother
North Korea has announced that it now has nuclear war-
heads to sit atop their new Taepo Dong II ballistic missiles,
capable of reaching our western mainland. Just to round
things out, we still have hate-fueled Indians and Pakistanis pointing nukes at each other over Kashmir. Reports
are now that Pakistan has already built three long-range,
very quiet subs with nuclear missile capability, thanks in
large measure to technology and assistance from one of
our European "allies." This same Euro-buddy, predictably France, is now in talks as well with India to supply all
of their nuclear home deterrence needs. Perhaps most
chilling of all, our newest attack submarine is named the
U.S.S. Jimmy Carter. C'est magnifique!

Nuclear brinkmanship in the Cold War certainly
had its fun moments including the neat trappings of the
Space Age cocktail culture and some really cool movies
(the original 1964 "Fail Safe" is my favorite, but you can't
beat the image of Slim Pickens riding the Bomb down in
"Dr. Strangelove"). I never got to make out in a bomb
shelter like the characters in Donald Fagen's exquisite
1982 "New Frontier" music video, but it sure seemed

to make the risk of fiery annihilation worthwhile. The teacher didn't broach the whole scary aspect of radioactive fallout until seventh grade health class, by which time they had pretty much abandoned "duck and cover" and were telling us all to hide in the basement with water and canned goods for say, two centuries. Those were the days when MAD (mutually assured destruction) was the ruling doctrine espoused by Kissinger and the Politburo without anything major in the "oops" category. Of course we found out later there were a few little burps in the system: as Egyptian tanks stormed to the outskirts of Tel Aviv in 1973, Nixon and Brezhnev were actually talking on the Hot Line; U.S. nuclear forces were alerted in 1979 when a large Soviet missile attack was seen on NORAD screens – it was actually a computer drill that no one bothered to announce, but apparently quite a lot of vodka and Budweiser was consumed later that day; in the interest of détente, the Soviets goosed themselves in a similar fashion in 1983 AND 1995, with blessedly unspectacular results. And of course there was the Cuban missile near-dust up in 1962.

So the results of two great powers with bunches of nukes are interesting cultural accoutrements, lots of drama and tension, and probably a fair amount of cirrhosis. We still have ours, and the Russkis still have theirs. And though freedom tore the Berlin Wall down, we may now have a lot more to worry about. Brian Kennedy and Mark Clark of the Claremont Institute (www.missilethreat. com) describe in commendable detail the ongoing threat of good old fashioned ICBM attack on America, with a critical difference: the threat of MAD may not work on a nation of a billion people, or one led by an authentic Napoleonic-complex nut job, or on Al-Queda terrorists not limited to any one location. The published doctrines and statements of the leadership of the regimes in Red China and North Korea respectively, ascertain the worth of nuclear weapons as legitimate policy options in pursuing their goals. In 1996 China's Lt. Gen. Kai implied a nuclear threat to Los Angeles over Taiwanese sovereignty, and N. Korean defector Col. Choi described for Congress in 1997 his homeland's policy goal of targeting the U.S. mainland for mushroom cloud renovation. And we already know what Bin Laden's psychos would do if given the tools.

As tensions begin to grow and options disappear, it's worth considering the Israeli model. Their preemptive destruction of Saddam's nuclear reactors in 1981 was, proper, effective, and saved lives in the long run. The Clinton Administration's failure of nerve in 1994 lost us the chance to end a N. Korean nuclear threat before it began. Instead of dispatching the Peanut Farmer for hugs and goody gifts of 1000-megawatt reactors, Pyongyang's unfinished nuclear facilities should have mysteriously exploded in the dead of night. A flattened Tokyo, or San Diego may now be the wage of cowardice. Rather than arguing over the cost to domestic spending, we should have already built a ballistic missile defense, and should aggressively pursue one now. A lot of good the welfare state will do the charred corpses of a government that neglected its legitimate, primary responsibility for the sake of wealth redistribution. Such a defense system will not stop terrorist "suitcase nukes", and sadly we will live to see nuclear terrorism devastate an American city. This may be made possible courtesy of rogue states which sell nukes to terrorists in return for the hard cash that places like N. Korea or Iran desperately need.

Imagine your rage, you liberals, if W. (or now, Obama) comes on the tube to announce that there is a smoking hole in Tehran, or Pyongyang where their nuclear plant used to be. The world will go on alert, Putin will rage, the dictators of China will flood the Taiwan Straits with their ships, Uncle Ted will holler for impeachment, and we will all be pretty terrified. Now imagine instead, how you will feel if the television images are of a mushroom cloud in the center of Pittsburg or Seattle. Only the precise application of strength can avert this horror, which will make a joke of peace marches and hopeful intentions. Our leaders even now wrestle with such unsavory calculations."

In 2002, the film adaptation of Tom Clancy's novel The Sum of All Fears was released. All in all it wasn't bad, and had one truly terrifying moment: the look on the national security advisor's face, sitting with the president at the Super Bowl, that a terrorist nuclear bomb is about to detonate beneath them. A look of horror and clarity, he yells the code word to scramble, and the Secret Service hustles the commander-in-chief to the limo and away without so much as a backward glance. Minutes later, the stadium and part of downtown Baltimore is vaporized and the nation careens toward an orchestrated nuclear confrontation with Russia. In the movie the bad guys are, laughably, Nazis. That's right, the same idiots with beer bellies and lousy home-made tattoos that not even Geraldo takes seriously anymore have somehow garnered the cash, connections, and geopolitical know-how to place a bomb where it will entice the U.S. to obliterate the Russians, and vice versa. What was a fun James Bond scenario twenty years earlier ("Octopussy") was just plain dumb a year after the 9/11 attacks. So I ask you dear reader, why in the wake of an all too real Islamic attack would Hollywood change such a plausible enemy to such a dated caricature? I think we both know

*the answer. And for all their urgency to avoid offending some
preferred groups, it won't stop an inevitable hit...*

Nuclear War: The Home Version

"The long list of fun things society has created, from iPods
to microwavable pork rinds, includes Americium (Am-241)
a synthetic element derived from tickling plutonium with a
few spare neutrons. Where can you find this silvery-white
hi-tech Play-Doh? Am-241 turns up in all sorts of places,
from radiology labs and oil surveying kits, to the common
household smoke detector. Dr. Henry Kelly of the Federation of American Scientists testified before the Senate in
2002 that a small amount of Am-241 propelled by a pound
of TNT could dangerously contaminate an area of twenty
city blocks, with eventual demolition and cleanup costs
exceeding fifty billion dollars. Some claim the Federation has a decidedly left-wing slant, a generically reasonable supposition when dealing with scientists. So let's cut
Kelly's claim in half: ten city blocks, and twenty-five billion
smackers. Add to the potential contamination the wide-
spread, rapid panic that the reporting of such an event
would cause, and we still have an immediate catastrophe
and a long-term cleanup on all aisles. Last week the former
"Radioactive Boy Scout" David Hahn was arrested for stealing hallway smoke detectors. His visage was splashed all
over the news, pocked with the sort of skin lesion burns
one might see from crystal meth usage, or perhaps, gamma
radiation exposure. Ken Silverstein of Harper's magazine
had first written about Hahn in the mid-1990's, describing
the then-youth's fissionable fascination, and his attempts
to build various homemade reactors. Silverstein is unimpressed with Hahn's latest activities, and with the feds'

ransacking of the man's apartment only to find a few smoke detectors and no dangerous levels of radiation. The man was jailed, and poses no present threat. Just another nut job playing with atoms?

Technical details once classified have since been launched by novels into the standard fare of cable news, video games and the thrill show "24." It isn't the present threat of nuclear terrorism that surprises, but rather that it has not already occurred. Imagine a southern city that is a major international transportation hub, with a couple of million residents, and home to an international news network. The dirty bomb detonated somewhere between the airport and downtown will not destroy the network's broadcast capabilities, leaving it free to provide non-stop coverage of bedlam. The legitimate fears of fallout, amplified in a panic, would leave a strategic interstate, rail, and air intersection practically dead, with a vital economic region backed up and panicked. The billions lost regionally in halted commercial traffic would have national, and rapidly, international repercussions – think New Orleans, only much, much worse. Government leaders will thump and bellow, and finding no readily identifiable targets, will target the civil liberties of their subjects for their own protection. We will be given a new, larger version of the pointless Terminal Security Authority, the moron stepchild of 9/11. Last week in a speech to the national press club Newt Gingrich made a sobering point: "I am genuinely afraid that this political system will not react until we lose a city, [and] how rapidly we will impose ruthlessness on ourselves in that kind of a world. I think those of you who care about civil liberties had better be thinking through how we win this war before the casualties get so great that the American people voluntarily give up a lot of those liberties." Earlier in his speech, Gingrich lamented that, with respect to our present circumstances, we are not a serious nation. The early Nineties' Tom Clancy novel "Sum of All Fears" was a chillingly plausible scenario of Islamic nuclear terrorism in America; when the movie came out in 2002, the villains had incredibly been replaced with neo-Nazis, doubtless inserted to avoid the ire of Muslims. We are soon, sadly, to be in a fix when a U.S. city is irradiated. It will be our greatest challenge to date to rebuild and fight back, to preserve America and resist the temptation to descend into a police state. The average Americans with smoke alarms in their homes had better learn to recognize the threat from all enemies, both foreign and domestic, and be prepared to call them by name."

Fallout-dusted cities and civic self-immolation are not the only potential crises with which we may be visited. Rock star Sting wailed in the Glorious Eighties about "Oppenheimer's little toy" in his hit "Russians." Ol' Sting may not have noticed the irony of a nation that could produce thousands of nukes, yet had a chronic toilet paper shortage when he penned "There is no monopoly in common sense, On either side of the political fence; We share the same biology, Regardless of ideology; Believe me when I say to you, I hope the Russians love their children too." Would the aging crooner notice the irony of a nation about to acquire nukes that forces their women to cover their faces (Iran), or whose citizens are rumored to have resorted occasionally to cannibalism (North Korea)? For the time being biology in capitalist nations smell one hell of a lot better. But what if we weren't ready, and a single blow took us back to the 19th century? I love a good apocalyptic novel, but this one just plain scared the bejabbers out of me ...

One Scary Second

In June 1994 we had a near dust-up with the North Koreans over their desire to both sell ballistic missiles, and to acquire nuclear technology. Even as Pres. Clinton's wife was attempting to take over health care, the White House was frantic to prevent a war on the Korean peninsula. The ubiquitous Jimmy Carter rocketed over to work out a deal with dictator Kim Il Sung, who died the following month. The deal brokered promised the NorKos light water reactors, and interim energy aid in exchange for their good behavior, including liberal international atomic inspections, an end to short-range No-Dong 1 missile exports, and the supervised storage of their spent reactor fuel rods which could be converted to plutonium (the "boom" form of old uranium). Fifteen years on and the same old North Korea under an ailing leader now exports longer-range Taepo-Dong 1 missiles, has detonated its own nukes, and is rattling the sickle again. Ah the short cycles of history. I'm not saying that every time a Democrat moves to take over U.S. health care it causes nuclear proliferation, but someone should study the phenomenon. (It would be otherwise prudent to court order an electronic tracking device on camera hogging Jimmy Carter, but redundant).

As Pres. Obama contemplates his options vis-à-vis Iran and North Korea, he should include in his summer reading "One Second After" by William Forstchen (Forge Books 2009). Professor Forstchen's cautionary read is based upon the Compton Effect, discovered in 1925. Simply, particles called photons may be excited to such a degree that upon striking other particles called electrons, said electrons themselves roar off in higher energy states while the culprit photons scatter off to repeat the process. This was found to be a marvelous concept in developing diagnostic and therapeutic radiology. It was also discovered that at higher energy outputs – the kind you get with a nuclear blast – so many electrons are released that an instantaneous electrical current is produced, the electromagnetic pulse (EMP). EMP is a known feature of nuclear weapons that has been observed to fry all electronics a short range from the blast. Transformer relays short out, all vehicles with electronic ignitions stop, post-vacuum tube radios and TV's all go dark and silent. The earth's atmosphere is chock full of friendly electrons but; an intense gamma radiation blast from say, a nuclear weapon, above the atmosphere will amplify the scattering of the Compton Effect into an EMP that could blanket a continent.

What if one lives on a continent where all finance, health care, entertainment, environmental comfort, food production and delivery, and every major conveyance for communication are built upon an electronic infrastructure? What would you do if in the estimated 1 microsecond EMP pulse, you lost all electronics, and the electricity to power them permanently? What could you do for a loved one with a portable insulin pump, or implanted pacemaker?

Forstchen's novel for the most part avoids sensationalizing, preferring to begin the story in innocent questions about when the power is going to come back on, and why so many cars are stalled on the interstate. There are no mushroom clouds on the horizon or swirling clouds of fallout, and no cities are blasted. There is only a nation thrown two centuries back without the means for reliable sustenance, in a suddenly overpopulated landscape. If one or two of the characters' abilities are a bit too convenient, they are believable enough to carry the story and realistically describe the ensuing upheaval. By the time the damage is recognized, questions over whether the terrorist nuke was launched from a container ship in the Gulf of Mexico or the sponsoring nation was turned to glass have become irrelevant. What is immediately relevant is how this and subsequent administrations will deal with potential enemies before it is one second too late."

❖ ❖ ❖

The drive from Vegas to Phoenix was through a landscape beautiful and barren, desolate and mostly waterless. We did come upon evidence of a recent sprinkle near the Arizona-Nevada line, but the desert looked unimpressed. The American Indians knew how to make a go of things in these parts, before being dispossessed by pioneers no less intrepid but doubtlessly less knowledgeable. As we drove along toward the Joshua Tree National forest and Phoenix beyond, I was thinking about the rock and dirt wilderness that stretched southward, and of all the other intrepid types down below the border anxious to get up here to a better deal. I could not blame the average Mexican for wanting to leave behind the poverty and corruption of his homeland, whatever the legality of coming here; I do however, blame the hell out of an intellectually impoverished, politically corrupted U.S. government that lets them in willy nilly, and then turns to its own citizens to foot the bill. I do blame the hell out of those in the media, academia, moderate suburbia, the Catholic Church, and anyone else who cannot or will not look plainly at the damage an unsecured border is doing to this country. And if any American speaks up in protest, they are roundly accused of ignorance and racism, as happened on the Arizona border in 2005 ...

Ordinary Citizens Embarrass the Government

In his hilarious "Holidays in Hell", P.J. O'Rourke (okay, so I like quoting the guy) observed that the greatest change in the Third World in the 21st century would be that the United States would become part of it. The latest controversy surrounding the "Minutemen" border patrols confirms the seriousness of that prediction. Beginning last month, a citizen group known as the Minuteman Project began patrolling the Arizona border in an effort to call media and political attention to the farce known as "border" control between the U.S. and Mexico. Somewhere between one and two-thousand citizens, somewhere between Douglas and Naco, Ariz., have established patrols to spot illegal immigrants and inform the duly authorized Border Patrol agents to expedite pickup and (hopefully) return of the wayward travelers. Why on earth are these crazed right wing, gun loving nuts doing this?

The Center for Immigration Studies has documented an immigration rate of greater than 1.3 million immigrants per year since the 1990's, fueled by net increase of 500,000 illegal immigrants annually. The Census Bureau's estimate of 9 million illegal immigrants presently in our country, costs from $11 billion to $22 billion per year, according to the National Research Council, in large part due to "a higher rate of consumption of government services, both because of their relative poverty and their higher fertility." California is presently shelling out $ 3 billion a year for illegal immigrant services, mandated by a federal government which can never quite seem to find its checkbook when the bills arrive.

Attorney Dr. Madeline Cosman spells this out in real terms, describing how the 1985 Emergency Medical Treatment and Active Labor Act has helped those in need. This law which mandates care for every patient presenting to an emergency room regardless of their problem or inability to pay, has forced ER's to treat for free any illegal alien who shows up. Under pain of crippling personal and institutional fines, the nation's hospitals have to eat the bill for fat Uncle Sam's dinner. In California, this has contributed greatly to the closure of eighty-four hospitals between 1993 and 2004. As the federal government goes about the business of spreading misery equally, Dr. Cosman documents how our non-border is allowing new influxes of communicable diseases largely eradicated in this country, including – here's the really fun part – "drug resistant strains of tuberculosis, malaria, leprosy, plague, polio, Dengue Fever, and Chagas Disease." Hey, I'm all for diversity, but this is pushing it.

From Pres. Bush, to his bleeding heart opposition, and throughout the cocktail parties, soccer games, and morning chat shows of America, there is an aversion to seeming in anyway unsupportive of brave peasants struggling across the desert to pick our bargain-priced lettuce. The media as usual lead the charge to the safe position, admonishing us with cluck and consternation to not "oversimplify" a situation with so many complex factors. Financially wheezing, California boasts huge welfare and unemployment payments, while simultaneously encouraging the use of non-residents to work the farms. The reality is perverse, but hardly complex. And now brave reporters, politicians, and polite society begin to whimper at the site of dangerous militiamen on our borders, who are obviously racists and gunning for a fight with poor unarmed itinerants. Why are these crazies doing this?

Will the federal government, crippled by the compassion and ego of its operators, solve the problem? The Jewish World Review reports Department of Homeland Security figures citing, for the millions of illegal immigrants, "only 124 employers were fined in 2003 for hiring them." Mark Krikorian, executive director of the Center for Immigration Studies, says it would be simple to require employers to electronically check social security numbers. Instead, the Senate is considering The REAL ID ACT (H.R. 418), which passed the House, which would require states to adopt a standardized drivers' license, a national ID, in a database shared with Mexico and Canada!

As is often the case, there is an easily discernible thread here, which is expanding federal control at the expense of private citizens. In the 1990's militia-nut Randy Weaver was acquitted of all federal charges after federal BATF nuts gunned down his son and wife at Ruby Ridge. In 1991, at a B'nai B'rith meeting in Fort Lauderdale, chief state prosecutor Janet Reno said: "the most effective means of fighting crime in the United States is to outlaw the possession of any type of firearm by the civilian populace." The Branch Davidian nuts were quick-roasted in Waco to prove that she meant what she said. Now Arizona governor Janet Napolitano worries that "you can't stop the Minutemen from coming even though ... it's worrisome to have untrained people, potentially armed, performing what should be a law enforcement function." In Tombstone Rep. Ben Miranda, D-Phoenix, raised the specter of "(Klan) hoods out there", while activists with the ACLU are on the scene banging pots and screeching to denounce the racism of the Minutemen. "The Minuteman project has created a powder-keg situation with the potential to go beyond harassment and false imprisonment to real violence," said Eleanor

Eisenberg, executive director of the American Civil Liberties Union of Arizona. Equally unimpressed, the Border Patrol is complaining that the Minutemen are tripping sensors, and generally getting in the way. Reports from the Douglas area are that the usual traffic of 400 per day has dropped by 75%, but Gov. Napolitano says that the migrants are surging in other areas: "And until you have operational control of the entire Arizona border, you cannot say that progress has been made. And we don't have it, and the Minutemen can't give it to us," she said.

So democrats anxious to please their constituents, ACLU reps anxious to protect the liberties of NON-Americans, and federal employees made to look bad all denounce the Minutemen. The Minutemen Project volunteers may carry arms for self-defense, but there had not been a single shot fired to date. They do not physically threaten, but use binoculars and radios to alert the proper authorities. And where does our Chief Executive, the leader of the War on Terror, stand on the issue? "I'm against vigilantes in the United States of America," Mr. Bush said of the Minutemen at a joint press conference with Mexican President Fox. Pres. Bush went on to re-assert his support for legislation to grant guest-worker status to millions of illegal aliens already in the United States. That is why the patriots of the Minutemen Project are trying so desperately to send a message, before we join the Third World.

At any rate, I thought they were patriots. I wonder if 1600 or so years back saw anything similar? Were there retired centurions sitting in lawn chairs on the Germanic borders, sharpening their short swords, sipping wine, and sending runners back to tell the provincial governor that a bunch of skin-clad barbarians were wandering southward looking for cut-rate olive work in Tuscany?

*No doubt the newsreaders in the Forum and the patrician wives
lounging in the public baths clucked disapprovingly at the rubes
wallowing in racism, oblivious to all enlightened nuance, as the
borders began to crumble...*

Illegal Immigration is OUR Fault

"Historian Edward Gibbon gave 476 A.D. as the date
for the Fall of Rome, the overthrow of the last Roman
emperor by Germanic barbarians. The date of course
was not recognized at the time in Rome or tottering western civilization as anything special, merely the latest in a
series of structural failures afflicting the empire. A series
of political and military conflicts within the empire over
two hundred years led to a formally divided state, which
then fragmented under the weight of confusion, apathy,
and finally the nibblings of adjacent inferiors. It is generally agreed that a great deal of Rome's troubles were
begun in, or furthered by waves of corruption and egomania in the leadership, which undermined the workings
and effectiveness of the established government bodies.
Unprincipled leadership certainly furthered the problems and inefficiencies of running a large, multicultural
state with numerous restive minorities. With mounting
financial problems, the Roman government turned also
to appeasement, through an institutionalized welfare
state, remarkable growth in the number of state-spon-
sored holidays, and attempts to ingratiate themselves with
border peoples by relaxing legal, cultural, and eventually
military standards, as pertained to their frontiers.

If not a seamless analogy, it is at least easy to again
consider that historical cliché in so much popular history,

that America is a replay of Rome as the latter began her slide. Through the swirl of varied causes of Roman implosion, there is a general consensus of an overall societal apathy toward the central identity of the nation. It was the loss of identity that weakened the empire to the point that it became susceptible to barbarians which could not otherwise have threatened the intact state.

It is too easy to wonder at identity while contemplating Senator Kennedy exhorting the pro-immigration marchers on the Mall, pausing after each addle-brained blast for the Spanish interpreter to liven up the crowd. Many of the rally's speakers went on at great length in a foreign tongue, and those that spoke English used the same old tired Marxist language to excite the attending proletariat about "living wages" and "taking what is ours." After the first wave of such rallies on the west coast, the word went out about being camera-friendly, and all the Mexican flags were replaced with American ones. The CSPAN camera pans over the D.C. Mall to show a sea of red, white, and blue, to which must be spoken...Spanish. Much as a wall along our southern border might be a nice start, it must be admitted that even one across as confined a space as the northern marches of ancient Britain couldn't keep out blue-painted future scotch producers (which may explain Kennedy's stance). Again, Gibbon: "But the decline of Rome was the natural and inevitable effect of immoderate greatness." Tired for the moment of scouring graveyards, the Dems are rallying non-Americans to become their future supporters. Like the patricians of old, the Republicans are hoping the lettuce will still be picked, and the problem will just go away. Our problem is not immoderate greatness. It is the unwillingness of Americans of every ethnicity to insist on, and fight for our common identity that invites the present invasion."

Later in 2006, George W. Bush went on television to address, with great anticipation, the growing problem on the border – and blew it. The public was getting used to it...

Bush Sides with the Free-Rangers

"It is maddening that the rhetoric of American statecraft has become so nuanced. Mired in the rhythms of the mature and the thoughtful, the citizenry is again confounded by tough ideals that are muted by - heaven help - the post-modern rules of civility. This tepid rhetoric then becomes a self-fulfilling prophecy, a bowl of bland butterless oatmeal translated into policy that satisfies no one.

Bush began well enough, stating, "the United States must secure its borders." So much for the tough talk. He then described using "up to 6,000 Guard members" who "will not be involved in direct law enforcement activities" and whose presence will [not] "militarize the southern border." How exactly can one use the military and not "militarize" something? Predictably the Left led by the New York Times began shrieking hysterically that Bush is indeed militarizing the border as though that were proof of an innate evil. What precisely is wrong with "militarizing" our border? It's our border, and we are in a state of war with shadowy killers who are comfortable working in the desert, and would love a big patch of open U.S. dirt across which to freely wander. So what if our neighbor gets mad?? It's not like we're teasing the old USSR, where the wrong joke in mixed company could turn the cocktail party into a house fire. This is Mexico for crying out loud. What are they going to do, stop allowing their workers to come here? Or maybe they will put the squeeze on oil sales to us, simultaneously stimulating our homegrown industry and lessening their own influence. But true to form, we up the ante and offer to cover our opponent's bet while we hold all the cards.

Bush said, "To secure our border, we must create a temporary worker program" which "would match willing foreign workers with willing American employers for jobs Americans are not doing." Was he even aware of the shear incomprehensibility of those combined thoughts? Why does America have any unemployment or a welfare state at all? And why should American employers ever pay the wages that would make labor unions, Dems, and all the dumb workers' parties happy when they can be artificially propped up by Uncle Sam?

Because, W. & Co. will say, we "need to hold employers to account for the workers they hire", presumably making the employers pay more to cover Medicare SSI, etc, and converting shadow workers into taxpayers. This will doubtlessly lead to the creation of a new "Department for Guest Worker Affairs" along with legions of TSA wannabes complete with badges and forms, to hound the fruit pickers and restaurants. Why can't we just curtail hiring noncitizens and point our welfare recipients toward the waiting opportunities? Oh I forgot, these are jobs that "Americans are not doing." Does that mean the jobs will still be done when the non-Americans become sort-of-Americans, or will we need a fresh batch of illegals? The most painful line in the speech began: "It is neither wise nor realistic to round up millions of people, many with deep roots in the United States." So a government that can keep tabs on millions of taxpayers, and threaten them with an IRS intrusiveness that knows no bounds can't ferret out a few million illegals given the time and will? And why should we care whose roots are deep in our country, if they aren't our countrymen? We should have expected better from this president, but sadly, are learning not to.

On Election Day that November 2006, voters rewarded the GOP for their leadership on the border and in other endeavors, and kicked them to the curb. Insofar as any hope that the Democrats would do any better at border control, well, they were Democrats. What should voters have expected? 2007 saw an ineffectual Bush Administration and feckless Congress collaborating to continue more of their good work...

Build The Damn Fence!

The arguments have been advanced, flung, parsed, chewed, and recycled concerning the immigration bill now in the Senate. The debate shows are a-flurry with second-tier candidates using opposition to the bill as traction, and with establishment pols seeking an opportunity to shore up their foxholes. The most baffling, disturbing feature of this bill is the zeal with which the White House is pursuing its passage. Beset with war troubles, the lame duck president compounds his incomprehensibility by supporting legislation guaranteed to harm his stated interests. There is much argument over whether the provisions of the bill will improve or worsen our long-term immigration problem; what seems obvious to all but the bill's congressional supporters is that the bill will anger most of Bush's enemies and friends, an achievement whose rewards leave simpler minds scratching their heads. What is certain is that Republican interests will be harmed for not protecting the country, and Democrat interests advanced in direct proportion to the number of unskilled and fertile migrants we can attract.

Will the "fence" provisions work? Last year legislation signed into law by W. ordered the construction of over 800 miles of new border fence, two miles of which have been built to date. The president is taking the "half & half" approach to fence building: his '08 budget allocates about half the money needed to build (less than) half of the fence required for our Mexican border. Given his penchant for spending time on his ranch mending his own cattle fences, Bush sure must have a lot of loose cows.

The new legislation calls for "Z-visas", stay-in tickets received for shelling out a few grand and returning to the mother country while the paperwork clears. Bush and his GOP lackeys join with senators Ted Kennedy and Dianne Feinstein to present a marvel in bipartisanship: it draws ire from forces both in favor and against a sovereign American nation. Right-wing conservatives who actually want to preserve our nation are furious at the amnesty that the establishment is pleased to euphemize as a "guest worker" provision. Lefties including Hispanic advocacy groups and the Roman Catholic Church who believe America has no right to enforce her borders are furious at the punitive expectations of fines and waiting lists. And athwart our ideological divide strides big business, La Raza, and sober, mature senators seeking to be a bridge for illegals into our economy and our weakening political structure. This bill will grant immediate amnesty, and public wailing and gnashing will later defang any monetary burdens on aspirants.

The president states that the immigration bill "upholds the great American tradition of welcoming those who share our values and our love of freedom." He cannot be so stupid. The bill is contra-Constitutional in that it does not protect the borders, and worse, gives the appearance of doing just that. It will provide border control in the same sense that the Terminal Security Authority makes flying safer, which is to say, not at all. Sen. Lindsay Graham (R-SC) scolds "colleagues who come to tear this bill down with no alternative." It is axiomatic that compromise window dressing is seen as such a positive by a government that cannot smoke out 12 million illegals yet is nonetheless is happy through the IRS to constantly track its productive citizens.

This bill undermines the American principle of a shared dedication to the rule of law; by implicitly accepting squatters' rights for those who can swim the river or climb the fence, and by attacking legitimate civic values with inappropriate religiosity. This bill undermines the physical notion of America by refusing to control the border outright. By pushing this bill the president is directly acting against American interests and Constitutional requirements. The constitution requires impeachment to try for "Treason, Bribery, or other high Crimes and Misdemeanors." Could willful dereliction of duty rise to this standard and qualify Bush for such consideration? Please?

We hit a rare, spectacular gully washer of a storm between the Joshua Tree Park and Phoenix, picking our way along the interstate between dark brooding mountains falling away finally with the rain as the city outskirts started lighting our way in. To the south of us lay the border that two years later would be twisted in narco-gang violence following the trails of illegal migration into our country as surely as a Anglo-Saxon pioneers first picked, then thronged their way into Kentucky. One can love the Spanish influence from down south in our music, dress, architecture, art, and food, and still love America. It is not racist in the slightest to insist that we defend the greatest, warts and all, country in human history, or that we demand a common language (English, in case you wondered). It is pertinent to note that the American Indians two centuries ago had a lousy immigration policy, and they paid the price for it.

❖ ❖ ❖

In the grips of a presidential campaign in 2008, we were faced with a choice of establishment, non-sexy foreign policy pragmatism, or a high-spoken, idealistic vision of a new international cooperation. Okay, I'm being generous. They were both lousy choices. But to conduct effective foreign policy is high on the presidential job list, so I thought it proper to consider what the two views of the two aspirants were regarding foreign policy. At any rate, it would have been fun if any serious reporter had ever pushed these questions...

Time For A Grown-Up Foreign Policy

"Let us stipulate up front that all adults do stupid things. Sometimes Daddy drives drunk. Occasionally Mommy will buy into a pyramid scheme and fill up the garage with boxes of all-natural herbal products that she can't unload. But the grownups' mistakes do not automatically confer wisdom and expertise on the kiddies, nor should it put them in charge. A lot of us may be mad at W. over Iraq, but do we really want to give the Democrats the keys to U.S. foreign policy when they can barely hold a learner's permit?

We are in the heady days of an election year and next week the Democrats will gather to nominate their latest hero to wrest control of the White House from the war mongers. At this writing it appears that the Obama campaign has passed on the nomination of Virginia senator Jim Webb, himself a combat veteran,

former Secretary of the Navy, and father of a still serving combat Marine. Senator Webb stood to add considerable foreign policy and military expertise and heft to
the feel-good naiveté' of the Obama campaign which
still seems to be floundering in its attempt to enunciate a cogent foreign policy. While John McCain had
come out unequivocally on the side of the Georgians,
Senator Obama couched his criticism of the Russian
actions in U.N. terms, calling for a condemnation from
the Security Council. Does Obama know that the Russians have a permanent seat, and a permanent veto on
this council?

The 21st Century offers an important opportunity for
the presidential candidates to state their foreign policy
philosophies. Vladimir Putin's post-revolutionary bear
has awakened and we're all ready to party like it's 1979,
Afghanistan, and Jimmy Carter all over again. The video
images of Soviet, er, Russian BMP personnel carriers
and the sunken ships in Poti harbor are testament to the
resurgent threat. A few questions beyond Georgia come
to mind for the dueling senators:

- Are you prepared to use military force to preserve the
territorial integrity of Taiwan in the even of an attempted
Chinese invasion?

- If a nuclear/chemical/biological weapon is activated
in a U.S. city and the assailant is linked to, or is a foreign
nation, would you respond with military force?

- Do you favor the inclusion of the Ukraine, the Baltic
States, and other former Soviet satellites into an expanded
NATO?

- If the Soviets, sorry, the Russians subjugate Georgia, they will control all oil flow from the Black Sea; does this represent a strategic threat?

- To what extent, if any, would you stand by South Korea in the event of aggression from North Korea?

- If a cyber attack against U.S. financial or energy institutions is identified as originating from a foreign power e.g. China, how would you respond?

- After the election, if an ongoing terrorist-backed opposition is identified and acknowledged by a Congressional bipartisan consensus would you favor remaining in Iraq; withdrawing all forces; or leaving a token force to support an Iraqi government?

- Prior to the outbreak of formal hostilities in World War II, there were increasing reports of oppression and human rights abuses later shown to be the foundations for outright genocide. Do you favor the use of U.S. military force to stop such oppression within the borders any sovereign nation, just certain nations, or none at all?

- The Bush Doctrine, stated after the 9/11 attacks, is based on an official policy of preemption, the officially sanctioned assault on parties deemed to be an imminent threat to the U.S. or its citizens. Do you favor a policy of preemption?

- Do you view oil – its acquisition and free market flow – as a matter of national security, and what would you do to guarantee its access? Would this include accessing domestic sources?

A grown up candidate or party serious about foreign policy needs serious answers to these questions, among others."

And we all know how that turned out. It's easy to understand why the electorate didn't give the nod to McCain in 2008. But we still have ongoing trouble spots in the Middle East, Latin America, the Far East, and along our border. It's fair enough for you anti-war voters to have criticized the latest President Bush for a confused and wasteful, even dangerous foreign policy. But when you same doves excitedly elect as chief executive someone who goes to Berlin to call himself a "citizen of the world", and to Cairo to apologize for the his own country – well, you get what you deserve. And the rest of us get to laugh at you.

❖ ❖ ❖

Afterthought and beyond:

Can Space Be Free?

It is tough to make a libertarian case for Mars exploration with – gasp – government as the catalyst. Natural law libertarians like John Locke and Ayn Rand might have to take a back seat to the pragmatic school of Friedman and Hayek when considering the proposition, but could there be room for both on the Red Planet? An interesting article, praise Google, on such deliberations comes from a 1999 issue of Reason magazine by John Tierney. The author described the swirl of ideas at the first Mars Society convention in Colorado, and wondered at the direction of it all. Would there be good commercial prospects for and following settlement? Rather than an extension of our own sclerotic government, could Mars colonization be an opportunity for a new, enlightened society that learned from, but was not shackled to earthly bureaucratic drudgery? Mr. Tierney made a good point that Mars offers libertarians a rare chance to be for something, rather than just against limited government. Libertarians could cheer the settling of a new world established along the lines of truly free markets and actual civil equalities not presently known found in our own oppressive licensing regulations and tax code.

So how do we get there? Mars can be gotten to through private enterprise, say by hooking up Sir Richard Branson with Bill Gates and letting Ted Turner broadcast the whole thing. But combining enormous expense with poor prospects for short-term returns is not quite how the super moguls got where they are today. Ideas floated by the Mars Society range from government bonds (ugh), to an international Mars Lottery, whose grand prize winner might actually get to go on the trip. This still leaves government as the only feasible first agent of transport, along with the real probability of statist contamination. Can government kick-start an exploration that then becomes commercially successful? From Isabella and Columbus, to Lewis and Clark, there are successful examples of government catalyzing capitalist-based expansions, whereupon the businessmen rushed past the bureaucrats in settling the wilderness. But having gotten us to Mars, can we then get government out of the way for all but basic protections of life and property?

Why should our nation venture to other planets? In the long term, there may be un-imagined economic benefits in heretofore-undiscovered natural resources that might rattle the periodic table. There is certainly the constitutional role of national security, and it might be prudent to have an off-world colony about the time Gore's disciples start returning us to medieval agrarianism. And how better to reassert superpower status over the U.N., mullahs, Hollywood, and the rest of America-haters than by claiming an entire planet for ourselves? As a depressed person must be gotten to return their gaze from crippling introspection to outward wonder, so there are the socio-cultural intangibles to gain in keeping our eyes ever upward and not focused on our daily plod.

From a strictly pragmatic approach, any nation committed until recently to spend nearly $1 billion in the next decade on erectile dysfunction drugs for government beneficiaries should certainly be able to find the cash for these nobler endeavors. Un-libertarian conservative George Will noted a few years back that the federal government should take the lead role in Mars exploration, because it is the only entity that can actually do it. In 2004, Pres. Bush's speech on space policy called for the International Space Station to be completed by 2010, with manned missions in the Crew Exploration Vehicle commencing in 2014, and a return to the moon by 2020. In the days of the conquistadors, the famous motive was "God, Gold, and Glory." The modern American version might be "Freedom, Foraging, and Fun", but for this disgraceful NASA timeline. If politicians put half as much chin music into space exploration as they do ethanol subsidies, we might already be there. Can a libertarian case be made for government leading the way in interplanetary exploration? I'm not entirely sure. For now it might be enough to convince ourselves that we need to go, and see where this leads us."

❖ ❖ ❖

Part 3

"I am dying from the treatment of too many physicians."

Alexander the Great

"One finger in the throat and one in the rectum makes a good diagnostician."

Sir William Osler

Medicine, Health Care, and the Compassionate State: Can't I Just Have a Shot to Kill the Pain?

*What's the Deal with the Hippocratic Oath? * Dammit I Have to Make a Living! * Medicare: Another Compassionate Failure * A Dispatch From the Dark Side (Down Under) * And While We're on Medicare… * A New Fountain of Youth * The New Reservation * You Cant Still Have a Bullet to Bite On * Primary Care Can Work * One Big Con * P4P Continued * (More) Too Big to Fail * The Beeper * More Gov't Care * Doctors Roll Up Our Freedoms * The Rise of the Machines * Rolling Blunder * Vengeance of the Disabled * One Ugly Structure * Creepy Kids Want More than Candy * Who Do You REALLY Want In Charge? * Just Like They Made Housing Affordable * The Price of Pork * The King's Coin * I'm Going Back for Seconds * A Policy Cornucopia * Our Plate is Full * Last Thought – Blame the Patient*

The "business" point of the trip out west was to attend the annual meeting for the Associate of American Physicians & Surgeons, that year in Phoenix, Arizona.

The story however began five years earlier when Todd and I went to New Orleans to attend the convention of a different organization, the American Academy of Family Practitioners. By 2003 Todd had already established a successful cash-only clinic charging $35 per visit, cash, check, or charge. (And no, that charge is not a misprint) After several years in a traditional third-party insurance morass, he was feeling frustrated, worn down, and generally dissatisfied with a career for which he had already spent a decade to prepare. The first AAFP convention we went to was in 2001 in Atlanta. It was fun walking through the kiosks and exhibits (Prevacid, a heartburn drug, had a booth making all you could drink cappuccinos. I love capitalism!) As the week progressed we split up to take in the lectures and instructional courses that held our particular interests; Todd hooked up with a group that would be his eventual gateway to a year's work in New Zealand, while I took a course in basic office plastic surgery procedures. One interesting fellow we were very fortunate to meet was Doug Farrago, M.D. Back then Doug was a plucky, free-thinking family practitioner in an industry not amenable to such, who was walking around hawking his new publication with free copies to any takers. The magazine was the "Placebo Journal" dedicated to medical humor, and taking the bold step of laughing at doctors, patients, and the entire silly business of modern medicine. The free issue was hysterical and I still have my copy. Ten years later, Doug is a nationally sought public speaker with a few major news interviews to his credit, a critically acclaimed blogger, and whose magazine now sits in doctors' offices and hospital lounges in all 50 states. And yes, Dr. Farrago is a dedicated physician who still sees patients full-time.

It was a real inspiration to meet a colleague working outside a box so many had fought actively to remain in. The other really notable event occurred over lunch one day. Between lectures, Todd and I met for lunch and decided to stretch our legs with a walk across the street to the Turner Building. After killing a half hour in the food court, we browsed in the bookstore, and I thought about all the time I had bragged to Todd about a great book I had read a couple years before. In a moment of inspired genius I bought that same book for him with my most cheerful endorsement. I might as well have stood my friend on a cliff and given him a swift kick. Within six months he had quit the long-established, hometown group practice that had actively recruited him throughout medical school and residency. It wasn't a purely financial question. On the horizon Todd saw, as most doctors now do, mounting debt, and increasing pressures to stay on an accelerating treadmill for as far as he could see. The old guys in the firm understandably wanted him to buy in as a partner, for big bucks. Recouping that investment, in money and years, Todd saw would wear him out, and would not be worth it. And this, the reader must understand, was itself a very successful practice that had even been written up in trade journals for its manage-rial and financial excellence. Todd took a few months off, leased a small building, refinished the inside himself, bought some used clinic equipment, and opened up with minimal investment. As mentioned before, the charge was $35/visit, and NO third party insurance. He would see a Blue Cross or Humana patient, but would not file their claim, nor talk to the insurance company. He would not see Medicare or Medicaid patients ever (the govern-ment programs for the elderly and poor, respectively) due to the increased costs he would incur, and due to fear of government intrusion and sanctions. Did it work? Within 2 years he had opened a second clinic and was seeing over 10% of a prosperous county, and boasted that not once, ever, did a patient ever wait more than twenty minutes to be seen.

Within another two years, in admiration of Todd's bold move and with growing trepidation in my own conventional insurance practice, I had walked away. I moved on to full-time ER work for an hourly wage. Call it rationalizing if you like, I don't care: it was my "cash-only" solution. A great inspiration passed on to me by a fellow resident several years earlier had then provided the same to my friend, who's subsequent action then reverberated to my own new direction. Good ideas, or bad ones, do that. As for the book that catalyzed these developments, prepare do-gooders and limp-wristed purveyors of pitifulness, to wail and gnash. The book was, of course, <u>Atlas Shrugged</u>. The last day of the Atlanta convention, while the rest met in a large auditorium to congratulate and confabulate about the future of a self-shackled industry, Todd and I ducked out early for a more appropriate celebration of active minds and joyful hearts. We hit The Cheetah gentleman's club in downtown Atlanta, where the beer is cold, promptly served, and the scenery is honorably, cash-only.

❖ ❖ ❖

But back to New Orleans: two years after our first AAFP convention, we decided to go attend the one in New Orleans. The admission fee would buy us some continuing education credits, and we hit a few lectures of interest. Of greater importance however, inspired by Farrago, Rand, and ever in search of a good time, we had a mission. In the preceding two years, the federal government had begun to implement one of the truly dumbest ideas to hit medicine since stimulants for appetite control. The Health Insurance Portability and Accountability Act had been passed, ostensibly to protect the privacy of patient medical information. As may be said of so much that Uncle Sam favors: "what a joke!" Not only has the law been shown to make it easier for the various federal agencies to access a person's information, but it has also made it incredibly harder for all health care workers to access and share data to improve patient care. *This clumsy, high-handed government "protection" has led to the worst sort of idiocies on every level. Only a couple years before, when stumbling bleary-eyed into the hospital to begin early morning rounds before a long clinic day, I could find my patients simply by looking for their names on the doors. After HIPAA, the names came off and I had to track down each individual chart (which the nurse might have in the patient room). The original law was only supposed to govern the transmission of electronic data. The end result was that out of fear of government fines and penalties, hospital corporations panicked and voluntarily removed patient names from everything. Mind you, hospital doors heretofore only said "Mr. Smith", not "Mr. Smith has raging genital herpes and thunderous bloody diarrhea." All your pastor, mistress, or mom would ever know is that you were in the hospital, not a particularly obvious violation of one's privacy. Of course your privacy was protected against a sleep-deprived physician groping to find your room before dawn. In every town, pharmacy, office, hospital, ER, ICU, residency-training program, crystal shop, and sweat lodge, one would and will still hear variations of "I'm sorry, I can't tell you that, it's a HIPAA violation." The money spent on redundant computer networks, additional encryption software, HIPAA compliance officers and endless seminars, and the absolute incalculable man-hours wasted on complying or skirting this garbage has added up to billions of dollars in lost productivity.*

The foregoing explanation was necessary to set the scene for New Orleans. Todd knew his way around print formatting, and ginned up a fun pamphlet decrying the loss of freedom in medicine. An essay on his successful cash clinic was accompanied by suitable quotes from Ayn Rand and Pink Floyd, with which we hoped to stimulate interest, conversation, and maybe stir the pot just a bit. For my part, I came up with a brilliant T-shirt befitting my artistic talent: two stick figures. The first wore a doctor's head mirror, and was bent over. Standing behind offering tender attention was a smiling stick Uncle Sam, with goatee and stars and stripes hat, giving it to the poor doc. The caption was "Got HIPAA?" Sophomoric? Yes, and proudly so! Wearing the same T-shirt we entered the convention, and offered our pamphlets to any and all. The T-shirts sold for a reasonable price, and we sold every one of one hundred and fifty. And it was a scary revelation into the mind of modern U.S. health care.

Similar to Doug Farrago two years before, we were met with looks of disbelief, disgust, and even fear, yes fear! More than once I saw a physician marked plainly by his name tag look at our ridiculous, hilarious shirts, start to smile, then look around rapidly to see if he had been noticed, and dart the other way. We sold not a single shirt to any doctor that day – all of them were purchased by pharmaceutical representatives who laughed out loud and called us to stop at their booths as we walked the aisles of the convention. Why would drug reps laugh, and not the people most targeted with this insanity? Why the hell weren't the doctors in this convention having a good time and laughing at themselves? Had I read this a few years before I would not have believed it and would have scoffed at the hysteric writing it. But I know what we saw, and it was ugly. The attitudes of U.S. physicians for decades now have been molded and homogenized to fit into accepted norms by a society that sees physicians as a commodity to which they have a right. A great deal of U.S. medicine, and primary care in particular, is encumbered by a professional Stockholm Syndrome wherein the beaten are increasingly happy to be allowed to approach the third party table for a few more reimbursement crumbs.

At the convention we visited booths selling this or that medicine or office tool, often by physicians trying to get out of traditional practice. Other booths proffered the virtues of working on Indian reservations, and of Medicare. Why in hell was the taxpayer shell-

ing out big bucks for a booth in an expensive convention to push a mandatory government health program (the first "government option" of later parlance)? One vendor, an ENT surgeon by training, was selling a new-fangled ear cleaner, and bemoaning the modern clinic experience. He was amazed to hear Todd's description of his cash only clinic. As he asked repeatedly "but how do you take call", I heard tiny gears grinding and saw smoke coming out of his straining ears as my friend patiently repeated, "I don't." The convention was self-important and subdued, presumptuous without joy, and dour. It contrasted all the more dramatically with the city in which it was staged, the over-the-top, ongoing celebration for the senses and mind that is the Crescent City. It was no surprise, emblematic even, that on the last night of that convention, the big shindig planned featured as a headliner, in the primordial birth swamp of jazz and blues...Kenny Loggins.

❧ ❧ ❧

The year after our good time – sad convention display notwithstanding - in New Orleans, Todd had a great idea. He refused to waste any more time or money on such a lousy time (and I was inclined to agree, with one exception: if the AAFP ever held a convention in its natural city of Branson, MO, then we should blow the money for our own booth and really take it to 'em!) But my friend came up with a new, great idea. He had found out about another group, one that promoted physician independence, a disdain for and reversal of third party medicine and government interference in health care. That was definitely a more interesting track, and October 2004 found us flying out to Portland, Oregon for the convention of the Association of American Physicians & Surgeons. First impressions being ever important, Portland is a city with fantastic microbrews, more high-rent beer than either of us had ever before enjoyed in one place. Arriving the day before the convention and the day of a major rally for vice presidential candidate John Edwards, we got to see thundering herds of thoroughly committed, wild-eyed liberals all decked out in multi-tint hair dye and SEIU shirts, hollering for fair-trade, all-vegan abortions for illegals. It was great fun, bless their hearts.

The convention itself was something new. There were no kiosks, other than one table where a doomsday nut was pushing some books and videos, but he was quickly shown the door. The agenda included topics that dealt in a general theme of mistrust for government, and removing that kind malevolence from health care whenever and wherever possible. One of the most interesting talks (every year) came from attorney Andrew Schlafly, an attorney who defends physicians against the authoritarian intrusions and yes, prosecutions at the hands of the government. That year physician-speakers included an ophthalmologist accused of $16 million in Medicare fraud, a charge later reduced to $44,000. For that, he lost his license and spent over four years in maximum-security prison. Another physician, a pathologist, told how his teenager had been terrified while eating cereal, when armed federal agents stormed his house in search of Medicaid fraud evidence. For not getting the paperwork done in a timely fashion, his multiple examinations of the placentas of Medicaid patients was deemed fraudulent. When the government sent him a check that they later determined to be incorrect, the doctor was charged with mail fraud for receiving the check in the mail. The federal judge upheld the charge and convicted him. These were not the sort of stories we were used to hearing at the AAFP conventions where they extol the virtues of government kindness.

Todd and I were excited to have conversations with both headline speakers, conservative activist/columnist Starr Parker, and future senator Pat Toomey, from the Club for Growth. It was refreshing to actually meet and converse with others who shared the view that not all goodness emanates from government. The lectures were mostly interesting, all given in a single conference ballroom or during lunch. It was great fun exploring the streets of Portland in October, and our last night we were treated to a wonderful dinner by an insider lobbyist attached to AAPS. The lobbyist thought our story of the "Got HIPAA?" shirts was great, and by good fortune I just happened to have a spare with me. Our host later emailed me to report that he had in fact given our protest shirt to Rep. Nancy Johnson (R-CT), one of the authors of that moronic law. I hope she wore it with pride.

❖ ❖ ❖

Over the next couple of years we went to the AAPS conferences, next in the D.C. belly of the beast, and after that in Phoenix, then in New Jersey. In Washington we were able to lobby our elected representatives, and I tagged along with Todd and his fellow Georgians to see their congressmen. We argued in vain with Rep. Nathan Deal to reverse Bush's "Free Drugs For Old Folks' Votes" program enacted the year before, and good party man that he must be, Deal defended this naked (and ultimately unsuccessful) bribe. Later that afternoon it was more gratifying, if sobering, to enjoy a long interview in the office of Rep. Tom Price, himself a physician and AAPS member. He was not as I recall a supporter of the big bribe, and warned of more dire accelerations of government health care to come. That evening we enjoyed a cocktail reception in the Rayburn Building, and an informal Q&A with Senator Tom Coburn, also a physician. I had the very good fortune to personally put a question to both Rep. Price and Sen. Coburn during the separate meetings. To both physician-legislators I asked, what would happen when enough physicians, because of poor pay and regulatory/prosecutorial burdens, refused to continue seeing Medicare and Medicaid patients; what would the political result of such a critical mass be? Both gentlemen answered, in separate meetings, identically: the government would move to take over all of health care. That left an impression.

And so it was that September 2008 found us driving from Las Vegas to Phoenix for yet another AAPS get-together. Maybe it was just our perspective, but it seemed to us by then that the organization was losing its focus, being swamped by the tide of Bush '43 fecklessness and rising neediness among the electorate. Todd and I shared the views of the majority of conference goers, but lesser and admittedly fringe topics had continued to find space on the agenda, and were diluting what should have been the concentrated drive of the organization: to demonstrate the toxic effect of government involvement in health care, and push to reverse and eliminate its presence wherever possible. Egos and infield squabbling were accomplishing what they too often do for great ideas, fracturing any momentum into ineffectiveness. We were under no great illusion that America would suddenly awake to the danger to our freedoms that our collapsing health care system poised. On the other hand Phoenix is a blast. We found a couple of really good bars, one where the microbrew and from-scratch pizza are out of this world, and the other where the comely waitresses all wear short-skirt Scottish kilts, bless their hearts. A tour of the Frank Lloyd Wright museum at Taliesin West was fantastic, as were the steaks at the Pinnacle Peak Patio Steakhouse. (As to the latter, I was in training, and so hit a 32-oz. with all the fixin's. No problem, scarfed it down in less than a half-hour, beans, bread, and beer included. It was a piece of cake, and I looked in fine shape of for the big show in a few days in Amarillo.)

❖ ❖ ❖

Medicine in the Western tradition, has ostensibly called the best and brightest of society to serve in its rolls. The training process is arduous, the dedication required is substantial, and the commitment of a substantial portion of one's life to this lifestyle often stamps an identity on those taking this journey. Of course there have been the occasional nonconformists, problem children who finding themselves swirling around the porcelain bowl of primary care in America, who saw their colleagues swimming in vain against the quickening current – and vowed to climb out before someone lowered the lid.

A great deal has been written over the millennia about the role of physicians in their societies, relationships which have led to not just to the evolving technology of medicine, but the evolving regard of the individuals who provide the care. Naïve aspirants approaching the medical school application process are motivated by well meant, yet poorly grounded altruism, and a desire to accept and meet challenges that loom all the larger against the backdrop of those solemn, awe-inspiring gentlemen and ladies who went before. Many in medical academia reckon that the peak of competitiveness for medical school slots was reached in the early 1990's, and has been steadily declining since. The headlines that screamed twenty years ago that we would have too many physicians, especially too many specialists, now cry over coming shortages and the loss of enthusiasm for many to undertake this career track. Is there really such a problem, and if so, what are its origins?

A couple of months back, a colleague relayed this anecdote: this full-time E.R. doc and I had graduated together from medical school nine years earlier, and since he had taken an active interest in serving on the medical school's alumni board. Apart from glad-handing at barbeques and football games, these members'

duties include serious fundraising efforts on behalf of
the school and particularly for the medical students.
Well beyond any nostalgia trips of the good old days of
cadavers and lecture halls, these physicians are bound
together by a sincere love for their institution, their
profession, and a desire to impart this feeling to the rising generations of medical students. My friend was discussing the state of the profession prior to a meeting
with the association's director of fundraising, and was
attempting to impress upon her the point that things
had definitely changed for the worse. He explained the
growing pressures on physicians, not the least of which
has become the uncertainty of making a comfortable
living upon completion of training. He described the
hunted mentality that more and more of our number
now suffer, caught between government regulations
and ravenous lawyers. He tried to paint the picture that
medicine was losing the sense of enjoyment that had set
it apart for its practitioners from all of the other professions. The fundraising director could simply not believe
the problem to be so great, nor the gloom so deep. The
alumnus-doctor held up his hand, caught the attention
of those assembled, and asked how many *actively practicing physicians* would recommend their children embark
upon a medical career. Of the ten around the table,
nine stated they would actively discourage their children
from such a course. Of course this was not a scientific
survey. But the fundraising director for the medical
school was shocked to see this nearly unanimous stance
against pursuing that which they had all gathered to
nourish and further. Though not a representative sampling by any stretch, who should be more enthusiastic
for the medical profession than those gathered to raise
money to support its furtherance?

So are we talking about an actual shortage, or just a pessimistic current running through some physicians? On 3/2/05 USA Today reported the Journal of the American Medical Association's 1994 prediction of "a surplus of 165,000 doctors by 2000", and the Congressional action to cap federal payments to residency programs to "to save money and prevent a doctor glut." This article then reported revised concerns that "the nation will have a shortage of 85,000 to 200,000 doctors in 2020 unless action is taken soon", based on growing demand and falling supply. The nation is aging and as the Baby Boomers age, their health problems (and not coincidentally, their demands on government) will increase dramatically. This will occur while many currently practicing doctors from that generation will begin to scale back or retire altogether, prefiguring an interesting double whammy for those who want to see a doctor. (The April 2005 edition of Family Practice Management magazine ran the numbers from the U.S. Census Bureau and predicted the need for well over 150 million *additional* annual physician visits by 2020, based on both population increase, and population aging.)

Upon graduating from the Tallahassee Memorial Hospital Family Practice Residency Program in June 1999, we knew we had walked out of a long tunnel into the sunlight. After over a decade of study, sweating test results, long nights awake, living off of student loans, periods of seemingly constant criticism (self-, and from others), uncertainties galore, and general irritation, we had finished. I was off to set up a cushy family practice office in a beautiful, up-and-coming resort area while my buddy Todd was off to Calhoun, Georgia, his hometown, to join an acclaimed, very successful group practice which had been courting him for the past six years to return as a full partner. I was envious of Todd walking into such a great practice, and he was envious of me living on the white sands of the Florida panhandle. We had a high old time the night before following the graduation ceremony, a long night of loud laughter, too much beer, delicious cigars, and reminiscences long into the night. The only tears were those of laughter, and a unanimous happiness enveloped those of us who refused to let the night end, determined to savor the last page of the book before closing it and heading off to our new lives. It was great!

I met Todd the day after graduation in the parking lot of a video arcade center where his kids could play, while we sat and nursed our hangovers. There were some more laughs, and mutual congratulations over a successful evening, but the tone was definitely more somber. We had had some great times together but it was time to go our separate ways, and both of us were sad to be living further apart. A handshake, hug, slap on the back, and I pointed my pickup westward while he loaded up his wife and kids and headed north. I would be passing his way in another two months on my way to Virginia, and we promised to keep in touch. Life was as it should be, and the expectations and realizations of finally achieving our respective goals after over a decade consumed my thoughts as I cruised along I-10 through the beautiful rolling scrub of the panhandle, staring into a blazing summer sun. We had, each of us, made it. The rest of the story, yet to be written, nonetheless seemed foolishly predictable...

The medical school application process is a fairly long process, fraught with pitfalls and undue aggravations. With variations depending on the given school to which one applies, a certain set of pre-requisite science courses must not only be successfully completed, but the student must excel i.e. make 'A's" in order to compete for a coveted admission slot. The typical courses are biology, general chemistry, organic chemistry, and physics (a year of each), with calculus thrown in for some of the snootier schools (no one EVER works out a long differential equation during med school). Back in the great old days when they told each class entering medical school that 50% of them would be gone by Christmas break; most students had scientific undergraduate degrees. According to some of the graduates of those bad old days, highly scientific, introverted nerds with rather extensive communicative challenges ran much of medicine. For the past decade-plus, medical school admission committees have had a change in heart, seeking a greater breadth of experience and motivation in their students, encouraging the applications from non-scientific backgrounds. Many of these folks were on their second or third careers. Those applying still needed to ace their prerequisite courses, and score competitively on a nationally offered MCAT (Medical College Admission Test). The competition remained tight, with acceptance rates to top-flight schools often below 5% of total applications well into the mid-nineties. To grab a plumb spot in a medical school of good reputation was a mark of high achievement, the opportunity to learn a permanently marketable skill, and conferred if not a guarantee, the expectation of a certain level of success and material comfort for one's sacrifices. This is not to negate the humanist motive that all medical students voice on their applications and interviews, and that the great majority sincerely felt. But it would be blatantly dishonest for all but the most unrealistically ideological to neglect mentioning the expectation of living in a material standard commensurate with one's investment in terms of wealth (student loans, deferred income) and time (a decade or more). Everyone of us had individual, though often shared reasons for walking down this road; but all of us who did began the journey under a set of rules, mostly unwritten, by which we were forced to play. The long hours and financial sacrifices far out of proportion to many with lesser education were understood up front, and there was generally little complaining. As an esteemed and truly beloved medical school dean often remarked: "We ain't running a prison here." For all of their faults (and they are typically many), medical students approach the process with certain stoicism and optimism, accepting sacrifices as challenges and ready to play the game.

My dad went to medical school the traditional way, straight out of college, beginning in 1958 with the clichéd "Look to your right and left – one of you won't be here next year" speech. Professors and students wore white coats and ties, and the female contingent of the class was very slight. Academic halls were scenes of great formality and jocularity as were the gross anatomy labs and medical wards. The Calling of Medicine, professionalism as a great collective understanding, was understood, inculcated, embraced, and celebrated in speech, dress, manner, and action from day one. These were the "old school" doctors, many of which are still in practice, the ones who accepted, refined, and passed down the Hippocratic traditions of Western medicine. Internship and residency training was hard, unquestionably harder than today. My father tells tales of his intern year when as a married man with a toddler he would enter the hospital on Monday morning and re-emerge on Saturday evening, to spend Sunday with the family and begin the cycle over the next day. The interns of that day were paid poorly, just above diddlysquat, and doubtless had to endure tales from their professors over how tough they had had it in the preceding generation. Entering medical school, I knew for certain that I would never duplicate my father's feat, and had no desire to do so. That generation of physicians worked harder than most of us can comprehend, and accomplished feats of good for the patients in our society that were a credit to their calling. They also accomplished great harm.

After finishing four years as a naval flight surgeon, and another four years in ophthalmology residency, my father was ready to establish his practice and begin to enjoy the goal for which he had worked for the previous sixteen years – solo practice as a surgeon in a location of his choosing, under basically his own rules. I grew up in this environment, with this role model. Childhood in a surgeon's house is nothing mystical, just a set of household environmental parameters like any others to which one is accustomed. I never remember a house without the phone ringing at 2:00 AM, the hurried or missed supper, the extra efforts on the part of both parents to accommodate ball games, school, playmates and the like. I could hang out in my old man's office whenever I liked, and was often invited to watch him operate on his patients or assist other surgeons with theirs'. I was from an early age comfortable in the hospital, knew the nurses by their first names, and had a long continuous observation post on the life of a physician for good and bad. My old man loved, and still loves the practice of medicine and though not subsumed by it, certainly embraced his profession as a noble calling and identity with pride and gratitude. Despite the not infrequent taunting from schoolmates that I was a "rich doctor's kid" (Hmm, they never said that to the lawyers' kids), I knew that what my dad did as the only ophthalmologist for forty miles around was both valuable and cool. He worked hard and played hard, on his own terms.

I thought the medical environment was so cool that I actually worked for a summer as a hospital orderly two years after I had made the decision to forgo the pursuit of a career for which I knew I didn't have the stuff. The summer of '82, between my college junior and senior years gave me an expanded, enhanced understanding of a life in medicine. I worked days and I worked the grave-yard shift. Back before tightening economics relegated nurses to such menial tasks, hospitals hired orderlies to take scheduled vital signs, run errands, and generally help out as directed. I had a blast. Walking the halls of Johnson Memorial Hospital in the small town of Abing-don, Virginia gave the chance to harass growling night nurses, have psychotic patients fling knives at me (okay, it was a closed penknife), and generally feel important as I walked around with my blood pressure cuff and stetho-scope. I learned how to assist in catheter changes, wipe rear ends and change beds in record time. Just because the old man got me the job didn't mean I was playing the part of a spoiled snot-nose – hell, I enjoyed the work! A friend and fellow orderly and I had a wonderful time con-versing with a gentleman in acute alcoholic get-the-bees-out-of-my-closet withdrawal, and I really enjoyed hanging out in the ER whenever my duties were lighter. I mopped up after a delivery and marveled at the placenta in the sink as the nurse explained the structures and function to me. One night when a Code Blue was called, I ran to assist as the physicians in-house rushed to start chest com-pressions on the man whose chest was held together with rows of staples. The father of a childhood friend, a radiologist, directed the team as they tried in vain to revive the sallow body. I had never seen someone die before, but I left the room more focused on the calm power and expertise demonstrated by the physician. It was a great summer. I had seen and done a lot, far more than I had expected, and I left for my last year of college with a paradoxical regret. I had decided that I could not pursue medicine, that I would never be good enough academically, and that those like my dad whom I had watched perform their artistry were on a plateau forever out of reach. I bragged to my buddies in college about the drama of a Code Blue, watching a thumb re-attached in the ER, and the delightful company of cute female orderlies who also worked the night shift. My plans had been laid to pursue a career in as a naval aviator after graduation, and I knew that my little summer job had been a mere diversion, fun and interesting, but allowing only wistfulness when contemplating a career that could never be. I had gone as far toward the calling as I was allowed and it was time to come back to reality.

Or not. Despite being chided by a family member for years following that I "needed to join the real world", I was pretty damned happy to be avoid it as much as possible. Life as a naval flight officer in the mid-eighties was fun, really too much fun. I grew up in a politically conservative, pro-military family, and had been influenced by my father's service to try that as a career. Getting paid to travel, fly in high powered carrier aircraft, and generally avoid an office-based culture seemed like a great deal long before "Top Gun" was made, and it was every bit so. Due to no talent or brilliant decisions on my part, I found myself in the fall of 1985 flying antisubmarine missions as part of a truly great squadron based on an aircraft carrier in the Mediterranean. Over the next three years I traveled to beautiful places I had never imagined, participated in real-life international incidents, and above all had more fun than I thought possible, or that I can adequately describe. My reckoning of things political was too simplistic, happy with the flow and tone of the Reagan years, always in favor of a strong military, lower taxes, laughing at weenie liberals, and proud of tracking the submarines belonging to the godless Communists. Had any of us cared about the state of health care, our parties would not have achieved such Olympian proportions, and I paid little mind to the domestic questions raised in the eighties beyond whether or not anybody wanted to raise my taxes. My great influence in those brief, fantastic years was my squadron C.O., a boisterous, career pilot that daily inspired affection and absolute exasperation among his junior officers. He was handpicked on his last flight from our carrier to fly a secretly-captured Islamic terrorist non-stop from our ship in the Med to Washington, D.C., an assignment reflective of his skills as an airman and leader of considerable esteem. His advice to me once was simply: "Whatever you do in life, if you aren't having fun, get out!" A year after he had left the squadron and I was struggling with my future plans, his advice was my focal point. The squadron was changing, with new guys coming in and the old crew breaking up – such is the way in a navy squadron. As my time to rotate out of the squadron was drawing nearer, I was suddenly faced with the realization that I had accomplished all of my goals, that I had no desire to move up the competitive chain of military promotion, and that my most fun days in the military had passed. I had no idea what to do.

After contemplating one or two fairly silly ideas, the overriding question was obvious: "Why NOT try medicine?" My biggest reason for not trying was a fear of failure, a phobia common to many considering this particular track. After several months of pondering the options, the plan gelled. I would kill my flying career, transfer to a dead-end desk job, complete my academic science requirements, and roll the dice. My time in naval aviation taught me that life was about adventure, doing new things, living life as an absolute refusal of boredom. If I couldn't continue the geographic and physical adventures of carrier flying, then, I reasoned, it was time to pursue intellectual adventure.

❖ ❖ ❖

Several years ago while working as an emergency room physician one busy Friday evening, I was given the chart of the next patient to see. There were a couple of chest pains, a sore throat (it is common medical parlance to use the complaint or presumed diagnosis as a noun to describe patients in exam rooms as your workload. Like any other field, the idiosyncrasies of the language arise from a desire to expedite, often taking on their own dark humor). So I was given a chart for a patient with the stated complaint of "back pain", no doubt chronic form his medication list notated on the chart. Well, as we always say in the ER, we gotta keep the train moving. I went to Bed #8 to find a middle-aged man wearing jeans and a tractor ball cap, obviously in no acute distress, one who assured me that he had a "high tolerance for pain" (they always do), who had run out of his narcotics and needed a refill until his appointment with his regular doctor... *next month*. That is not how the game is played in the

ER, where acute problems are treated and chronic pain absent any recent injury or apparent exacerbating cause is referred back to the patient's family doctor or pain management specialist. Chronic pain patients know this very well. This particular patient's history included no recent trauma or repetitive motion injury, and he spoke in calm, even tones. His blood pressure was normal (folks in acute pain typically have elevated blood pressure) and his heart rate was also normal. My exam revealed nothing, not a single palpable or reproducible area or action of tenderness. In fact, this guy looked quite comfortable. I finished, made a show of reviewing and then regurgitating the chart info to demonstrate completeness to the patient, prior to telling him that, NO, I was not going to write for him a prescription for narcotics. The patient set his jaw, fixed me with a glare, and asked, without a trace of sarcasm: "Mister, did you ever have to work for a living?"

❖ ❖ ❖

On a dark, wintry night in Virginia Beach I was on the phone with my then-fiancée, who was projecting her particularly bitchy evening on to me. She was still working in Jacksonville, Florida, anticipating moving north in two months, and didn't want to hear about any of my wanderings to the movies or local bars. She jabbed a verbal point, inquiring whether I had even bothered registering for my medical school pre-requisite courses for the coming summer. I admitted that I had not quite gotten around to that and she exploded with: "Pat, your whole life you've just showed up!" I had to admit that she was right, but what the heck, that method hasn't failed me yet. Nonetheless I scheduled an appointment to talk with the pre-med advisor at the local college, shelled out the grand for registration and my first semester of courses, and tied to ponder what the hell I was in for. I had been a history major in college because I liked history, and because it was sufficient to get a naval officer's commission. We lofty minds in the liberal arts eschewed such fancy studies as calculus and organic chemistry; my one significant accomplishment in our "Betty Crocker" chemistry class was taking a huge whiff ammonium hydroxide, and losing my sense of smell for the rest of the day. Going into a real college science course left me anything but cocky. Most medical students develop burgeoning obsessive streaks somewhere along the line, and I started mine by going to class three hours a night four nights a week, watching movies on Friday night, and studying like a fiend weekend, pausing only long enough for the guilt to drive me back to the books scattered over the dining room table. I kept hopping up to scan CNN the weekend that the Ayatollah Khomeini croaked and the Tiananmen Square festivities were ramping up in Beijing, but otherwise it was a tough, nervous summer. When I got my first test score back, I was utterly shocked. I had worked as hard as I knew how on that stupid chemistry test and there it was, a 74 percent score. No one had ever explained that there was a curve. I had the highest grade in the class, and only five minutes of relief. Because back in the late Eighties, when competition to get into med school was still very tight (more about that later), every test counted. If you blew a test, you would get no higher than a "B" for the course or possibly lower, and "A's" in the pre-med courses were the currency needed to gain the coveted medical school interview. Whether you were tired and wanted to quit studying, or you had a weird psychotic former study partner memorizing social security numbers to check on your posted test score (true story), or your car battery died on the way to class for the fourth time that hot summer and you were trying to revive it with baking soda and a Pepsi because you had just learned about electrolyte solutions – there were no excuses and all sacrifices were worth it, because you had to get that interview.

This, in itself, was a surreal experience. The medical school interviews come after completing 17-20 hours of hard science course work, scoring respectably on the day-long Medical College Aptitude Test (MCAT) festival, surviving the hangover the next day, and filling out long applications complete with essays on why one wants to be a physician who will be more suitable for saving mankind than the next joker. Then the envelopes hopefully arrive inviting you to an interview, for which you shine your shoes, put on your best tie, and prepare to enter the competition with the other ten percent or less of those applicants who were similarly selected. Apart from being a little unnerving, the process also has its humorous twists – like when your interviewer inquires whether one has ever been tested for a learning disability in math. But a focused sense of mission, a stiff upper lip, and a lot of luck can still win the day, and one day the mailman arrives with the most important letter of your life, declaring that in fact you have somehow fooled them all and gotten accepted to medical school. And that is, truly, the best day of medical school.

On opening day, the auditorium is packed with a bunch of undergrads used to making straight A's and being academically superior to those sadder chaps with whom they have previously been associated. Not bad company, until you realize that someone in your group will have to be I the bottom-third, *someone* is going to have a tougher time – someone here, for the first time ever, won't be the best. And that someone will hate that fact, whether or not they can accept it. Medical school begins in novelty and apprehension, and then takes on the tedium of intellectual trench warfare, where the bombs and artillery burst of facts to be memorized explode in voluminous sheets over the numbed students until the Big Test, when it is all regurgitated, everyone gets drunk...and they do it all over again. That was the first year of medical school, and the second was just more of the same, revving the students' factual grasp up to the level of surviving the first medical board exam, a two-day, stopwatch-timed affair run by proctors as kind as any Buchenwald guards ever were, necessary as the first of several examinations given on a national basis as pre-requisites to getting state medical licenses. Not that any of us cared about that completely abstract notion at that point in the game. The goal was to get unscathed into the much-anticipated Third Year, the clinical year where we would run around in white lab coats as *real* medical students seeing real patients and becoming exposed to the different basic areas of medicine. It was on the basis of these brief, highly variable experiences in the clinical rotations (e.g. in OB/GYN, general medicine, general surgery, psychiatry) that one would plan their elective rotations in the fourth year. These rotations were used to set one up favorably to apply for a residency slot in the specialty that the student thought he would most enjoy. Our dean, who had been responsible for shepherding students toward their ultimate specialty choices for more than thirty-five years, was unshakable in his belief that the suitability of the overwhelming majority of students to their chosen fields never ceased to re-affirm his decision not to consider atheism. I have no substantial criticism of the system for in truth I cannot think of a better or more efficient way to train medical students, and then to handle the mass selections which will place one highly talented and ambitious student into an unimaginably competitive neurosurgery slot while another more lackadaisical type might become a highly successful pediatrician. The infamous "Residency Match" combines written student preferences and individual residency program preferences (for certain students) into a big computer blender, punches "Puree", and on the given day every one of the sorry lot finds out exactly what they will be doing for the rest of their lives. Maybe. As I said, I do not criticize this system because I haven't the slightest idea on how better to fairly place sixteen thousand or so medical students in a process which allocates tens of millions of dollars in the short term and which will significantly, irretrievably alter the lives of its subjects. But it's a sobering thought that there are the highest statistical probabilities that after you complete your residency which will determine what you will probably do for the rest of your life, you are likely to actually reside within 200 miles of where you completed this training. Sobering indeed, in that decisions of such magnitude are made based on the experience of a few short months in medical school.

Two months or so after Match Day, it is time to graduate from medical school. Everyone's family blows into town, there are dinners and toasts, and you prepare for the one single, other great day in medical school. Everyone is glad they were here, glad that they did it. And no one is sorry to be leaving. A couple of weeks before graduation, I was invited along for a leisurely drive to lunch with a classmate and his wife. This classmate, an exceptionally polished speaker, had been wisely selected to be the speaker for our class at our commencement. During the hour-long drive to the restaurant, we reminisced about the steps taken to this threshold, the hours and years spent on goals we could not yet accurately perceive or fully comprehend. Many students had pursued their pre-med studies as undergraduates while some, like my friend and I, were coming back for a second career and had spent more than three years apiece preparing for our four years of medical school. We talked about not having the luxury in those pre-med years of screwing up one test, *not even one*, about rushing from our day jobs to be on time for classes which were no sure thing, as nothing really worthwhile in life ever is. We recalled long nights getting ready for board exams, the incessant, impersonal yet malevolent clang of the timer bell during the gross anatomy exams, the long nights on call taking crap from know-it-all, burned out residents while we were dumb enough to be paying tuition for the abuse. We talked about how we had paid our dues, earned our stripes, had made the cut, and we were glad and proud to have done so.

My friend heard a theme he liked in that afternoon-long conversation, and he wove it into as fine a speech as I ever hope to hear. There on the stage in front of thousands of friends, well-wishers, faculty, and classmates, he spoke of the long road walked to get to this pointing descriptions and tones that touched those in the audience with no medical experience as deeply as those new physicians on stage. Telling a parable about the most expensive coat ever made, he reached behind the podium to pull out a freshly pressed and starched long white lab coat, the kind real doctors wear. To the enraptured assembly he described the dues paid to wear that coat, not in whiny, self-serving terms, but with somber pride and the recognition of how much had been done by so many present to arrive at this precise moment. "This", he said of the white coat, "is the most expensive coat ever made." The standing ovation was thunderous and genuine, leaving most family members and now-former medical students proud and a bit misty-eyed, and it ended our medical school days with as positive an exclamation point as has ever been struck in such a proceeding, while we shook hands, hugged, posed for snapshots, and prepared to enter medicine as physicians.

I can't help but think of those moments and of that speech with pride, and with a residual fear of those years of uncertainty. It was for some of us a huge gamble, an accruing of large debt, and an investment of many years with no guarantee of success. And to date I had never been bitter or felt shortchanged regarding those investments. I had yet to face the long nights and endless days of residency, thousands of hours more of training and hard, sleepless work often at minimum wage rates, more board examinations, often with their own fair share of scrutiny and recriminations from the system which has evolved to train physicians, and which I entered and exited freely, with a cheerful heart. After a long decade, an angry man from whom I had never taken anything sat before me and questioned whether I had ever "worked for a living." Was this angry patient merely an aberration, or emblematic of something larger? Had it always been this way, or had medicine changed?

❊ ❊ ❊

What's the Deal with the Hippocratic Oath?

On Graduation Day brand new physicians-to-be everywhere gather in their academic finery, in a crowd of laughter and nervous shuffling at the closed double doors leading into an auditorium. The scene is repeated at medical school graduation ceremonies nationwide as joyous students prepare to share with family and friends their supreme accomplishment, when the hand is shaken, the diploma accepted, and the solemn green academic hood draped in over the grinning student's shoulders. The flashbulbs pop, camcorders jostle over their neighbors' shoulders for the best shot, and the graduating class sit attentively listening for the final words of challenge and congratulations. The greatest symbolic moment for the students, the one holding the hush of an audience witnessing an almost mystical moment, is the taking of the Hippocratic Oath, the joining of the ancient western historical tradition whereby the student is so consecrated to declare himself a physician.

The Oath deals with physician integrity and behavior, prescribing and proscribing the boundaries for a position held in a society which itself held a very distinct view of the physician. The Oath binds the profession, past, current, and future members all, together in ties of obligation that rise above simple guild or union rules. Of course, the actual oath has been a little altered, a little massaged over the years, to accommodate the new physician's changing environment. Let us consider then, the Hippocratic Oath, Classical Version:

The Oath begins with some standard nod to the applicable deities - *"I swear by Apollo Physician and Asclepius and Hygieia and Panaceia and all the gods and goddesses, making them my witnesses, that I will fulfill according to my ability and judgment this oath and this covenant"* and immediately sets a promise. Requirements thereof included training costs, and even the collegial obligation of helping a fellow who is financially down on his luck: *"To hold him who has taught me this art as equal to my parents and to live my life in partnership with him, and if he is in need of money to give him a share of mine, and to regard his offspring as equal to my brothers in male lineage and to teach them this art - if they desire to learn it - without fee and covenant; to give a share of precepts and oral instruction and all the other learning to my sons and to the sons of him who has instructed me and to pupils who have signed the covenant and have taken an oath according to the medical law, but no one else."* Here again we see the physician called to a standard of behavior prescribed by nothing but his own moral judgment, bound in a promise before his fellows and purposefully set apart from the rest of society. *"I will apply dietetic measures for the benefit of the sick according to my ability and judgment; I will keep them from harm and injustice."* This telling injunction regarding therapeutics orders the subscriber to operate "according to *my* (italics added) ability and judgment," without regard to whether a patient's herbs or goat entrails needed for recovery were covered by the Blue Spartan and Shield formulary, or whether the word from the Parthenon had forbade the use of such pending Xerxes' report on the studies in Persia. Keeping the individual from "harm or injustice" in context obviously means "as a patient", otherwise the ancient doc would have been obligated to all sorts of economic and judicial rescues for which he would have been as poorly suited then as he is today.

"I will neither give a deadly drug to anybody who asked for it, nor will I make a suggestion to this effect. Similarly I will not give to a woman an abortive remedy. In purity and holiness I will guard my life and my art." Physician-assisted suicide was strictly taboo, ironically enough, in the society that gave hemlock its most famous introduction. Likewise abortion is strictly forbidden in the original classical oath, however many newly graduating doctors also give that admonition a miss with their modern promise. *"I will not use the knife, not even on sufferers from stone, but will withdraw in favor of such men as are engaged in this work."* We've pretty much been happy to leave all of the cutting to those who have completed a surgical residency. *"Whatever houses I may visit, I will come for the benefit of the sick, remaining free of all intentional injustice, of all mischief and in particular of sexual relations with both female and male persons, be they free or slaves."* The whole anachronism of slavery aside, there is a very clear volitional expression here. The physician will behave in a certain fashion in whatever house he MAY visit, which obviously leaves with him the decision of whether or not to visit a particular client. There is NO mention of an obligation to treat certain patients or society as a whole, despite the widely held notion from the lay public, to hospital administrators and insurance executives, to politicians and bureaucrats to the contrary. The whole privacy issue is dealt with unequivocally: *"What I may see or hear in the course of the treatment or even outside of the treatment in regard to the life of men, which on no account one must spread abroad, I will keep to myself, holding such things shameful to be spoken about."* This directive guided

physicians through the Roman Empire, the Middle Ages, the Age of Reason, the Industrial Age, and the post-modern neuroses of the early Information Age, yet it came to be regarded as inadequate until the U.S. Congress passed onerous HIPAA laws to teach doctors how to keep their mouths shut. The Oath ends in grand fashion: *"If I fulfill this oath and do not violate it, may it be granted to me to enjoy life and art, being honored with fame among all men for all time to come; if I transgress it and swear falsely, may the opposite of all this be my lot."* It calls to the individual to make the investment, take the risk, endure the sacrifice, and bear the burden, for which he will be rewarded by a society which recognizes the value of professional who is bound by something far greater than insurance rules and Congressional mandates.

The Oath if valid, presupposes a societal context that recognizes the value of a highly ethical physician bound by his word. Recently I heard a hospital CEO decry a specialist who was hesitant to take ER call, exclaiming "but dammit, he took an oath." But is that necessarily on point? Did the doctor in question swear before Apollo, his state medical board, the local Rotary Club, or some other interested party that he would be at anyone's beckon and call? Did this specialist even take the classical Oath, or was his some variation that allowed him to perform abortions on the side, drive a spare van for Dr. Kevorkian, or share intimate details on a patient with their insurance company or the government even against the wishes of that patient? Times, and technology, have changed and so has the view of the Oath by those who take it. "The original oath is redolent of a covenant, a solemn and binding treaty," writes Dr. David Graham in JAMA, the Journal of the American Medical Association (12/13/00)."

By contrast, many modern oaths have a bland, generalized air of 'best wishes' about them, being near-meaningless formalities devoid of any influence on how medicine is truly practiced." Many in the medical profession see the Oath as not specifically relevant, but more broadly a touchstone for the moral and philosophical basis for those who care for the sick. Karen E. Geraghty of the AMA Institute for Ethics wrote: "All these changes raise doubts as to whether the ideals of a centuries-old text accurately reflect the ethical concerns and values of 21st-century medicine... the meaning of the Hippocratic oath for contemporary physicians may exist less in what it says than in what it stands for, although this by no means implies that the content of the oath is irrelevant. Rather, the shifting content of some aspects of the oath reveals its dynamic relationship with the changing context of medicine throughout the centuries. From the outset, the Hippocratic oath functioned to establish physicians as a moral community and delineated obligations and responsibilities specific to the medical profession." Fair enough so far, as Geraghty continues: "Despite changes in the content throughout the centuries, the fundamental role of the Hippocratic Oath is to demand that the medical profession, first and foremost, view itself as engaged in a moral enterprise. Rather than seeing the changing content of the oath as proof of its inadequacy for 21st-century physicians, these changes can be understood as reflecting the medical profession's struggle to define its moral position in the society of its day. By swearing to the Hippocratic Oath, therefore, medical graduates commit themselves not only to the content specific to their contemporary practice but also to the ideal that medicine is, at its most fundamental level, a moral enterprise." And here, as the chronological crow flies, we may see some significant shift of emphasis.

There is no doubt that the classical Oath was a moral directive, and so it is presently regarded. But Hippocrates's original call to a higher individual moral standard is now co-opted to the institutional service of society. Whereas the individual defined his moral position and behavior in his profession via the Oath, now new members of the profession use some facsimile of the Oath to accept the collective moral position expected of them. Geraghty: "The patient-physician relationship has been substantially altered in the past 50 years, with a decline in physician paternalism and an increase in patient involvement in treatment decisions. Medical specialization has diversified the practices and interests of physicians, as have increasing societal and legal obligations (italics added). The emergence of the field of bioethics has broadened the dimensions for ethical consideration, seemingly beyond the content of the oath." She is correct that the obligations of the physician, as perceived by society and by large portions of the profession, have reached far beyond the Oath. But have physicians consciously, willingly accepted these new burdens?

Shortly after the terrorist attacks on the U.S. in 2001, the American Medical Association published a "Declaration of Professional Responsibility", grandiosely stating "Medicine's Social Contract with Humanity." Within it states that physicians must act "together across geographic and ideological divides... [that] Humanity is our patient." That is a far piece from old Hippocrates calling for high standards of personal morality and not messing around with the household servants. Again, the American Medical Association adopted a declaration that begins "We, the members of the world community..." which obviously purports to philosophically commit all physicians in the AMA to a larger world collective of medicine. Do U.S. medical students, upon taking some permutation of an ancient Greek promise, realize how organized medicine commits them by inference to the ideology of "world" medicine? What is that ideology? The Declaration affirms commitment to:

1. Respect for all human life and the dignity of every individual. *(Okay, who could be against that?)*

2. Refrain from supporting or committing crimes against humanity and condemn all such acts. *(Does this preclude physicians from supporting their country in wartime, or even from serving in the U.S. armed forces if the opinion of international medicine states otherwise?)*

3. Treat the sick and injured with competence and compassion and without prejudice. *(Non-judgmental treatment of those seeking care is a basic tenet of popularly accepted medical ethics, and pretty darned hard to argue against. But who determines prejudice? If the U.S. government ratchets payment for Medicare services down to the point of being a serious money loser, isn't the physician guilty of being prejudiced against old people when he stops seeing Medicare patients? Is not the OB/GYN who declines to continue delivering babies for fear of predatory lawsuits guilty of prejudice against the next crop of women in labor that must languish in the county health departments and emergency rooms for their pre-natal and labor care?)*

4. Apply our knowledge and skills when needed, though doing so may put us at risk. *(The potential in this statement*

is enormous. The foresworn to this provision, if taken literally, obligates the physician to practice whenever needed – and there is always need – even to his detriment. This might not just apply to mission doctors treating Ebola virus in the Congo. Is not the physician in question obligated to operate in areas of high legal risk, or poor areas where the physician might go broke? This very broad, very altruistic statement has at its core the implication that a physician, by definition of his existence, has surrendered the right of free choice.)

5. Protect the privacy and confidentiality of those for whom we care and breach that confidence only when keeping it would seriously threaten their health and safety or that of others. *(This certainly seems reasonable if we're talking about a psychotic patient on the loose. On the other hand, some of the qualifiers might allow a benevolent insurance corporation or government entity to breach one's medical privacy for their own good.)*

6. Work freely with colleagues to discover, develop, and promote advances in medicine and public health that ameliorate suffering and contribute to human well-being. *(Pretty harmless, though the "work freely" bit does seem to clash with some of the previous, sterner admonitions.)*

7. Educate the public and polity about present and future threats to the health of humanity. *(Going on the CNN and warning the nation about the coming new flu strain might be a pretty good idea. But the nation is now all too aware, via special interest groups in state capital rallies and on CSPAN, of the agendas behind many that perceive their particular cause de jour as a serious public health*

threat deserving of new legislation, and of course, government money.)

8. Advocate for social, economic, educational, and political changes that ameliorate suffering and contribute to human well-being. *(Will the drafters of the "Declaration of Professional Responsibility" consider physicians who call for free-market systems to supplant government programs to be in good standing equal to those advocating socialized care?)*

9. Teach and mentor those who follow us for they are the future of our caring profession. *(If this simply means teaching science and the art of patient care, then the rationale is self-evident. Or does this also include the teaching of ethics that reflect a "dynamic relationship with the changing context of medicine"?)*

We make these promises solemnly, freely, and upon our personal honor and professional honor." *(As opposed to the personal honor implied in the Classical Oath).*

So where does this leave us on the question of medical oaths? The public's perception is such that the Hippocratic Oath represents an absolute commitment to service, which physicians shun to their ethical peril. But the truth is that physicians do not unanimously espouse nor adhere to the original Oath, and new versions, interpretations, or entirely separate oaths are now as much if not more so in practice. Moreover, there is no explicit language in the original Oath that requires "service at large." It may be rationally argued that the various oaths, declarations, and promises holding the affections of today's doctors are in fact more reflective of today's society, in that these various pledges reflect what society as a whole wants doctors to be. It may also be reasonably projected that against a rising tide of government regulations and barrages of predatory lawsuits, physicians find themselves awash in a world that by its actions increasingly defines its doctors as the problem or at the very least, only a commodity.

A society that increasingly resorts to legislative assurances for quality control likely places little value in oaths taken by those so regulated. Of what use is a doctor's word to a patient predisposed to access the tort system for a bad outcome? Whatever polls may suggest about the public's attitude toward physicians, or whatever the sweet little old lady down the street may think of her doctor, the actions of society belie significant trust for the members of the profession. Does this mean that the Hippocratic Oath holds no value for the layperson?

No. The traditional basis of the Oath is the word of the individual, which is rendered worthless to anyone unwilling to trust that word. The Oath or its permutations is not now valuable as a symbol of trust in a professional dedicated to carrying out nobler ideals. It is now valuable to the layperson to use as a shackle to the doctor, to remind them of some ill-defined or even fictitious promise to care for the whole world. When a physician declines to take emergency call, or to see certain types of patients, or simply demands to be paid, the layperson can shriek that "but dammit, he took an oath" even though they are unaware of the contents, context, or basis of that oath. Thus the doctor's own bond will be used by others to bind him. His promise is used not according to his highest ideals and to his own purposes, but by those who did not take such an Oath and who themselves bear no obligation. Is there then any utility to the individual taker of the Oath? If the maker of such a promise recognizes it to be subject to the exigencies of the day, then why would he assign any transcendent, permanent value to such a declaration? The biggest change in the Hippocratic Oath is not likely a blind eye toward abortion or euthanasia. The oath now does not so much fasten the individual practitioner to higher permanent ideals based on his own developed sense of ethics; it now reflects the wishes of society, in a "dynamic relationship with the changing context" of modern medicine.

❧ ❧ ❧

Dammit I Have to Make a Living!

On a beautiful September evening, we gathered for our five-year medical school reunion. Everyone was in suits or dresses milling about the open bar, recognizing friends and laughing at each other's newfound gray hair, or beaming at being introduced to a new spouse. It was a real pleasure to reunite with old classmates and trade stories from residency programs spanning the continent. Predictably the undergraduate fashions of some of our number ("Birkenstock formal") had given way to more conventional business hairstyles and dress, as was the case with one chap whom we'll call "D". D was a likable and easy-going, hacky-sack and backpack kind of guy in med school, an excellent student and always pleasant. Often during the first two years of school between innumerable lectures, students would gather in the adjacent courtyard to gulp caffeine and converse for a few minutes. Being on the extreme right wing in outlook, I often enjoyed jousting with my younger classmates over what I thought to be their starry-eyed, save-the-whole-world idealism. Like his closer friends, D. leaned toward the idealistic left regarding the delivery of health care, which gave us great opportunities to exchange views. Sometimes the passion of the exchange, though never with any personal animosity, would rise. This was 1994 and the country was absorbed over the fight in Congress of Hillary Clinton's proposed restructuring of the entire health care system. Naturally I had my problems with this whole notion and was not shy about saying so (if memory serves, I believe I referred to it, quite correctly, as "communism"). While enjoying one such mini-debate, I argued with D.'s assertion that doctors were making too much money. Like D., I too had already chosen to pursue family practice and knew very well that I would not get rich in that field, but I expected to make a decent living. When I pointed out that D.'s claim was wrong and groundless, he exclaimed: "Damn it, you've got people in this town sitting in the gutter while doctors are driving around in Mercedes!" I immediately pointed out to my classmate the absurdity of implying that somehow one had anything to do with the other, as though the doctors had stolen their cars from gutter bums. I would remember D.'s outburst all too well several years later.

There has for many years been a long-standing joke among medical students and former medical students that the greatest two days of medical school are the day that one is accepted, and the day one graduates. This bit of sardonic humor is more an expression of the comradeship of the years of intervening travail, rather than actual complaining. For all of the griping, the medical students showing up on Graduation Day to receive their degrees continue by and large to be a happy, humanistic bunch who are excited about the future, and that is as it should be. The soon-to-be residents (especially the prospective surgeons) know they're in for a rough go over the next several years, but they are excited about the prospect of learning and performing the new skills to make people feel better. They are not concerned on that day with how they will make a living for their families or pay back the debt that they have accrued. Every medical student nationwide for decades has at some point been admonished to achieve and practice the Three A's: ability, availability, and affability. And every resident doctor has been told by their instructors, senior colleagues, family, and friends, some version of an identical and logical concept: just concentrate on your studies and on doing the best job you possibly can, and the rest will take care of itself.

The Three A's approach, while only common sense, is excellent advice (particularly so for younger medical students not yet exposed to mortgage payments and the need to succeed in full-time employment). But unlike many of their non-medical counterparts, medical students buy into a rather unspoken concept once held but which now has no basis in reality. For many decades, all one had to do was run the obstacle course of medical training and a comfortable living and relative security was assured, provided one adhered to the Three A's. This made sense and was the reward society evolved to bestow upon those whom it needed. The lay reader may immediately think "Oh sure, a bunch or rich kids work for a few years, and they think they're guaranteed big houses and Mercedes and Wednesday afternoons playing

golf while regular people pay all the bills!" In fact physicians have been saddled with, and have often earned
such stereotypes. Far beyond the great majority of their
contemporaries, doctors defer an enormous amount of
gratification for which after many long years they feel
deserving.

The lay person may at this point also inwardly exclaim
"Geez, are these guys about nothing but money?" No,
and that is the portion of the stereotype which is unde-
served. The average doctor after medical school works
another 3-6 years, putting in hours for which, if averaged
out, he would make little better than minimum wage
(with the recent mandating of maximum allowed work
time of 80 hours/week, it would be about $8.50/hour).
But that is not a topic of great complaint among residents
who know the rules going in and accept this as part of
the dues one must pay. Generally residents are not afraid
of hard work, and many will moonlight to supplement
their incomes, gaining valuable clinical experience along
the way. Thus far, they operate within recognized parameters, and respond to the market they find exactly as anyone else might. And whereas an attorney, engineer, or
other professional with graduate training might expect
a payoff after surfacing from the training course, so to
does the emerging physician. As with other professions
it is not merely a matter of income, but what that income
represents, not merely the material benefit, but the sense
of accomplishment and self-respect that one expects after
long exertion. I have never heard anyone (apart form
politicians) complain about a successful businessman,
lawyer, engineer, or athlete who made and expected to
make a very good living after investing years of hard work
at low pay.

Yet as a group physicians have allowed their human-istic impulse to become a strange sort of guilt which converts their expectation into a reflexive apology. It is often dealt with in polite conversation and in the media as though the lay public has a legitimate say in how much a physician should make. Several years ago I watched multi-millionaire television commentator Bill O'Reilly exclaim: "C'mon, no doctor needs to make more than say, $400,000 or so!" For starters, that is a rude and immoral statement when applied to a neurosurgeon who has just undergone seven very tough post-doctoral years in order to achieve excellence in his art. Beyond that, why does a multi-millionaire feel he can give a legitimate opinion on a non-government employee's earning power? There have been numerous talk shows, news shows, and CSPAN panels on which have appeared physicians and non-phy-sicians claiming that they should be able to set physician salaries, and even assign them where to practice! Much of their arguments seem to be based on the sizable por-tion of medical education which comes from public mon-ies, yet medical students are generally not required con-tractually to reside in any certain locale, nor enter any particular field (there are scholarship exceptions, but the students know the conditions ahead of time, which is only fair).

And therein may be a kernel of the truth. More and more, physicians are regarded by the lay public (and sometimes themselves), sub-consciously or otherwise, as government employees to be moved, assigned, paid, and dealt with as the public requires. Politicians especially in their public pronouncements and policy decisions, make plain that they believe the members of the medical community must dance to their music. While I find this personally abhorrent, it is fair to recognize that there are many of good will that feel this way. But if this be the case, then they should state so forthrightly and allow up and coming students complete foreknowledge before saddling them throughout their careers with presumptions of obedience. And physicians compound the problem greatly through blissful ignorance in their training years, and then expediency intertwined with genuine compassion once entering private practice. Medical students are typically indoctrinated in their medical ethics classes regarding "equitable resource allocation" and "non-judgmental" provision of care for all regardless of expense. Yet there is truly so much that must be covered in medical school that these impressionable, idealistic pupils have no time to learn about the nuts-and-bolts of the system for medical funding in this country. As resident doctors many begin to get a rudimentary knowledge, and then a superficial grasp of the basics of the system. They start to learn about formularies, lists of medicines that various insurance providers will or won't pay for. They learn about inclusion and exclusion criteria for Medicaid and admission (to the hospital) criteria for Medicare. Residents will hear about co-pays, deductibles, and preexisting clauses. They will try to keep their eyelids pried open through the occasional lecture regarding managed care, HMO's, PPO's, and a host of other equally uninspiring acronyms.

They will be introduced generally to the whole quirky, wheezing structure, but they won't pay it too much heed. They will be thinking about how to prepare for morning report and hospital rounds, about the busy afternoon clinic, about upcoming board exams, or about the delicious Saturday off they have coming up that week. In short they will focus more on their lives and on what they understand their jobs to be. They will focus on how to provide the best possible care through accurate diagnosis and effective treatment, not on how it is to be paid for. This is not to dismiss that question as trivial, but of what other professional is it demanded that he figure out for the client how the bill is to be paid? The resident physician is likely in the busiest time of his life learning how to practice medicine. Many residency programs attempt to teach the fundamentals of health care financing to give the resident some knowledge basis prior to private practice, which is certainly appropriate. But through no fault of their own, the various residency programs cannot adequately prepare their residents to pursue the goal of making a profit. Actually they may deter the resident from that goal by inculcating in him an acceptance of the parameters of the third-party payer system, which lies in wait.

When our intrepid resident graduates and embarks upon private practice, he will likely have made a deal. The days of a brand new doctor simply getting a bank loan and hanging up a shingle are largely over. The extraordinarily high cost of setting up a primary care office rises even higher for specialists, who must purchase very expensive equipment and often hire more highly trained personnel to assist them. But new American-trained doctors are very much in demand by hospitals and the communities they serve. For a hospital to function, they must have patients. These patients either come to the emergency room that is nearest in times of illness or injury, or they seek out one on recommendation. Often that recommendation is the simple knowledge that their particular doctor is on staff there and will be able to attend them. Like all corporations hospitals always seek to expand their business, and to do this they need doctors to provide this referral base. And obviously, hospitals need doctors to admit patients and treat them until they are well again. And doctors often need hospitals in which to perform invasive testing or surgery, or to practice internal medicine and intensive care for which they trained so many years. So a very natural yet symbiotic economic relationship springs up between a hospital and its physicians. The hospital constantly assess its needs relative to the community and tries to attract doctors accordingly to join their staff and practice in their community. To that end they recruit: this often includes invitations to visit the area, introductions to prospective colleagues, and inducements to come to the area, including financial incentives to assist in starting up a new practice. In today's environment hospitals which take federal Medicare or Medicaid money – and that's all of them – are tightly controlled by the government in the way they offer these incentives (Consider that the expenditures of a private corporation which accepts clients whose bill is paid by the government may then be controlled by that government. So as with physicians, the government now de facto regards hospitals as quasi-federal institutions.).

The doctors on the staff of a hospital may seek to expand their own practices, or need someone to share the workload and they too may offer recruitment incentives. So our new doctor entering private practice will likely talk to a hospital, a group of similar specialists, or both in laying the financial support for establishing his practice. If the new physician joins a group, he will likely be sharing their call and starting at lower salary, until he can increase the size of his practice to pull his share of the group practice's load. Often the junior physician will then be offered, encouraged, or even required to buy in to full partnership as is the case in many other professions. Any acceptance of such a relationship with the group will generally obligate the new partner to all standing contractual arrangements with private insurance companies, Medicare/Medicaid and other government programs, and the local hospital. As with other businesses, the production targets are set for the new partner to meet as part of his own financial obligation. So far so good.

If the new physician does not join an existing group he may try to set up a solo practice or form one with a partner or two, usually with help from a nearby interested hospital. In return for this financial backing (now generally required to be made under federal law as a "loan") the aided doctor must agree to serve for a defined period on the hospital staff and take call to admit patients to the hospital and accept referrals from the hospital to his office. Of course this is a good thing because this is what the new doctor has trained to do. And to fulfill these duties, the young physician must accept the operational parameters of the hospital, becoming an extension of their agreements with the various levels of government and private insurers. The new staff member must accept Medicare and Medicaid, and therefore must accept all of the rules, restrictions, potential for audits, and constantly changing rule-minutiae that define the acceptance of government medicine. But of course our recently graduated resident has heard about all of this and is prepared to go with the flow, assuming that the system will work to his benefit provided he is able to exert the Three A's and do his best. This is the way his forbears did it and they got along just fine. He will attend staff meetings where he will be told about the latest rules and restrictions handed down regarding federal privacy restrictions, and about how and when he may or may not access medical records on his own patients. He will hear about how the hospital spent cash in multiples of six figures to hire consultants to prepare for an inspection by agents from JCAHO (Joint Commission on Accreditation of Health Care Organizations), an inspection that must be passed for the hospital to continue to receive federal funds. In that same staff meeting our new doctor may be dismayed to hear that his patients were transferred from the ER to a nearby hospital for want of beds, because there was no money in the budget to hire the needed additional nurses.

Three or four years into private practice the hospital subsidy may have run its course, or it is now time to put up a lot of cash to buy into a partnership. Suddenly the newer physician may be juggling his school debt and house payment with a relative loss of income as he begins to stand on his own (again, as one might in any other business).

Our young physician wishing to alleviate some of these restrictions may discover that his contracts with private insurers requires him to continue to take hospital call, even though his malpractice insurance premiums rise significantly if he practices any in-patient hospital medicine (In the current spiraling malpractice crisis, many physicians find themselves caught in this trap, unable to quit hospital work yet barely able to afford continuing it). This same doctor might wish to refuse taking on any new Medicare or Medicaid patients because he is losing money seeing them, but might be prevented in that course by his contract with the hospital which requires his subsidized practice to remain open to them. As the cost of doing business rises for our novice businessman, he will seek to do what his contemporaries do, which is to recoup his lost revenue by passing the cost on to his customers in the form of higher prices. And here is where doctors depart from the rest of the crowd. Physicians cannot set their own prices, but must accept what Medicare/Medicaid or third-party insurers such as Blue Cross will pay them. "Third party payers" are entities that charge a fee to their clients, and then pay the doctor or hospital for their clients' medical bills at rates previously agreed to by contract. The doctor is paid not by the party he treats, but by a separate agent for that party. His natural interest then becomes split between serving the patient, and the party that pays his fee (a feature remarkably in conflict to the Classical Hippocratic Oath discussed earlier). It is not admitted, but widely known throughout medicine that these third-party payers, private and government, routinely engage in delaying tactics to slow the payment of money already earned by the doctor.

And all of this happens amidst a steadily rising cost to do business in a medical practice. The doctor/business owner must pay sharply rising, sometimes skyrocketing malpractice premiums. Based on the latest round of government mandates, the practice might have to absorb the cost of hiring more staff to handle the increasing administrative burdens of new government directives, to be compliant in order to receive payments and to be prepared in the case of audits (violations noted in which, may result in civil or even criminal penalties). This tedious spate of concerns adds up to this: doctors are faced with the combination of fixed unit prices, and rising operating costs. The only way to preserve a profit in these conditions is to increase volume, i.e., to see more patients in the same amount of time.

Once several years back during a lull in the emergency room, I was able to spend a great deal of time with a gentleman and his child, the latter who had been brought in frequently with rater specious and unlikely complaints. On this latest visit, after a thorough history and exam, including labs and x-rays, I finally had to explain point-blank to the father that I thought his child a hypochondriac. We discussed the conditions at home, the similarity of complaints with the child's mother, and how the child was likely emulating what she had seen in order to get attention. The father saw the light and was genuinely grateful for this insight and the time spent, and then suddenly angry. He was angry that their family practitioner, whom they had seen only that morning, had just "breezed in, thrown some antibiotics at us, and rushed out", not even spending five minutes with patient and parent. Ah, I said, I understand why. I explained to the patient's parent the reality of medicine in general and of primary care in particular: the doctor is dealing with falling profits per patient visit, and must make up the loss in higher volume. So his brusque, quick fix manner did not reflect an ambivalent disregard, but a need to hurry to put food on the table. I described for the parent how many practices face costs of $30-$40 *just to put the patient in the exam room, before any cost is recouped!* (For minor complaints, the gross payment may be $40-60, and often delayed for weeks). I spelled out for this well-meaning parent how his family doctor was also likely a parent and husband, with bills to pay, a family to support, and how he probably had to rush room-to-room just to keep up. The gentlemen with whom I was speaking shook his head, and gave voice to the usual sentiment: "Man, you know, like everybody, I always think of you doctors as all millionaires, driving Lexus' and playing golf all of the time." This was a sincere statement without malice, reflecting the general consensus. This example also reflected how the system has changed, economically preventing a well-meaning doctor from spending the time necessary with a patient and parent to make the proper diagnosis and effect the proper treatment.

Nationwide patients are growing angrier at longer waiting room times, shorter visits with their doctors, and the rising sense of an impersonal, rushed relationship governing their care. Yet very few of them grasp the essential piece of the puzzle that it is not the choice of the physician but the conditions set forth by the third-party payers that actually call the tune of the dance. Some ignorant or rude lay people might exclaim that "doctors just want to make a lot of money, they could make a little less if they really cared about people!" But this sentiment ignores that the physician has the very same concerns and obligations as any other lay person, and that it is completely ridiculous to expect that physician to forgo the rewards for many years of competitive selection and longer than average working hours in an environment many would not tolerate. Doctors are also growing angrier. In economic terms, they are daily losing control over their medical decision-making, business practices, and the way they can manage their daily lives. In trying to keep a steady income by seeing more patients, they are merely responding to the altered environment as best they can, exactly as any reasonable person might. Yet in doing so, they incur the anger of frustrated patients, ignorant of the real costs of medical practice, who simply wish to receive care yet are willing to buy into the stereotype of rich uncaring doctors rushing to get out to the golf course. In the emergency room, I know a number of specialists who make a great deal of money, who have undergone years of specialized training to provided specialized diagnostic and therapeutic procedures to counter the ravages of illness and injury. Many of these specialists drive very nice cars, live in beautiful waterfront homes, and take very nice vacations. But each of them in turn is on call, available when I call them at three o'clock A.M. to rush to the E.R. to take a patient to surgery before an appendix bursts, or to perform a coronary catheterization in a patient clutching his chest with angina. One day I will be a patient requiring these services and this expertise, and I want it to be available. Knowing what these men and women have invested and sacrificed, it would be the height of hypocrisy to expect that they not be paid adequately to be ready to aid my family or me in time of crisis. Yet increasingly, this is what is expected by an angry and confused lay public.

Where does this leave our new doctor only several years out of residency? He probably enjoys his work and his proud of the quality of service he provides. But he is also worried about his income, even though it is substantially higher than that of most people, as he sees his costs and workload increase daily without any increase in income. He is probably getting frustrated with the lack of time spent with his family, and with the longer hours put in around seeing patients, trying to untangle the jungles of red tape to satisfy patient requests and to ensure payment for work that may have been done weeks before. This doctor may assess the situation to find that he will be personally better off if he limits his workload and removes himself from taking call at the hospital, which will dismay the hospital administrator who cannot understand why someone would want to do less work and have less business. The evolving physician will truly come to understand the gut-level meaning of the phrase "time-is-money" as he tries to carve out protected areas of time for family and personal rejuvenation. This will not be received kindly by the mother of a sick child late on a Friday afternoon, or and elderly lady sitting at her husband's bedside in the E.R. while he suffers with a stroke, only to find that no, their doctor no longer admits patients here. I have never met or spoken with a single physician who applauds this situation or views it with any pleasure, but it is the reality of modern medicine in a country where control was taken out of the hands of doctors and their patients. Yes some doctors are simply cold and avaricious, but these are far fewer in number than a frustrated public is willing to believe, and the growing number of practicing physicians seeking to limit their availability (and there income!) supports this assertion.

Remember our friend D. from the beginning of the chapter, the young student so angry at the apparent injustice of Mercedes-driving doctors and gutter-dwelling indigents? I did not see D. again after medical school until our five-year reunion. He was smiling, dapper in a new suit, and proudly introducing his wife and young child. It was great to see him and we joyfully shook hands. I told him he looked great and asked how he had been, and whether he was family practice out west where he had completed his residency. He returned the compliments, and without missing a beat – his first question to me, on a night to reminisce, discuss hobbies, and have a big time - he asked with obvious interest how the payment rates were where I lived.

❖ ❖ ❖

Medicare – Another Compassionate Failure

A topic of great political and social significance over the past forty years has been the federal government's program to provide health care for the elderly, known as Medicare. The zany idea of free guaranteed care based simply on age goes all the way back to the 1930's, where a lot of American socialism began. Dr. Thomas Parran of the Public Health Service recommended tying such care to Social Security, an idea that re-surfaced in the 1950's among Social Security officials trying to protect the economic vitality of the nation's elderly. As part of Pres. Lyndon Johnson's "Great Society" initiative, the Medicare Bill (H.R. 6675) is Public Law 89-97 (79 Stat. 286) was passed in 1965 with great fanfare to ensure that our senior citizens would be well cared for. The following remarks were made Independence, MO on July 30, 1965 on the occasion of the signing of Medicare Bill (Transcript from the Lyndon Baines Johnson Library and Museum). Former Pres. Truman was in attendance and offered the first remarks: PRESIDENT TRUMAN. "... This is an important hour for the Nation, for those of our citizens who have completed their tour of duty and have moved to the sidelines. These are the days that we are trying to celebrate for them. These people are our prideful responsibility and they are entitled, among other benefits, to the best medical protection available. Not one of these, our citizens, should ever be *abandoned to the indignity of charity. Charity is indignity when you have to have it* (italics added). But we don't want these people to have anything to do with charity and we don't want them to have any idea of hopeless despair." After some introductory remarks Pres. Johnson paid compliments to

Pres. Truman for planting "the seeds of compassion and duty which have today flowered into care for the sick, and serenity for the fearful" and evoked the "painful wrath at the injustice which denies the miracle of healing to the old and to the poor." Johnson praised "the great leadership of men like John McCormack, our Speaker; Carl Albert, our majority leader; our very able and beloved majority leader of the Senate, Mike Mansfield; and distinguished Members of the Ways and Means and Finance Committees of the House and Senate–of both parties, Democratic and Republican" as proof of bipartisan complicity. The entire program was defined as any government charity is, in terms of need: "There are more than 18 million Americans over the age of 65. Most of them have low incomes. Most of them are threatened by illness and medical expenses that they cannot afford." And then the critically false assumption: "And through this new law, Mr. President, *every citizen will be able, in his productive years when he is earning, to insure himself against the ravages of illness in his old age* (italics added). This insurance will help pay for care in hospitals, in skilled nursing homes, or in the home. And under a separate plan it will help meet the fees of the doctors.

During your working years, the people of America–you–will contribute through the social security program a small amount each payday for hospital insurance protection. For example, the average worker in 1966 will contribute about $1.50 per month. The employer will contribute a similar amount. And this will provide the funds to pay up to 90 days of hospital care for each illness, plus diagnostic care, and up to 100 home health visits after you are 65. And beginning in 1967, you will also be covered for up to 100 days of care in a skilled nursing home after a period of hospital care. And under a separate plan, when you are 65–that the Congress originated itself, in its own good judgment–you may be covered for medical and surgical fees whether you are in or out of the hospital. You will pay $3 per month after you are 65 and your Government will contribute an equal amount. The benefits under the law are as varied and broad as the marvelous modern medicine itself. If it has a few defects–such as the method of payment of certain specialists-then I am confident those can be quickly remedied and I hope they will be.

No longer will older Americans be denied the healing miracle of modern medicine. No longer will illness crush and destroy the savings that they have so carefully put away over a lifetime so that they might enjoy dignity in their later years. No longer will young families see their own incomes, and their own hopes, eaten away simply because they are carrying out their deep moral obligations to their parents, and to their uncles, and their aunts. And no longer will this Nation refuse the hand of justice to those who have given a lifetime of service and wisdom and labor to the progress of this progressive country. And this bill, Mr. President, is even broader than that. It will increase social security benefits for all of our older Americans. It will improve a wide range of health and medical services for Americans of all ages. In 1935 when the man that both of us loved so much, Franklin Delano Roosevelt, signed the Social Security Act, he said it was, and I quote him, "a cornerstone in a structure which is being built but it is by now means complete."" That last remark was instructive indeed.

The system was proposed as a simple payment-transfer whereby the currently retired generation would have their medical care paid for from the taxes of those presently working; who would then have their care paid for upon reaching their retirement years by future workers, and so on. The entire contraption was based on a wrongheaded premise and on false assumptions. *Charity is indignity when you have to have it,* according to LBJ. When would one need charity, except when they ... needed it? The premise was that someone should have his health care expenses paid for simply by virtue of reaching a certain age, generally touted by such adherents as a necessary condition of a "civilized" society. The faulty assumptions were (1) that demand for care would remain constant and (2) that the ability of each generation to pay for the care of their respective retirees would remain constant. The false assumption of constant demand was laid bare with the carnival bark of "free health care" that led to unrestrained demand, and consequently, more money being spent on health care. When granny has a sniffle, an ache, or feels blue, there is no reason not to seek attention, because it's paid for! Unlike everyone else the elderly person has no reason to prioritize minor health concerns with his other necessities because he won't have to pay for it (at this point the reader will think me very cold hearted, but hang in there!) So as there is unrestrained demand leading to more money being put into the system, we now get the natural response: a rise in price. Normally a rise in price leads to a curb in demand, but not so when the demand is for a guaranteed goodie. The price is met, and met again, in an inflationary cycle with no end.

Charitably, Pres. Johnson's initiative was only wrong in its ignorance of economics and human nature. It was political genius. Initially Medicare wouldn't pass: Repeatedly in the early 1960s a coalition of Republicans and conservative Democrats defeated Medicare. According to Steven Hayward and Erik Peterson in <u>Reason</u> magazine (1993): "The key figure in this perennial drama was Wilbur Mills, the legendary chairman of the House Ways and Means Committee. Mills refused to pass a Medicare bill out of that key committee, supposedly out of concern that Medicare would threaten the integrity of the Social Security program (to which Medicare is attached). Following the Democratic landslide in the election of 1964, which gave Democrats a 2-to-1 majority in both houses of Congress, President Lyndon Johnson exerted his influence to stack the Ways and Means Committee with new Democrats sympathetic to Medicare. Wilbur Mills changed his mind and embraced Medicare. "Mills can count" was the explanation given for his flip-flop. This new political landscape virtually assured that Medicare would sail through Congress with huge majorities."

From repeated defeat and frustration, the new Medicare program would be put on track by those whose belief that the government should provide health care (or who were unwilling to oppose such) would not be denied.

Richard L. Taw, M.D., President, American Private Physicians Association, gave the following explanation in February 2004: "Few people realize that Medicare is the legacy of John Fitzgerald Kennedy. In his 1961 State of the Union address he proposed a mandatory hospital insurance plan for the elderly. When this issue got political legs, the Republicans countered in 1963 with a "Better

Care" program. Arguing that seniors already had access to hospital coverage, "Better Care" would have covered outpatient and physician's services. The AMA also countered with "Eldercare" which was a program for the poor elderly. Both of these programs were voluntary.

The single individual who put all of this together was Representative Wilbur Mills. Medicare is called his "3 Layered Cake". Mandatory hospital coverage became Medicare Part A. A voluntary outpatient coverage program became Medicare Part B. A voluntary healthcare program for the poor of all ages became Medicaid. The frosting on the cake and the brilliant political strategy was *linking this to Social Security* (italics added). *Signing up for Social Security benefits automatically enrolled someone in Medicare Part A and immediately terminated private health insurance* (italics added). And seniors had not had an increase in Social Security since 1959. This bill came with a 7% Social Security increase. Therefore, it was extremely popular with seniors and all the stakeholders got something out of it."

A master vote counter who always sought to consolidate political power, it was more likely that Johnson saw this program as another way to cement a Democrat voting bloc. Though Johnson feared that an illness might "crush and destroy the savings that [the elderly] have so carefully put away over a lifetime" he established a system that would force the elderly into its rolls, or deny them money that they had earned (the mandatory link to Social Security "benefits). Johnson badly wanted to prevent the younger generation from losing "their own incomes, and their own hopes, eaten away simply because they are carrying out their deep moral obligations to their parents, and to their uncles, and their aunts." To that end he exploded the growth of government and increased the taxes necessary to pay for that government, all on the backs of these very same younger generations! The families he proposed to aid have seen four decades of rising tax bills and the increasing need for two-parent incomes, thought by many to be a major contributor to the disruption of the modern family. But these are small concerns when elderly voters need their medical bills paid.

The second false assumption is that we would always have basically the same number of working folks taking care of basically the same number of retired folks. This was compounded by the first falsehood of constant demand.

Hayward and Peterson: "The hospital-insurance portion of Medicare was to be supported through a payroll tax shared equally by employers and employees. The voluntary Supplemental Medical Insurance was to be financed by premiums paid by the participants with dollar-for-dollar federal matching funds. The mechanism for increasing revenue for the hospital-insurance plan, when necessary, was the raising of the taxable earnings base. To keep solvent, the Supplemental Medical Insurance system would adjust the insurance premium until premiums and matching funds covered expenditures. Congress generally dismissed fears of cost overruns. Rep. Claude Pepper (D-Fla.) said: "The cost will not be greater than our present inefficient [sic] and wasteful fee-for-service system. According to experts the charge to the average family under a national health-insurance program will actually be less than it pays now, partly because the employer and government will contribute to the fund." It is consistent, and consistently amazing, how the advocates of large government bureaucracies always (1) decry the "inefficiencies" of free market relationships, and (2) find it appropriate and proper to saddle the employer with increased "contributions", never dreaming that these new costs will be passed on to the customer.

But Congress' assumptions were double-edged in their ineptitude. Hayward and Peterson: "A 1965 House Ways and Means Committee report on the actuarial basis for the hospital-insurance program proudly declared that "Congress has very carefully considered the cost aspects of the proposed hospital insurance system" and that "Congress very strongly believes that the financing basis of the new hospital insurance program should be developed on a conservative basis." The report acknowledged that hospital costs were rising faster than wages. "It is inconceivable," the committee report says, "that hospital prices would rise indefinitely at a rate faster than earnings because eventually individuals–even currently employed workers, let alone older persons–could not afford to go to a hospital under such cost circumstances...." Yet that is precisely what the advent of Medicare set in motion.

A brief interlude seems proper, to assure the reader that the point of throwing out dates and figures is not to become embroiled in historical Beltway wonkishness, nor to serve as a primer for Medicare. The chronology, data interpretations, and motivations of the major players will be spun in different ways depending on the prevailing ideology (or paycheck source) of the given speaker. But the important fact, the "take-home message" as is commonly referred to in medical school, is this: irrespective of motivations, Medicare was an ill-conceived expansion of government into the private sector, where all the good intentions in the world could, and can not be paid for when demand outstrips supply.

And speaking of rising demand… "The 1950 Census showed that the aged population had grown from 3 million in 1900 to 12 million in 1950" and had doubled as a percentage of the overall population. And between 1950 and 1963, the elderly population grew by 5.5 million, while the cost of hospital care rose an average of 6.7%, well above the average increase in cost of living." The rising demand of a growing elderly population, with an increasing life expectancy seemed not to concern budgetary forecasters one whit. Of course the life expectancy continues to rise, and there is no political will to anger retirees (a reliable voting bloc) by now extending their working years and forcing them to wait longer for their "free" care. The ratio of retirees to working citizens continues to grow with no end in sight, and, it becomes progressively harder for the workers to cover the bill for the retirees. The truth is, they can't. The actuarial system upon which Medicare financing was founded was already a bust in the program's first five years. Hayward and Peterson: "The Medicare hospital-insurance program was already out of actuarial balance and about 50-percent underfunded by the early 1970s, requiring in 1972 the first of several increases in both the payroll tax rate and the wage base against which it was levied."

This unpleasant fact has led to leading to constant funding formulae re-jiggering ever since, as well as a delicious government doublespeak. Politicians in both parties for years now have simultaneously advanced the idea that we must "control costs" even as they defended the notion that the growing body of elderly should have all of their care paid for by a taxpayer base increasingly unable to do so. The conclusion that this dual argument represents a logical contradiction, and therefore impossibility, is quietly ignored by those making policy. Worse still, leaders in both major parties continue to expand the benefits of a system already broken. Pres. Clinton's Secretary of Health and Human Services Donna Shalala upped the bidding in her remarks on the anniversary of the Medicare Act in 1995. She praised the administration's assault on the ever-present "fraud, waste, and abuse" which always attends such programs. She cited a new law extending Medicare benefits for disabled people, and promising to push enlarge these to lifetime eligibility. She cheered the addition of preventive benefits and a "Smoking Cessation Project" as a cost saving measures. In the face of rising budgets unpaid for as far as the eye could see, Sec. Shalala pronounced: "Of course, if we truly want to ensure the promise of Medicare for future generations-if we truly want to modernize the program-then we must still add the one benefit that has become an essential element of high-quality medicine: prescription drugs... We need an affordable, accessible, comprehensive prescription drug benefit-and we need a drug benefit now." Foretelling George W. Bush's disastrous "Free Drugs for Old Peoples' Votes" program in 2003, Shalayla resorted to the familiar political language of a promise made to some to be kept by others: "The addition of a prescription drug benefit will undoubtedly enhance the promise of Medicare. It's a promise that we-as a nation-cannot break." The egalitarian impulses oft-echoed in medical ethics discussions were given rein: "Truman, and the heroes of '65 knew that Medicare-along with Social Security-would be the twin pillars supporting the true equality of all Americans...[proving] not how good we are-but how good we can be. And, above all, Truman and the heroes of '65 knew that Medicare confirmed the greatness of America."

No it did not. The notion that the nation could, *and should* pay for the health care of the elderly is a lie, in that it was sold as expanding freedom rather than reducing it. The practical expectation was that the program could fiscally roll from one generation to the next in an endless conveyer belt of retirees who had already pre-paid for the care. This concept was shown to be false in the rising prices and rising demand that grew out of this new "right." As retirees' life expectancies and demands for care grew, the money they had put into the system has been progressively unable to cover their costs. This money is now taken from working citizens, in a huge inter-generational transfer of wealth, *transferring accumulated wealth to the demographically wealthiest generation* in American history! By forcibly taking money from the younger to pay for the older, the Medicare program is antithetical to freedom. (And the doctors who initiated and presently support the continued existence of Medicare embrace the worst of collectivist ethics. Contrary to the personal autonomy of the doctor-patient relationship, modern doctors now abet the taking from one patient to give to another. They unwittingly have become the celebrants of group preference over individual choice.)

Medicare is a budget nightmare out of control, but that should concern recipients and taxpayers, not doctors- right? Wrong! Doctors led by the American Medical Association in the early 1960's opposed the inception of Medicare, correctly fearing that it would lead to full blown socialized medicine. In the late 1950's the AMA lobbied strongly against such any national health program; in 1960 AMA executive vice-president Ernest Howard, MD warned against negotiating with the program's proponents as "the surest way to total defeat." Shortly thereafter the AMA launched a PR blitz against "the most deadly challenge ever faced by the medical profession." Interestingly enough, the AMA now boasts a six-point plan to save American medicine, which includes "Strengthening Medicare."

As the battle lines formed, U.S. labor unions led by the AFL-CIO supported the side of government-provided care, as a primary legislative priority. The American Hospital Association (AHA) also supported the creation of government care, as a way to pay for the growing number of elderly whose care was being absorbed by hospitals, and which was thought to threaten the rest of the private health insurance system. These were joined in turn by the National Farmer's Union, the American Nurses Association, the American Public Welfare Association, and the National Association of Social Workers. On the other side were the AMA, the National Chamber of Commerce, the National Association of Manufacturers, and the American Farm Bureau Federation (as well as the health insurance and pharmaceutical industries). In gross terms, the special interest groups divided up along the lines of those in need versus those who produced. The AHA was blunt in its 1962 assertion that identifying HOW to pay for new Federal funding was "of secondary importance."

The initial concept for Medicare was that it would pay only for the hospital expenses of the elderly. The AMA attempted a tactical trick and decided to fight the program on the grounds that *it didn't do enough* [get reference], declaring that for the program to work it would need to cover the outpatient, doctor's office-visit expenses as well, initially dealt with through their "Elder Care" program. This premium-funded voluntary program was later proposed in conjunction with Medicare Part A (hospital coverage) and Medicaid (coverage for the poor) in the famous "3-layer cake" legislation. Ways and Means Committee Chairman Wilbur Mills, anxious to pass a bill, eagerly accepted this notion, and the passed bill included the three realms (hospital, out-patient, needy) of care envisioned by its architects. The AMA's bluff was called and their opposition wilted. Since then the AMA has not only accepted but embraced the existence of Medicare in its lobbying efforts, and has made the viability of the program a top priority. Is this to protect the interests of the elderly or the pocketbooks of member physicians? Actually it doesn't matter, since both are groups that feel trapped into participation with the program through financial necessity.

The elderly were fed, and then fed themselves, on foolhardy promises that could not pass the basic economic smell test of time. And the doctors who viewed the new program with a wary eye were at first delighted not to have to ask elderly patients to pay the bill, and were happy to accept the government checks for their care. Costs soared and legislators frowned at growing budgets. In 1983 Medicare adopted a system of DRG's (diagnostic-related groups) introduced to organize payments for certain patient groups, to more efficiently control costs. "Controlling costs" and reining in "over utilization" were of course buzzwords for attempted rationing, the natural result of declaring a good or service a "right." What it meant for doctors who mainlined government cash into their clinics was that their practices became hooked on revenues that came with a whole ball of red string attached. The costs were of course not controlled, because the root causes of the inflation – unrestrained demand in a growing population of beneficiaries – were not addressed. So the doctors grumbled under the increasing administrative workload and occasional audits, and continued to accept payment for work legitimately done but paid from shaky ground.

Now that we've slogged hour way through the rise of Medicare, we might ask how this affects our bright young doc fresh out of residency. For starters, unless he or she joins a group, they will have absolutely no idea what to start charging patients. Is a sore throat worth $50? Will $100 sew up a two-inch laceration? Unless very astute, the physician new to private practice will not have a good way to wrestle the smoky fog of physician office charges often referred to as "usual and customary." Eventually our intrepid healer will find out what the fee scales are, from the major private insurance companies that service a given area, all of which will have tied their fees to what Medicare pays, somewhat in the manner that individual bank lending rates mimic the prime rate. Our new practitioner will assign the fees as best he can, and start submitting bills to the third party carriers, private insurance and Medicare/Medicaid. Whether the patient has private insurance or is a government client, the bill submitted will claim payment based on a numerical code, one of tens of thousands of codes developed by – of course ! – government. These codes are compiled in the dreaded International Classification of Diseases, Tenth Edition, or ICD-10. This thick, expensive codebook, updated over and over along with another ridiculously Byzantine tome called the CPT manual, dictates how a physician is paid.

By now I can tell dear reader, your eyes are glazing over from the tedium of this description. Why, you are asking, am I troubling you with these minutiae? Take a breath, go get a drink, have a stretch, and allow me to explain.

Physicians apply for, and go through their medical training to do something that they think is interesting, cool, useful, and hopefully, fun. None of them rack up six-figure loans and go short on sleep for years to operate at the whim of government bureaucrats who come up with the latest five-digit decimal code to describe whether Granny fell out of bed or off a toilet seat; dammit, she broke her pelvis! While the government and private insurance companies hold the doctors' finances through this ridiculous system, they charge each doctor's office big bucks for these stupid codebooks, published annually, marketed, and distributed by...the American Medical Association. Yes dear friends, the same AMA that claims to look out for physicians and patients, makes millions annually by coordinating with the federal government to keep both parties trapped in an administrative and financial trap. The same federal government that forbids individual physicians from price fixing on pain of criminal penalty, itself fixes prices.

Upon opening an office, and hiring a staff, the physician intent on treating patients to his best ability must also reserve extra resources to hire additional staff to do the billing, which is to say, look up codes, fill out forms, transmit claims to third-party payers, and re-transmit the claims when some of those are rejected because the decimal place was misplaced, making it appear that Granny broke her pelvis because she was thrown from a horse instead of falling off the toilet. Neither the doctor or Granny care, of course, because either way she has a busted frame; but the paperwork must be correct, or our young healer won't get paid, which can have deleterious effects for his staff come payday, and negative comments from his/her spouse when the mortgage is in arrears.

Stop your whining, I can hear the reader growling, it's part of the cost of doing business just like in every other job. And you are right, in part, for thinking this. The civil engineer learns his craft to measure grade densities and calculate dynamic thermal material contraction ranges, not how to beg for county zoning board variances. The hotel manager has to learn not only holiday flex-scheduling to maximize his productivity and minimize overtime, but has to comply with OSHA, EEOC, and all state regulatory costs which he then passes on to the customer... exactly. Other professions, other service industries, other commodity suppliers simply pass increased costs along to the customer. Not so, the doctor.

Care to guess what happens if, because your power bill, or your malpractice insurance costs, or your employee health plan costs go up, you pass the increased overhead on to your patients? If you raise the cost of treating a typical strep throat, the bill will be refused by the patient's insurance company which, if you press the point, might threaten to drop you as one of their "providers", thereby cutting you out of part of the local market.

If the private doctor tries to pass along an increased cost to a government patient (Medicare or Medicaid), then he runs the risk of fines, and even criminal penalties. Yes we have all seen the occasional news reports of occasional bad actors being perp-marched out of offices for committing Medicare/Medicaid fraud to the tune of millions, but that is not what we address here. Our glorious federal system for providing care to the elderly and the poor presumes that physicians are not to be trusted, and subjects them both to a set fee schedule and severe penalties to see those fees enforced.

On any given day the government's men in black can show up to a doctor's office, announce that they are "here to help", and do a chart audit. The auditors will look to see if the documentation for a given charge (to the government) matches their criteria, which is constantly shifting. If they believe a physician to have submitted a bill for more than the visit was worth, then they will want the difference back, in addition to a fine. So if a doc spends and extra ten minutes talking to a senior about home safety or smoking and doesn't record it all, but reasons that he spent more time and therefore should be paid more – uh-oh! And here is where the fun begins, with the government practice of extrapolation. Let's use some round figures: If a doctor sees 1,000 Medicare patients, the auditors might pull 50 charts. If they perceive even minor over-billing errors in say, five charts, then they consider that an error rate of 10% - which is then applied presumptively to the doctor's entire panel of Medicare clients. Now the government can demand repayment for an "overcharge" for 100 patients, plus an administrative *fine for each patient.* In medium sized practices, helpful government visits can add surprise administrative penalties in the tens or even hundreds of thousands of dollars, which invite criminal charges if the doctor refuses to cough up the cash. Some doc's hire a lawyer and fight for a reduced settlement, but either way they are still out a considerable amount of cash, money that they believe they earned and for which no fraud was committed. In the private sector, disputes over payment may go to court, but the seller still has a right to charge what he wishes for his services before they are rendered. Not so in health care, where the actual burden is on the doctor to prove his innocence, and cannot react to changing conditions by passing his costs on to the customer.

So a doctor well trained and eager to care for senior citizens will now submit himself to be essentially a government contractor, with no union benefits and no additional protections afforded to other federal drones. The doctor will have to accept what he is paid, cannot adjust his prices as he sees fit, and will be subject to whatever fines, restrictions, new rules, directives, guidelines, and whims handed down by the Center for Medicare and Medicaid Services. A specialist recently told me of how Medicare has to certify an ostensibly private clinic must be "certified" every ten years, or the government will simply withhold payment. So an office that had been in practice for over three decades could not be trusted by you the taxpayer to operate up to snuff, unless the government certified it to be so. To that end Uncle Sam was withholding $180,000 *for work that was already done*, until the doctor paid for some little parasite to certify his office. In what other industry is this sort of abuse tolerated where society allows the government to essentially steal from a private citizen?

But wait, I can hear the reader say, health care is a right and as such, deserves special rules and protections. To which I say…well, the editor won't want to print it.

I reject utterly the notion that health care is a right, anymore than housing, advanced education, food, heating oil, transportation, cable TV, or comfortable shoes are "rights." To define as a "right" any good or service automatically makes a slave of those who produce that good or provide that service. That is why popular society and even academia has allowed the perversion of the original Hippocratic Oath, to serve ends for which it was never intended. That is why LBJ's evil masterstroke set seniors and their families against doctors; that physicians themselves participated in their own subjugation was just a bonus. If Medicare (and by extension it's idiot step-brother Medicaid) was such a great deal, then why all the rules and fines?

But you may ask, can't a doctor just quite Medicare if it's that lousy? The short answer is yes, but... A great many of those requiring medical services are past fifty, and an orthopedist will go broke treating hip fractures exclusively in the under-65 crowd. Similar may be said of cardiologists, ophthalmologists, internists, and so on. The government and their Vichy buddies in the AMA targeted and held a critical demographic for doctors, and a very successful voting bloc for incumbents who favor Medicare. In fact they created a monopoly, the very sort of arrangement deemed to be unfair and inefficient when practiced by AT&T and Microsoft. We consumers fat, dumb, and happy had better pray that government never discovers a "right" to cell phones or PC's. Why? Because demand will skyrocket – a right is free, after all – and with it prices. The generous provider of that right, the tax-payer, will want cost controls, which will lead to restrictions in supply, R&D, increased regulatory overhead, and soon enough, rationing. That's exactly what happened with Medicare.

Think Medicare isn't a de facto monopoly? All but a handful of private hospitals scattered across the nation accept Medicare, which means, they play by government rules. They will not grant staff privileges to any doc not in Medicare's good graces, and any emergency room or in-patient work involving someone 65 or older will go according to the government. A critical care specialist will be told (true story) by a nurse manager that, according to Medicare guidelines, the antibiotic ordered for an ICU patient is wrong. The specialist will have in hand lab cultures, hard clinical data, and years of hard-won experience to support her choice; Medicare will counter with cost tables that tell the clinician what would be most cost-effective and –here's the kicker – will refuse to pay for the patient's expensive stay unless the doc gets in line. This small-town doc of whom I speak was trying to care for a very sick patient, and then faced with a horrible choice: do what is right for the patient, and deny to the hospital money that should be paid for work legitimately done, or; support the hospital for all the other patients in need of it's care, and hope that the individual patient responds to a less-optimal antibiotic choice. Treat the patient correctly and the hospital loses; protect the hospital and community, and hope the patient survives. And don't think for a second that helpful attorneys are not lurking in the bushes outside the waiting room, with expert witnesses ready to pounce in case the patient doesn't pull through. "I was trying to support the hospital" or "Medicare made me" will be lousy defenses in court.

Physicians on the staff of a hospital accepting Medicare (again, over 99% of them) will themselves have to have offices that comply with Medicare guidelines and inspections. So can a physician refuse to accept Medicare? Sure they can, but they will likely not be able to provide inpatient care, will be financially harmed, and their reputations well suffer in the eyes of the community, and patients who cannot understand why they can no longer see their doctor. Increasingly some primary care doctors are limiting the number of Medicare (or Medicaid) patients they will see; many are quitting hospital duties altogether to be free of these restrictions, and some are even refusing to see Medicare patients in the office in order to escape the tender mercies of the government's men in black. And who suffers ultimately, but those very patients who have a "right" to health care?

The very existence of large government programs designed to disburse compassion to the citizenry is antithetical to the individual and to the concept of freedom. Some of you dear readers may yet remain unconvinced. Some of you may still think health care is a right because a hallmark of a compassionate society is that its citizens care for each other. Okay, then let us consider the view from one who has "been there, done that, and got the T-shirt." My dear friend and residency classmate Todd West has never been afraid to stir up the soup, and in 2005 he did just that. Burned out after several years of working in a multi-specialty practice, and then an urgent care clinic, he thought to take an opportunity to see the world and broaden his daughters' education. After making the proper contacts and inquiries, Todd packed up his family in the fall of '05 and headed off for a year in New Zealand to work as a primary care/ emergency room doctor in a small town short on such talent and long on scenery. They had a blast, brought back hundreds of stunning photographs of the landscape, and had great stories of a truly life-changing experience. New Zealand is of course a land of socialized medicine, where it is all "free" (which is why of course, they have to bring in doctors from overseas). What were Todd's impressions of working in the sort of health care environment to which all Democrats and too many Republicans aspire? Here, an on the spot report:

"A Dispatch from the Dark Side" (Down Under)
By Todd B. West, M.D.

"Here I am, in paradise! Not exactly. I am in fact living in a very beautiful country that I enjoy very much, but certainly not paradise. I am in the Bay of Islands of New Zealand. I came here to get away, to take a break from the ordinary, to escape the frustrations that were gnawing away at me ever since becoming a doctor, to have a chance to rest and recover from my own ambitions and decisions that didn't turn out exactly as planned, and to live surrounded by beautiful scenery and slow the pace of my life down long enough to take a deep breath.

I knew that New Zealand has a two-tier medical system and that I was taking a job working in a publicly funded healthcare system hospital. I knew that socialized medicine was the primary of the two systems and that, entering the belly of the beast, I would get a first hand look at what the future of American medicine could possibly become. I knew that my anti-socialist sentiments made me a less than ideal candidate for the job. But still I willingly came. I was puzzled and curious about what life would be like in the South Seas island country that had undergone significant social and economic reforms in the mid-eighties. And I wondered why these overwhelmingly successful results did not lead to the reversal of the socialization of medicine amidst the rising economic tide.

One of my biggest surprises was to discover that the welfare and economic reforms (referred to deridingly as Rogernomics after Roger Douglas, MP) that were enacted in the mid-eighties and appealed so to me are largely scorned by the average citizen, and looked upon with remorse even though no subsequent government has overturned this legislation to restore the previous state of affairs. The reforms that have opened New Zealand markets to the world and diversified it's economic base as well as stabilizing their currency, the reforms that thrust New Zealand ahead of the United States in economic freedoms, the reforms that reduced individual income taxes from an average of sixty-six percent to thirty percent, are thought to be a huge mistake and an embarrassment. New Zealand was in fact one of the first countries in the world to socialize medicine, and prides herself in very progressive policies concerning social and welfare reform. And yes, the average resident of New Zealand does in fact consider health care a right! So now, even though I still can't fathom why they regard economic progress as a mistake, I can at least say I have had a good exposure to what one of the best-tested socialized medical systems in the world has to offer, and what we may have to look forward to in the good old U.S. of A.

New Zealand is a small country. Barely four million people live here and most of them reside in the three major cities Auckland, Wellington, and Christchurch. The rest are spread out in rural communities and smaller cities. This in fact gives us a chance to review what a small population, with a surplus government budget, and with decades to develop, experiment, and refine their policies, can deliver in the way of government-funded medical care.

The best aspect of the system is the AAC, Accident Compensation Corporation. This is a national accident insurance company that covers all residents and visitors to New Zealand that encounter an accident of any kind whether in traffic, at home, or work related. The government-owned company is funded by payroll taxes levied upon all employed persons in the country. It completely covers all medical care and prescriptions, all inpatient as well as outpatient care, and both acute as well as continuing care or rehabilitation that may be required. It has some aspects that remind me of America's workers compensation insurance, but with much less paperwork, fewer abuses by patients (i.e. workers wanting to get out of work or collect disability), and less cost. Of course the catch in this scheme that works so well to reduce the cost of the accident coverage is the fact that all doctors are automatically indemnified from lawsuits for providing medical care to accident victims. I think that of all of the government meddling I have ever encountered in the provision of medical care this one at least works reasonably well, and makes pretty good sense as long as the provision for physician indemnification remains intact. The other catch is that the care provided is still delivered within the confines of a socialized system with limited resources (to be described in more detail below). Also as with any large bureaucracy, the check is in the mail for months on end before it finally arrives in the hands of the provider.

For any New Zealand resident that so chooses, public medical care that is free, can be supplemented with private care from private physicians and private hospitals, and which can be paid for with individual funds or with private insurance coverage. The funny thing is that when people know they can get it free if they wait a while longer, most patients tend to do so rather than pay for it themselves. Because of this apparent sentiment, private hospitals are not over-run with demand and specialty services are subsequently less available than one might expect, i.e.

supply equates to demand. Where the demand is high, as for neurology consults, even in the private system the wait can be several months long due to a cumbersome credentialing process, and a payment scheme which, combined, form a serious disincentive to come here and increase the supply. Most New Zealand trained doctors go to Australia or abroad because they can earn more money elsewhere.

So now what does demand unlinked to supply beget? For one thing it develops a good deal of patience on the part of the patient because you just can't get in a hurry to get anything done around here. At my hospital, a small twenty bed facility that is located about 70 kilometers from the next larger tertiary hospital we have very limited capabilities. After 4 P.M. during the weekdays there is no x-ray services available. Also, most of the weekend x-ray services are unavailable, or only partially available if a tech happens to be on call. Laboratory services are available only twice daily for most lab values. A courier takes specimens to the tertiary hospital lab once in the morning and once in the afternoon during the week and only once a day on the weekend. We do have the ability to do a blood gas, CBC, Troponin I, and sodium/creatinine using an iStat machine. However, the machine frequently is broken and has to be shipped out for repairs and often provides values that vary widely from the base hospital lab values, leaving me to question its accuracy. If you have the need of an ultrasound, CT Scan, Exercise Tolerance Test, Echocardiogram, or other diagnostic test it must be discussed with a consultant, and if approved the patient will be sent down for the next available appointment, which may be days away. For an angiogram the patient will have to go directly to Auckland, the only hospital within a three-hour drive that can perform that procedure. Of course there is helicopter transport when the level of acuity warrants it and when the weather or other situations do not preclude its availability. To my knowledge there is only one Neurosurgeon in the entire country and he is located in Auckland. You had better hope for no head injuries or aneurysms if you are anywhere outside of the vicinity of greater Auckland. Primary care physicians have virtually no diagnostic tests available in the office, and are restricted to diagnosing based solely upon the patient history, clinical examination, and impressions.

These primary care physicians and small hospitals do a relatively good job with uncomplicated problems or with palliative care. However, there is no national formulary and the regional formularies can be severely limited. There are often no reasonable choices within an entire class of medications, where the obvious best choice is often absent. Sometimes even the least expensive choice is completely missing from the formulary and a more expensive and less efficacious choice is substituted. A significant portion of hospitalizations for uncomplicated pneumonia, pyelonephritis, and cellulitis could be avoided if just one decent fluoroquinolone were available. Advanced diabetic and hypertensive medications are unavailable but dialysis units abound. Unlimited stroke rehabilitation is easily obtained but Plavix is absent from the formulary.

One important aspect of this system that allows it to work seems to be the indigenous cultural response, which might be found lacking in America. To state it succinctly, patient expectations are not too high and there is subsequently more acceptance of a less than optimal outcome. In other words, when certain tests or procedures that would help guide the diagnosis and treatment of patients are either postponed or are completely unavailable, I have found that this is generally accepted by the patient and their family with a certain amount of resignation. I shudder to think of what the average American consumer of healthcare would say or do, what threats of litigation would be invoked, if a diagnostic test were needed and not immediately available to the patient at any time of the day or night. That is, in my opinion, a major reason why socialized healthcare in the U.S. is slated to be an unmitigated disaster. Americans want first-rate care at a cut rate-price, NOW!!! We can either have better care or cheaper care but not both. You can't have filet mignon on a McDonald's budget. The federal government faces the prospect of delivering medical care on a limited budget to a population with an unlimited demand. That is a certain recipe for disaster.

I continue to grow in my belief that the ultimate salvation of American medicine will come from a free-market system that, like in every other aspect of the economy, will eventually deliver the best service at the best possible price. Innovation always costs more. Therefore the best care will always be a moving but ever improving target in market competition. This competition will fuel newer technologies that will become less expensive as demand provides more competition and an entrepreneurial drive to find better or cheaper ways to deliver the desired product or service. (Remember the first Sony Walkmans? Now think iPod). By continuing to turn away from the natural wins and losses of the marketplace, I fear that we as American citizens had better learn to be more resigned in our expectations, and more contented with the outcomes that will result from the care received as a consequence of the mistaken premise that healthcare is a right.

From what I have seen of the differences in U.S. and New Zealand expectations, I conclude that the present course in my homeland is leading toward a transition far more painful than its proponents can foresee."

Allow me to restate, for emphasis, the chilling line: "patient expectations are not too high and there is subsequently more acceptance of a less than optimal outcome." Is this what you would wish, or even accept for yourself or your loved one?

❊ ❊ ❊

And While We're On the Topic of Medicare...

The preceding chapter has been neither to make one an expert on Medicare, nor to serve as a be-all blueprint for taking the system down, however lovely that would be. The point is to consider health care with an eye to individual freedom, and the pitfalls to which we are all subjected when this freedom is not our highest goal. For several years I maintained a website called "Doctors For Freedom", with two or three dedicated readers and some excellent photo-shopped editorializing pictures, all rendered by yours truly. It was a fun place to rant about medical politics and since the target audience was health care professionals, the commentaries there might have been a bit "in the weeds" for the lay person. There were some good topics for the general public to consider, for instance, this piece entitled "Welcome To Medicare":

"Numbered among the more chilling phrases one might hear is "Welcome to Medicare", the greeting of Uncle Sam's forced hug welcoming you to your dependent years. Not only is admission to Medicare mandatory in order to access YOUR MONEY in a totally unrelated social security account, but it makes you a de facto supporter of a program that is bleeding productive Americans dry, even as it strangles doctors desperate to escape.

The current issue of Family Practice Management magazine features a comprehensive article on "How to Conduct a 'Welcome to Medicare' Visit." Brrr, I feel the chills.

Immediately the article notes that "you might need to reframe your thinking about what constitutes a physical exam", including "seven elements ... as much of a conversation as it is a physical exam... [to] identify modifiable risk factors." Then there is some blah-blah about planning your routine to optimize your time. Mighty helpful, but I'm betting the average clinician is already well aware of that particular requirement. The history elements therein suggested are already well known to any competent Western physician. The guide pushes screening for depression, including asking: "Over the past two weeks, have you felt down, depressed or hopeless?" and "Over the past two weeks, have you felt little interest or pleasure in doing things?" Anyone being thus welcomed will likely answer in the affirmative, is psychotic, or is dangerously non-conformist and should be treated as though psychotic.

The harried Medicare-greeter physician will be called to include a "Review of functional ability and level of safety", which can then put you on the hook for not recognizing granny's poor balance or early Alzheimer's. No problem, when she falls down after forgetting to turn the stove off, the family's friendly attorney will be most helpful, with the backing of Uncle Sam's Welcome, Etc. guidelines. The review of functional and safety, etc. includes all sorts of pertinent questions regarding the physical accoutrements and safety features which should be featured in any depend-, sorry, "beneficiary's" abode.

And on we go. Want to get an EKG? (same thing as an "ECG") "If the patient is sent to another facility for the ECG, the order must read "ECG as part of the Welcome to Medicare Physical, codes G0366-G0368. Medicare has instructed that physicians must order the ECG in a manner that helps to prevent use of codes for ECGs not related to the initial preventive physical exam." Of the 11 preventive services now authorized under Medicare Part B, "some services are covered at 100 percent of the Medicare allowable charge, and some services are covered at 80 percent, [and] some ... only if medically indicated." How should you bill for this hazy cornucopia of medical comprehensiveness? The Center for Medicare and Medicaid Services (CMS) will allow a level-one or level-two E/M code with a -25 modifier attached, or perhaps a Level-3 later on if you think that would be more appropriate. Warning intrepid Medicare doc, you had better choose wisely, lest you appear to defraud when the rules change.

Any new paperwork required? A checklist of the seven elements of the initial exam "must" be in the chart. And you are "required to give your patient a written plan for obtaining the appropriate preventive services." I always try to inject snide comments and similar humor into these commentaries, but this is just plain making me angry. Why aren't America's physicians completely insulted by this asininity? What the hell happened to our pride in our individual minds? Like the repeated bullhorn instructions in a reeducation camp, our conditioned Medicare provider is told "over time, you will become more adept at completing the initial preventive physical exam in a reasonable period."

CMS allots its servants time "equivalent to a 30-minute 99203." The auditors pace, the searchlight passes over, and the bullhorn continues: As you perfect your Welcome to Medicare exam routine, you should also refine how your office handles this new benefit before patients are even in the exam room ... Schedule the patients in a timely manner ... Perform some of the screening before the face-to-face encounter ...The initial preventive physical exam is an opportunity for you and your newly enrolled Medicare patients to start thinking about Medicare-covered preventive services." The goal for this newfound organizational acumen?? To "help physicians deliver the initial preventive physical exam in a financially sound manner."

So for all of the new opportunities to be accused by the government of fraud, for all of the responsibilities assumed to be the physician's, for all of the new hassle, anger, and unearned demands for your time and investment, what is the payoff? The exam will be paid at a rate equal to a level 3, new patient office visit, about $97, and the EKG about $28.* (*Note: this is gross, not net, and a pittance compared to rising office costs*) This should certainly encourage you to trim your overhead, but don't dare short the billing manager – you'll need her on the witness stand.

(*Both the exam and the ECG must be done for either one to be paid, and the Centers for Medicare & Medicaid Services (CMS) plans to issue relevant billing instructions. I can't wait.)"

If I have put too fine a point on it thus far, I hate Medicare and the lie upon which it was built. A terrible, deeply hurtful byproduct of this program has been its effect on the consciousness and perspective of the nation's seniors, who now equate oppositions to Medicare with hatred of the elderly. In 2006 I went on to an American Association of Retired Persons forum and posted some stern, but accurate thoughts on Medicare. The responses were, mildly put, shocking. My original post:

"Medicare is dying, as well it should. It is dying of its own weight, increasingly unsupported by the terrible philosophy from which it rose.

The "greatest" generation, having beaten totalitarianism overseas, then returned home to ensure its continuance here. Today's seniors voted themselves a huge benefit that they never earned and could never pay for. The Medicare program was so ill-conceived that is was financially unsustainable within 5 YEARS of beginning, requiring increased funding and deficit spending ever since. The inflation in medical prices from Medicare and its idiot stepbrother Medicaid have led to medical price inflation which:

(1) Increases the cost of private insurance, making it harder for people to afford, so...

(2) More people end up on the rolls of government assistance, increasing the demand for these programs in a vicious cycle

(3) Scared by reduced pay and increased government harassment, more doctors yearly flee the program or retire, while fewer students are interested in medical careers.

(4) The nation's total debt continues to skyrocket - this will have to be dealt with and paid for by the grandchildren of the wealthiest generation, American seniors, in world history.

This program is dragging us into full-blown socialization, a guarantee for permanent mediocrity. Freedom-loving Americans should oppose this and seek to return to honest medical care, where the services - AND PAYMENT - is between the doctor and patient, without the interference of a government check. We can have excellence in health care, or we can have it for "free", but we can't have both. www.DoctorsForFreedom.com"

Here were the unedited responses:

"I would suppose you'd like for us who depend upon it, and who's lives have been saved by Medicare benefits to die also?

"You are a selfish human being, and if you are a doctor, God help your patients"

"Ya just gotta love these folks who have a political philosophy consisting of "I've got mine, so the rest of you". It's reminiscent of Hyenas and other dog eat dog critters, but fortunately, as civilized human beings we can make the choice to lend a helping hand to the needy and lesser among us. This is the route we have chosen to take in America despite those who wouldn't mind watching the helpless and elderly die for want of a little help. It speaks volumes about BOTH, no?"

"The elderly–Eskimos used to sit on an iceberg and drift away rather than be a burden on the younger folks. The icebergs aren't there any longer in great enough numbers for that so —what do you propose to do with all old people now?   Put them in a pasture and shoot them like some do to old horses?"

"This country that can give ISRAEL a trillion dollars since the 1970's and the country of IRAQ will cost a trillion dollars before all said and done— and that's just a SAMPLE of our generosity— - I think the USA can do more for their OWN people than kick them in the butt. Seniors are the ONLY reason you are even here today— and SAVED this country for you taking it through wars and depressions."

"Methinks Dr Freedom should lose his medical license and forbidden to practice medicine furthermore....... if he does have a license.

"Or maybe there should be a firing squad for anyone over 65 who gets sick or requires medical attention, especially for those who are not wealthy enough to help these greedy doctors to make the payments on their BMW's."

"I owe my life to Medicare......3 life saving operations that I couldn't afford, costing up in the tens of thousands...you would have me dead according to your post, which fits in with gist of your posts."

"If you are indeed a doctor, then by your charging exorbitant fees, you, yourself are responsible for the high costs of medicine, yet you blame it on Medicare."

"And by your posts, it indicates the inhumane feeling you must have for your patients, caring only for the fees they can pay. Tell me this, why should a doctor charge $175 for a less than a 15 minute visit for a throat infection, where all he did was prescribe anti-biotics and an OTC decongestant?"

"You are the problem, not Medicare. It is the cold hearted doctors."

"What is your purpose in posting this here, if not to raise anger? Like MamAndMam posted, you need to take this to a 20's something board and quit drumming up high blood pressure business on a forum like this."

"Payment between Doctor and Patient, that's your gripe with Medicare. Your entire protest is based on the fact Medicare will not allow you to rip off your patients with exorbitant office visit and other medical procedure fees."

"My suggestion is that if you are not making enough, that you switch to another occupation and quit complaining.... a used car salesman or insurance salesman comes to mind as useful outlets for your talents."

"It's not cold-hearted doctors that is the problem, but a doctor that goes on a senior's forum and denigrate the program that keeps most of us alive. And if you think it's free Mister, you are wrong...we pay dearly for it each month, plus the co-pay amount. We all aren't exactly on the millionaires list."

"BTW you offer $35 office visits and the world will beat a path to your door step" [I responded with a post that my friend Todd had indeed begun a cash-only clinic, and charged $35/visit, was seeing over 10% of his county in less than two years. In fact they were beating a path to his door. Todd took now private insurance and, to escape government interference, refused from Day 1 to see Medicare patients]

"Dr Freedom seems to want to be free from criticism so he can roll in all the dough he wants."

"The website you provided has to be a joke"

I posted a response that said, "No one's life is automatically worth more because they are elderly, or infirm, yet that is the underlying premise of this cruel program." And then got this gem of a response:

"When you are old, on your death bed and in real pain .... I hope someone sends these kind words back to you."

"From that statement and the link posted in your original post, it seems that you are self serving and have no thought for those who are not independently wealthy.

Please don't respond to me again, as I believe you don't have the interests of the public as a whole at heart, only your own interests which you are trying to persuade us to subscribe"

And last but not least...

"If I could point to only one flaw in our medical system I would point to the fact that the current system of medical schooling is set up to limit the number of doctors. People go to medical school expecting to become rich.
We should have medical schooling available to ALL who are qualified to learn and not limit the number of doctors the way we do now. Doctors should not expect to become rich. That would bring the cost of healthcare down.

"Dr. Freedom,
You said: "Where we disagree, I think, is that the economic point is separate from the humanistic point." Yes,

indeed we do disagree. I think that people are so utterly unique, so valuable that they are, each and every one of them, "priceless". I believe every human ever living a life on this planet, from beginning to now, was here for purposes each individual, himself or herself, decided before they schmooshed themselves into a physical body to function on this dense, heavy planet. So, "economic" has absolutely nothing to do with it. Evolution is the name of the game, and that deals with intangibles, spiritual issues and the "real" us, which is not a physical body at all.

You said: "slaves are separated from the economic rewards of their efforts, and are thereby devalued as individuals worthy of compassion and respect."

I could not disagree harder or more! Those slaves are the ancestors of people on this planet today who are so valuable you could not count enough zeros to write out their worth in dollars! What is more, thanks to DNA, we are discovering there is no "pure" race, and by and large, everyone is a little of everything! Slaves separated from economic rewards of their efforts are not devalued as individuals! The fact that they were slaves has nothing to do with their worth! It has everything to do with the utterly flawed SYSTEM - not the individuals! In fact, in the face of something as degrading as slavery, I think those men and women so inspired and so exemplified courage as to INCREASE their value in the intangibles that count! Why, I'm not even a Christian, but I would be incensed if I was. Jesus was not a wealthy man - he depended upon others to support him, did he not? You may wish to rephrase this slaves separated from economic rewards devaluing them as individuals idea!

You said: "in a system of finite resources - would you deal with those who over-consume i.e. take more than their fair share?" Unless you are God, you cannot define "fair share" any more than I can. How about thinking about it in a startlingly new way?

How about giving to each, as they NEED. If you need less, good for you. If you need more, why and where is it decreed that you should not need more? If we want a kinder, gentler world, your ideas will surely not get us there. I do not mind giving more to those who need more and less to those who need less. I'm sorry that you do.

What is more, I disagree that we have finite resources. We may not have in place ways to DISTRIBUTE resources, but it is not a case of "grab it quick before it runs out"! This world has supported life of such diversity it boggles the mind, for billions of years. Our resources are not finite. Actually, WE are the ones who are finite! We only stay here a short time, and then we depart! If we think oil is running out, we have choices and options of other energy sources that CANNOT "run out". We are never without choices.

You said: "In a "one world that cares" model, is any line ever drawn to say no?" and I don't understand your question. In a "one world that cares" model, what line COULD be drawn? And why would anyone want to deny another who needs anything?

Bottom line, right now, all too often, money is the unit of value used to define people. It is one of the primary pieces of evidence that we are still a very primitive species. It does not have to be that way, but until people can

(1) see that it doesn't have to be that way; and (2) then decide to change it, it will continue in full force and effect.

What if we are drastically shortchanging ourselves by insisting that money dominates everything? Because I think that's just what we are doing. Every human is so much MORE than we are normally led to believe. SO MUCH MORE. Why, if we tried to pay for the value of just one of us, there wouldn't be enough money in the whole world to equal that value!

Thistle"

I don't smoke pot, nor imbibe other illegal substances, so I had a tough time processing Thistle's amazing essay. Tezon Blanco is delicious high-end tequila, poured from a fetching bottle with volcanic rock stopper, and imparting flavors of citrus and black pepper. Several generous glasses of this delicious diversion however, while allowing me a good night's sleep, did not make so much as a dent in trying to understand the other-worldly, karmic consciousness contained therein. If anyone could have divined the nonsense in John Lennon's classic "Imagine", I'm sure Thistle could.

❖ ❖ ❖

Undeterred, I continued to have fun jabbing big government's hug for Fred and Ethyl. Before Sarah Palin ever heard the term "death panels", there was a case to be made that economics could not be wished away...

A New Fountain of Youth

"We have an aging problem in this country, which is to say, the average age of the average American is increasing, or in the popular parlance, the population is "graying." People are living longer – how on earth could this be a bad thing?

A brilliant British sitcom from the 1980's, "Yes Prime Minister", broached the topic and its perils. In untangling the lines of cronyism surrounding the tobacco lobby, the argument is successfully fleshed that a ban nationwide ban on smoking would not only cut tax revenues, but increase average life expectancy, along with the monies paid to old age pensioners, all of which would leave Her Majesty's government strapped. A government disposed to care for both the health, and the additional social welfare of its citizenry has a vested interest in – ahem – encouraging expedient living. The episode culminates with a chain-smoking, cough-wracked former tobacco lobbyist being named Minister of Health.

The "American Medical News" tells of study results from following the attitudes of 20,000 Americans ages 54 – 71, since 1992. The cohort was divided into four parts, proposed to measure the self-reported health in each sub-group. Researchers were surprised to find that the 45-59 year-old "youngest group reported having more pain, chronic health conditions, drinking and psychiatric problems than did people at that age about a decade earlier." Apparently the younger Boomers complain more of daily physical tasks such as climbing stairs and standing up from a chair. The story quotes possible causative factors. While obesity and the perils of a sedentary lifestyle are mentioned, greater weight is given to the emotional vector. Increased health expectations, growing intolerance of poor health, and a decline of stoicism are all cited (any primary care doctor who has had to deal with the cholesterol fears of a hand-wringing 65 year-old marathon runner will acknowledge this last bit). It would be redundant to add "neurotic" to the Boomer descriptors.

And a new industry has sprung forth to accommodate history's most grasping generation (though to be fair, they did churn out the best music). The CNN Health site tells us of the growing trend in patients seeking anti-aging therapy, and the obliging doctors willing to provide such. Founded in 1993, the American Academy of Anti-Aging Medicine (A4M) accounts for "19,000 members in 90 countries", and anti-aging products now comprise a "$45.5 billion industry growing nearly 10 percent a year." Biochips, total body scanning, and microscopic nanobots are all hawked.

A4M is "dedicated to educating physicians, scientists, and members of the public on anti-aging issues... that the human life span can be increased, and the quality of one's life improved as one grows chronologically older." The group is clear that it does not "promote or endorse any specific treatment nor does it sell or endorse any commercial product." Their site also contains the interesting objectives: "Assist in the funding and promotion of critical anti-aging, clinically based research. Government outreach, education, and advocacy for anti-aging medicine." Funding? Government outreach?? This is starting to become worrisome. If nervous ex-hippies want to gobble handfuls of Coenzyme Q10 and seaweed extract, or buy disposable do-it-your-self colonoscopy robots that transmit the images to the gastro guy in the office, then be my guest. But let the latest crop of presidential wannabes get hold of this and get ready for Medicare Part E. The fiscal health of our nation, and the bottom lines of doctors depending on government payments are at serious risk.

But there may be a way out. An excellent letter from David Wells, MD in this month's Family Practice Management magazine (http://www.aafp.org/fpm/20070400/letters.html) points out that the initial Medicare screening ultrasound for abdominal aortic aneurysms is limited to patients age 65-75; who have smoked at least 100 cigarettes (that is hilarious on its face). But the catch is that this benefit is part of the "Welcome to Medicare" physical which must be completed in the first 6 months of Medicare eligibility. Dr. Wells astutely notes that the only patients eligible for this screening would by definition be aged 65-65½ years old. So the government has creatively relieved the taxpayer of paying for all those needless screenings for those older than 66. Most aortic aneurysms don't blow, and if they do, the expenses after that are pretty limited.

One of the researchers in the AMNews article said "I think it's rising expectations and the greater use of health care services. The more you see a physician, the more you are likely to find a problem of some sort."

Exactly. As it stands anti-aging medicine is a lose-lose proposition, where the taxpayer and doctor take a bath, while the early elderly get madder and more anxious. We have a generation predisposed to find problems shrugged off in earlier years, for which a new industry has been developed. And this industry poses a double threat to our economy, and our physicians' incomes. If this anti-aging stuff actually works, Medicare recipients will be living even farther beyond their willingness to pay for themselves, and will drive us further into bankruptcy. As the elderly clientele grows it will find new and more frequent reasons to see the doctor, which, under the terms of the Sustainable Growth Rate alchemy, will accelerate the drop in physician's incomes. It may be that the only way out is to preemptively declare anti-aging visits, treatments, etc. to be guaranteed Medicare benefits. Doing this will cause a rush amongst the legions of anxious Boomers to get the latest Methuselah regimens, which will then drive up the price of anti-aging specialist visits, and their prescriptions; Medicare will have to contain costs, and will be forced to curtail anti-aging reimbursements. Devices such as making anti-aging treatments part of the "Welcome to Medicare" package would curtail some of the loose spending. The NIH or VA could even gin up a study or two to demonstrate that if the anti-aging stuff isn't begun by age 66, it would neither significantly increase longevity, nor prove cost effective. The anti-aging docs will lose money and move on to other lines of work, and the beneficiaries can return to their government-approved life spans. Can you imagine the traffic jams in Arizona and south Florida if we don't nip this in the bud?"

Three years before the first of the Boomers became Medicare-eligible, a crisis was already apparent. Before President Obama had been taught the phrase "shovel-ready", and before the '08 real estate crash and recession, we already had crushing entitlement debt for elderly health care that has only accelerated. Ever an optimist, I offered a workable solution to protect the promise to our seniors...

The New Reservation (Where are the slot machines?)

"What to do about the deepening crisis of Medicare? Access to doctors is dropping for seniors, as not coincidentally, payment is declining for those very doctors to care for the elderly. The population is "graying", which is to say that the average age is on the rise, as more Americans will soon be enjoying their golden years. What to do?

Inspiration comes from a letter by Harry Neuwirth, MD in the American Medical News (4/16). While considering the effects of moving more seniors into Medicare-HMO's, Dr. Neuwirth succinctly describes the breakpoint: "We cannot realistically expect that doctors will continue to provide services as Medicare payments lose ground to office expenses or that taxpayers will agree to foot the bills for our increasingly strident and populous gerontocracy...It is therefore time for the rest of us (non HMO providers) to begin a graceful exit from the Medicare system. Next year's anticipated 9.9% cut undoubtedly will be partially mitigated and can be made up by transitioning from participating to non-participating status come Jan 08. The next 12 months will be well spent in restructuring our offices so that we can dramatically limit our exposure to Medicare or completely resign as Medicare providers come 2009." We have a rapidly increasing demand for senior medical care, dwindling financial resources to pay for that care, and what can only be described as political dementia in our politicians' approach to solutions. Dr. Neuwirth is to be commended for his use of the wonderfully apt term "gerontocracy", which sums up these political obstacles to any serious solution.

Sometimes the solution to a problem lies not in resisting unwelcome circumstances, but in rolling with them. The federal government cannot actually solve the Medicare problem, so they must instead devise a "solution" and for this they already have a framework. When faced with the burden of displaced native populations, the feds created reservations to care for the American Indian.

When inner city poverty ruffled the national sensibilities, kindly Uncle Sam developed urban ghettos for the disadvantaged locals. A way to "solve" the Medicare crisis is to embrace what the program began: the elderly were marginalized from the medical marketplace by making them a client population of the government, while still setting policy as if they were actual consumers. This led to price inflation, cost overruns, shortages, and all the rest. What is required now is to complete the process and move grandma and grandpa on to the medical reservation. The federal government could establish a national network of exclusive Medicare clinics, staffed by hired Medicare-only providers to care for the elderly and thus fulfill the program's primary mission.

With the enormous Medicare bureaucracy already in place the transition would be relatively simple. Use agents from the Centers for Medicare and Medicaid Services to purchase existing clinics for use as exclusive medical homes for the elderly. With the number of primary care doctors going out of business or living on the edge, this should be easy. The next critical phase is to stimulate demand among physicians by making Medicare attractive again. The only way to accomplish this is to make being a provider financially attractive once again. Newly (re)acquired Medicare doctors must be paid well, thus encouraging competition among U.S.-trained FP's and internists to care for the elderly. Recognizing Medicare as the charity population it is might also serve as the logical justification to carve out reduced-tax zones, or give lawsuit indemnity protections a' la sovereign immunity. With the prospect of making say, $200K, the new Medicare clinics would have no problem filling all of their staff positions in short order. Once the buildings are procured and staffed, all that remains is to open the doors. Administrative costs could be streamlined by confining meddlesome audits, inspectors, and directives by only accepting Medicare patients (why should the taxpayer pay for filing their supplementals?)

A critical point of this new approach is that once the new Medicare clinic network opens, no other private clinic may see a Medicare patient under any circumstances. Hospitals and their emergency departments will still toil along under the same conditions. Once the new Medicare clinic network up and running, it will be a simple manner for the government to declare success and co-opt some out-patient surgery centers along the same lines (it will also be more palatable to use happy primary Medicare providers to give a PR counterbalance to specialists upset over the loss of their investment potential).

The Medicare Trustees and Congressional Budget Office both report comparable figures: Medicare expenditures will DOUBLE by 2030, while the worker: beneficiary ration will decline by over 30%. And last week, the Medicare Trustees reported that for the first time ever, Medicare was funded over 45% by NON-Medicare revenue in consecutive years. And the Baby Boomers – soon to hit dependent status – make up nearly a third of the population. To sum up, we cannot afford this stupid program now, and when the Boomers enter their golden years, well…

A medical reservation for seniors can provide immediate economic benefits. It can help the government get a handle on spending, uh "cost control", by having the oldies queue like everyone else. The AMA will have less to complain about, as the perennial Sustainable Growth Rate complaints will be rendered moot. The AAFP will love that seniors appear to have a medical "home", and electronic health record vendors can all vie for fat government contracts. Politicians of all stripes can claim not only that Medicare was "saved", but also that it now delivers modern, more efficient care. Private doctors can get behind the concept too. Sure, they'll lose some Medicare concession, but they could also lose the additional administrative overhead burdens and fear of prosecution that come with the privilege of serving the elderly. The medical reservation can economically segregate the aged from the rest of a society desperately seeking to slow medical cost inflation - a fire break dug while we load up the HSA's and pharmaceutical research in the pickup. Granted the wait times for appointments at the Medicare-only clinics will lengthen to months, but this can be sold to the seniors as better than having no access at all.

So can our new "medical reservation for the elderly" provide care for all of our deserving seniors? Of course not! But neither can Medicare, and the medical reservation can provide what Medicare now fails to deliver: good PR. The real purpose for Medicare is not really to cover all the elderly, but to appear to, much as the TSA appears to provide safe air travel. The medical reservation can give politicians and their organized medicine lapdogs a new way to extol the virtues of government compassion in the same sort of way that a former communist superpower used to brag about crop harvest projections. Socialist democrats and spineless Republicans can use video shots of happy seniors entering bright shiny new clinics for their "free" care, and run nifty commercials about all the new wellness benefits along the lines of the taxpayer-funded Medicare D rah-rah spots. They can film those same lucky beneficiaries exiting the building, happy to have received comprehensive care in a modern facility from cheerful American-trained doctors. (naturally the government will want to keep the camera off the growing lines in ER waiting rooms). Of course the AARP will have to be brought to heal, but they can be bought off with some goodies for their leaders, more meaningless promises for Social Security, or maybe some early bird special coupons. To actually provide bumper-to-bumper medical coverage from the government for the nation's elderly, the original intent for Medicare, was never really possible. The program is insolvent, and everyone from Families, USA and AARP all the way to the GOP knows it. The only practical purpose for Medicare now is to placate elderly and pre-elderly voters. Getting the shuffleboard set on to their very own medical reservation may at least achieve that lofty goal."

In the years since this was originally written, the Boomers have begun to hit 65 and dependency, the Obama health care initiative was both supported and castigated by the oldies, our annual deficit has more than doubled, and our national debt has skyrocketed. And still every year Congress has to enact emergency measures to halt radical, programmed cuts to doctors' Medicare payments to prevent a collapse of the whole system. The money will get ever tighter, the lines will grow longer, and any physician new to the game or still in it may expect the penalties for providing taxpayer-funded compassion to grow as well.

❧ ❧ ❧

When Care Ain't Primary

We have all heard a lot in the news these past few years about the necessity, magic, cost benefits, and all around sense of "primary care." By primary care we loosely refer to family practitioners, internists, pediatricians, and depending on who s defining, OB/ GYN's and ER doctors. In short, we mean the docs who see you for a problem first. I know a little bit about the field. I thought the entire concept made sense, and that it would be a fun and not too difficult way to practice medicine. The rewards are a wide spectrum of systems, disease processes, and people within which to practice. The downside is that the primary care doc is almost never the final expert for a great many conditions that require referrals to cardiologists, orthopedists, endocrinologists, psychiatrists, or social workers. The pay is less, but the hours are generally better, and the training track while strenuous enough, is admittedly far easier than the death march of a surgical residency. I was excited to graduate from medical school and begin working at a well-respected family practice, where I received excellent training. The work included extensive patient contact both in the clinic and in the hospital, and after the first year I supplemented my income and training with extensive work in urgent care clinics after hours, and later, in local small town emergency rooms. After graduating from the 3-year program, I went into private practice with a classmate from residency, and continued to moonlight in emergency rooms while we got the clinic up and running.

There is a lot that makes sense about primary care, and patients by and large love having easy, reliable access to their primary care doctors. Most ailments, boo-boos, and conditions can be handled quite well by a good family practice or internal medicine generalist. Throughout the 1990's while I did my medical training, politicians on both sides extolled the virtues, values, and benefits of a robust primary care workforce as the backbone of health care. And being politicians, they had no clue why primary care after the late Nineties began to drop sharply in popu-

larity among those providing it, and among those trying to decide which field to enter.

You Can Still have a Bullet to Bite (If It's Pre-Authorized)

"John Wayne's last role, that of a gunslinger dying of cancer in <u>The Shootist</u>, also featured Jimmy Stewart playing a crotchety old country doc who delivers the bad news. He recognizes in the gunfighter a scared man who needs the reassurance of the facts and a sympathetic hand as he walks the dark road. Perhaps more than any other specialty, family docs always seem to have been attracted to that pursuit by the chance to extend the personal touch tempered with common sense to a person in need. Of course the movie was grossly inaccurate by modern standards: before Jimmy could examine The Duke, he would have to advise him of his privacy rights, and then have him sign an Advance Beneficiary Notice if he were a Medicare patient, or otherwise verify his insurance. The doc would have a girl tied up on the telegraph in the other room verifying insurance, and another girl would be in a side office getting an earful from the blacksmith about how he got his statement back on the evening stage which showed the doctor had grossly overcharged him, and that the charge for the whiskey and bullet to bite on was not covered by his plan. When prescribing some rudimentary painkiller, the doc would need to get back on the telegraph to find out whether that was on the Retired Gunfighters' Group Plan Plus formulary list, check with the local apothecary to make sure The Duke wasn't getting dope from the local tribe's medicine man, and weigh whether this treatment would raise suspicions sufficient for the Drug Enforcement Agency, Western Territories Branch, to direct the boys in F-Troop to seize the office records. And even though The Duke was dying of cancer, Lauren Bacall would have been able to sue the pocket watch and carriage off of Jimmy Stewart if he didn't also check and document Wayne's cholesterol, prostate, and warn against the dangers of smoking.

Primary care in this country appears to be changing rapidly, both in its accessibility to patients and its appeal to practitioners. Family doc's and general internists constitute the body of primary care, including most clinic care and most hospital admissions. This is the group that takes care of a kid's sore throat, treats his sister for anxiety, and admits their grandma to the hospital for pneumonia. A recent online poll in <u>Medical Economics</u> magazine reported that a whopping 73% of respondents are "sorry" they went into primary care. And two years ago only 47% of new family practice residents graduated from U.S. medical schools (and applications to U.S. medical schools dropped 6%). When I began medical training in 1992, the Clintons and legions of concerned do-gooders were all pushing "Primary Care" as the wave of the future, whose "gate-keeper" practitioners would essentially control health care access for the betterment of all.

The Numbing Nineties proved interesting in the evolution of health care. The HMO/gatekeeper model of primary care that attracted many physicians and promised to save health dollars, is now discouraging and scaring away many physicians by saving dollars from those earning them. A national survey of physicians find family doc's paying an average of 57% overhead, and the Merritt Hawkins research firm finds their average salaries have not kept pace with inflation (3% increase over the past 3 years, 2000-2002). A legion of newer, better drugs became available, "MRI" became common parlance, and "legal settlement" became a viable alternative to honest work for enough plaintiff-patients to drive malpractice sky-high. In the course of trying to research how much the prevalence of malpractice suits has risen in Florida, I have encountered opposing arguments from insurance groups, physician organizations, and concerned "patient advocate" groups, all trying to point the finger of blame away from themselves to explain rising malpractice costs. But the facts are that malpractice costs are rising in Florida to the point that many physicians working on the margin must choose between ever-decreasing income, going "bare" (doing without), or simply closing up shop. And after examining my own recent malpractice premiums, I can assure you dear reader that the increased cost of malpractice insurance is very real, and very painful to absorb.

Insurance reimbursement payments i.e. what the doc begs to receive for work already done, have flat-lined and even those often seem curiously delayed (but just try delaying the paycheck for your employees the same way). Complaints of any level of severity from patients can bring swift retribution from a state Board of Medicine whose judicial temperament would have done the Spanish Inquisition proud. The Feds have now invented an entirely new "privacy" industry with which to invade offices and the lives of private citizens, and there will be increased pressures for physician audits for "fraud", what with the impending implosion of Medicare. Physicians cannot legally write off losses attributable to patients who won't pay their bill, while those same patients may still sue with abandon. Overhead in every facet is rising, while profits are dropping.

Ok, I hear some of you in the back row: "Martha, he's just another rich doctor whining about not making enough!" Certainly not. Fewer, less competitively-selected physicians will be available to care for growing numbers of patients, and care will suffer due to decreases in access and excellence. The simple fact is that none of us can expect physicians to act independently of market forces. I leave you with a quote from a colleague's letter published in the AMA News: "With declining reimbursement and physician income and increasing responsibilities…it is no longer worth it to many of us to always be available to our patients…The world is changing and medicine will change along with it. The old days are gone, so we should stop whining about how good they were." Sounds like advice a crotchety old doc might have given to an aging gunfighter."

By now, if you are wondering whether I am anti-primary care, then allow me to reiterate: primary care as an academic discipline, and as a way to care for patients, makes sense. But it has been used by third party payers, private insurance and the government, to "control costs", with unfortunate and predictable results. Around about 2005, the state of primary care was bleaker still…

Primary Care CAN Work – If It Serves Itself

"This year a physician on staff at our hospital retired, after practicing well over half a century in our small Gulf Coast town. This gentleman has lived the life and practiced the art that exemplified the very best to which generalist family medicine has aspired. In his earlier days he rode his motorcycle through wooded paths to perform emergent amputations at sawmills, delivered babies and performed appendectomies, and was the sole reliable source of medical care for many years. Past his eightieth birthday he renewed his family medicine board certification yet again, and has imparted the very finest example of professional excellence, courtliness, and personal equanimity to his far less-experienced colleagues. There are few of the old-school generalists left in practice, and fewer still able to practice in the capacity for which they had trained. A friend and I who went through training together were musing on that very point, and on how today's family doctors differ from our generalist forbears. It seems hard to dispute that the old country doctors prior to the suburbanization of America were far more capable in the ways that matter most, of delivering care to their patients. Whereas today's family practitioners have a vastly superior pharmacological and imaging armamentarium from which to draw, we have simultaneously diminished in our ability to rapidly intervene, diagnose, treat, and reassure. This is based largely on fear.

Today's FP doc, more than any other colleague of another specialty, walks in a landscape sculpted increasingly more from negative incentives than from positive ones. A budding family practice resident is taught about the intricacies of in-patient adult medicine with its intellectual challenges, excitements, and opportunities for procedural interventions. But out of residency, many will find these skills, if used, to be a greater threat than benefit. The hospital-going family doc will have not only the inconveniences of call, but will have to submit to hospital by-laws, contracts, and turf wars which will more often than not intrude directly into his private office practice. A hospital presence will ensure a wider variety of experiences, and increase the probability of new legal experiences as the FP who takes call increases his potential malpractice footprint, along with increased hospital-mandated coverage which will be chum in the water for circling plaintiff attorneys.

The 21st century family physician will still care about his work, and will take joy in care well delivered. But it will not be enough. We are now all too familiar with the office fears our intrepid clinician will face. He will contend with a steadily rising overhead, from employee benefits to malpractice premiums, from mandated HIPAA compliance, to delayed third-party payments and the ongoing threat of audits. The new FP will lace up his running shoes and jump on the treadmill, trying like hell to live up to the edicts of his residency, organized medicine, the government, and a society which all continue to promise him stability if he will only work a little harder to eke out a profit margin. He will learn to keep a running comparison of average cost per visit with average reimbursement per visit, and he will learn to turf the unprofitable complaints quickly away, or else he will founder. Throughout medical training, our family doc has sacrificed time and treasure for years – the temporary loss of control over his daily life – in order to achieve a greater long-term goal. At the other end he will expect to regain in great measure, control over the course of his life. It will be a bitter lesson when he finds that, in both the hospital and office environments, he will continue to sacrifice the greater portion of his professional autonomy in hopes of preserving a decent income in the face of a tightening economic noose.

A declining interest in primary care among U.S. medical students tells the tale as - SURPRISE - financial disincentives encourage them to use their brains in more profitable ways. The America Academy of Family Practice trotted out a "Future of Family Medicine Project", which confirmed the very worst assumptions underlying this dying specialty, showing a degree of denial that would make a crystal meth addict blush. Their platitudinous prescriptions for a "team approach", a "basket of services", and "elimination of barriers" are so much chin music to teach stressed FP's to shine their beggin' bowls a little brighter, and darn it, try to buck up and work a little harder. What is the future of family medicine? Low pay, frustration, a haven for foreign medical graduates, and a willing cadre being shaped to support the complete socialization of U.S. health care as a way to pay their bills.

But it need not be so. The specialty of Family Medicine (and indeed primary care) can be saved and here is how:

1. Adapt scope of practice to one's environment. New family practitioners must leave training assuming that they will have a tough go early on, and be ready to adapt their practice styles or type of work to their local medical landscape. A boutique clinic in an affluent area makes sense, but a low cost cash-only might flourish better in a small town.

2. Establish financial autonomy from the start. **Today's new family practitioner should accept as a condition of opening a clinic that it will fly or fail on a cash-only basis.** To be financially viable, new family docs must seriously consider "going bare" without malpractice insurance as a pre-condition to opening a practice.

3. Minimize regulatory interference. By refusing to accept any third party money (especially the government's!), overhead may be dramatically reduced, along with patient wait times, and customer satisfaction improved. The sustainable family practice should be able to greet any government auditor at the door with a smile and refuse them admittance with complete confidence.

4. Return honesty to the physician-patient relationship. Coding, adjusting, re-submitting, and discounting are all fundamentally dishonest practices. Treating a common complaint should cost the same, and command the same respect for the customer no matter what his insurance status.

5. Recognize and celebrate the original philosophy of medicine, that places the autonomy of the patient and the physician as equals, above all else.

Today the AAFP and American Board of Family Medcinine, seek to mold family doctors into a mindset instead of encouraging innovation. When family doc's complained of more interference, the AAFP suggested electronic "interoperability" to speed up that intrusion. When FP's lamented shrinking paychecks, the ABFM gave them more mandatory certification testing, that would not increase their worth to clients. NONE of this should encourage any intelligent medical student to choose family medicine.

Showing family medicine to be a specialty that celebrates individual autonomy, innovation, and true sustainability is the way to use positive incentive rather than fear, to resuscitate this waning profession."

The parlance on the cable news shows is now "Pay For Performance" for teachers and cops. That is fine with me, as these are government employees and we taxpayers should be able to hold them to account. Note how easily however, it was for the government and its organized medicine lapdogs to treat primary care doctors as government workers with the same mechanism...

One Big Con

"Whether one is selling hamburgers, computers, insurance, or medical care, capitalism is the most moral, and therefore the most fair, option available each and every time. When I plunk down extra bucks for a good steak or an imported cigar, I am acting in full support of better pay for better quality. On the surface, the trendy Pay-For-Performance (P4P) wave sweeping Congress and organized medicine seems to conform to this standard of value-for-value, thriving in a competitive marketplace of rising quality and availability. And who could argue with that? But as with most great movements that are contrived (as opposed to those which evolve), there are a couple of irritating little problems with this latest savior of modern medicine. Under the surface of the P4P solution is a nagging little implication. We are told that to get the benefits – i.e. MONEY – of meeting P4P standards, physicians must meet set management goals scientifically shown to be the best for managing chronic conditions. So any physician meeting the standard of care would get a cash register 'A', right? Therefore it follows that anyone not meeting the standard of care (and the lawyers will surely interpret this as the standard of care) will get a less than perfect score, manifested in less than perfect payments. But wouldn't every physician seek to meet the standard of care irrespective of payment, and according to his best judgment, in each case? Old Hippocrates gets a little inconvenient in the face of P4P, and the negative implication is staggering. AMA Board of trustees Chair Duane Cady, MD states that there is "no debating the rightness of the position" of P4P, and extols the ethics of programs that "link evidence-based performance measures to financial incentives." Again, doesn't the classical Oath of Hippocrates require "best judgment" once a physician elects to contract with a patient? Free-market capitalism is always the best and requires no apologies; but isn't its logic perverted when it is used as a substitution, rather than an adjunct, for a physician's judgment? And isn't the implication from the purveyors of P4P that one will only do their best when paid for it? Where were these guys over the past decade when excellence was expected for seniors despite falling Medicare reimbursements? Why wasn't better pay linked with higher quality care then??

Here's why: because as any honest physician bloody well knows, this whole damn fashion show is designed to PAY DOCTORS LESS! Joel Finklestein reports in AMNEWS that health care costs are projected to keep rising at 8.2%, having leveled off rather than dropped as predicted in 2003. Well no wonder. More dependents are being created daily thanks to Medicaid; more seniors are living longer, and fixin' to get free drugs for voting the right way in '04; and humanity's most grasping generation, the Boomers, is ready to round the corner to and embrace full seniority and all the freebees. Based solely on demographics or only on inflation – and we are going to super size that combo – health care spending will continue to skyrocket. And with it the budgetary pressures will continue to build on spineless legislators to wring "fraud, waste, and abuse" out of hapless doctors who bought into this dishonest P4P scam.

And where are the guardians and protectors of all that is right and good in western medicine? Organized medicine is being led by the AMA and American Academy of Family Practice to an acceptance in principle of P4P, which will soon lead to an enthusiastic embrace quicker than you can spell "Vichy." Organized medicine will fight for a change in payment formulae, and is trying to wheedle Uncle Sam out of computer money to be more compliant with the office invasion yet to come. But once the basic idea of P4P is accepted, a great many doctors will expect more money and practice as they always have, to the best of their ability. Then they will be paid less, or have to justify being paid correctly via more audits, forms, and other onerous efforts (extra work for which they will NOT be paid). The budget will continue to explode under the compassion of government-supplied care. More doctors will face charges of fraud, fewer will take Medicare/Medicaid, and the whole wreck will wheeze closer and closer to full nationalization. Then America's patients will really get to see what performance based on pay feels like.

P4P Continued...

The stupid application of P4P as a way to cheat honest doctors was highlighted in 2006. And it took a nurse to point it out. First the prestigious **Duke University** closed their Family Practice residency program even as the cover of the 6/19/06 "American Medical News" sported the headline "Primary Care Doctors in Demand." Later in the same AMNews issue is an article titled "Study confirms shortage of critical care doctors." This piece stated "not enough young physicians are willing to take on the long, demanding hours of a critical care doctor." Their source clues us in to a report that claims "lifestyle and reimbursement as the biggest barriers to boosting medical resident's interest in the subspecialty." [THIS COMMENTARY WILL NOW PAUSE FOR 30 SECONDS TO ALLOW YOU TO PICK YOURSELF UP OFF THE FLOOR AFTER THIS STUNNING REVELATION]. The article recommends a two-fold improvement: increasing the supply of critical care docs by improving pay and loan forgiveness offers; expanding the J-1 via waivers to allow more foreign doctors to practice in underserved areas."

The June, 2006 Medical Economics magazine article by Ken Karpay called "Drop That Mug, Doc" tells of the 15 or more states who legislatures are getting upset about doctors receiving pens and coffee mugs from pharmaceutical reps – what is referred to as "marketing" in every other sector of the economy. He quotes Massachusetts state senator Mark Montigny who equates Caribbean vacations and free pens as equally dangerous to in there ability to warp weak-minded doctors, and seeks to illegalize ALL drug company gifts. Doing their usual good work, JAMA intoned that "even small gifts [are] a powerful influence", provoking USA Today to pronounce doctors "sufficiently well-compensated that they can live without pharmaceutical freebies."

Other [current] stories included a reminder of the approaching deadline to apply for your National Provider Identifier, obtained through the NPI Enumerator (kinda reminds you of Frank Zappa's "central scrutinizer").

There are all the usual stories about the perpetually forecasted cuts in Medicare physician pay and rising practice overheads; CMS planning to increase primary care payment rates at the expense of specialists; and laughable, and sad call by the American Academy of Family Practice for "Thousands of FP's for Historic Capitol Rally."

A story in Family Practice News recounts an episode from the annual meeting for the American Association of Clinical Endocrinologists. The deputy chief clinical officer for the Center for Medicare and Medicaid Services, Dr. Trent Haywood, called for support for Payment For Performance (P4P) thusly: "The thing is for clinicians to work with us and get on board. We don't want to design a program and not have clinician input." *(But we will if you don't play ball!)* A fellow traveler, Aetna executive chairman Dr. John Rowe airily sighed: "My fear is that the P4P train is leaving the station, and the doctors aren't on it."

What do prospective physicians, especially the handful still considering primary care, face in their professional development? A country that continues to devalue them, undercutting their worth through declining pay and increasing expectations; a society demanding to trust their bodies to physicians whom they believe to be so weak-willed that they cannot be trusted with a drug rep's pen; an unholy collaboration of government coercion and corporate bribery to force doctors to swallow the self-defeating P4P. Who stands up for the doctors? Certainly not a government stooge and Big Insurance lackey who cajole and threaten doctors to acquiesce to their dishonorable positions, selling out their profession in the process. Who stands up for the doctor?

At the very same meeting, the panel included a nurse, Twila Brase, RN, president of the Citizens Council on Health Care, which advocates competition and scorns P4P. Ms. Brase slammed P4P and evidence-based medicine as a sure road to "budget-based care, not customized care." Denouncing Medicare and big insurance as the real villains, she urged doctors to cease their participation and charge patients cash. While doctors in organized medicine, government, and Big Insurance shamefully sell out their profession *and their patients,* a nurse stands up for the Hippocratic Ideal. Dr. Haywood, hopefully embarrassed by her honesty, responded: "This is the first time I've been on a panel where someone advocated the abolishment of Medicare and Medicaid. It's a shock to me." Hooray for the clear-headed Ms. Brase, and shame on our cowardly profession for remaining under obligation to anyone but our patients and ourselves, in an honest and completely voluntary relationship."

The P4P train continued then as it does now, on wobbly chasis, down rusty rails of inevitability ...

(More) Too Big to Fail

"And the laughter continues for Pay-For-Performance (P4P). If life imitates art, it also imitates a joke. Increasingly physicians have joked darkly that Medicare might offer them the opportunity to work at a loss, and now it is really coming true. I only wish I were making this up. As is chronicled for anyone with a half-wit's grasp of logic,

Medicare is failing – badly. The projected budgets are always under-projected, and cost overruns are ho-hum normal for the wonks in D.C. Every year there is a threat to slash physician Medicare payments, always averted at the last minute with much fanfare from the impotent AMA about "preserving access for our seniors." Now we are told by our federal masters that P4P is coming and we WILL all play ball, in order to reduce costs and preserve resources by managing patients better and reducing the need for hospital admissions and expensive procedures. (Pausing for laughter here, this is really tough to write with a straight face) Of course we already knew that this was a huge con to give cover to the real goal of reducing payments to doctors. Not content to live under this flimsy cover, the American Academy of Family Practice (AAFP) again roars to the front of the line for self-abusers and masochists who think themselves to be "humanists."

   In the latest issue of Family Practice Management we read about "a Medicare pay-for-performance program in 2007. Under the program, physicians would be paid 99 percent of the "Medicare economic index," which reflects what Medicare figures it actually costs physicians to provide services, with the remaining 1 percent awarded for meeting quality and efficiency standards." Take a breath, wipe your eyes, and blow your nose – I know this is almost too funny to continue. One of the leaders of the FP implosion weighed in: "AAFP Board Chair Michael Fleming, MD, recently sent a letter commending Rep. Nancy Johnson (R-Ct.) for introducing the bill, but he cautioned that the bill's implementation schedule may be too aggressive, not allowing small practices enough time to prepare for pay for performance. He also recommended that the bill focus on practice

performance, rather than individual physician performance, to promote a team-based, practice-wide approach
to improving patient care." This is so funny on so many
levels that Dr. Fleming and Rep. Johnson should get
their own zany sitcom. They are pushing a bill designed
to promote more doctor visits, which will in turn lower
the amount allowed to be paid physicians in the future
under the Sustainable Growth Rate alchemy. They actually commend each other on a bill that will pay a doctor – if he is really good – exactly the cost of seeing the
Medicare patient. Now I'm not to good at math, but
as this is written, wouldn't that mean the doctor would
make NO money from seeing the deserving senior? And
that is a best-case scenario! And what about the bill's
implementation being "too aggressive" for small practices to prepare? As a former marina-owner acquaint-
ance of mine points out, "I would never need to wait
for someone to give me more money. If this is such a
good deal, then why wouldn't practices want to implement it immediately?" I know, the new overhead costs
for HIPAA-compliant electronic medical records, data
tracking software, and all the rest must be in place before
Medicare can award the bountiful P4P. So absorb all of
those costs, and continue to accept Medicare under the
threat of audits, criminal prosecutions, and rising overhead. And if you are really, really good, you just might
be reimbursed just enough to cover your costs. Don't
spend it all in one place."

*A couple years earlier, I had to think long and hard about my
role in primary care. As that role crystallized in my mind, I took
decisive action, and later wrote about the experience, published in*
Medical Economics *magazine:*

The Beeper

"It's been thirty years, but I can still see it plain as day, dull silver, bulky, ever present on my old man's belt – the beeper. It was the kind that let out a shrill series of beeps, a burst of static, then the voice of the clerk at the E.R. instructing my dad where to call. It was there when he went to the office, clipped above his jeans when he went out to work on the farm, moved back and around out of the way from the swinging limbs and brush and tools which would injure it. The old man would slip his sport coat off to pre-flight his small plane before a weekend trip, reaching into his back pocket for his trademark red bandana to wipe away a spot of oil or grease, stuffing it into the back pocket below the waiting silver box. I remember it most clearly, in its sharpest visual relief, contrasted against the blue of my dad's standard button-down oxford blue shirt, winking from its belt perch when the blue blazer slid back as the owner twisted in the pew to reach for a hymnal. For some reason my strongest memory of the beeper was from church, I suppose because it represented an oddly permissible disruption to the solemnity of the service. Sure, the old man cussed it on most days and in every possible venue. The implacable little box with its little hidden voice could break dad's reverie and escape no matter where, no matter when. He could hear it over the tractor engine, and knew the sound even when the boat was fully revved, flying across the lake on a previously unspoiled summer afternoon. I don't remember the beeper ever spoiling a shot, but many autumn afternoon bird-hunting expeditions were cut short by the random hand of his electronic friend. Nor do I remember seeing him actually hurl the beeper at anything, but he often verbalized the desire to do so, and the loving adjectives applied to his companion have remained generally, unprintable.

My dad continues to practice as an ophthalmologist and facial surgeon from the storied "old school", whose graduates still adhere to the stylistic regimens of crisply starched white coats, neat ties, and courtly manners, all to reflect their genuine sense of high purpose in their endeavors. And I know he outwardly hated the damned beeper, but I suspect inwardly he was proud of it, not as an ostentatious status symbol, but as a tangible sign of his responsibility and special place in the community. In the 1970's, after Vietnam and during Watergate, when "Internet" sounded like fishing and "cell phone" sounded like biology, almost no one had beepers. Before anyone in a small town in rural Appalachian Virginia had ever heard of crack or Oxycontin, before beepers were a business tool for drug dealers and cool for grade schoolers, only doctors carried them, making the little tags as identifiable with the hallowed traditions of medicine as the stethoscope. The man, or more rarely, woman, who wore a beeper in those days, was marked. They were the ones who would duck out of cocktail parties or anniversary dinners to assist patients and colleagues in the throes of emergencies. These were the professionals who, by and large, lived up to the high expectations established by society, each other, and themselves. They complained out loud sometimes, but to no one in particular. They raised and supported their families, at times sacrificing their own physical and mental health with appalling casualness while adhering to their professional code. Many of these beeper-bearers of thirty years ago paid sometimes inordinate, ridiculously high dues to be what they had aspired to be. Their choice to seek excellence, even perfection led some of their brightest minds into gross excesses of stress, work, and indulgence, even as they expanded the frontiers of diagnoses and therapeutics at fantastic rates. They made the choice, accepted the rules that changed constantly, and stood on the wall to defend all of us against the unforeseen and frightening assaults on our bodies and lives. Even as grade school classmates confused me with their sneers and teasing about my "rich" dad, I understood how much they depended on the only ophthalmologist for forty miles around, and how lucky they were to have the one facial plastics surgeon who would forgo a Sunday afternoon to reconstruct someone's face because he was the only one who could. There was the one call after midnight on Monday morning from the ER for a patient who had stuck barbed wire in his eye four days earlier, and came in because it was starting to hurt. At two in the morning, the old man dressed, put on his tie, and drove the thirty minutes to the hospital to examine a patient who cursed and berated him for making the gentleman wait. It was apparently a real learning experience for the patient when a doctor pushed the slit lamp aside and offered him a choice: he could shut up and be examined, or the two of them could settle their differences in the parking lot. The patient sat quietly for the rest of his exam, and received the excellent care that my father's tradition demanded for all patients, whatever their shortcomings. Even when suffering abuse, the physicians of the old school who carried those first beepers put their patients first.

I couldn't measure up to that standard I thought, as I began my undergraduate years. I swerved away toward a completely different career, based on the youthful desires of nonstop fun, adventure, and a desire to keep distant from the serious, mature bindings of adult responsibility. The plan worked for a few years, but as I was forced to reconsider my long-term goals, my challenges so long un-confronted loomed up from a childhood awe of those who carried the beepers and stethoscopes, who were needed at all hours, the ones who embraced adventure for the benefit and to the respect of their fellow men. It was a naïve and idealistic perception, but grounded in the truths which I witnessed as someone raised in that tradition. I didn't know, could not have grasped, that the great generation of physicians who had done so much to elevate the level of care in our society had sewn the seeds of destruction for all that they had accomplished. I had no understanding that the physicians of the old school had, through unwitting arrogance and avarice, used their code of professional ethics to bludgeon themselves and their patients into a socialized system that would far outweigh their good work in its degree of dehumanizing destructiveness. It was, and remains wrong, to accede to the fantasy notion of free care for all based on taking from others, and the doctors whose job it was to care for the individual should have recognized the larger consequences of forcibly taking from one patient to give to another. My inexcusable hero-worship of the old school graduates blinded me to the truth, that so many who shirked their duty to stand firm and stop the socialization of medicine were content at first to accept easy government cash, and later comfortable in shrugging at the system made inevitable by their failure to stop it dead in its tracks. I knew growing up that lawyers were basically the spear's point of evil and that malpractice was a growing threat – what I didn't know, couldn't know, was the gut-punch agony of saving someone's life, only to have them sue with malicious delight to right a wrong never committed. Those were black clouds on a far horizon when I graduated from medical school, gratefully wearing my old man's hood, a garment from the old school that I treasure still.

A month later, in a crisp white lab coat and tie, in my first intern day, I accepted my very own beeper with fear and, yes, pride. I too would be one of those who answered the call, who could be proud of my ability and willingness to do what few others could or would do. Naïve, idealistic, prideful? Yep. But ego is required to be a physician (at least I knew that!) and I was long since cynical enough to avoid the laughable idealism of my younger colleagues who entered residency still arguing that money didn't matter and that all patients deserved the best care at all times no matter what. The first time the beeper went off we were rounding on our very first patients. A nurse who certainly knew more than I was calling to get a Tylenol order, for a patient assigned to me, whom I had not yet seen. After four years of high-priced graduate school, clinical rotations, and two board exams, I was absolutely terrified. What was the patient's history? Would he have a reaction with another med, was there liver disease that would become failure when I authorized the fatal Tylenol? I set my jaw, girded myself, and did what every intern ever born had to do at some point – I faked it. Yes, I said with absolute confidence, give the Tylenol. The damn beeper went off at least five times within the next ten minutes, and by the end of the week I was ready to shoot it in the back yard. But as the weeks, then months of residency passed, it didn't seem so bad. When I clipped the little black friend to my belt before going out to supper, I knew that people were counting on me, and that I was upholding the very standards that I once thought I could never meet. The beeper called me to patients with respiratory distress, for emergent deliveries, and for a brain-dead patient on a Saturday morning that first month of internship, whose family needed counseling prior to choosing to pull the unfortunate's tube and let him go. Later that day my wife wanted to visit a local imported car dealer for a test drive. Riding in the back of a cushy BMW whose cost far exceeded its worth to me, the dealer noted my beeper and smugly assured my wife that I was a doctor and I could afford it. I refused to ever visit that dealership again.

When residency ended and I moved off to the Florida Panhandle to begin a new practice with a friend from residency, one of the first things I needed to do was purchase a new beeper. And for the next four years I faithfully kept it with me wherever I went. I would sleep with the beeper on the nightstand, and curse myself when I left it in the other room, only to awaken the next morning to see unanswered pages on the tiny screen. My partner and I traded off weekends, trying to scrupulously keep an open ear to our patients' weekend concerns. The calls were minor most of the time, an otitis media here, and a kid with a fever there. Once "911" appeared in the little beeper window, the corresponding number to which I responded with haste. It was a judgment-impaired boyfriend calling about his girlfriend's itchy psoriasis, prompting a very focused conversation with the boyfriend on the meaning of "911". The E.R. was the usual stimulator of the beeper, more so of course, on call days. Call was never too bad in our small town E.R., just the same type of admissions that primary care types get everywhere: chest pain, nursing home urosepsis, overdoses, unassigned patients whose apathy over their own care had caught up with them, and with us. An admission, as any primary care physician knows, usually initiated the stream of pages for constipation, insomnia, requests to smoke, and the need to deal with family members' questions and neuroses. While establishing an office practice by day, I continued my E.R. moonlighting begun in residency, and often fielded pages from our office patients between seeing E.R. customers. The balancing act was no big deal, and I grew accustomed to the strange rhythms of living in a half-clinic, half-E.R. twilight while waiting on my clinic practice to grow.

It would surely grow in the affluent resort community we had selected as a location, following the years of medical training during which we were told by countless sources that the demand was and would remain high for family doctors, dedicated to the "lifelong learning" now trumpeted by the FP organizations. And learn we did. We learned about the incredibly high overhead for a medical practice. We learned that no matter our motives or desires, no matter our constraints or costs, we had to try to protect ourselves. We learned that Medicare didn't pay worth a damn, but that Medicare patients demanded prohibitive amounts of time and exposed us to greater federal scrutiny. We stopped accepting new Medicare patients two years into private practice, and never considered accepting the (often) lazy self-destruction of Medicaid into our office. We learned that hiring an outside billing company, as a way of dealing with our fears and ignorance over billing, was a stupid money loser. We learned what it felt like to be sued. And then a residency classmate of ours threw off the yoke, opening a modest cash-only practice to the mutual delight of both physician and patients. His income dropped a little while his free time and job satisfaction soared. He took no call and wore no beeper. And beyond my envy for my friend's courageous move, I began to focus on what I was doing. Our office staff was routinely berated by very well-to-do patients over twenty dollar co-pays, while we struggled to keep the doors open, waiting a month or more to be paid for work already performed. We had to listen to elderly patients just off of the golf course complain about their medicine costs, then complain more when they still met the unstoppable infirmities of aging. We had mothers too busy to bring in a sick child on Friday, call for antibiotics on Saturday, and then complain because we insisted on examining the child on Monday. We had the ever-present threat of the E.R. call schedule hanging over a free Saturday meant for football watching, a Sunday dinner with friends, exercise, or any other battery charging available to patients. The beeper didn't really go off that much, but when it did it always represented the same thing: loss of control.

The traditions of Western allopathic medicine called us to be ever ready and willing to help those in need. And the warp of societal expectations and the heavy hand of government over the past generation have summoned us to the E.R. not just for those in acute need, but for those repeatedly choosing to destroy themselves, or those abandoned by their families, or those for whom simple comfort alone should have been given long ago. For the privilege of providing in-patient care, I had to submit to the stupid governmental regulations familiar to all of my colleagues, suffer the increased liability exposure common to hospital work, slog through yet more paperwork, and wait weeks for reimbursement checks that were never commensurate with the effort expended. I came to understand that the Hippocratic Oath was not just a code of conduct for the physician, but represented one-half of a contract with the society from whence it sprang. Physicians failed their duty of leadership through financial greed, and by subjugating their relationships with their patients to large, dehumanizing corporations and clumsy bureaucracies. Society broke their half of the compact by expecting convenience and perfection on pain of great retribution, at cut-rate prices. And finally I have learned what the beeper has come to represent.

On a brilliant sunny day in June, I was joined by a couple of friends for a day out on the water. It was wonderful enjoying more free time out on my sailboat since leaving my private practice for full-time work at the E.R. two months earlier. Trying to run a private clinic was no longer attractive for many good reasons, highlighted in contrast to my present situation. I enjoyed having a predictable cash flow, paying no overhead, and having no responsibilities outside of my scheduled shifts. Whenever patients complained about the cost of the visit, or tell me they have Medicare/Medicaid, or griped about their insurance, I could enthusiastically embrace my rationalization and answer them that I don't get into all of that, my only concern is making them better. I don't really worry about educating them on a system that will soon crash, in part due to their own weight. They will find out soon enough, as E.R. lines continue to grow. My friends and I drank cold beer, enjoyed the sun and the music, told stories, and embraced a beautiful day. That afternoon we pointed the boat south into the Gulf of Mexico, our forward horizon only a clear sky over a deep, soothing blue. I went below to the cabin, and got my beeper. I thought about the noble tradition of medicine, and about how, when I have a crisis there may be only incompetents, or no one to stand guard, to man the wall against my frailty. I thought about how we could save the system, and how because of cowardice, we won't. I looked at the little black plastic device without malice or anger against those who would choose differently, because that was the essence of it all. Because I have learned that it would not matter how many people I could help, or how much pain I could ease, or how many lives I could prolong, and it would not matter whether anyone was there to help me in my time of need. None of that would matter if I sacrificed my life to an unthinking machine that would consume me, if I did not choose to live and die a free man. I was grinning ear to ear when I climbed back up on deck and handed a camera to my friend to record the moment. I walked to the bow, took a breath, and a last look at the last beeper I would ever wear. And I threw that sucker as far out into the Gulf as I could. Then I turned the boat north and headed for port, a freer man."

And I never had a moment's regret.

❖ ❖ ❖

More Government Care

It has infuriated my left-leaning friends and family, from "moderates" all the way over to the flaming red progressives, how I characterize the adherents of liberalism. Inasmuch as diabetes is long established as a disease of blood vessels, so liberalism (and its various synonyms) is properly characterized as a disease of self-esteem. No one who wishes to think well of themselves wants to be told that they have poor self-esteem, but this is not a time or place for pulling a punch. Liberals divide into two basic groups. The first are those tender-hearted souls who seek to do good for any and all, who cannot stand the thought of pain in the world, and who believe in supporting large, herding, collective programs designed to shower compassion over the less fortunate and unenlightened. This first group uses their votes to preferentially (and that is key!) extract money from some to give to others. This is different than gas taxes or highway taxes, which apply to all more or less equally. The application of preferential taxes is wealth transference; the first type of liberal engages in this to feel really good about him or herself, by using someone else's money for their good intentions. We may refer to these as "bleeding hearts."

The second type of liberal is the supremely confident, often over-educated, preening intellectual and/or community organizer that herds smaller groups into larger ones, always exhorting for bigger movements, more organizing, and ultimately, bigger government. This type of liberal even more than the bleeding hearts, will not shrink at the thought of using the coercive power of government to force their will on any and all. In fact they revel in using centralized power to do good, rewarding their followers, and in so doing aggrandizing themselves. They will demagogue any who oppose them not usually on issue grounds, but by character assassination. Their opponents will be called racists and elitists and greedy, while the truly greedy liberal amasses even more power. This type we shall call "bullies."

The common point between bleeding hearts and bullies is that neither can leave their fellow man alone. Whatever their stated intentions or goals, liberals of both camps share in common, and may be recognized by their non-stop, incessant need to boss other people around. Whether through oozing buckets of compassionate and big-hearted good wishes, or punitive laws, an iron fist, and barbed wire, the need to force others in order to feel good about

307

*one's self is the very definition of a deeply flawed self-esteem. And
as such, it just lends itself to being a health care busybody in the
extreme. And I'm not just picking on politicians here; physicians
are themselves some of the most scurrilous of a rascally lot, as I
noted in the last of the W. years...*

Doctors Roll Up Our Freedoms, and Smoke Us

"Doctors just can't seem to help themselves. Someone
waves what sounds like a good idea in front of them, and
by virtue of their profession the docs take the predictable, easy stance. Then the good idea becomes a program proposal, with advocates, spokespersons, a congressional hearing or two. And then the proposal becomes
law, receives funding which locks in allies, which fight for
more funding, and so on...Then the program becomes
its own raison d'etre, and its supporters become enslaved
to the program, seeing all else as subordinate to their
good intentions. And then the doctors become tyrants.

It seemed like a good idea to many a decade ago to
begin a national program to expand health care access
for children. Seems there were a lot of families too poor
to afford health insurance and too rich to qualify for
Medicaid. In 1997 a Democrat president and Republican
congress reached a compromise and cooked up the State
Children's Health Insurance Program ("compromise"
increasingly being understood to mean the enlargement
of the state and the diminution of the individual). SCHIP
became a block-grant way for states to soak up more federal dollars and as such, became popular with elected
officials on both levels. In Beltway-speak, an assistance
program's success is defined NOT by getting people off

the dole, but by increasing its number of "clients". The fans and supporters of SCHIP cheer the program's rousing success of increasing its client children to over 6 million, and as fallout, an additional increase in new Medicaid children by over 6 million. SCHIP and Medicaid adherents have much to cheer for, as more clients mean more need, more lobbying, bigger budgets, expanded eligibility criteria, more clients, and so on into a never-ending upward spiral of consumption.

National Review Online explains the downside in "S-Chipping Away at Free Markets." NRO describes how the program has grown beyond its original mandate, and now covers children from increasingly affluent families, as well as 700,000 adults. The longer term negative is the SCHIP impact on the free market: as the Democrats push to enlarge the program, it is predicted to further move children off the more expensive private insurance rolls into the arms of the loving taxpayer; and acts as a disincentive to increase one's earning power for fear of losing benefits, an effective tax increase. To pay for all this compassion congressional Dems are seeking to shell out $ 50 billion over the next 5 years, while the White House wants a trimmer $30 billion, with caps on income levels. A budget fight is ensuing – enter the hand wringing doctors.

The American Medical News opines on the side of full SCHIP and therefore, against promoting a free market for children's health care. The AMNews wants mores kids covered, and even suggests efforts to "reach out to families already participating in other state and federal relief programs." It is AMA policy to encourage maximum SCHIP enrollment, and the organization now fronts a

large group of the organized concerned publicly calling on Congress to increase taxes to fund this program.
Never ones to hold back from the trough, the American
Academy of Family Practice has chimed in with the AMA
in pushing for tax increases. So U.S. doctors through
organized medicine want to increase the state and federal tax burden on individuals in order to pay for kids, a
sure fire political winner on par with supporting puppies
or sunshine. Or as Senate Finance Committee Chairman
Max Baucus said: "When given the choice between standing with big tobacco companies and standing with kids, I
stand with America's children." What a swell guy!

Remember when the concept of "sin taxes" – on booze
and cigarettes most often, and with fatty foods more
recently – really gained new steam in the 1990's? The
failed Clinton Care plan was to rely heavily on tobacco
taxes, and the subsequent class-action lawsuits against
Big Tobacco scored billions for the states. These billions
were to defray medical expenses borne of smoking and by
the taxpayer, and many states promised to dedicate their
cash prizes to anti-smoking education. Doctors including
the AMA applauded and called for even higher smokers'
taxes, and now they get to do it again. When compassion
needs to be funded you don't ask whether the revenue
source has any connection to the problem. If you are a
lobbying do-gooder, you plunder any unpopular source
you can find and tobacco has served admirably in the role
of perennial tackling dummy. Let me interject immediately that I am not in favor of, will not advocate smoking,
and that is NOT the point of this commentary. The AMA
"along with 66 other medial associations, hospital organizations, consumer groups and insurers" is calling on Congress to up ciggy taxes $0.61 per pack, with the hoped for

collateral benefit of reducing smoking particularly in the pediatric population.

Should the federal government be in the business of providing health care to children? Of course not, any more than it should be empowered to steal from taxpayers to pay for the elderly or the poor. But federalism survives only in the mouths of Republican politicians during the primaries. It seems pretty obvious that money doled out from D.C. commands more lobbying and leads to expenditures far above that originally projected. When doctors advocate for these programs, they become extensions of the government, which means they intrude into the lives of private citizens. These physicians aren't sitting in their clinics and offices waiting for a patient seeking help; rather they are walking uninvited into the homes and pocketbooks of private individuals and FORCING care upon them. When an individual chooses to smoke, why is that anyone else's affair? "But when he gets COPD or lung cancer we all have to pay" will be the response. But why is the responsible party always the taxpayer, and never the smoker?

And now for the newest, worst outrage. A story recently featured on the Rush Limbaugh show detailed the plan by congressional collectivists: the proposed tobacco tax may include raising taxes on premium cigars by as much as $10 per cigar! The story he quoted from Tampa raised the salient question: "How do you oppose a sin tax Congress has rigged to help sick kids?" Fine cigars, one of the last surviving vestiges of western elegance, are now threatened by the grubby little hands of U.S. doctors anxious to fund health care for kids by taking from others. Cigar smokers do not threaten kids, nor do they cause 99.99% of the little tykes' ailments (maybe there is one grandpa firing a stogie in a car full of kids with the windows rolled up, but if spotted he would probably be shot on sight). But when it comes to universal coverage – and universal payment – U.S. doctors care only where the money is, not who it belongs to.

All of this begs another question: in the end, what is the point of achieving universal health coverage through coercion and the shackling of peoples' good times? Does the quality of life U.S. doctors claim to champion apply only to AMA-approved wholesome pleasures? The western tradition of medicine has through the centuries promoted the individual patient above all else, and it is only in recent decades that the collective good has radically supplanted this concept. Where once an American doctor by oath would never consider of forcing a treatment on a capacitated adult, now U.S. doctors will force smoking cessation as their way of making patients and taxpayers do the right thing – for the children."

When doctors and politicians collaborate, the result is almost always bad. The ranks of both avocations are full of bleeding hearts and bullies, and the unjustifiably large egos seemed determined to outdo each other in bothering their targets de jour. Meddlers from Ted Kennedy to Newt Gingrich to whoever was the current president of the AMA (they're all the same) all coalesced in the mid-00's over putting electronic medical records (EMRs, now also called Electronic Health Records) in every office. All of which had a chilling familiarity to it ...

The Rise of the Machines

"They lived only to face a new nightmare...the War Against the Machines"

...Sara Connor, Terminator 2

By now we all know what happened. For over a past decade, seemingly independent and disparate entities began to adopt computerized operating systems to improve their efficiency and interoperability, in order to protect the welfare of the greater population. The system designed to benevolently achieve new levels of safety, excellence, and cost-savings began almost immediately to operate according to its own interests...as the previously private systems were linked into a centralized government network, the new network began to ruthlessly seek out entities deemed to be inferior, forcing their assimilation, or their destruction...

A very large, very malevolent push is underway to computerize all of American health care and those physicians still able and willing to resist this trend should do so. Who is interested in the establishment of electronic records as the norm? Exactly the same entities interested in controlling doctors as the commodities they have become. Private third-party payers are furiously pushing electronic medical records as a way to improve efficiency, improve outcomes, meet standards of care, and improve documentation – the latter ostensibly for the purpose of helping physicians to be paid at higher levels. Did any of us really believe this voodoo? It has been evident from the start that the interest private insurance carriers have had in electronic records has never been in paying doctors more, but in containing costs. If the doctor works primarily for the patient, then he diagnoses and treats; if he works primarily for the insurance carrier, then he contains costs. We should have seen what would come next.

Medical Economics reported a chilling example, that
of HealthAmerica withholding $20,000 and threatening
worse, for a family practice group judged to have submitted too many 'Level 4' charges, following their adoption
of electronic medical records (EMR). When shown to
be baseless, HealthAmerica altered the accusation, suggesting that some of the charges weren't in the "spirit" of
Level 4's. The same article makes clear that the coming
trend will be that those who adopt EMRs with an expectation of higher coding, will suffer more frequent audits.
The auditors will seek "a pattern of generic notes", and
then attempt to deny payment by claiming, "you've got
the same note here, and there's no meaningful clinical
observation. You're just cutting and pasting and sticking
it to us. " Consider the HUGE contradiction here: we are
increasingly told to practice evidence-based medicine,
in which all patients' diagnoses and treatments will be
generically categorized; yet the validity of these catego-
rizations will be more suspect due to their generic quality. Does the insurance company expect to base payment
for clinical service based on an EHR line describing how
"Aunt Sally still enjoys picking peaches"?

Organized medicine, as they so consistently do nowa-
days, is working hard to undercut the interests of doctors
interested in maintaining any semblance of independence. The AMA is publicizing its efforts to "ensure health
IT standards are established to allow physicians, hospitals
and other healthcare professionals to share and exchange
data" and will "work with Congress and insurance companies to align incentives as part of the development of a
national health information infrastructure so physicians
are not stuck with a disproportionate financial burden
when they implement these technologies."

Uncle Sam's legislative assembly line is also busy launching ICD-10 and a new Office of the National Coordinator for Health Information Technology, in what Rep. Nancy Johnson (R-Ct) says will "overcome key obstacles that have slowed our progress toward adoption of a national, interoperable electronic system." Exactly. Published goals of the Center for Medicare and Medicaid Services include a "focus on quality issues"; "public reporting of data to be made available to physicians and patients"; "[creating] incentives for providing better quality care"; "encourage electronic health records and prescribing, and; "promote evidence-based approaches." Government lapdogs at the Institute of Medicine (the same guys who started the whole re-certification industry) agree, and recommend "broader adoption of electronic prescribing and other measures to cut down on the number of patients who get the wrong drug, dosage or mix of medications." Their report was funded by the Center for Medicare and Medicaid Services.

A voice of dissent, the Assoc. of American Physicians and Surgeons, is warning all who will listen, on the dangers of the latest development. On July 27, the U.S. House of Representatives passed a bill to create a national database of patients' medical information to "lower costs, improve patient care, and reduce medical errors." AAPS Executive Director Jane Orient, M.D. correctly opposes this ominous very bad idea: "A national health information system would effectively eliminate any and all patient consent to the release of their records by placing the records online. Patients would have virtually no control over who can sneak-a-peek at their very private and sensitive medical records."

Even in a small solo practice will cost tens of thousands up front, with thousands yearly in software updates and IT support necessary for interoperability with third-party payers. This cost is expected to be offset by increased revenues, money from submitted bills increasingly under suspicion precisely for the efficiency with which they are generated. Any doctor accepting EMR's will be subject to HIPAA rules, P4P guidelines, increased demands for data collection, and the involuntary dissemination of clinical results for national scrutiny. By allowing the outside access to their records, doctors' work will be judged against national averages, rather than by those they are supposed to serve. These same doctors will then be mislabeled, sanctioned, and begin to "teach to the test", dumping problem patients and skewing their clinical decisions to satisfy abstract standards. And woe betides any doctor whose office is hacked into and patient records accessed. A past-perfect storm of organized medicine, "patient advocates", the government, and the insurance industry has coalesced to computerize and link all U.S. doctors and their patients. Is there no hope for the independent doctor to withstand this irresistible tide? In fact there is.

The one hope is for those independent doctors, who can, to refuse to accept EMR's. In the very near term this will necessitate the refusal to participate with all private and government third-party payers, who will condition payment on the adoption of such systems. This is NOT a call for a return to primitivism, but a recognition that we have gone too far. The greatest computer in the office is still the physician's brain. Records are required, but only those needed for the good of the patient. If the doctor believes that an electronic record will enable him to do a better job for his patients, fine. But adopting EMRs – and the changes in behavior and thinking that comes with them - for the purpose of cooperation with private insurance or the government only diminishes the importance of the individual patient. In the "Terminator" series, the omnipresent computer system SkyNet used cyborgs, flesh-covered machines, for their de-humanizing purposes. The forces behind the EMR movement do not seek simple robots. A robot could follow narrow ICD and CPT codings, submit bills, and be paid accordingly. Medicare, the Blues, et al also want cyborgs – robots responding to evidence-based directives and formularies, wrapped in an outward skin of compassion, willing to morph to fit each yearly change in fee schedules and allowable procedures. And when "Med-Net" is fully implemented, supported at state and federal levels, it will begin to seek out and destroy those entities not in compliance. Then our only hope may be that future resistance fighters will send someone back through time to teach us how to use a ball-point pen."

That warning went unheeded and to date, hundreds of millions have been blown nationwide as hospitals and office nationwide have been forced to adopt electronic records as yet another cost of doing business with the government. Medical care has not been measurably improved, but we all have looked a whole lot busier.

Giving great big hugs with government cash just seems to take on a life of its own. Back in the Glorious Eighties, folks got rightly incensed over $600 wrenches and pricey toilet seats contracted by the military. But where has the outrage, trillions of debt later, been over medical overcharging? Back in 2005 the deficit hawks should have been ready to pop wheelies …

Rolling Blunder

(It would be too easy for those so inclined to infer that I was making willing to make fun of handicapped folks, which I am not. The only purpose of this piece was to ponder the inefficiency, and absurdity of the present system.)

"Last September, Big Medicare grand poobah and Finance Chairman Sen. Chuck Grassley (R-Io) wrote an upset letter to HHS Sec. Mike Leavitt on the "Fraud and Abuse in the Power Wheelchair Program."

He noted that in FY 2003 the Feds expended $1.2 billion for power mobility devices (PMDs). He described the establishment of a National Coverage Determination (NCD) requiring a revision of the Healthcare Common Procedure Coding (HCPC), which may nonetheless have added an "unnecessary degree of subjectivity to this process." Got it?

(I added for pure humor purposes, other acronyms covered including: Certificate of Medical Necessity (CMN); Mobility Assisted Equipment (MAE); Local Coverage Determination (LCD – itself 18 pages in length); Durable Medical Equipment Regional Carriers (DMERCs); RESNA (Rehabilitation Engineering & Assistive Technology Society of North America) and Assistive Technology Partner (ATP); DMEPOS (??). His stirring inquiry also listed that although CMS projects the add-on G-code payment will cost $5 million annually (is that like a G-spot?), this does not include the cost of the additional physical exams. Showing world-class leadership, Sen. Grassley requests that CMS "Provide a crosswalk from the 49 codes released on February 2005 to the 63 codes released on September 14, 2005" including detailed explanations of each.)

In recent years the subject of powered wheelchairs and whether and how the government will pay for them for its dependent citizens has become a hot topic, zooming around the corridors of power on new tires with a long-life battery. It is axiomatic that whatever government wishes less of it taxes, and whatever it wishes more of, it subsidizes. Well the government apparently wants a lot of folks in wheelchairs because it has been subsidizing the hell out of them. MarketResearch.com reports "In 2004, there were 68.9 million obese persons in North America and this number is expected to increase to 74.7 million in 2006." This leads to a projected increase in Bariatric Mobility Aids (chairs for people>250 lbs.) These chairs are "made for heavy people, [which] manufacturers are expected to lay special emphasis on performance, maneuverability, and solid construction." Cooper & Cooper from the Univ. of Pittsburgh documented an increase in wheelchair sales from 1996-2000 of 30%, and a similar growth rate for powered scooters. MarketResearch supports this, noting "Bariatric products are projected to be the fastest growing mobility aid segment in the near future." We have an aging population, with more chronically ill people living longer, including an enlarging population segment of the morbidly obese. And more of them will want to get around.

The physicians for these patients will continue to be called upon to support their claim for wheelchair/ scooter provision from the government, which shelled out

$1.2 Billion in 2003 on these devices. Medicare now requires a face-to-face examination with your doctor, along with a written prescription for the wheelchair/ scooter, within 30 days before applying for a device, for which it will pay 80% of the cost. Medicare also requires the doctor to provide medical documentation to support the claim that the patient cannot otherwise move around sufficiently in the home (thankfully a therapist is no longer separately required to certify that the patient can steer a scooter. Now the doctor can as well)... The final rule scheduled to go into effect June 5. 2006 allows for an additional payment of $21.60 for the extra compiling and documenting; and stipulates that the wheelchair/ scooter vendor must receive the prescription and medical documentation within 45 days of the exam or hospital discharge.

Paul Wenske in the Kansas City Star reported recent FBI investigations in four states that uncovered "hundreds of millions of dollars in bogus billings" filed with Medicare, involving power wheelchairs, "which cost the program $5,000 compared with $2,000 for scooters."

There are a lot of ill or disabled folks in our country who need wheelchairs to sustain a decent quality of life. Their needs, laid bare through a clumsy bureaucracy, provided an avenue for unscrupulous doctors and other con men to bilk the system for millions. This in turn led to another round of new rules, interim rules, fact-finding, and the absurd acronyms, G-codes, and crosswalks scrutinized by Chairman Grassley. When this all filters down to the individual practitioner, it will be one more avenue for inadvertent fraud or waste.

Now consider this same mindless template applied to prescription drugs, physical therapy, out-patient drug administration, "wellness" exams, and a host of other things. How can people continue to support such a system, barring denial and willful ignorance? We certainly do not wish to withhold wheelchairs from the sick and the poor, who deserve our sympathy. But we do have to recognize that this mess is just another day in the life of government-provided care."

And now six years later, a news story has just crossed the wire of a doctor charged with Medicare fraud in the millions, including prescribing and billing for a powered wheelchair for a blind patient.

When the bleeding hearts and bullies team up, compassion leaks in through every drafty crack of the health care shack with the trillion-dollar roof...

Vengeance of the Disabled

"Have you ever heard of a man named Robert Fogari? He lives in Hudson County, New Jersey where he practices as a rheumatologist, a medical doctor specializing in autoimmune and inflammatory disorders. Last month the AMA News published an account of Dr. Fogari's experience with the evolving American Dream where rights are ever expanding for the fashionably aggrieved. Dr. Fogari was sued by one Irma Gerena, a sufferer of lupus, who saw the rheumatologist for 18 months and twenty visits. Ms. Gerena "made no allegations of medical negligence." Rather she sued claiming a violation of the Americans with Disabilities Act because the doctor refused to hire a sign language interpreter to accommodate her deafness. Ms. Gerena, who persuasively claimed that she was the victim of inadequate communication regarding her care, corresponded with her doctor via written notes with the help of family members who were always present. The cost of the specialized interpreter would run according to the defense, $150-$200 per visit, while the reimbursement to the physician would be a Medicare-blessed $49. Result: the jury found for the plaintiff to the tune of $400,000, half of which was for punitive damages.

The Fogari episode is a marvelous microcosm, a core sample if you like, of the shifting social and psychological strata upon which we now attempt to anchor new assumptions. Dr. Fogari has practiced for four decades, making him one of the "old school" generation of physicians responsible for the astounding leaps in healing via new diagnostic and therapeutic technologies and modalities. He is also a member of that generation of doctors that vehemently opposed the creation of nationalized health care – Medicare and Medicaid – and then spun on their heals, hands out for easy government cash, when the fix was in. Compassion had rarely been so profitable. Of course the warnings over government creep into medicine came true as the unrestrained demand for services from the retirees and poor have crashed federal and state budgets, causing government to strangle doctors and hospitals with increasing layers of bureaucracy and reduced payments for legitimate services rendered. But this story is not merely about the cruel self-delusions of nationalized care. In 1992 columnist Pat Buchanan, catalyzed over the support by Pres. G.H.W. Bush for the Americans with Disabilities Act, led a mini-revolt among conservative ranks, which weakened the president, leading ultimately to his reelection defeat. Buchanan understood correctly that whatever good the federal government might like to do for the disabled, it could not justifiably force at the expense of business owners. As we have witnessed in the intervening eighteen years, the term "disabled" is highly variable however much one may be cautioned against questioning some who claim the label.

But this story is not just about a high-handed government slapping down a business owner. Yes our case is of a private citizen price-capped by the government, unable by law to pass on increased overhead to his customer, and then required to work at a loss. But it is also about the barbarism of class warfare, where clubs are exchanged for lawyers and the greater plunder is from the psyche. Ms. Gerena's attorney argued that the annual cost of the interpreter amounted to a tiny fraction of Fogari's income, asking the court therefore to accept the notion that the patient had a claim to part of the doctor's income. Is Fogari a nice man? Who knows, and who cares? Whether he is filthy rich or just getting by is none of our business. Why because Ms. Gerena is deaf, should she be afforded more rights than a business owner unlucky enough to render her an apparently adequate service? This case has a lot: the false compassion and cost of creating new "rights", the tyranny of a gluttonous government, our primal instincts to take what is not ours, and the wages of timid principle. These are things to consider as we embark upon an increasingly stimulated federal activism."

And we had such activism aplenty, at both state and federal levels. Republican governors followed W.'s lead with results ranging from ineffective to disastrous, though always laughable...

One Ugly Structure

"Before building an edifice cumbersome enough to obstruct the view, a foundation must first be poured and a framework erected. Unbeknownst to many, United States health care is approaching an accelerated (de) evolution into socialism. The foundation was Medicare, along with its stepbrother Medicaid. By guaranteeing health care to target populations, the government created an ever-enlarging clientele, which itself serves to drive up health care prices for everyone. Two major developments underway in national health care policy today are now serving as the framework for a true eyesore.

In the scramble to curry public favor, two Republican governors are pushing their own statewide plans. California Gov. Schwarzenegger intends to launch a program that will require all Californians to have health insurance coverage through a fun mixture of mandates, taxes, garnishes, and confiscations. Business owners with more than 10 employees must cover them OR shell out another 4 percent of their Social Security wages to a state fund to provide insurance for the otherwise uninsured. Patients will have new costs to complain about, as their hospitals attempt to pass on the cost of a tax on 4 percent of gross revenues. Doctors will each be assessed 2 percent of their gross revenues, which will hardly act to increase their supply within the state. Schwarzenegger hopes that spending more on Medicaid will trigger more federal matching funds, leading to Medicaid payment increases to doctors and hospitals that will more than offset their new taxes. But for that scheme to be successful, the rest of the nation will have to pay MORE to keep Californians healthy. Seem fair to you? Add in the planned expansion of Medi-Cal and the Golden State faces premium inflation and perhaps, a flight of insurers; both of which will encourage more employers to turn their charges over to the state for coverage.

A leading GOP name for the 2008 GOP primary race is former Massachusetts Gov. Mitt Romney, whose plan for universal coverage in his state has drawn mostly applause. This plan also intends to cover everyone, with said coverage reaching consumers through (more) market-based approaches that will activate the miracle machine of capitalism. So far so good. The state will establish a medical stock exchange called "The Connector" to allow small businesses and self-employed to access group plans, and use pre-tax dollars (something not previously possible under Federal law). These positive innovations are (also) balanced by a state-imposed employer mandate which certainly will encourage business owners to make do with fewer employees; Medicaid will expand eligibility to more children, which will worsen the state budget woes, and be a disincentive to encouraging families to pursue the now-more accessible private plans. And contrary to the basic notions of freedom and individual responsibility is the "pay or play" rule that fines a person who does not buy into any plan at all.

On Capitol Hill, the Dems are pushing through the ability for Medicare to negotiate drug prices directly with the manufacturer. This will allow the behemoth entitlement program to crack the whip over evil pharmaceutical companies and force them to sell at lower prices to Medicare, or be left out in the cold. This reduction in profit margin will also allow the drug makers to invest and research less, and turn out fewer new drugs otherwise breathlessly anticipated by the Boomers. The little-acknowledged Democrat ally in this has been Pres. Bush, whose description of Medicare and Social Security as "commitments of conscience" prepares the way nicely for the Pelosi-Clinton enlargement of the dole, which W. himself exploded with the Free Drugs for Old Folks' Votes Medicare "Reform" Act of 2003.

The governing class, the media, and select sub-populations have already raised the girders, and are adding on floors. True to form, as the state plans fail their scaffolds will be adopted nationally by a system that cannot see Medicare as a failure. And soon we shall see less of the horizon, as an ugly, expensive building takes shape."

In 2006 the absolute refusal of the Republicans to give a viable alternative to the Democrats would catch up with them as they were deservedly bounced from office. That Election Eve, the view for freedom in health care was as scary as ever...

Creepy Kids Want More than Candy

"Halloween is nigh upon us and the little bunnies and goblins, witches and super heroes that show up on the doorstep will be scarier and more dangerous than ever before. For centuries the traditions of mummers, latter-day druids, Guy Fawkes wannabes, drunks, and rascals prowled the streets of the British Isles looking for hand-outs and threatening mischief. In my trick or treating days we feigned terror at the stories making the rounds about LSD in the candy bars and razor blades in the apples – and then headed out into our completely safe neighborhoods to scarf as much loot as our stuffed bags could hold. Oh how the jack 'o lantern turns. Social engineering and dark do–gooderism have once again turned the kids into the terrors in the night as the adults cower behind their doors.

Think that cute gypsy princess on the porch is here for a Snickers? Or that the midget robot is here for a peanut-free, lactose-free, carob-coated broccoli bar? The little dears don't even know the game. The kids are weapons in the hands of evil forces that are here for as much of your money and freedom as they can stuff into their flame retardant, lead-free, Pelosi-approved bags.

On October 3, Pres. Bush vetoed the Democrat attempt to radically expand the State Children's Health Insurance Program, created to insure the children of those too poor to afford insurance and too rich to qualify for Medicaid. The bill sought a 5-year, $35 billion enlargement of the commitment that you must pay for your neighbor's children whatever the season, well over the $5 billion increase proposed by the White House. Congressional Dems chose a political gambit easily consumed by an emotionally motivated public as likely swayed by legislation in favor of puppies or sunshine. Naturally the AMA and the AARP, always eager to enlarge the reach of government for our own good, have jumped in to denounce this rare instance of Bush frugality as a mean attempt to deny care for "our kids." They won't tell you that this program has dwarfed its original mission, whose over 6 million clients now include 700,000 adults, nor that it was the very existence of this program that increased the cost of medical care and subsequently private insurance premiums, making both more difficult to afford and driving increasingly well-off families into SCHIP's loving harms. Too late,

W. has correctly characterized SCHIP as a very large, very real plank in the platform of nationalized health care.

In addition to the meddlesome AMA and AARP we have the American Academy of Pediatrics, a socialist bastion hand-in-glove with the federal government happy to trample any individual in the promotion of "healthy kids." Boston columnist Michael Graham enlightens us on the good work organized pediatrics under Medicaid guidelines is pursuing, fearful over "what happens when you send your kids to the doctor and what the doctor starts asking the kids about you." Graham recounted how his 13-year old daughter's doctor interrogated her on her parents drinking, smoking, and gun-owning habits. Frighteningly, the girl was asked in private "if, well, Daddy, if you made me feel uncomfortable" without suggestive history or physical findings. Graham describes how another parent's visit included the pediatrician extracting detailed information on the law-abiding family's guns (numbers, types, locations) which he then reported to law enforcement. We live in a topsy-turvy world where hospitals –literally- no longer put patient names on chart covers or doors for fear of federal privacy regulations, yet nosy doctors can report your guns to the local police as though a crime had been committed. And in their minds no doubt, a thought crime at the very least has occurred. This Halloween parents aren't the only ones waiting out on the street, sending the little tykes on to your porch. There are other sinister shadows, anxious to take your money and your freedoms. Boo."

With no counterbalance to the force of collectivism, the bleeding hearts and bullies only got bolder. The George W. Bush years, a mess in so many ways, were especially generous in the realm of big government care. The specific program initiatives and general rhetoric went hand in glove with an absolute refusal to reform Medicare/Medicaid spending – what the hell am I saying, W. INCREASED it! In fairness the minute the GOP tried to trim any of the health care fat, they would have been beset by Dems and most of the media for killing old people, starving kids, and drowning puppies. But still they should have tried, and there was no excuse to increase the expenditures. In the 2007-08 Democrat primaries, Saint Hillary of the Blessed Plan tried to push her image as THE health policy burning bush, only to be snuffed out by Barak Obama. President Clinton's wife repeatedly tried to push a bigger, scarier version of the Mitt Romney "all in" plan that was already using universally mandated coverage as a way to bankrupt Massachusetts. She promised to attack the wealthy, Big Business, Big Pharmaceuticals, and Big Insurance, exactly as Obama would do a year later. Obama attacked Hillary for mandating individual coverage, exactly the path he would choose once inaugurated.

In January 2009 and during the preceding election, the claims of the winning candidate were preposterous – and it didn't matter. The bemused, painful earnestness of the faces in the cold Inauguration Day crowd just knew that this guy could pull off the impossible...

Who Do You Really Want in Charge?

"In saying that it is time to move forward on health care, President Obama is correct, and there is only one sensible way to do it. The most logical, most significant reform that could be accomplished is simply, to put doctors in charge of the entire process. After all, why should patients without the benefit of medical training be allowed to make such complex decisions? When grandma gets sick, as the president noted, maybe expensive surgery is not the right call when cheaper, palliative medicines could giver her a pretty good comfort level for whatever time she has left. For years medical professionals led by such as the American Medical Association have publicly wrung their hands over the fair allocation of limited resources – the sort of questions medical school ethics classes pose that wonder whether the half million or so spent on one bypass surgery would be better sent to the local health department for kids' vaccines. It is high time for doctors to assume the mantle of authority for which they are eminently prepared, and start making the tough decisions for patients. Medical dollars, tight enough already, will become far, far scarcer in the coming years and it should be up to the healing class to tell patients what is good for them. Doctors should be able to determine - without the subjective distractions from patients and their families - whether the development of pricey treatments for the more virulent cancers makes sense. Freed from the worries and complaints of their clients, healers could do the most good for the most people more in accordance with our budgetary constraints and collective will. If you or a loved one do not get what you want or mistakenly think you deserve, then you should have the good grace to bow to the wisdom of the majority.

Have you had enough? If you aren't angry at the ridiculous notions just proffered, then Democrat health care will be just right for you, and you may be beyond hope. If you think that what was just proposed is stupid and cruel, then one has to wonder: why would you accept those same callous, de-personalized judgments from a government employee with no expertise in patient care or clinical skills? When the President tries to imply that the free market has failed patients, he won't tell you that there has not been a free market in health care for more than forty years. He will laud the efficiency of Medicare, not the fact that this program was actuarially out of funding within five years of its inception. The Democrats will tout all sorts of cost savings from eliminating fraud & waste, and never admit the fraudulent philosophy at the heart of Medicare and Medicaid: it is impossible to mandate universal, affordable, high-quality care.

We fear government making medical decisions, or rationing care as if those intrusions had not already come to pass. Federal guidelines already force doctors to choose certain antibiotics, or meet certain criteria before admitting patients to the hospital. Failure to comply means the parent hospital is not paid. Poor pay and high administrative overhead have already closed many clinics to Medicaid and Medicare patients. Layers of regulation and perpetual quasi-governmental inspections lead to the idiocies that drive up hospital costs to funny-money levels, for which they, not government, are blamed.

Why do a president and party that oppose the market innovations of health savings accounts and interstate insurance portability want to expand the framework of what is long since a proven failure? Why add trillions to a budget that cannot even meet its current health care obligations? In 1965, We the People decided that being poor (Medicaid), or old (Medicare) should be attended with free health care. These programs have been financial disasters, have led to increasing shortages of physicians, nurses, and hospital beds relative to the population, and have become a springboard not to reform, but to more of the same. ObamaCare promises to be the most expensive "free" prescription ever filled."

As Obama started to intone specifics on his looming health care plan, he repeated, reemphasized, and retorted to items from his campaign website health "plan," really a rehash of the entire Democrat approach for the past several years. He had to make an adjustment here or there. During the primaries, he excoriated President Clinton's wife for advocating mandates requiring the individual to purchase health insurance; those same mandates would however, become the foundation of his plan once the election was over. The Obama plan was hailed by far too many as just what was needed, and it's opponents were labeled greedy, racist, backward, and just plain mean. I tried to warn them...

Just Like They Made Housing "Affordable"

"Watching the news this week one would think in the midst of this latest government-created financial crisis that Americans are split between those who want a big reassuring hug from the government, and those who, like the abandoned child, wondered why they haven't gotten one all along. Health care seems to be on the back burner, but since this electorate loves to write its own sub-prime loans, let's not let the cost of things worry us. Amidst the HOPE and CHANGE of the Obama supplicants lies a big hug in the form of health care reform, along the lines of giving a cigarette to an emphysema patient in an oxygen tent (cue the Talking Heads' "Burning Down the house).

Obama promises to cover all Americans with a new plan based on a national insurance program, that will increase the government's role in the present market, furthering the good work of LBJ and W. Benefits will be guaranteed as will eligibility. "Portability", the ability to take insurance coverage unbroken from job to job and state-to-state, is also promised (curiously, Dems have repeatedly blocked GOP attempts to provide this for private insurance). Premiums will be affordable to all, and if they are not then whosoever is tapped as deserving by a compassionate government will get a subsidy. Remember that we will invariably get more of what is subsidized – people on government assistance – and less of what is taxed, in this case, taxpayers.

And taxpayers will get a long, painful punch in the nose from the Obama plan. Despite his assurances of "simplified paperwork and reined in health care costs", we may count on the opposite. The plan touts a National Health Insurance Exchange to screen plans for minimal benefits and quality, and connect prospective clients to these plans. This same plan enacted by then-Gov. Romney in Massachusetts has now run into the red several hundreds of millions, and will certainly be more expensive on a national scale. Obama believes that employers have an obligation to provide health care, and those who do not wish to "will be required to contribute a percentage of payroll(s) toward the costs of the national plan." The establishment of Medicare and Medicaid has led to significant medical price inflation, a fact ignored by those who are otherwise concerned with the uninsured. As more sign up for subsidized care, the premiums of the dwindling number of private plans will rise faster than the rate of inflation, causing bosses to prefer paying the (cheaper) penalty and moving even more into the government-sponsored plans.

Medicare spending has (conservatively) doubled in the past 15 years, with a projected rate of growth expected to remain in double digits. The Obama plan does nothing to address this budget nightmare, or the inflation it will worsen in the increasingly non-private "market." Instead the plan calls for a laundry list of new programs, electronic records systems, and incentives linked to results as guarantees for better quality of care, a bait-and-switch tactic already in full cry nationwide, and used to excuse paying hospitals and doctors less, even as their costs continue to rise.

The gist of the plan is to coerce more of the market into a government-backed macro-industry, and – sit down for this – I believe it will work. Oh it won't actually accomplish its stated goals anymore than the TSA increases actual passenger safety. But it will allow greater numbers to delude themselves that things are better even as services diminish and ER waiting lines grow. And if you think big government-sponsored industries are so great, I offer these two words: "Fannie Mae."

Honest, really, I did try to warn them all. But no, Obama and his glassy-eyed media acolytes led the Democrat lemmings into the most painful passage of a bill since Uncle Fred hit the Mexican buffet. Amidst the threats, name-calling, lies, cowardice, fear, and rush, the Dems went and created for themselves an entirely new villain with which to whip up their draining support – the Tea Party. Voters with a choice only of irrelevant Republicans and crazy Democrats struck out for a grass roots option that they hoped would provide, if not a new direction in U.S. politics, a brake on the wreck about to happen on Capitol Hill. There was cajoling, 'round-the-clock media speculation on dozens of channels, bribes for recalcitrant pols, and utter disdain for the protests flooding into congressional offices. Too late the voters realized just what they had unleashed by putting Democrats in charge of everything, and that this latest crop actually meant all the anti-American, anti-freedom, pro-socialist garbage they had spewed throughout the campaign. Too late voters learned (again) of the high, high price of nominating a moderate, unprincipled GOP careerist. As the smiling Democrats followed Speaker Pelosi and her enormous gavel toward the capitol steps, angry throngs yelled themselves hoarse in protest. Polite chin tucking, suburban moderates and liberals took their talking points from the Washington Post and New York Times in their disdain for the Tea Party protest. The same crowd that always drooled about "dissent being the highest form of patriotism" when it was a GOP war didn't really seem to mean it when it came to Dems socializing health care. The Tea Party was castigated as backward rubes, the racist products of incest, who had no real claim to be so angry. Surely, there were a couple of fools in the Tea Party ranks waving signs to "Keep Government hands Off My Medicare." But whatever their faults, nothing excused the lies told and repeated about violence and racist slurs during the Obamacare protest. The very nature and magnitude of those lies told how desperate the collectivists were to pass what amounted to a coup, an overt overthrow of expressed popular opinion by a majority representing, ironically, a minority. I was working in the ER on the coast, in Apalachicola, Florida that night and thought long and hard about what had happened ...

The King's Coin

"Back in the days of wooden ships and iron men, the Royal Navy had a lot of ocean to cover and occasionally ran short on sailors. A favorite recruitment tool was to drop a coin in a tankard of ale which, when discovered in the bottom of the mug by lurking members of the press gang, was determined to be an implicit acceptance of employment by the poor sod holding the empty. He had in the parlance of the day, "taken the King's coin" and was summarily hustled off to one of His Majesty's ships for the duration. Over the years, the pewter ale mugs started being made with glass bottoms so that the discerning patron could examine his beverage before draining a potential contract. So it has been for centuries, that taking the king's coin has impressed, even stolen many an otherwise happy life.

Forty-odd years ago, U.S. doctors betrayed their profession, and their patients by taking the king's coin when they accepted the eventuality of government medicine in the form of Medicare and Medicaid. Men and women trained to deal in facts, statistical projections, and hard choices were unwilling to tell the nation what it needed to hear, and instead invited Uncle Sam into the exam room in exchange for what was then a nice chunk of cash. It was easier to do good for the elderly and the poor with someone else's money, and to feel good about themselves for having done so. That mindset is now triumphant in Washington, D.C., by all respects now the capitol of the enemies of Americans and freedom. The Dear Leader and a Congressional majority desperately disdainful of its own rules and founding document are busy feeling really good about doing for some by stealing from others. They know, and yet do not care, that Medicare has not been financially solvent since 1972. These anti-Americans know that Medicaid is breaking numerous states, even as they plan to add millions more to the rolls. Obama and the Democrats know that they cannot provide good care for the entire population; the trick is to provide the illusion of care, "coverage" for all in order to build a permanent dependence in the numb-skulled minds of an increasingly benighted electorate. Republicans who rolled over for W.'s obscene bribery of seniors with promises of free drugs were deservedly stripped of power, and are now left on the ineffectual sidelines to watch the wreckage they helped sow.

A decade or more back, Medicaid recipients were issued gold cards that resemble credit cards. Anyone familiar with the ER environment has heard many times able-bodied, smiling beneficiaries in no distress exclaim as they check into the ER for a minor complaint, they "have the gold card" and that all is covered (without a thought to who is paying the tab). The other night, just after the Democrats increased nationalization of health care, I sat in a small town ER, talking with a lab technician, an x-ray technician, and a nurse. It was emblematic that the two patients in the ER were an elderly person who by age and ailment list would have long since run through any money that could have been contributed for her care during her lifetime; and a child whose parents spoke no English. I noted this as a microcosm of where we have come, four taxpayers at work, in part to pay for the care of two government patients. If you think this a harsh description, it is only because no doctor or politician has yet told you the truth. If you think I am being mean, then look at our deficit, the tax increases in this heinous bill, and the rising unemployment level.

Our x-ray tech laughed ruefully and exclaimed "We all have the gold card now." I looked, and sadly, my coffee mug did not have a glass bottom."

Whatever may be the future of government provided health care, it will be increasingly worse, and an accelerating threat to us all if we do not learn to call facts as they are, and make the hard choices.

❖ ❖ ❖

America The Fatter

In my line of work, you get to the point where you can spot certain trends. More often than not an ER doc can look up at the reception window and predict with good accuracy whether the patient checking in is here for chest pain, trouble breathing, or an exacerbation of anxiety. Sometimes it's even easier than that. Now don't think me cruel or callous, but when a 350 lb. gentleman checks in because of knee pain, the list of possible causes slims down quickly. The discussion over how much a patient's behavior contributes to his health problems, and who should be held responsible for paying for those problems, becomes all the more relevant the faster health costs rise. In 2007 the question was becoming more strident than ever ...

The Price of Pork

"Some companies penalize for health risks" reads the 9/9/07 Associated Press headline, of a story that elaborates "Now companies are penalizing workers who have high health risks such as obesity and high blood pressure or cholesterol as insurance costs climb." Who could have seen this coming? For more than 50 years it has been a growing corporate tradition in the U.S. that the boss should pay for his workers' medical care as a way of improving the output of the work force, of incentivizing workers, and of well...caring for them.

"The businesses are deducting from employees' pay-checks, adding insurance surcharges or offering insurance discounts or rebates only to low-risk workers." Huh? What exactly does "low-risk" mean? According to <u>Forbes</u> magazine in 2006 "Six in ten people in the United States are overweight, with a third crossing the boundary into obesity. The extra weight leads to at least 100,000 deaths annually. Obese people are at a much higher risk for heart attacks, strokes, diabetes, arthritis and some cancers." Is being a blob the only reason for the boss to stick it to you? The Centers for Disease Control and Prevention claims an economic cost of smoking at $3,383 per smoker per year—$1,760 in lost productivity and $1,623 in excess medical expenditures. The CDC also attributes 417,000 premature deaths annually to the ciggies, along with loads of chronic and expensive secondary pathologies including emphysema, heart disease, cancer, and one supposes, terminally bad breath.

Indianapolis-based Clarian Health will start reducing pay for employees in its health plan by $10 per paycheck if their BMI ratio is in the obese range of more than 29.9; and $5 per check will be docked if they don't meet required cholesterol, blood pressure or blood glucose measurements. Cincinnati-based Western & Southern Financial Group adds between $15 and $75 monthly to the insurance cost of health plan participants according to their BMI scores. Scott's Miracle-Gro Co., a lawn and garden company based in Marysville, Ohio, charges $40 more per month in health premiums for employees who don't complete annual risk assessments. The company charges $65 more for workers who don't try to reduce any high health risks that show up. Weyco, a Michigan-based health-benefits-management company, fired four employees who refused to quit smoking (the company stopped hiring smokers in 2003, and required then-puffers to punch out and depart the premises to light up). In 2006 Weyco began monthly tobacco testing, charging $50 a month to workers who tested positive or refused testing.

Is all this nagging from your boss a good thing? A 51-year old in the AP story was quoted thusly: "I knew if I wanted to be healthier and pay less, it was up to me to do something about it" as he lost 54 pounds and lowered his BMI enough to earn refunds the past two years. A CNBC report in July described how a New York UPS office hired a "health coach" for a pregnant diabetic employee. The health coach "redesigned her diet and helped her stick to it by frequent counseling," resulting in a healthy birth and return to work. So everyone wins, right?

While National Work Rights Institute director Jeremy Gruber cheers the prospect of healthier workers, he still worries that it will be accomplished "on the backs of employees by charging them money and punitive assessments." Employee advocates voice fears that anti-discrimination laws such as the Americans with Disabilities Act won't cover the person who is 20 or 30 pounds overweight, and corporations are already tailoring their policies to take advantage of the differences in various state laws. "It's a backdoor approach to weeding out expensive employees," Gruber said.

Weeding out?? Being a chubber or a smokestack are unhealthy choices, but what does that have to do with the employer? Isn't that outrageous?!

No, not at all. The Kaiser Family Foundation and Health Research and Educational Trust reported that employer health-insurance premiums rose more than 11 percent in 2004, a fourth consecutive year of double-digit growth. The study cited rising health insurance premiums in the preceding 3 years as a significant contributor to 5 million fewer jobs providing health insurance in that period. During that time employer-sponsored health insurance costs rose around five times the rate of inflation and earnings (The cost for single-family coverage has risen 78% since 2001). The rising costs are eating into the employers' profits. So the employer must take a cut in profit, pass his new costs on to the customer, or place the burden back on the employee. That is the price a free market demands of employees who think the boss exists to pay their medical bills.

Over the past half-century the majority of the workforce came to see health care as the responsibility of employers. During the past four decades, a growing segment of the population has come to rely on government for their care, fueling the belief in a "right" to health care. The more that people believe their own health to be the responsibility of their employer, the more benefits they will attempt to attach to their jobs. And the more people see government (e.g. Medicare) as the appropriate manager of our earthly woes, the more burdens they shall seek to give up to the benevolent bureaucracy. And the line between employer-provided care and government care will become less distinct as the angst wells up over the rising price of health coverage. But how can we have health care as a new right, and still expect to maintain a right to privacy from whoever pays the bill? Answer: we can't. In fact the Feds have already entered the game via the Health Insurance Portability and Accountability Act, stating that rewards or penalties could not exceed 20 % of the total cost of employee health coverage. Apart from the completely arbitrary standard, does anyone remember when HIPAA was first sold to help protect privacy?

The forthcoming election season (2008) has predictably heated up the perennial hand wringing over universal care and the government's role in that care. Governors in several states including Massachusetts, Colorado, Pennsylvania, and California are all implementing mandatory health care programs. And under the dictates of federalism, these would be harmless enough, failing to infect any innocents across state lines even as they fall flat on their respective faces. But when the big dog gets in the game, look out! Last week presidential candidate and protectors of the weak against evil doctors John Edwards made a statement that should have scared far more than it apparently did. Speaking in Iowa, Edwards said that his universal health care proposal would require that Americans go to the doctor for preventive care: "It requires that everybody be covered. It requires that everybody get preventive care," he told a crowd sitting in lawn chairs in front of the Cedar County Courthouse. "If you are going to be in the system, you can't choose not to go to the doctor for 20 years. You have to go in and be checked and make sure that you are OK." He said that women would be required to have regular mammograms to find "the first trace of problem." Edwards said his mandatory health care plan would cover preventive care, including mental health, dental and vision coverage for all Americans. Would there be mandatory mental health screenings, perhaps prompted by this year's rampage at Virginia Tech? What if someone were found to be the disagreeable sort, would mandatory mental health intervention be necessary? "The whole idea is a continuum of care, basically from birth to death," Edwards said.

Edwards said his plan would cost…oh forget what it would cost, we can't afford it anyway and that's not the point. Edwards said, "In my view, everybody is worth health care." He might have added "whether they want it or not." Sure that's just one candidate, but how many so-called Americans might share that point of view, so long as it's good for you?

But doctors would never back such a violation of personal choice, would they? Last summer in Chicago, the American Medical Association voted Tuesday to support a health care reform plan that would mandate all Americans to "obtain" health care coverage. This was a big change for an organization that heretofore had refused to back any mandatory coverage. So now the AMA is lobbying to support legislation that would require individuals and families earning 500% of the federal poverty level to obtain both catastrophic and evidence-based preventive health care coverage "using the tax structure to achieve compliance." Families and individuals earning less than 500% of the federal poverty level would also be required to obtain coverage after "implementation of a system of refundable tax credits or other subsidies." Those other subsidies could include vouchers for the purchase of health insurance.

How bad could it get? What if do-gooderism from the likes of Edwards got AMA backing, a slick marketing campaign, and lots of congressional support? When a non-covered citizen comes to the ER, might the hospital or even the ER doc be held responsible to report him to the state so that they might provide the unfortunate some coverage? And would not reporting the patient leave one open to sanctions? The AMA said last year that they would not support tax penalties against citizens who won't play ball. That is the same AMA that famously opposed the creation of Medicare, right up until it passed. Upon seeing some cash in it for doctors, the AMA has been a four-square Medicare supporter ever since. Obviously mandatory universal coverage will have the same sort of appeal for the fabled House of Medicine because they will perceive it to be good for their bottom line. And this path to universal compassion will be flower-strewn by those who want their boss, the government, or anyone other than themselves to be responsible for their own health."

The John Edwards presidential campaign fizzled, but his lawyerly quest to have his supporters blame others for their troubles never lost steam. A few years spent in private practice plus a whole heapin' helpin' of ER time had given me a good look at the result of our ongoing national buffet, results tailor-made for displacing the blame...

I'm Going Back for Seconds (2005)

"It's often easier to tackle a subject with the appropriate theme music. The twisted lyrics and howling gravel pipes, and insane ambience of Tom Waits serve well to consider the insanity of American obesity. (One moment please, yes ma'am, I'd like two, with extra cheese). I love laughing along with our own local morning sports-radio show when the chat turns to porky little kids and their Sony Playstations. While I haven't found a scientific, double-blinded study demonstrating a direct relationship between electronic gaming and blubbery rug rats, I have no doubt that the laughter is well aimed. A fitness coach friend who routinely works with children sees a clear link between the surrogate parenting provided by electronic devices and kids' difficulty with basic levels of physical fitness as a major obstacle to their best mental and emotional development (whew that sentence wore me out - better grab a snack). Given the truly American instinct toward doing things "Big", I was reassured for the culture to learn this from the Journal of the American Medical Association: our presently greater-than 9 million pediatric porkers have swelled their ranks by over 300 % over the past twenty years. That's a lot of Happy Meals.

But my basic aversion to bipeds less than 4 feet tall aside, the pork problem has been grabbing headlines this year as our good friends at Medicare try to wrestle with the (apparently cumbersome) problem of the overweight elderly. Health and Human Services Secretary Tommy Thompson declared, "obesity is a critical public health problem in our country that causes millions of Americans to suffer unnecessary health problems and to die prematurely." I can't help but think that private concerns such as Pizza Hut and Taco Bell might differ with Mr. Thompson. The purveyors of all that tastes good, the Krispy Kremes, KFC's, Budweiser, and L'il Debbie snacks probably view all of this as, well, a growth industry. The MSNBC report that declares 34% of Americans to be overweight, and an additional 31% to be obese has to be regarded as a clear market signal from legions of well-sated consumers. (I'm betting that for all the hell that HHS raises, it will have zero influence on the various agricultural subsidies that help to keep food cheap and available for the not-quite-starving masses).

HHS Medical Officer Dr. Sean Tunis stated "...we have shifted the focus of medical obesity-related treatments to whether or not they can be shown to improve health outcomes, rather than whether or not obesity can be considered an illness." Was there any controversy over whether the effects of obesity on body systems and longevity constituted an "illness"? Center for Medicare/Medicaid Services Administrator Marc McClellan explained, "Medical science will now determine whether we provide coverage for the treatments that reduce complications and improve outcomes." Which is...sorry...(Mom always said don't write with your mouth full). So a benevolent government will now consider how to help the obese, providing the scientific ducks all line up – preferably with an orange glaze, and wild rice on the side. But wait, if we try to dent the American gut, who will fund the countless self-help, get-happy diet and exercise machine infomercials clogging up the tube at 2 AM? Don't these has-been models and actors, "fitness celebrities", and the like, also need a chance for "improved outcomes"? And if arrogant government bureaucrats are so willing to help Medicare beneficiaries with their waistlines, can't they deal with a more serious burgeoning health crisis and encourage young Medicaid recipients to duplicate their genetic material a little less freely?

I'm reminded of Jay Leno a few years back making fun of Domino's large pizza deal, whereby for a little extra they could "make it a meal" by throwing in some breadsticks, chicken wings, and 2-liter soda. In an age that SHOULD feature smaller budgets, we are paying Washington chowderheads good money to worry about whether a bunch of fat people really are more ill and whether they should be helped via government …largesse. Instead they may threaten the very foundations of our modern 21st century economy if Adkins products stocks start to fall.

A timid perusal of the web site for the National Association to Advance Fat Acceptance (www.naafa.org) is almost too much to swallow. There are various tip-links on how to file grievances with airlines who charge extra for extra seats; how to write a successful complaint letter if one is outraged by a "fat-bashing commercial"; a "Declaration of Health Rights for Fat People"; a description of a lawsuit by a San Francisco woman described as a 240 lb. "fitness enthusiast" denied employment as an aerobics instructor. The banner at the web page top cheers that the 2004 NAAFA convention was a "resounding" success. I wonder if the banquet was all you can …never mind.

The American Obesity Association's web page (www. obesity.org) has an entire page devoted to explaining the tax breaks American face-stuffers can receive by itemizing expenditures aimed at reducing their girth. I knew it! It always comes back to someone wanting someone else to foot the bill. If one seeks to gain most-favored trading status with Dairy Queen and have their little chubbers waddle in for free sundaes for life, then it's none of my business. But now America's well-fed have tax breaks and want new medical treatments including bariatric surgery covered by the taxpayer. As we collectively waddle toward socialized medicine, consider: the government that pays for your care will be able to direct your care. What if you LIKE cheese sauce on your ice cream and hate exercise?? We now witness a society ready to adopt the schizophrenia of suing McDonald's for addictive French fries, and then paying for the stomach stapling of the plaintiff. And we are also treated to the high comedy of a special interest group that seeks special consideration and treatments for a condition inferred to be natural, absent diet and exercise."

Thanksgiving became my traditional time to write about America's government-sponsored waistline, but it wasn't my fault. In 2006, with the leaves on the ground, anticipating the smoker's heavenly aroma, I just couldn't help myself ...

A Policy Cornucopia

"The leftover candy is almost gone from the clinic and ER break rooms, and most of us can do with a little less chocolate for the next couple of weeks. The holidays are approaching fast, which is great timing for a response for a recent last commentary. A colleague who uses the nome de plume "Frank Edematous" wrote in to offer some friendly critique of both our central theme, and tone. His final point was succinct and direct: "You sound callous and uncaring and you are a doctor. You sound like the kind of guy who might deny care to an obese person and truly believes that he/she is worthless because of their obesity."

His comments were much appreciated, especially for their timing. As my regular readers know, Thanksgiving is the traditional time to examine the fun surrounding

America's institutionalized obesity culture and the idiocies it spawns. So load up your plate – extra gravy now! – grab another roll, and consider...

This fall MSNBC reported that "31 states showing an increase in obesity. Their source, Trust for America's Health, advocated such fixes as employers paying for nutrition counseling and subsidized health club memberships for their workers; government mandated screenings that measure the fitness of Medicaid beneficiaries (presumably when not giving them free-for-all food stamps), and PAY them ("subsidize or reimburse") for participating in exercise and fitness programs. The TAH report also wants local level, governments to zone and legislate land use laws to "give people more chances to walk or bike", followed with "Local governments also should set aside more funding for sidewalks." Talk about eminent domain with a side of hash browns! TAH executive poohbah Dr. Jeff Levi summed up the approach of modern big-group/big-answer medicine, saying "a lot of the things that the government tells people to do about their weight aren't realistic, which makes obesity a societal problem, not just a personal problem."

Not content to shut up while he was behind, Levi proceeded to depict unsafe streets and the costs of fresh produce as contributors to porkiness over which the sufferer has no control, the exact same logic which organized medicine has used to characterize handguns as a preventable health hazard. The common thread is a complete de-emphasis of any personal responsibility for the problem. Levi finished with "we're not asking them to take responsibility for something they have control over" i.e. it's YOUR fault you miserly taxpayer! Once again, we have a doctor – sorry, provider – telling one group of patients how they must regard and treat another group of patients.

In March '06. CNN reported the Centers for Disease Control and Prevention estimation that "two of every three American adults, and more than one in six children and adolescents are considered overweight or obese." The CDC also noted that the percentage of chunky Americans has DOUBLED over the past 20 years (supersize THAT!). In that report Prof. J. Eric Oliver of the University of Chicago (talk about a town with great pizza!) said the real obesity problem is due to all of us "not adjusting to modern life and choice, essentially being able to eat what you want, where you want, whenever you want." Okay prof, you had us there, but then you too kept talking: "That's consumer capitalism catching up with where we eat," he said. "Ultimately, the real problem is that we don't seem to be very biologically equipped to deal with the contemporary lifestyle." Is he suggesting that it really isn't our fault that potato chips and HD TV are so cheap? If the problem really isn't our fault but our biological adaptability, then isn't that a shot at capitalism? Note how every time a "health policy scholar" opens his or her mouth, it involves telling someone else what to do, and taking their money.

An expert in those two activities, former-president Clinton, wants to "stop the increasing prevalence of childhood obesity" in the United States by 2010 through a partnership between the William J. Clinton Foundation and American Heart Association. They advocate starting children on the path of proper diet and exercise, so that they'll grow up to be healthy adults and reduce obesity-related health costs. Who could argue with that? Clinton et al also want to "work with" the food and restaurant industry and the media and increasing physical activity and improving lunches in schools (read "coerce private business, while giving more tax dollars to academic types in government medicine and education unions to study the problem). Bubba said "lawmakers should take a greater involvement in the fight – setting higher standards for school lunches and eliminating junk food in school vending machines, and called on the fast-food industry to shape up." Geez, let a guy get a bypass operation, and he just has to get into everybody else's grocery bags.

Across the nation, stories about the all-you-can-eat society, and attempts to rein it in, are erupting like succulent Portobello mushrooms. Fox News has reported that "Many young children are too heavy for standard car-safety seats, and manufacturers are starting to make heftier models to accommodate them." ("We don't recommend that a parent use a restraint system for a child that has outgrown that system," said Eric Bolton, a spokesman for the National Highway Traffic Safety Administration. "It is risky.") Articles in serious medical publications this past year have detailed the rise of patients so fat they can't fit into CAT-scan machines to diagnose their pulmonary emboli or evaluate their acute belly pain. (No word yet on whether the NHTSA is mandating heavier-duty shocks, or whether HUD is seeking funding to study reinforced toilet seats).

(Please excuse this interruption, but the timer went off and it's time to take the pie out of the oven)

New York City's health department plans to require some restaurants to list the calorie content of their food on their menus. The rule would apply only to businesses that serve standardized portions and already disclose calorie information voluntarily – not the sort of restaurants where concerned uptown do-gooders eat, but the fast-food chains where the rest of the mob dines. Health Commissioner Dr. Thomas Frieden, another government provider, said diners deserve to know up front when a meal has the potential to pack on pounds (because they're just too stupid to know all on their own!).

New York, Maine, Maryland, and California have all attempted to institute "Twinkie taxes", punitive measures to coerce customers away from legal products such as soft drinks and fried foods. Inventor of the "Twinkie Tax" concept, Yale psychology professor Kelly D. Brownell, complains that tasty, low-nutrition foods are too cheap, and should be taxed, with said booty then used to subsidize healthier alternatives. (Contrarian Southerners may at least take temporary comfort living in the homeland of the Krispy Kreme, where any county fair now boasts of deep-fat fried...Twinkies).

Just this past week, there were two prominent fat stories in the news: In New York KFC is being forced to discard high trans-fat oils in their foods, possibly removing the "good" from their "finger-lickin'" ...) This move is in response of course not to their customers, but to the government. And in Winter Haven, FL. Police Chief Paul Goward was fired for his memo telling the department's "jelly bellies" to shape up. The memo used no names and singled out no officer, but apparently hurt feelings are worse than cops suffering MI's while chasing suspects. This recalls last year's brouhaha in New Hampshire, where Dr. Terry Bennett faced the sanction of his board of medicine for telling a patient she was fat and needed to lose weight.

The interested factions have really gotten their hands around all sides of this issue. Organized medicine wants to steer people in the right direction, but may want them to fork out some cash to do it. The American Academy of Pediatrics wants their doctors to advocate for some pretty reasonable things, such as school wellness counsels and the vigorous protection of compulsory PE classes. But then they join the mob and demand exercise-promoting "Social marketing", funding for research in the prevention of childhood obesity, and "the construction of safe recreational facilities, parks, playgrounds, bicycle paths, sidewalks, and crosswalks." The AMA passed a resolution that would work with the Congress "to create an incentive program for individuals working towards or living a healthy lifestyle as measured by BMI and waist circumference." (Does this mean we can get our taxes lowered if we jog regularly?)

On the other side of the table we have the good old National Association to Advance Fat Acceptance (www.naafa.org) who, no lie, offers a national merit scholarship. Applicants must submit an essay on topics including "The importance of fat acceptance in the year 2006; Personal Fat Activism; Another fat related topic on approval."

So what happens when the National Association of Pay-For-Performance Acceptance (the AMA) runs afoul of the NAAFA? Who wins when the pro-fat camp has to see doctors whose payment is determined by meeting obesity reduction goals? That's a sumo match that will be worth watching.

I led off talking about the response of "Dr. Frank", with whom I had a pleasant (really!) exchange. We will continue to promote the joust of ideas and welcome all critique, and it is important to state that of course I'm not down on obese folks here at all. What I am FOR is freedom, the kind between doctor and patient that truly allows the latter to pursue his or her own interests with the benefit of honest counsel from a trusted expert. But patient choice is no less important to good health than meeting blood pressure and HgbA1c targets, and providers who feel otherwise are wrong. Patients who suffer obesity need compassionate, honest evaluation and treatment, which should not include the direct force of tax increases and banning certain foods. Such care should disdain the indirect force of government funding physicians' choices for their patients, which dehumanizes the latter to a commodity to be manipulated for gain. So as politicians, public health scholars, and organized medicine join us at the national table this Thanksgiving to gobble down tax dollars and free choice, let's encourage them, at least, to chew with their mouths closed."

The whole darned topic tasted so good I went back for seconds in 2007...

"As our regular readers know, Thanksgiving is the traditional time to examine the fun surrounding America's institutionalized obesity culture and the silliness it spawns. Our nation's physicians are increasingly besieged on the one hand by insurance companies and government do-gooders threatening to cut their salaries through Pay-For-Performance, which sets milestones for patient performance including blood pressure, and of course, obesity. With the dollars on the line will the onus for slimming be placed on the patient, or will the doctor be held financially responsible for another's exercise and diet habits? Will any physicians seriously argue what a P4P obesity target implies? That short of incentivizing providers differently, keeping one's patients fat and happy results in more visits, therefore more revenue, and is good for the, uh, bottom line.

We approach the joyous day when the gobbling of millions of American turkeys will be forever silenced in the service of gobbling at the dinner table. A growing conglomerate of the concerned, ranging from organized medicine and employers to the federal government and climate control advocates, is focused on the costs of American chubbiness. What better occasion than this day of national feasting to reflect on just who is paying attention to our waistlines?

With health care costs swelling quicker than a waistline after the pumpkin pie, bosses are cracking down on more expensive employee behaviors when it comes to cigarettes and the table. Professors M. F. Jacobson and Marion Nestle claim in a recent Journal of Public Health Policy describe obesity as "the new smoking." The problem may be a heftier one to tackle: "While three in five Americans (61 percent) believe health insurance should cost more for smokers, only 40 percent believe it should cost more for those who are overweight because of poor lifestyle habits."

By multiple estimates, obesity costs the national economy billions yearly in direct medical costs, progressive conditions that lead to future costs, and lost productivity. MSNBC reports that West Virginia's proclivity to plumpness cost taxpayers nearly $200 million last year. This has inspired the state's largest Medicaid provider UniCare to offer doctors and their staffs training in obesity prevention and body mass index measurement. UniCare has even offered Weight Watchers membership free to some of its Medicaid clients (no word on any reaction by taxpayers who have to fund their own Weight Watchers dues). A similar program exists in California, and will soon expand to 13 additional states. The Trust For America's Health ranks West Virginia second in the percentage of children who are obese (An unenviable achievement in a nation whose percentage of children on oral diabetic medications doubled from 2002 – 2005, according to the American Public Health Association).

The Journal of the American Medical Association just published a study that finds being overweight does not increase the risk of dying from heart disease and cancer; but it does increase the risk of acquiring morbid obesity, which DOES increase the risk of heart disease and cancer. Northwestern University professor of medicine Dr. Robert Kushner responded: "You should not take heart in the idea that if you are only overweight you are OK ... there is a high likelihood you will be obese because people gain weight as they age in this country." He concluded with "We've done very well at medicating people to keep the medical [obesity] complications at bay, which allows people to live longer." So not being obese can lessen the co-morbidities, and therefore the need for expensive medicines and care? The question hangs like the gravy and biscuit aroma in the kitchen: why didn't U.S. doctors think of that?

In other funny fat news...

Our Plate Is Full

Is it The End of the World? Last week the Associated Press reported a new push by public health experts that "Cutting calories, carbon dioxide can help save lives and the planet." "The U.S. Centers for Disease Control and Prevention is considering public promotion of the "co-benefits" of fighting global warming and obesity-related illnesses," said Dr. Howard Frumkin, director of the CDC's National Center for Environmental Health. "The American Public Health Association is seeking to connect obesity and climate change solutions," said executive director Dr. Georges Benjamin. Forget climate change, it will be Armageddon if they take away our steaks! Dr. Robert Lawrence of the Johns Hopkins School of Public Health said, "A diet shift away from heavy meat consumption would also go far [to reducing greenhouse gases], because it takes much more energy and land to produce meat than plants. This dovetails with a United Nations report claiming that the meat sector of the global economy is responsible for 18 percent of the world's greenhouse gas emissions. But what about all the rogue cows, pigs, and sheep still blasting dangerous methane into the atmosphere? Shouldn't they be killed and eaten to help save Mother Earth?

❖ ❖ ❖

Doughnuts to the Oldies...Patrons of several senior centers in Putnam County, N.Y. were up in arms in August. The reason: officials had decided to ban the delivery of free day-old doughnuts, cakes, and pies to the senior centers. "Officials were concerned that the county was setting a bad nutritional precedent by providing mounds of doughnuts and other sweets to seniors." One resident decried this "Lack of respect" which implied seniors were too senile to make the choice for themselves. But another responded "I think the senior center did them a favor by taking [them] away." "Senior citizens can walk down to the store and buy doughnuts. Nobody's stopping them," said Michael Jacobson, executive director of usual suspect The Center for Science in the Public Interest (the same crowd that got traditional movie popcorn butter banned, and tried to claim that hot dogs cause brain cancer). However, Jacobson added, senior citizen centers, nursing homes and assisted-living centers should not be worsening the health problems of seniors. Putnam county officials compromised: Small amounts of doughnuts, cakes and other baked goods could be served at the centers — *but they have to be eaten elsewhere.* Once again our seniors want to be cared for and guarded against all harm-and they want it done their way. We can only imagine how much fun this will be as the Baby Boomers start assuming their long-sought permanent residence.

❖ ❖ ❖

And in the "No Further Comment Needed" category ...
"Press Release October 13, 2007:
Stop Referring to Kids As Obese

Oakland, CA – The National Association to Advance Fat Acceptance joins the Weight Realities Division of the Society for Nutrition Education, and the Association for Size Diversity and Health in urging our government, the medical industry and the media to stop using the words "obese" and "obesity" with reference to heavy children and adolescents."

After that last bit, I'll admit, I was full.

❖ ❖ ❖

A last thought on health care ...

In the course of my lifetime and just a bit before, health care has become largely viewed as a right in the U.S. As health care became a guarantee owed citizens by their government, those that actually practiced it became in the public mind, an arm of that government. In that course and in great part due to their own shortsightedness, physicians have increasingly come to be viewed as such, as government employees. And there is a dark, murderous logic to what might follow: the government that giveth can deny, and may use its agents to enforce edicts for the greater good. Society through its politicians, malpractice attorneys, unhinged false compassion, and unrealistic expectations has put the burdens on the doctors, nurses, hospitals, pharmaceutical industry, and all other professionals actually trained to deliver medical care. But the evolution of medicine, from the ancient inception of the Hippocratic Oath to just recently, has had as a foundation the mutual respect of the relationship between the patient and physician. Now that the trust inherent in that compact has been abrogated, society foolishly seems to think that only doctors will pay the price...

Blame the Patient

A recent (2007) <u>Medical Economics</u> article "What About a Crackdown on Patients?" hinted at the real problem – and the real opportunity. The nation is spending nearly $7,000 per capita annually, with no end in site for the growth in the ranks of the elderly and those on the dole, our favorite dependent populations, Medicare and Medicaid. The nation is going bust, and politicians everywhere are scrambling to cut costs any way they can. The "Crackdown" article described a timid West Virginia proposal to tie certain "expanded" Medicaid benefits to patient compliance in hopes of improving health and (surprise!) cutting costs. Nice try Mountain Momma, but it is time to look this bull in the eye.

The nation is faced with paying ever-rising costs for two growing groups, the elderly and disadvantaged, neither of which has any incentive to access the health care system any less. Neither group is paying the freight nor has any reason to contain costs, and so for their own good physicians must step in to guide and discipline them. And why shouldn't we? The rational implication for Pay-For-Performance is that doctors cannot be trusted to do what is right or competent in the best interests of their patients; therefore the "true" patient advocates in Congress, statehouses, and the AMA must devise friendly coercions to get the very best out of U.S. physicians. Under the cloak of quality improvement the deceitfully contrived P4P scheme celebrated throughout the halls of government, Big Insurance, and organized medicine is nothing if not a cost-containment plan. Since society at large now accepts the notion of tying specific actions to remuneration in medicine, it's time for doctors to see the benefits of playing within such a framework.

Will better compliance cut costs? That depends with which standards the beneficiary is called to comply. West Virginia started with the Medicaid population, so let us begin there as well. It is not undue stereotyping to note the vast usage of deadly tobacco in the ranks of the disadvantaged, and the legal triumphs of the late 1990's successfully tied smoking to great sums paid out by over-burdened states. Now that we have got Big Tobacco with physician support to do its part by shelling out billions for (ostensibly) smoking cessation programs, it is time to turn to the consumer. Require the Medicaid recipient to abstain from the cancer sticks, or place them on a national data base absolving ER's from seeing them for respiratory and cardiovascular-related complaints. It is well-known by all taxpaying health care workers who regularly treat our subsidized youth that certain preferred groups feel relieved of the burden to practice any sort of DNA dispersal discipline i.e. birth control. How then to attach consequences to this profligacy? Orphanages will only extend the cost and leave the parents free to make yet more decisions with other peoples' money. The only sane solution is to limit each mother (couples are so hard to quantify any more) to one government-supported child; extra progeny would not me eligible for Medicaid, SCHIP, or the associated free prescriptions and late-night Tylenol from the ER. A would-be mother who learns from others the consequences of multiple simultaneous earaches might be given pause. Diabetes? Hypertension? These are ailments easily tracked and managed with multiple treatment options, usually to very good effect in the properly motivated patient. So let the patient decide! If the individual beneficiary chooses not to take his medicines, then respect his choice by allowing him to retain its full benefit. So you have a morbidly obese patient who can't seem to consume less than 4,000 kcals per day? This is a patient whose free office visits and meds in turn free him from the burden of prioritizing. As physicians sworn to do all we can to promote the health of our patients what-ever their objections, we would be remiss to allow this to continue. And in select cases, a call to the local WIC or food stamp offices might be in order. Our present system makes an enabler of the doctor, as well as the taxpayer.

And what about the elderly? Through the miracle of Medicare, vast numbers have managed to far outlive an age when they could actually pay for themselves, and have turned to their benevolent juniors to make up the difference. In this societal judgment physicians were willing accomplices and, upon perceiving their incomes directly affected, have become vocal proponents. Neither physicians' groups nor the government have dared incur the nuclear wrath of the AARP crowd and accordingly Medicare expansions have continued without end. The institutionalization of health care as a "right" for the retirees transformed physicians and hospitals into extensions of a government that must provide without complaint. The establishment of Medicare Part D confirmed for the golfing set that they should not have to bear any cost they don't wish to. Medicare recipients have no incentive to contain costs, and what fun that spawns. Are you nervous in the middle of the night? An ER visit for a complete cardiac workup is free to you if you have lived long enough. Constipated and over 65? Abdominal CAT scans won't cost you a penny. Are you an overworked nursing home staffer, worried that your demented patient bedridden for a decade moved a little less today? No problem – Medicare, suddenly watchful family members, and teams of helpful lawyers will help encourage you to send your patient to the ER where an equally encouraged doctor will do the million-dollar workup. But the nation's elderly have a reputation for toughness and we should not insult them by leaving them out of the solution. As with our Medicaid friends, smoking is a no-no, and continued free choice on the part of the patient should be met with the choice of the hospital not to treat the associated recurrent complaints. Of course this will impact the hospitals' bottom lines, but we can't let something like that stand in the way of cost containment – oh, and improving the health of our seniors. If a patient had a clean coronary catheterization within the past year, then recurrent chest pain is likely just anxiety and should not warrant admission no matter what the risk factors or history. The elderly could be required to carry a standardized state or federal medication list, laminated, and hanging around their neck upon presentation. Failure to have this readily available could justify refusal to treat all but the direst condition until someone went home to retrieve it.

How could we deal with out-patient expenditures? Members of both the dependent populations could easily be limited to a set number of visits per month, adjusted by medical complexity or average coded visit level. Example: a smoker with metabolic syndrome, average systolic greater than 160, greater than 130% recommended weight, with depression could easily be a 99214 on any visit. This patient could reasonably be limited to 3 visits per month, and pay for any additional care herself. Any attempt to seek fertility treatment at the taxpayer expense would, once reported to the central database, reduce this person's allowable visits to 2 per quarter. If she is over 65, she could receive an additional psychiatric referral. The Congressional Budget Office reports that nearly $2 billion will be spent in the next decade on male impotence drugs alone ($90 million was spent in 2006). Is Uncle Ray's good time on a Saturday night really worth bankrupting your children? Is granny's urge incontinence medication really that necessary, when she can well afford diapers in bulk?

Vast and organized forces are marshaled to force doctors into generic, impersonal treatment regimens that greater powers deem "best practices" and "evidence-based." Failure to comply will earn enmity, lower pay, and possible criminal sanctions. Compliance will infuriate patients as they are swept more into the ever-tightening swirl of budgetary goulash designed to spread compassion evenly, while attempting to combine the oil and vinegar of excellence and cost-containment. Those patients who have been trained to believe they have an absolute right to our services have lost all respect for the medical profession – engaging them a bit more forcefully will help restore that respect through a new set of incentives. By limiting, sorry, streamlining available diagnostics and therapeutics, we can delay the fraying of this critical piece of the national fabric.

Holding patients to blame for their predicament makes practical sense, but also passes the philosophical smell test. Decades ago physicians signed on to the idea of health care as a right that justified government intrusion into the exam room and OR suite. Perhaps this is something we should no longer fight. By accepting government provision of care and ourselves as the designated providers, we made our "best judgment" subordinate to larger concerns over scare resource allocation and national macro-targets. After betraying the Classical Hippocratic Oath forty years ago, isn't it disingenuous to try to climb back on our collective high horse and complain about the individual patient's interests as though they exist in a vacuum?

As cruel and foolish as the above cost-containment suggestions seem, they would improve the behavior of patients which is otherwise gorging itself on the nation's economic health. The poor and the elderly waste billions every year through their own choices, frivolous visits, unplanned pregnancies, minor aches, and general nervousness. We as doctors accepted, and then promoted this system. Until such time as we are courageous to enough to admit our guilt by overturning this awful system, we should put the blame in the next best place – our patients. It will be after all, for their own good."

I am not in any way advocating this sort of cruel, dehumanizing outcome. But society is pushing for it whether it knows or not.

The AAPS conference wound down on Saturday morning that September 2008, after which was held the annual board of meeting. As an elected board member Todd was ensconced in the conference room a few hours more, while I was able to enjoy blue corn nachos, college football, and several delicious India Pale ale drafts while waiting to head out. I was learning a lesson about politics and packaging watching the AAPS over several years, a good organization that has good ideas and principled members. They also have – as does every group – just a couple of weirdoes that take up too much floor time, and promulgate fringe ideas, some of which make it on to the agenda. The fault therein is to dilute the important central message, and give opportunity to their detractors. This is not to slight or defame the AAPS, for which I have great respect. But at a critical time for the defense of the individual in the swirls and misinformation of the health care debate, the group philosophically best placed to educate the public had no business wasting time discussing shaken baby syndrome, intelligent design, or teen sexual abstinence. The nation's health care system was being further weakened and usurped by a weasley Republican, setting it up to be swallowed whole by a socialist successor. This was a long-odds political battle that required better public relations, more effective lobbying, and a concerted focus on the central cause of fighting government involvement in health care. I support their founder, and the larger tenets of the AAPS, but they appeared to have been overcome by events after missing a critical window of opportunity. Like the Republican congressional takeover in 1994, a lack of clear, informative message discipline, with steady follow-up, will be defeated by a hostile media and ignorant public.

❖ ❖ ❖

The administrative niceties and lunch finished, we hit the road north for Flagstaff on as pretty an early fall afternoon as they make out in Arizona. A bit north of Phoenix the terrain starts to cut between mountains and gullies, then gains elevation on to broader plateaus as the desert starts to fall away. By the time we were nearing Flagstaff, we began to see the occasional stream, or patch of trees already sporting golden autumn leaves, few and far between, but a real contrast with the desert behind. We hooked a continental right in Flagstaff on to Interstate 40 and head just a bit east for the first stop, the Canyon Diablo Meteor Crater. It's also known as the Barringer Crater after Daniel Barringer, the first guy to suggest that this 4,000 foot wide, 170-foot deep hole in the ground, was caused by a meteor. My first thought was that Mr. Barringer must have been a savvy turn of the century entrepreneur who made big bucks pointing out the bleeding obvious to greenhorns in the newly settled west. Or maybe he had to disprove some quack notion of a bothersome Al Gore forerunner who was trying to blame the geological mystery on global warming from too many whale oil lamps burning in San Francisco. But no, Mr. Barringer was actually an engineer who owned a mining company and thought the crater would be a line on a 100-million ton, extremely lucrative buried iron deposit. There is a permanent research facility in the bottom of the crater, and a little museum and typical gift shop, where you can buy sweets to stuff into your noisy children while you try to read the explanations of the unusual geology found in and around the hole. The best part though is to simply stand on the edge and drink it all in. The crater is big, no, absolutely huge, and gives the visitor on the rim the urge to fly down into the middle and swoop around like some mad cliff swallow on really potent psychotropics. From the top one can look across a 360-degree vista of the high desert, breathtaking browns, reds, and a little sparse-growth green in distant patches in the mesa shadows, the warm September sun and an early autumn wind fighting for top billing on the rim top.

Barringer never found the iron mother load, which later scientists proved had actually been vaporized and scattered all over the surrounding countryside. On the up side, he got a really cool tourist site named after him, and no Luddite protest rally stopped the cable cars from inspiring pre-packaged rice six decades later. Capitalism wins again.

While it may have sought to harvest the blasted mineral riches of natural phenomenon, capitalism actually had to create our next stop. Sometime back in the 1880's a railroad terminal started growing from a stopover to a small town, a \$2 million hotel was built there in the teeth of the Depression, and then one tiny mention in a country rock hit over forty years later put the town on the map. Of course we speak of Winslow, Arizona, made famous in "Take It Easy" by the Eagles. The song was written for the group by Jackson Browne of whom Todd is, to be understated, a huge fan. And so, part of the westward tour had to include standing on the famous corner in Winslow in homage to great music. The famed corner features a life-size bronze statute of a *guy with a guitar presumably "takin' it easy." Behind him is a tromp-l'oeil mural of a window reflecting a girl (my Lord) in a truck that we hope is slowing down to take a look, and on that block a very real flatbed Ford just like the one in the picture. The place looks like a little dusty, half-forgotten railroad town as reminiscent to my mind of Jimmy Buffet's "Ringling, Ringling" as anything. There were two or three bars and restaurants in the old downtown, and a movie theater, but most of the traffic was out on the highway. Having my picture made on the site of a great piece of Americana, call me a tourist if you like, was worth the effort to get there. We by no means saw the whole town, which I'm sure is charming, but the sun was setting, and it was time to coffee-up and head east. A mile down the road and we were on the outskirts. The convenience store was moderately busy with Saturday evening traffic for gas and beer. I wondered what it would be like to live in Winslow, that looked like not much, a long way from nowhere. There were a few Caucasians in the store who were all speaking English. The other folks in here all appeared to be of Latino persuasion, and were all speaking Spanish. Maybe the latter were all Americans, speaking Spanish the way other Americans speak ebonics as a way to preserve a sub-cultural identity in our vast melting pot. Maybe they were all documented guest workers whom I should have thanked for low food prices. Maybe they were all illegals and I should have called ICE. I don't know. We topped off the gas tank, got the largest size coffees available, and headed east into the night. It was one big, star splashed sky over a dark interstate desert, with a hell of a view in a beautiful land.*

❖ ❖ ❖

Part 4

"Where liberty dwells, there is my country."

Benjamin Franklin

"I'm not saying you're not good at what you do.
I'm just saying I'm better"

Hank Hill, "King of the Hill"

Awash in America – Revels in the Land of "Number 1"

*Real Men * Return to the Holy City * The Purple Death * And Then They Came for the Cookies * I Don't Give a Damn Where You are Registered * Indoctrinating the Next Generation * Stupidity = Terror * Our Own Worst Enemy * Keep Your Kid, and your Senator Away from My Video Game * Warming to the Kiddies * Off to See the Mouse * American Self-Destruction: We're #1! * Two Movies, One Lesson * A Moral Malfunction * Our Best * Lighten Up*

*Holiday Notes: Thanks All Around * Warm The Planet, Chop That Gobbler * Christmas the Illogical * Christmas the Unpredictable * Not As The World Giveth **

369

One reason, maybe the biggest of all that I entered into my rendezvous with culinary destiny at The Big Texan is the sheer size and magnificence of the entire production. For all the sniffing by supposed sophisticates and the staff at the Huffington Post, we are a big splashy culture that kicks big ass. At our best we have built the biggest and best of everything, from cars to rocket ships to cable sports programming to statuesque jiggly models with large platters of hot wings and huge pitchers of beer to wash it all down. Doggone it all, America likes to have a good time, the bigger the better, which is the entire and sum total explanation behind the Super Bowl, tractor pulls, Victoria's Secret, and those beads they throw on Bourbon Street.

Only capitalism could create our glorious and glittering, mad electrified rush into and through the arms of excess. Only a nation so awash in liquor, riches, and passion like nowhere else, a birthplace of smashed dreams and weekend lies that leave everyone smiling, at least a little, could give rise to the farce of "Celebrity Rehab with Dr. Drew." Only a free market could create such a place, and such a market could only grow from a society that wanted to have a good time. Can we possibly imagine the original Plymouth Puritans creating a Las Vegas? Nope, that gene pool had to be washed out liberally with incorrigible Scots and liquored-up Irishmen to loosen up those hat buckles. Dubai and the super-rich aside, the Arabs are not exactly famous for their fun side. The Africans are too susceptible to tribalism, and the Latins have too great a penchant for generalissimos. The Chinese have spent too many centuries trying to turn everything they can get their hands on into some sort of powdered aphrodisiac, which may say something about their population problem, but the inventors of fireworks did not have enough rocket power to invent the $4 midnight surf & turf buffet. The Russians? Too cold, probably too drunk, and too worried about the Germans. The French? Ditto. The Germans? Are you kidding me? But put all *of these ethnic groups together under the banner of freedom, steal some Indian land, and you get yourself the only permanent party cool enough to attract the likes of The Rat Pack, give birth to a Louis Armstrong, and build the Ford Mustang.*

As George C. Scott growled in his immortal "Patton" speech, "Americans traditionally love to fight. All real Americans love the sting of battle. When you were kids, you all admired the champion marble shooter, the fastest runner, the big league ball player, the toughest boxer. Americans love a winner and will not tolerate a loser. Americans play to win all the time." We kicked out the British for, incredibly, far less then we passively tolerate now. But when we had a country to build, we blew across the continent, ripped off the Mexicans twice, had the world's biggest living room wrestling match over states' rights and slavery, committed the afore-mentioned theft from the Indians, and settled California. We had Texas cattle drives, Kansas City stockyards, and Chicago steakhouses. Will Rogers famously remarked on the first ever car ride to poverty, and after a late start, we beat the damn Commies to the moon. We were the birthplace of blues, jazz, and rock (sorry about that rap garbage), and no nation or people can top the beauty of South-eastern Conference coeds. We are the loudest, most deservedly egocentric country in the room, even if we do occasionally have one too many and gobble up all the fried shrimp before we spill oil all over them. It is no coincidence that America when at her best has the greatest culture on the planet. We have a lot to be proud of, but also a lot to lose.

Quoting "Patton" will call down accusations of misogyny and simple-mindedness, and advancing themes like American Exceptionalism will invite pseudo-intellectuals to say one is not sufficiently nuanced. Those who offer such criticisms have clearly not seen a U.S. Navy Blue Angels air show in person.

The heroic, manly affect that played such a large and vital part in the development of our collective psyche is under continued assault from lesser, envious types whose poor self-esteem offers only the recourse to tear down what works. And that's how we got the daytime talk show...

Real Men

"One of the drawbacks to occasionally working the night shift is that one can spend the next day in a semi-wakeful, discombobulated fugue, the mind wandering between trying to remember whether this is a day off, or time to get ready for another shift. And the reactions aren't as good. Recumbent in a post/pre-work stupor on the couch last week, I flipped on the tube to surf mindlessly. Tragically, I just couldn't work the thumb fast enough on the channel button, and I was stuck momentarily on "Dr Phil." Now I know better than to watch this drivel and put much-needed IQ points at risk, but as stated, I was still trying to wake up. Dr. Phil was facing a couple with two twin baby girls, discussing who-knows-what, with the rest of the audience ooing and awing in sugary clucks and murmurs. The wife of the couple was beaming with swimmy-eyed gratitude at Dr. Phil, while the husband was blubbering away, nodding to embrace whatever debasement the collective seemed to have agreed on. The two baby girls sat each in a parental lap like Democrat primary voters in infantile obliviousness, matching pink bows stuck on their bald baby noggins as though they could tell the difference. In expansive tones, Dr. Phil sat back with hand-on-his-knees finality, grinning widely: "Folks, what we've got here is a '*feel goood*' moment." I really wanted to vomit, I swear, but just couldn't (plus, I would have had to clean up the couch). Whatever the topic or complaint, here was ostensibly a "man" delivering to his two future delinquent daughters a video record of his emotional meltdown cast as some sort of accomplishment.

We all saw this pathetic trend taking shape in the otherwise-Glorious Eighties with the rise of Phil Donahue and the pathfinders of the therapeutic society, marking the drop-zone for Operation Oprah. Much has been written about the re-education of the American male, raising "sensitivity" above leadership and equanimity in the face of adversity, as the prized state for a man. From these sages of afternoon chat-TV to the new generation of holistic self-help internet gurus, we have legions dedicated to refining, softening, making pliable, and basically unmaking men in society as a way to fulfill their ideal of what a "real man" is. But unlike the philosophy of Marine Corps boot camp wherein the individual is broken down and then raised back up as a stronger, more focused being trained for higher works, the new re-modeling of today's Y-chromosome carriers is accomplished in non-threatening pastels and low-cholesterol rhythms designed to make them more palatable to…women. Which is completely nonsensical.

I do not claim this as an original idea, but enthusiastically embrace the comments of earlier enlightened pundits who note the basic dissatisfactions in modern feminizing trends as the result of self-hatreds transferred to men; a vain attempt to improve the subconscious collective female self-esteem which has like any good collective move, only succeeded in spreading misery equally. Now women convince themselves that the new feminized men sporting more overt neuroses, haunting delivery rooms, driving mini-vans to soccer practice, and swallowing ideas as stupid as "compassionate conservatism" are not only better lovers and providers, but by comparison make themselves feel more accomplished in having tamed the brutes. Hogwash.

It was not always so. Long before the Cocktail Generation accepted has-been status by embracing the immodest label of "Greatest", before the Baby Boomers were revealed as their greatest mistake, before LBJ inaugurated the "Great Society" as history's biggest bribe, the Cocktail Generation was the motive force driving America to its cultural apex. After whipping Fascism they had saved Western Europe from the Communists, stopped them in Korea, and had set our sights on the moon (back when Democrat leaders embraced heroic ideals). George Will has described the cultural scene of New York City in the early sixties as the last flowering of "Babylon on the Hudson", in years when Rat Packers crooned the soundtrack to a time when the glittering technology known as "space age" was an inexhaustible mine of hope and dreams for the world and rocket ships soared from the consciousness of little boys into the cosmos and back again, when the national gaze was up and out and confident, not inward and afraid.   I was a mere toddler then, with only shadows of memory to touch, faint visuals of the grandparents sipping martinis to a neon background while I sat in a little coat and tie, enraptured over a plate of fried shrimp; blue runway lights glimmering through thick cigarette smoke hanging in airplane cockpit air presaging travel and adventure; a G.I. Joe in silver space suit, riding in a Mercury capsule. We little boys who watched our grandfathers and fathers saw men who smoked, who drank too much, who sometimes did not acknowledge the intellectual gifts of their female companions. We saw men who despite their repressions and undiagnosed depressions were unapologetic for their roles as leaders and providers, who actually strove to refine and improve on individual images of projected strength. We still have such men aplenty, but our culture insufficiently celebrates the value of their natural chauvinism, and their unspoken honor as protectors. Theirs' was the task to set the example not of undirected machismo, but of manliness to the next generation, and in doing so won wars and built empires. The message from the popular culture today might well be that the warriors on the Normandy beachhead were fighting for guaranteed child care and a higher minimum wage, but I do not accept that. They fought and died as heroes because that is what men did, and still do. So this D-Day anniversary, tell a boy about Pat Tillman, or buy him a copy of <u>The Longest Day</u>. Just keep him away from Dr. Phil and the "feel good" moments with which the day is laced."

Self-reliance, the much-derided "rugged individualism" of American mythology was once upon a time quite real and the basis for much success and advancement. The key word of course was "self", as in "self-interest." Give a kid a car, and he will eventually settle for a Yugo. Demand that he work for his own, and he might be the kid to work nights and weekends, start a scratch company that ends up creating hundreds of jobs and millions in tax revenues, and along the way he will have a loaded late-model Corvette. The difference is one of motivation, the kind available only to those who honestly work for their own ends...

Everything I Needed to Know About Economics

"In the 1965 film "McLintock", John Wayne plays a wealthy cattle baron in the rapidly settling Old West. His fortune earned by cow punching between bouts with Indians and the elements, Wayne's character waxes both practical and philosophical as he dispenses advice to younger homesteaders. In an early scene Mr. McLintock confronts said homesteaders busily loading up lumber for their would-be farms that the land baron advises them not to build. His advice is based on local knowledge of water runoff patterns, yet he is publicly castigated by a local bureaucrat, himself seeking to profit from the homesteaders. The bureaucrat incites the crowd by impugning McLintock's wealth and vast land holdings. An earnest, poor looking sooner hollers up wondering if that is true, and why a rich man would begrudge land given to them by the government. Not missing a beat, the Duke scowls his answer: "The government never gave anybody anything. There's no such thing as free land – if you make these homesteads go, you'll have earned every acre of it!" No it's not high-falootin' rhetoric, neither coiffed like the flaming red-head Maureen O'Hara nor fastidious like the town's chess-playing shopkeeper. But the point is made. A hungry yearning for personal betterment drove tidewater colonials across the Blue Ridge and the Mississippi into the West to seek better lives. Yes they stole land from the Mexicans and Indians, and many innocents died in the great migration. But the vast majority or settlers, cattlemen, prospectors, merchants, and laborers on nascent railroads laid a path on very clear lines: one's prosperity was directly the result of one's efforts, and was never guaranteed. Enlightened self-interest (well, in most cases) settled the West. And the story of that great settling became a romantic tale of rugged individualism that reverberated back across the continent to stamp its rhythms, fashions, and good old simplistic morality plays into the American psyche. Sure most gunfight scenes were apt to be of the seedier variety, more akin to Clint Eastwood in "Unforgiven" than Gary Cooper in "High Noon." Solitary pioneer women survived in sod huts through blizzards that killed grown buffalo near their door. The rigors of dust, ice, locusts, childbirth, starvation, dysentery, solitude, and hard work built a great American legacy. And the common thread through that legacy was self-interest, the beauty of voluntary exchanges of value for value. There is no more American story, because that is THE American story.

In "McClintock" a young homesteader is reduced to pleading for a job from the wealthy cattle baron, and then attacks him in a fit of self-disgust. After being thrown to the dirt, the homesteader admits that he should be grateful that the older man gave him a job. "Gave?!", the Duke bellows, "I don't give jobs, I hire men." The younger man straightens himself, his pride returning: "I'll certainly deliver a full day's work" to which McClintock retorts "For that I'll pay a full day's wage. You won't give me anything and I won't give you anything. That way we both hold up our heads." If one truly comprehends that brief exchange, all of honest capitalism is explained. Last week the fools in the Maryland state house voted to force Wal-Mart to pay a portion of its payroll into health care for its workers. Coming between employer and employee thusly betrays the American story, and proves that the Duke's simple explanations were well over the heads of the Annapolis city slickers." I contend that McClintock's explanation to the homesteader encompasses everything one needs to know about a free market economy, if there is but the courage to heed it."

Back in high school, for some odd reason, I decided that I wanted to go to a military college just to see whether I was tough enough to hack it. Whoever said they preferred luck to skill certainly got that one right. Years before it was targeted for destruction, The Military College of South Carolina, The Citadel, caught my interest. Associating myself with the great traditions and friendships of the school in her last years was the luckiest move I ever made...

Return to The Holy City

"With the skyline of the "Holy City" as backdrop, one wades ashore through the oyster beds and black sucking mud of Castle Pinckney, the site of a long-defunct gun battery commanding the inner harbor approaches upstream from Ft. Sumter. The locals call it "pluff mud", a stinking, sucking goo that will pull the shoes off the wearer without effort or warning. Pluff mud on one's deck shoes defies all but the most determined attempts at rinsing and rubbing, sticking with the tenacity of the Carolina mosquitoes. Memories like malevolent, grinning ghosts rise out of the muck with the same rotting primordial smell that assaulted us on humid, sticky spring mornings long ago, borne on the waves of swamp gas erupting from the flats of the Ashley River. The stench was worse on warm mornings, wafting in steamy swirls through the drenched irritated ranks of teenagers dripping in sweat and frustration, awaiting another round of the physical and verbal insults that characterized "knob" year at The Citadel. Only a city of Charleston's elegance and arrogance could breed the tradition necessary to give rise to such an institution. Pat Conroy's etchings of the school reveal his sense of its iron darkness, and belie his irrepressible love of the phenomenon that binds its graduates one to another, tighter than any school has before or since. The traditions of the lost school mirror the surviving traditions of Charleston, a city of hurricanes, Old World depth, slavery and pirates, insular graciousness which bids welcome with an open hand that also warns of a permanent distance to those not to the manner born. A native of this anachronism and his two out world friends (granted temporary access by virtue of attendance to the South's greatest military academy) stood under leaden skies, casting against the bank for flounder and trout, pulling in the same and greedy crabs, a string ray, and drinking in the celebrations of the bonds renewed that no damn Yankee federal court system could undo. Serene and implacable, the Holy City rested in the arms of its river boundaries, smiling demurely from the Battery into the brisk sea breeze.

The natives of Charleston discuss the outside world, and worry about the rising threats from within and without. They love their new bridge, an architectural marvel leaping over the Cooper River, an almost crystalline artery pumping into and from the heart of the old city. Many Charlestonians celebrate the loss of their navy base in favor of the new industry and jobs that took its place. More than one of the natives born of old Low Country families curse and bemoan the influx of 'Yankee realtors" but bask in the leaping real estate values, new restaurants, and shining upscale growth which burnishes the South's most exclusive city. And there is something to that, something that makes the contradiction believable and palatable in a way only Charleston could pull off. In their innate superiority of aristocracy, the natives assume that beauty and benefit should simply accrue, because they always have, in the only American city with such unrehearsed defiance of convention. New York has given itself to the world, and San Francisco is a spoiled brat on Ritalin, constantly screaming for attention. Charleston is happy for you to visit, and expects you to marvel at her charms. But she really doesn't care whether you do, because the visitor who fails to so genuflect merely betrays his own unworthiness. The new stores and high dollar neighborhoods, unlike similar blooms in other areas, do not alter the local character but bow to it, and are·absorbed as subordinate to the Spanish moss, lowlands, and hidden porches South of Broad that whisper patronizingly "Shh, mind your place...we were here before, and we aren't moving." Even the non-native imposters who now complain about the growth adopt the style and graces of the authentic natives. There are more cigars smoked in the bars now, and more fusion cuisine graces the menus. The displayed wealth of the restaurant patrons and King Street shoppers is staggering. But the khaki pants, golf-as-life sensibility, and constant descriptions of family ties still ease the talk of deals and dollars, laughed at in lilting musical notes by the new belles of an Old South not as dead as some believe. One need only taste the saltier seafood on the banks of Shem Creek bars, or watch the beauties play volleyball on the Isle of Palms to see through the new condos and Gap stores to a world whose heart has yet to change. Walk down through the Old Slave market and have a bowl of she-crab soup to feel a pulse unchanged by Black Beard himself, civil war, or the modern day stupidities dragging the rest of the country into ruin. Stroll the Battery among the ghosts, past the silent guns and homes more arrogant than any real estate on the Cote d'Azur to feel the truth of the city that sniffs with diffidence: "Please come see us…and remember, we don't care how you do it at home." This is why Charleston better resists the condo terra forming of generic family entertainments and retiree sensibilities that are homogenizing the rest of the costal south.

A child of the city was killed years ago, murdered by the very land it revered second only to the South. The nation's most politically targeted school, The Citadel, poisoned by the acceptance of federal dollars, succumbed to black robed assassins more concerned with the hateful egalitarianism of modern feminism than with the evolved traditions of a school as patriotic as any service academy could ever hope to be.   In its place, a feminist-friendly clone was inserted, brilliantly corrupting not only the mission of the school, but the traditions which served to improve the minds and lives of so many of its graduates. The three friends fishing in the harbor disagree stridently over whether the school should exist, and the one holdout knows this fight against the exigencies of "diversity" is lost. But no school craving favors of federal policy will ever weld a bond like the one shared over beers on the banks of Shem Creek after catching two of the smallest flounders ever landed. That bond was forged in a school now dead to its nature, yet born of a city that ignores time. Only the fire of such a tradition could forge that bond, and it is a crime that forthcoming generations will be denied the same. As the plane lifts away from the Low Country, my heart swells with pride at having been allowed in, if only for a short time. Tradition, like pluff mud, sticks."

After the Schizoid Sixties and Stupid Seventies, America was due to hit another high point (by which I mean apart from Haight Ashbury). The Eighties comprised, in my completely informed observations, the greatest decade in human history thus far. America never kicked it better than in the Eighties and by the middle of that magical time, a lot of us were having more fun than we could possibly have imagined. Twenty years on, there was a lot to be nostalgic over...

Money for Something

"Too many opportunities or great moments are only recognized for their true value in the rearview mirror. One such moment occurred for me in Chicago, in 1995, in the lobby of the Palmer House hotel. There was a tie, an unseemly, gaudy print, that I left hanging on the rack to my eternal regret. As most of us look back we enjoy the nostalgia, but cringe over the intervening years felt to be lost if we have not lived them well. Alternately, a moment can be so great as to tower over the subsequent moments, and nostalgia for it washes the color out of time that was not so bad in its own right. Few years have the good fortune to be as superlative, as streamlined, as sunny, chrome-shiny, and downright fun as 1985.

Next week a re-mastered version of the English band Dire Straits' "Brothers in Arms" will be released for the album's twentieth anniversary. The album was the band's greatest commercial success; with some of its lyrical and thematic complexity admittedly replaced with slicker production and singles more amenable to radio pop commercialism. And yes, much of the haunting guitar riffs and wistful lyrics of their earlier work, more evocative of late-night bars and alleys, had become more a sax and synthesizer soundtrack for a Mother's Day brunch. But it was still a great album and, hang the critics, especially so for it's' signature song. P.J. O'Rourke noted that one of the remarkable features of the Eighties was that it began on time; in that vein I give credit to 1985 for having its very own, very distinctive theme song: Money For Nothing. You know the words and the melody, and even you moon-eyed socialists seeking to massage your own egos with ostentatious compassion can be caught at stoplights singing along to this awesome tune. "Now look at them yo-yo's, that's the way you do it, you play the guitar on the M-TV" (kids, they may not tell you in history class, but there were a few short years when MTV was not the void of conformity-as-rebellion, faux intellectual, gay rights, anti-capitalism commercialism, but in fact played really great music videos. I'm sorry you missed it). The song fronted a paean to blue-collar sensibilities, "that ain't working", and the derisive signature, "Money for nothing and your chicks for free." Perhaps the lyrics were an attempt to degrade the evil commercialism of the Greedy Eighties, when the fortunes and (paradoxically) government involvement were of a lesser degree than in the Feminized Nineties. The (briefly) Music Television touted the accompanying video as the first to be entirely computer-generated, and so it is understandably crude in retrospect. The imagery, visual and lyrical, is of crass materialism ("we got to install microwave ovens, we got to move these refrigerators ... color TV's"), wispy boy singers with private jets, and a Madonna clone slinking around provocatively. Maybe the lyrics were an attempt to impugn all of this easy wealth and seemingly careless, causeless optimism and improved living standards stalking the nation during the horror that was the Eighties. If that was so, some of us were just too dumb to get it. 1985 like all years had highs and lows.

Reagan had been inaugurated for a second term, easily rising above a hostile media's befuddled caricature to ambush Gorby in Geneva and set the stage for the collapse of the USSR. Ricky Nelson died before his time in a plane crash, the Walker spy ring was broken after leaking inestimable secrets to the commies, and New Coke was introduced as the silliest hoax in our popular culture until Sean Penn became an intellectual. Riding the wave of 1985's "We Are the World", Bob Geldof's Live Aid Concerts were a showcase for fantastic musical talent and do-gooder impotence, simultaneously lining Ethiopian warlord pockets AND making American adolescents feel good about themselves. Harry Belafonte gave an angry press conference live from Ethiopia to deny the charges that the charitable donations were going to a Soviet puppet – not noticing the Soviet Hind helicopter which flew past in the background during the press conference. Artists such as Bruce Springsteen skipped rational adult satisfaction and moved immediately to acute fuddy-dud status, moaning about the depression and homelessness caused by trickle-down economics, while happily accepting millions of dollars and adulations made possible by an economy reinvigorated by supply-side economics. A large ozone hole over Antarctica was discovered which apparently destroyed us all ten years later. Muslim terrorists hijacked the Italian cruise liner Achille Lauro, and were promptly brought to justice by the U.S. Navy before the French were aware there was anything to obstruct. In December, Congress passed a balanced-budget bill that has served as their example of fiscal discipline to this very day. The iconic movie moment of the year was bullet-spewing "Rambo." 1985's theme song recorded the year in bucketfuls of frivolity ("I should have learned to play the guitar…"), confusion ("yeah buddy, that's his own hair…"), sex ("look at that momma…"), with

Sting harmonizing with the background synthesizers about wanting his MTV. The visual style of the music video, like the year, was an optimistic blend of neon, retro-Fifties, and Miami Vice pastel, swirled into a booming economy which was an enthusiastic grasp by Americans of their own identity and intellectual birthright. It was the last decade in which America's citizens generally defined themselves as such through their actions and optimism, before accepting the moral torpor of a faction fight over government largesse. Whatever the intent of the lyricist, the effect of the song was a defiantly carefree smile, and ironic jab to the critiques of materialism.

I'll never forgive myself for not buying that tie in Chicago ten years later. The print over bright, gaudy, and sunny yellow was of objects. Included were a string of pearls, a glass of whiskey, a polo pony, and a yacht, all symbols of opulence, achievement, desire, and optimism. The middle of the tie featured a banner which simply said "The Eighties." If there could be a theme song for the optimism which soared over the heads of whiny artists and woeful op-eds, a worthy musical expression of the can-do which launched the economy that became the true bridge to the 21st Century, then the ironically titled "Money For Nothing" was that in spades. Indeed, it was money for something."

(A few years after this column was originally published, a kind reader ran across it on my website, and forwarded a link where I might purchase that very tie. I am proud to report that it hangs now in my closet, a talisman against progressive weeniness and reminder of great glories.)

Conspicuous consumptions, capitalism, overcoming communism, hot babes with big hair, and beer – there were the things, the

385

goals, and the logical rewards in a world that made sense. We had every reason to enlarge, amplify, and grow the good things of those years, to turn it up to Spinal Tap's "eleven" and rock the whole world well into the next century. But our own Camelot faded all too quickly, beginning on the day George H.W. Bush uttered the poisonous phrase "kinder, gentler" to separate himself from Reagan. Boy did that ever work. What began as harmless fumbling led to the two decades of Bush-Clinton-Bush, which left the nation as a drooling, confused mess. The philosophical confusion and loss of American identity however multi-causal left us in a perfectly exploitable state for resurgent liberalism and self-harm. Surely a horrible force was behind this unraveling...

The Purple Death

"Ah the miracle of capitalism! For the mere price of just $7.00 I was able to walk out of a local retailer last week with a DVD containing the first twelve episodes of the classic Flash Gordon serial. Filmed beginning in 1934, the thrills, the chills, the evil grimaces of Emperor Ming, and the steady hand of Flash guiding his rocket ship and his followers on to new adventures are all there. The inaugural episode, "The Purple Death", filmed in 1934, featured a fictional world united in fear of a new, evil technology, made in a real world not yet acquainted with the horrors of fascism, and willfully ignoring the evils of communism. The Great War was over and the morality plays of global conflict flashed in black and white, over Dr. Zarkov's quizzical dolefulness and Dale Arden's trusting glances. "The Purple Death" opens with a worldwide affliction, where seemingly random people are felled by a mysterious ailment, marked only by a purple spot on their foreheads. Panic sprouts in the major cities, and a world council is summoned to broadcast assurances from America, while sending out distress calls to Our Hero. Flash is located with Zarkov and Dale, orbiting the earth in a rocket ship, and fast closing on an enemy ship from the planet Mongol. Through his high-tech periscope Flash watches the intruder and notices a sinister peculiarity: periodically, spurts of a whitish powder plume from the ship's underbelly into the earth's atmosphere, presumably to filter down to the populace. This is no CIA cocaine sifted on to minority neighborhoods, nor Al Qaeda anthrax rained on the infidels. This is doubtless the real thing, the very cause of the Purple Death! Flash & Crew do battle with the enemy ship, feign their own crash landing, and plan an infiltration of Emperor Ming's fortress. Meanwhile Ming and his chief scientist plot in his most secret lab, on the verge of creating a far more sinister variant...

Here on Earth, Pres. Bush is on a speaking circuit, pushing the virtues of ethanol, switch grass, and other miracles, oblivious to the opportunity – and obligation – to pummel the Dems for blocking Alaska drilling. That Cynthia McKinney claims her silly hairdo and her ethnicity excuse behavior that would jail the average citizen is debated as a serious question. Millions of dollars in TV ad time support the latest up-to-date coverage on the doings of world leader Tom Cruise, whose religion of choice is most accurately dealt with by the ribald cartoon "South Park"; this same cartoon which routinely features Christ is then banned from depicting the more sacrosanct image of Mohammed in a subsequent episode. Perhaps we don't notice because that very week the media hyper-focuses on the musings of another great mind, Charlie Sheen, whose concerns over a White House conspiracy behind the Twin Towers attack entice the media on multiple networks.

And then morning chat hostess Katie Couric is tapped as the new CBS news anchor. Amidst a rising prevalence of pediatric diabetes, multiple grade schools have banned running on the playground.

Before Flash & Co. break into Ming's lab, the evil ruler and his chief scientist are examining their latest fiendish weapon. Prefiguring the evils of eugenics, a variant of the atmospheric death powder is developed, which will only kill the strong-willed, leaving the weak-minded alive to serve as slaves in Ming's growing empire. Was it just a show? Suddenly I am very afraid."

It was probably hard to see things fraying and crumbling amidst the plenty and good times still abounding. But by the early '00's there were subtle, yet unmistakable signs that the wheels were coming off...

And Then They Came for the Cookies

"Can nothing be left alone? The pilings of our cultural dock are becoming dislodged at an alarming rate, as demonstrated by the Girl Scouts of America. Forget the Waco, Texas controversy over whether the local Girl Scout chapter supports Planned Parenthood: there is darker work afoot here.

If not a man of compulsive habit, I am at least a creature who takes comfort in the rhythms of temporal rituality, the marking of the seasons as unique and worthy of note as they pass. Spring is my least favorite of the seasons, sometimes warm but often tentative liked the forced smile on the face of a world beaten by winter too long, and knowing what it will get if it opens its mouth just one more time. Valentine's Day is simply worthless, the obligatory fun of female peer pressure forcing beleaguered and henpecked males to engage in all sorts of gestures made pointless by their utter lack of spontaneity. Yes there are documented dopamine neurotransmitter release responses to combinations of chocolate, roses, and wine, but it's still an act. This is NEVER to be properly compared to St. Patrick's Day, where mythic drunkenness catalyzes rituals of laughter and lesser imbibing to evoke the genuinely spontaneous pleasures of living. No wives are holding guns to their green derby-wearing hubbies, forcing them to sit up straight as they order one more round, allowing the observer a more honest and obviously more entertaining view of human interaction. NCAA basketball I know, is a ritual for millions this time of year; for me it is a reminder to endure the yin and yang of yearly cycles, the bitter with the sweet, the lull with the foreknowledge of resumed football watching in a mere five months. Such are the milestones that mark the passage of the year, irritants or joys depending on the celebrant, but comforting in their dependability.

One of those little minor celebrations is the late February glucose explosion felt nationwide, Girl Scout cookies! I remember them vividly at least as far back as 1973, wandering through the frame of our future home, munching down an entire box while exploring the foundations and crawl spaces. We lived there less than two years, but the cookies remained a constant. The standards then were the shortbreads (ok), the peanut butter sandwiches (better), and the sine qua non, the Thin Mints! Thin, uniform, stacked easily, so addictive they would have become the preferred currency over cigarettes in WWII

POW camps if the Red Cross had but packed them. Over the years the new kids arrived, the chocolate and peanut butter combo "Tagalongs" and the gooey, chewy caramel-coconut "Samoas." They have always been fun to anticipate, savor, share, and trade, an American standard. That Brezhnev could steamroll Carter, Hollywood might squall over the homeless, and the Clinton Years would defile all sense of propriety and reason stung a little less for awhile when the cute little girls in green showed up with the loot.

When a friend at work asked if I would like to purchase some cookies from her daughter, another mark on the road of 2004 was reached. The boxes arrived, bright in their basic colors of red, green, purple – but something had changed. I had already downed a couple before I went back to the boxes, my first clue. The coconut-caramel, fudge-dripped "Samoas" were now the generic "Caramel Delights." This cookie is already famous for being caramel and delightful, and I don't believe for a moment that it is any need of new marketing. Why are the Girl Scouts changing the names? Why did "Tagalongs" become "Peanut Butter Patties"? Is the name felt to be insensitive to those in society who follow behind others? Are the GS trying to do their bit to foster a world where no one loses and everyone gets a trophy? Are the feminine tendencies toward meddlesome nurturing being advanced upon these unsuspecting innocents? What exactly is wrong with "tagging along", given that an alarming segment of the population seems to prefer that to actually earning what they get. While I never wished for the GS to develop a cookie named "Societal Leech", the established moniker seemed no great insult. If the GS wanted to embrace more multiculturalism with the new, admittedly tasty "Piñatas", then what happened to

"Samoas"? Who at GS Central Command feared ticking off heavy-set Polynesians, and why?

Ah but to seek the comfort of Thin Mints, the last refuge and…oh no. The idiotic randomness of a society that declared rap "music" and banned fine cigars from restaurants has now done in a blameless cookie. While the flavor remains unchanged, the cookie's appearance has been obviously altered. Gone is the reassuring, uniform smooth disc, replaced by one slightly thicker, with misshapen, deliberately irregular borders duplicated on the package, as though the GS were trying to improve the self-esteem of more homely cookies by defacing their sleek standard bearer.   Change for change's sake is the disorganized muddle of a John McCain subcommittee justifying its existence, ego as substance. And all so the Chips Ahoy can feel better about themselves."

Disturbingly, it is not only the cookies that are being messed with. Maybe it is just karmic, necessary balance and consequence for the most kick-ass society in human history that everything has to be bothered and fixed nonetheless.   A whole bunch of cultural traditions that had gotten along just fine, not perfect mind you, but fine enough had to be targeted by the easily offended and perpetually aggrieved. As a libertarian free-thinker actively practicing and refining the art of staying the hell out of other peoples' business, I had not been interested in writing about, much less observing, the Gay Movement. Instinctively I am opposed to any "diversity" endeavor, having been seen my college – The (former) Citadel – and my first career – naval aviation – suffer the tender ministrations of the diversity merchants, to their targets' great detriment. But hey to each his own, I have always tried to think, just let me be, to think what I want.   Back in the Seventies I went to the midnight movie to watch "The Rocky Horror Picture

Show", where we threw toast and toilet paper, and fanned away the fog from Susan Sarandon's on-screen lovelies. The whole thing was a lark, just one big joke, so it was cool and fun for everyone. I had no idea the movie would become a documentary, in hindsight. The late, great Lewis Grizzard observed that there must be one hell of a mess in the closet that he wished the gays would remain in, and that made good sense. He didn't call for persecution, or even rudeness, but only wanted the freedom not to accept gay lib as he chose. Were he alive today, I shudder to think what sort of Ellen Degeneres talk show mea culpa the crotchety old writer would have to endure. Times have changed to be sure, and the gay crowd may go where, and do what they will. And yet, readers have called me "sneering" and "mean" just for wanting to be myself...

I Don't Give a Damn Where You Are Registered

"Over the weekend, we were lounging around the hotel room in South Beach after a long day at the Miami Boat Show (c'mon winning Lotto numbers!). Earlier in the day we had walked by James Carville laughing into his cellular (something like "we gonna fleece these people, heh, heh"), and politics was the topic of the evening. C-SPAN was on the tube and we were immersed in discussing the issues of the day. After agreeing that all the consternation over W.'s national guard duty was hilarious given the high standards Slick Willy had set, my friend Letti asked, "Ok, what do you think about gay marriage?" "I don't give a damn", I answered.

The issue for me has become as tiresome as Janet Jackson's breast, obvious yet irrelevant. There has been quite a lot of verbal churning over this in the past few weeks, and it will only grow as a red-meat-base-unifier as the conventions near. The Sunday shows, periodicals, et al are all re-examining the surrounding positions, and most of the newspapers in the airport had some sort of page 1 story dealing with this. Personally I wake up ever day less concerned with respect to sexual preference/orientation tolerance, than for the Left's obvious lack of tolerance for citizens who prefer to profit and are oriented toward success (with exceptions of course for well-meaning entertainers and New England millionaire liberals). But it's topical today, so let's persevere.

Historical tradition aside, it is difficult to grasp why any government seeking the adjective "limited" has any legitimate say in marriage at all. Some of the greats of conservative opinion have inveighed that, regrettably, W. will be correct when forced to call for a constitutional amendment to federally codify heterosexual marriage to protect the family. Lovely. The very institution which has undercut the foundations of traditional family stability for nigh on half a century now seeks window dressing protections for the (relatively) superficial assaults from the gays.

Gasp, Shock! How dare you accuse gays of attacking the family unit when they only want tolerance, respect, and a chance to live as they wish? Easy. The recent history of gay pride as been nothing more than attempted forced assimilation, the pounding of the societal skull until it accepts as normal any behavior favored by those holding the mallet. Anyone personally tolerant of everything is a fool, incapable of action or clear decision, and the shoulder-shrugging embrace of gay-rights rhetoric by the mainstream media gains for them the same

title. When excruciatingly earnest looking lesbian couples appear on the talk shows to plead to adopt young
boys, they are concerned for their own self-esteem first
and foremost, else they would never pursue a second-
best option for the child. When gay men exchange tragic
glances in courthouse photo-ops designed to publicize
their pain, they too are begging, and demanding, acceptance as "normal." The desire of gay activists for legal
recognition has never been substantially about fair housing or equal tax status. It is primarily about forcing close-
minded straights to embrace them as equal in motivation
and desire. Force – focus on that word. Sometimes the
simplest way to defeat force is to simply let it pass by.

There should be no clumsy, reactionary federal legislation, as there need be no pointless state recognition
of marriage as anything beyond a property-sharing contract (this will protect the divorce-lawyers' industry). Marriage devised of religious instruction and thousands of
years' tradition evolved to promote better behavior and
better child rearing. It did not spring from the Koran
or the Old Testament solely as a way to protect survivors'
benefits or fair housing. We have as a nation caused ourselves only trouble by trying to pick and choose different
groups for encouragement, whether through the insult of
affirmative action or the pandering of child-tax credits.
In terms of who gets the survivor's cat or life insurance
payoff, any capacitated adult should be able to designate
whom he/she/they/it wish. Heterosexuals entered into
a faith-based ceremony need not fear how others regard
their own relationships; nor will they ever be compelled to
morally accept imitations of those relationships. A special
interest agenda, not the private behavior of individuals, is
the only problem here. Removing legal distinctions from

marriage might dispatch the straw man of "gay rights", and bolster our supposedly cherished freedom of association. As obnoxious and frankly rude as the more vocal gay activist groups have been, achieving legal marital bliss may be the last thing they really want. Once the gay crowd can cut its collective wedding cake, what can they complain about then? They get what they want and I can still choose to ignore them. Just because Steve and Ed had a lovely ceremony in no way compels one to ask them for dinner any more than the happy couple are obliged to behave with more consideration for the beliefs of their neighbors. Those who so choose should be encouraged by societal norms to adhere to their own beliefs, regarding such alternative couplings with whatever disdain seems good to them. "'Tolerance', I believe it's called."

A reader responded to the original publication of this column with a weirdly tongue-in cheek response column on the topic, celebrating the artistic virtues of the gay community so much that it envisioned a collapse of the marriage industry in their absence, if the gay crowd all began concentrating on their own weddings. In tiresome Lefty style, the defense of gay marriage wormed its way to the logical (I kid you not) destination of examining the link between Bush-Cheney, Iraq, and Halliburton!

One thing that has become nakedly apparent to any honest person is the stark intolerance the Left and its subordinate groups have for anyone unwilling to embrace their prescriptions and shifting standards. Some traditions were tragically placed on the executioner's block for our own good. Was the national psyche permanently damaged in the aftermath of the 9/11 terrorist attacks? It was heartening to see the furor in the weeks immediately following the attack, but it was equally discouraging to see some wanting to turn Ground Zero into a permanent monument, rather than two bigger, gaudier skyscrapers as twin middle fingers shot to our enemies. Predictably a national tragedy became an excuse to expand government, and restrict our freedoms...

Indoctrinating the Next Generation

"As the latest crop of holiday movies draws nigh, I'm licking my chops anticipating "Master and Commander", and the climactic "Return of the King." It's comforting that despite the onslaught of DVD's and giga-jillions of satellite high-definition channels, people still find immense pleasure in congregating to enjoy a new story together. We love the shared rituals of rushing to stand in line in anticipation, the previews, explaining to the employed teenagers that no, I don't want a 24 oz. "regular" soda but the small-,yes that one, the smallest size cup. And the popcorn. The big tub, laden with yellow synthetic motor oil and salt is a ritual must for true movie enjoyment. Those of us who can remember life before Ben and J-Lo even remember real movie popcorn, the coconut oil taste distinction that defined a worthwhile evening or Saturday afternoon. Even if your cute date was far more interesting than the onscreen plot, the popcorn never went uneaten. It was also the source of some really good laughs. On Christmas night 1977, in a completely sold-out theatre, I was down front trying to get back to my seat with two jumbo tubs just as the bright preview flashed on screen, and right into my eyes. I tripped, and upturned an entire tub of pop right on to an unfortunate gentleman's lap. The entire theatre roared with laughter as I tried to duck, hide, and apologize simultaneously. The man and his date just looked a bit sad, and left two empty seats for the entirety of "Close Encounters of the Third Kind." I felt kind of bad, but my buddies let me share some of their remaining tub, and the movie was pretty good.

The taste of old-fashioned movie popcorn was distinctive, comforting, and...I can't remember. I mourn that I can no longer remember the taste of good old-fashioned movie popcorn. I can't remember because over a decade ago some lousy do-gooder, nosey-nanny idiots out to save everyone's children got it banned. The meddling former hall monitors at the Center for Science in the Public Interest decided that there was too much cholesterol in that delicious coconut oil and got it banned from the theatres. The same bunch that a few years later would try to get hot dogs banned for causing brain cancer (seriously) struck a death blow at one of the nicest, most innocent underpinnings of western civilization. "Statins" are a class of medication that lowers cholesterol, as part of a multibillion dollar industry in the U.S. New statins are introduced every year, the medical literature continues to suggest progressively lower cholesterol targets so that we will all live to be old enough to utterly bankrupt everything and everybody with our entitlement demands, and yet we see an interesting (and wonderfully ironic) increase in the American per capita beef consumption. The point is that high cholesterol and heart disease in a sedentary society continue to be very prevalent, even though we rid ourselves of the hemlock of coconut oil. Could it be that the Center for Science in the Public Interest responded to a very real and ongoing threat to our health by attacking an aspect of that threat so miniscule that it made no real difference? I seriously doubt there exists any data on people coming to the ER with acute chest pain and no other risk factors but that they went back to the concession stand for seconds. Heart disease is very real, and a "growth" industry, but there was no drop-off in bypass operations after the killer popcorn was rehabilitated by whatever gunk they put on it now. So a very real problem (heart disease) was dealt with by addressing it tangentially, by scaring a public prone to hyperventilation into focusing on an easily eliminated scapegoat without making any significant dent in said problem. As usual, society inconvenienced itself, and felt better for it even as we continue to build both new cardiac critical care suites and Krispy Kreme franchises (Note: the author LOVES Krispy Kreme doughnuts, whose taste benefits far outweigh any niggling health concerns).

Society continues to choose feeling better by diffusing the *perceived* risk, even though there is no real risk reduction and the obvious direct solutions still remain the best. I had a lot of time to ponder these things in the airport check-in line last week while waiting my turn to be scrutinized by a helpful federal security official. While news reports and the evidence of our own eyes make it plain that air travelers are no safer despite armies of inspectors and sniffing gadgets, we have swallowed whole another inconvenience because we "had to" do something. Today's children will grow up without ever having tasted real movie popcorn. And they will be the first ostensibly American generation to grow up already comfortable with the idea of checkpoints."

While going through the security checkpoint at my local airport in 2005, my travel bag was searched, revealing a sealed disposable suture kit, filled with sterile dressings, drapes, gauze, and instruments to sew up minor lacerations. I was going to visit a friend who asked whether I would remove a mole from his back, hence the kit. The first Transportation Security Administration agent pulled it out, asked what it was. I told him specifically its contents, including a small disposable scissors for cutting sutures, adding that it was not so important as to miss my flight and he could keep it for all I cared. The agent said no, he would need to check with his colleagues; moments later three of these uniformed professionals were passing the sealed kit around, shaking it, holding up to the light, and regarding it as the apes in "2001: A Space Odyssey" beheld the bone. Finally they handed it back, and bade me open the sealed plastic box. I peeled the cover back to expose the contents, started to reach into the box, and was told quickly to step back. After careful examining the tweezers, clamp, scissors, and supporting materials, the lead agent closed the lid and handed the box back to me, told me I could proceed. Putting the box back in my luggage, I zipped it shut and walked away. Twenty feet later the realization hit me, and I doubled over, unable to stop laughing. In my haste I had packed a scalpel in the same compartment as the suture kit, a sharp blade and potential weapon completely overlooked by the TSA agents. Worried about a tiny, potentially deadly scissors, they had allowed me to board with a knife. But not even these little imperfections had by that time been able to stop the TSA mentality from becoming an earnest, if less than effective presence in U.S. air travel…

Stupidity = Terror

"Tragically, the modern airline system is fast becoming a leading training center for anti-Americanism. The flurry of hysteria over the latest al Qaeda attempt to blow up planes with liquid explosives has played predictably into the terrorists' aims. If violence begets violence, then certainly fanaticism inspires like foolishness. More infuriating than the Islamo-fascists (who still should be exterminated like the vermin they are) is the ineptitude displayed by a government too engrossed with unattainable visions of perfection. A couple years back some jerk tried to torch a plane with explosives in his shoe. This made foot fetishists of the idiots at the Transportation Security Administration, leading to the awful indignities of middle-aged businessmen hopping around in a de-shoeing pageant that has to have Bin Laden rolling in his cave. But how was the TSA so taken by surprise? We've known since the late sixties, courtesy of Don Adams and "Get Smart" that intricate machinery could be hidden in the shoe. And what if a would-be prince of Persia is found to have perfected an underwear bomb? The implications jar the aesthetics of the most jaded and hardened cynic, and one can already imagine the TSA twits rubbing their mitts in glee. Admittedly I never thought about the possibility of liquid bombs on board, because that's not my line of work. Had not the TSA already considered the threat? There are two possibilities, and neither is encouraging. Either the TSA never even imagined that liquid explosives could be employed, probably because they spend too much time looking at peoples' feet. Or they considered the possibility, and chose not to talk about it until events forced their hand, in order to preserve their image. Here we have the small minds of big government in perfect miniature: either unimaginative, or totally image conscious. Either is an invitation for true terror from without, and encouragement for mental enslavement within.

After the UK plot was uncovered, the TV screens were full of breathless reporters showing clips of herded passengers dumping lipsticks, bottled water, face creams, and baby bottles into bins provided by gleeful TSA union workers. My radical individualism recoiled in horror as one cowed woman, upturning her purse, explained: "I hate to lose all this, but it's for our safety, so …" It is NOT for our safety, I wanted to scream, but exactly the opposite! This stupid woman has more chance of encountering the Grim Reaper driving to the supermarket to buy her latest copy of "Oprah" magazine than she has flying to England once a week. This latest flurry of "safety" is a win for the terror-jerks, and a win for governments that like to control peoples' attitudes (that's ALL of them). The TSA continues to mull whether to ban insidious potential "remote" devices, such as Blackberries, and iPods. I love tuning out my fellow travelers, using the Pretenders or some Pink Floyd as the soundtrack to (now) wordless people watching in the terminal. If I am held hostage for four hours while behind me someone's carpet monster screams for her juice box that the TSA wizards confiscated, then a true act of terror will have been committed. If we have any aspirations at all of remaining a free people, then we must first preserve our instinct for freedom. And to do that, we must be willing to accept some risk – and pray no one develops a time-delayed deodorant bomb."

Years after writing this, much to my chagrin, an actual "underwear bomber" made an unsuccessful attempt to bring down a Christmas Day flight. While we are all glad that this idiot failed, it was nonetheless a small defeat of useful Darwinism to have missed the chance at his self-eviction from the gene pool. This incident spawned a new round of media furor and brought to the fore the new "body scan" industry, no doubt delighting all the boys lucky enough to go to TSA camp.

The whole TSA mentality is really just a resurgence of the deadly Puritan strain that stomped ashore nearly four centuries ago, bossing and ordering everyone they could find. For all the talk of throwing off the King's rule in the revolution, we have devoted an awful – literally – amount of time and energy trying to regulate each other's behavior in the pursuit of freedom. The War on Drugs, generally a bipartisan favorite, has been one such dragged out, failed effort...

Our Own Worst Enemy

"It was a hilarious picture. The man strapped to the gurney was really all right, and would be fine. But he had the singed, blasted look of Elmer Fudd after taking Bugs Bunny's exploding cigar to its necessary conclusion. To anyone in the biz, the preceding event was obvious: a crystal methamphetamine lab had exploded. I put this to our mildly crisped hero, assuring him of his physical and legal safety, and still got only the most ridiculous excuse for a cover story imaginable (the constraints of confidentiality, schools of snapping lawyers, and the federal privacy mandates notwithstanding, this genius claimed his cigarette had accidentally sparked a fire while trying to removed his girlfriend's toenail polish). As stupid as this poor fool's waste of his energies on these explosive toxins was, there is another endeavor every bit as stupid, and far more destructive: the U.S. "War on Drugs."

"I knew it Martha, this fool wants everybody to get high and do whatever!" Herewith, the required disclaimer: illicit drug use is self-harmful, the worst immorality of all, and there is no defense for it. And for the record, years ago, I rolled in laughter watching the bizarre 1936 "Reefer Madness" with some friends. All we had was beer.

The nut jobs of the Temperance Movement really got the ball rolling into the Gilded Age, reaching crescendo-then-crash during the Prohibition Terror. The

1914 Harrison Tax Act first got Congress into drug regulation by targeting dealers only for tax evasion. The Feds reacted to political pressure from the southwestern states by initially patterning legislation on the Migratory Bird Act (seriously), which ultimately became the Marijuana Tax Act of 1937. In 1930 the first director of the new Federal Bureau of Narcotics Harry Anslinger had some interesting views on "Negroes, Hispanics, Filipinos, and entertainers and their Satanic music, jazz, and swing" (where was Tipper Gore then??), stating "...the primary reason to outlaw marijuana is its effect on the degenerate races." The 1972 issue of the Archives of General Psychiatry details the growing international busybody trend of restricting mind-altering substances, fueled in the Land of the Free by concerned Caucasians purveying racist stereotypes to cow the respectable citizenry, leading to the general acceptance of a plethora of brand new federal crimes. The racism may be gone, but the instinct for the government to control loony behavior grew. In 2002 Pres. Bush 2, set "a goal to reduce illegal drug use by 10 percent over two years, and by 25 percent over five years." Fine, but why was this ever any of his, or the federal government's legitimate business? The President in early 2004: "I have asked Congress to provide an additional $23 million for high schools who want to develop and carry out drug testing programs. Random drug testing gives students a strong answer to the social pressure to try drugs." Super, now the price of encouraging students to use their minds is their further inculcation with the constant presence of government supervision. Again, what business is it of Washington's whether teenage n'er-do-wells are trying to look cool over a half-doobie behind the dumpster? Pres. Bush: "As we reduce demand for drugs, we're also preventing drug supplies from entering our country. Our military and law enforcement personnel are targeting the world's most dangerous drug trafficking networks... we are drying up the world's supply of illegal drugs at its source." This completely arbitrary approach to his defense responsibilities undercuts the President's seriousness over his constitutional responsibilities, foremost of which is border control, and demonstrates only political acquiescence. Bush would placate some in the southwestern states by meddling in their affairs rather than seriously control their (our!) border. The President's FY 2006 Budget provides for three drug war goals (Prevention, Treatment, Market Disruption), only one of which might be remotely constitutional under the grotesquely stretched canopy of interstate commerce regulation. This year's proposed bar tab will exceed "$12.4 billion, an increase of $268.4 million (+2.2 percent)", not counting the cost for over 408.000 drug arrests projected by the FBI for this year. Since 1995 the U.S. Dept. of Justice has recorded more than 43,000 NEW incarcerations per year, a quarter of these for drug violations. We are talking some serious federal and state dollars that might be better used for preventing the entry of terrorist nukes into our country, surely a constitutional obligation.

It is easy to read case after case of local, state, and federal abuses of civil rights including property seizure, the storming of homes, imprisonments to the horizon, and the occasional innocent shot down in the zeal of the soldiers prosecuting the Drug War. The education has been out there in forms ranging from grade school programs to fake White House-approved TV infomercials haranguing sports fans in the comforts of their living rooms, and still new users join the ranks of the self-destructive every day.

What of our crystal methamphetamine friend? The White House quotes statistics showing no significant change in usage among young adults since 1999, and an 11% increase in crystal methamphetamine-related ER visits since 1995. And the extraordinarily dangerous properties of crystal meth have been widely known since the mid-1980's. Now compare this to the national struggle to eradicate cigarette smoking – sort of – which has ensued over the course of my 44 years, and we have two excellent models of the real opponent in the War on Drugs: human nature.

Money taxed from you and I to educate, incarcerate, heal, and generally nag those engaged in self-destruction is a confiscation of our property, time, and therefore a violation of our rights. But wait I hear you say, those wild eyed, slobbering dope fiends will be out driving impaired, robbing, carjacking, murdering, and voting Democrat to pay for their drug habits! To which I answer: yes, but all except the last of those activities are proscribed by law and already punishable by severe sanctions IF enforced. Who cares whether one is robbed by a suave modern day Cary Grant cat burglar, or an unsavory crack head? Who cares whether one's loved one killed in an auto accident by a heroin addict, or a drunken senator from Massachusetts? From the opium bales in colonial Williamsburg, to the kid in my 5th grade class who died from snorting Pam cooking spray, to the idiot Oxycontin-shooters of today, a segment of the population will always seek to impair themselves. The trick is not to let them impair our freedom, a trick that we have yet to master."

The War on Drugs like so much that government pursues, is an effort at large-scale mind control. Regulating behavioral standards between free people is one thing; dictating acceptable attitudes, the proper purview of your mom or your preacher. Before Pres. Clinton's Wife was banished from the continent as an inconsequential Secretary of State, she carpet-bagged her way into New York (delicious irony, that) to become a U.S. Senator. In an unsuccessful attempt to gain more political clout by getting into yet more folks' business, the would-be Mother of the Nation pursued yet another critical issue...

Keep Your Kid, and Your Senator Away from My Video Game

"This is a great time of year. To blazes with Cindy, Dennis, and the other spawn of the South Atlantic, Time magazine's tendentious muckraking, Republican obsequiousness to the fantasy of government compassion, and the comparable stupidity of reality TV. The milestones of the year are passing, and one of my little favorites has just arrived. The annual release of EA Sport's NCAA 2006 College Football PlayStation 2 game has hit the shelf, a frivolous time-sucking harbinger of the greatest season if ever there was one. My team takes the field against an authentically rendered stadium backdrop, the crowd roars from the widescreen TV, and it's all I can due to keep my star receiver in bounds on the first long fade route against a hated rival. First down, the band strikes up, and the crowd roars again. The temptation is strong to get a six-pack and fire up the grill. This may be Japan's revenge for Hiroshima, but who cares? It is diversion, imagination, flashy lights and booming sounds, absorbingly interactive, and just plain fun. It is a wonderful escape from the foolishness of the do-gooder world and its legions of furrow-browed, ego-as-maturity churls fogging up my windows with their collective nosy breath. Or so one would hope.

Enter the junior senator from New York, the mother to the masses, to wave her heavy hand of concern over us all. Her baleful maternal instinct now targets an item of great significance to the nation: a video game. The target is this year's biggest video game release, "Grand Theft Auto: San Andreas" in which, according to the promo adds, one is a "gangsta" contributing to and trying to advance the general mayhem by gaining adeptness in evasion, assault, robbery, and murder. It is a cartoon, but reflective of the tastes of modern youth culture, both black hip-hoppers and white wannabees, sporting the ubiquitous backwards ball caps, neck 'bling', and Uzi-emblems of society's devolution. Don' t take this for snobbery – it's fun gunning down opponents and blowing stuff up on-screen, and for legions of America's little chubbers, the repetitive action of their proximal thumb musculature is the only activity they're likely to get other than the occasional trip to the kitchen for anther bag of snacks. Separated from the healthy discharge of youthful energies through the necessity of sports participation, these little dough balls can now enjoy animated sex thanks to the creativity of hackers who devised downloadable codes to insert X-rated activities into the on-screen characters' repertoire. (In the interests of full disclosure, my college football game does sport jiggly, short-skirted cheerleaders, but that is only to enhance the game day atmosphere).

Not that I really blame them, when their parents have abdicated their responsibilities in the face of growing economic pressures to work more to feed the growing demand for tax dollars from a government badly in need of gastric bypass. Enter Senator "Bill's Wife", a representative of the interests that sewed the seeds of this mess, now rearing up in moral outrage over "Grand Theft Auto." Oh I would dearly love to NOT write about this shrew and her quest for power, but she just will not shut up and go back to baking cookies. Consider the wearisome and predictable hypocrisy of Pres. Clinton's Wife's comment: "We should all be deeply disturbed that a game which now permits the simulation of lewd sexual acts in an interactive format with highly realistic graphics has fallen into the hands of young people across the country." Did we all forget that this very generation of minors was introduced to the intricacies of oral copulation when her husband fell into the hands of a certain beret-sporting young person only a few years ago, and she defended him?? Where was this harpy's famous concern for the tender sensibilities of our impressionable youth then? What if the electronic babes are the only ones these little couch-riding blobs will ever see? Video game industry publication <u>Gamespot</u> reports "Clinton, a vociferous critic of violence in the media, will be joined by David Walsh, president and founder of the National Institute on Media and the Family; Mary Bissell, fellow at the New America Foundation; and Kiersten Stewart, director of public policy for the Family Violence Prevention Fund." Now I don't know anything about these innocuous sounding organizations but you can bet the farm on this: they want to get into your business; they want publicity i.e. cash; they will push for the growth of government. So far, that gives them a lot in common with Mrs. Former First Lady. CNN reported the former Arkansas resident stated that explicit games were "spiraling out of control" and wants to limit the sale of games with strong violence or sexual content. The sort-of author of "It Takes a Village" wants to care for a big coast-to-coast village of kids, all of who need her so desperately to save their innocence before some awful game ruins it. The smartest-woman-in-the-world-ever wants legislation that will use the Federal Trade Commission to hammer retailers of such games with a $5,000 fine for selling one to a kid. Can't you just see the scene now? A couple of flabby n'er-do-wells with earrings and cell phones (looking disconcertingly like their baby boomer grandfathers), stroll in to the video rental boutique. They stroll too casually, stare at their feet, mumble, make their choices, wander, hesitate, and approach the counter. They don't make eye contact, clear their throats a lot, and look through the windows at their buddies in the car. In clear voices they state: "Yeah, um, we want, y'know, uh, TWO TUBS OF MICROWAVE POPCORN, SOME JOLLY RANCHERS, uh, a 2-LITER COKE, and rent, uh, THESE MOVIES, uh, FRIDAY the 13th XX: Jason Gets Medicare, GIRLS GONE WILD IN CANCUN Vol. 6, oh yeah, and a copy of Grand Theft Auto: San Andreas. The alarm sounds, the ruffians in the parking lot scatter before the approaching blue lights, and the Republic is saved, all due to a transplant New Yorker doing it all for the children, with no thought whatsoever of seeking higher office and more power, by butting into other peoples' business. Whoa, I just scored anther touchdown. If I ignore her she'll just go away, right?"

On occasion I have been accused of being anti-children, which is not strictly true. It is true that I never, ever wanted one of my own and am completely gratified at having accomplished this worthy goal. There are certain children of friends or relatives that I find tolerable and on occasion, even fun to be around. But spare me the fake, reflexive gooey smiling and baby talk that so many adults spew whenever a toddler approaches within ten yards. I find children before they begin to synthesize coherent thoughts at best are uninteresting, or worse, demanding and needy – hence the ease with which they are co-opted by Democrats. Though it is not actually the kiddies' fault, a large number if not downright majority of parents have elevated the worship of their particular child into the most pervasive narcissism with which they bully those around them. How many parents have you seen who will not control the squealing, running, and general fit-pitching now rampant in so many restaurants and airplane cabins? Oh he's just having fun, they will say, or she's just tired and cranky, poor thing. Yeah well so am I, but that doesn't give me license to rudely intrude into your thoughts by screaming at you from the next table that you do not deserve a damn child tax credit simply because you chose to exercise your genetics a bit more freely than you could afford...

Warming to the Kiddies

"As summer moves full sunburst into view and temperatures climb, it is apparent that quite a lot of Americans are worried about global warming this 4th of July. A recent cover story from conservative bulwark <u>National Review</u> entitled "Taking the Heat" is a sensible piece that advocates accepting the notion that mankind has caused some temperature increase; but rejects going Chicken Little with successful economies in order to assuage guilt over a problem whose effects are no where near quantified. The article correctly points out that the very solutions to this concern lay in free market solutions rather than in clunky government pronouncements sure to end up as little else but clumsy tax increases. Which got me to thinking: how come the very crowd that says we MUST do something because global warming MIGHT harm us in 100 years was so against invading a hostile nation that might have been developing nuclear weapons which would almost certainly have been used, and harm the environment immediately? But we digress.

The global warming gang was formerly the green flag ecology hippies that gave us the ponderous EPA and now wants to Kyoto us down to the economic level of Europe. Led by Wizard Al and his celebrity acolytes, we are scolded to use less gas, use less electricity, eat less meat, and use less toilet paper. That's a tough sell in the middle of summer when the kids want to go to Disneyworld and dad wants a steak and a ballgame on the plasma HI-DEF. We have it better than anywhere else, and the rest of the world wants to whine us out of our good time, mistakenly believing like all redistributionists, that it will improve their lot. And too many of us believe it. Too many nitwits believe that a Chinese citizen who uses half an American's energy per year has therefore half the latter's environmental impact. And too many of us believe that over-taxing the methane from cattle or the electricity to power a video game will somehow balance the clear-cutting fires and open sewers of the world's less developed peoples.

According to polls and politicians, a great many Americans have bought into the crock that they are more responsible for destroying the planet than your typical Saharan goat herder. For those who really fear global warming and want to be actively earnest in their pursuit, there is an immediate, economically measurable solution that will save scads of money and improve the lot of those around you: have fewer children. Consider that the ankle-biters use enormous amounts of resources in terms of diapers, SUV's to safely haul them to soccer practice, non-recyclable happy meals and juice boxes. I'm told by those with experience that the little tykes, in between producing all manner of greenhouse gases and carbon footprints, are enormously expensive, with recent surveys estimating about a quarter million a head just to get them to the point where you can legally kick them out of the house.

Whatever apocalyptic, morose imagery of the recent film "Children of Men," we are not faced with imminent pandemic sterility; but land is a finite resource. Look at a landfill, and tofu chomping green do-gooders with a couple of pups in tow deserve naught but scorn. Let Al Gore explain the ecological impact of his four children before pestering me about my barbeque habits. Technology allows us to do more, and have more of everything, with increasingly less human labor, our "guest workers" notwithstanding. Phooey on government pro-family policies to subsidize approved behavior, from Democrat WIC and Medicaid to GOP child tax credits. The same carbon footprint rules for a loaded Hummer should apply to kids: if you want one you should pay for it. That way the free market can let those who wish demonstrate their Earth-friendliness, reduce our share of global warming, and hopefully cut down on the noise level in the restaurant."

I suppose children might have some benefit if they came into the world already possessed of the skills to mow the yard or make a decent martini, but to date I have met none. Okay so in fairness, there are limited, and I do mean limited times when the ankle biters are not actively offensive. While W. was actively offending conservatives yet again by thinking out loud about his stupid, piddling little stimulus plan in the Summer of '08 and gas was zorching up to better than four bucks a gallon, I was headed down to of all places, Disney World. Yep, blight on the dwindling South, Mecca to homogenizing, complaining Yankees everywhere, the Almighty Mouse beckoned and southward I drove. An old college buddy who is raising two daughters on his own, being the great daddy that he is, promised them the big grand prize of a visit to the Magic Kingdom, but he sent up an understandable smoke signal begging for adult company. And being the team player I am...

Off to See the Mouse

"Riding on the packed bus discussing the events of the day, my friend of a great many years bellowed, "Why don't you ever write anything positive in your column?" My buddy is the exceptional single father of two splendid (really!) little girls, with whom I was invited to tour Disney World over Memorial Day. In his present status my friend is frequently short on sleep, and as such may be forgiven for not noticing that every column here presented is in defense of individual liberty, freedom, and fun, and therefore inherently positive. And despite his having invited a friend with a strident policy of personal childlessness, I being of an occasionally adventurous nature, thought exploring the Magic Kingdom and its allied provinces with the two princesses might provide some interesting observations.

As one might expect, the theme parks of Orlando were seam-busting full over the holiday weekend. The Magic Kingdom seemed filled to capacity, and there was no shortage of helpful, perpetually smiling staff available to guide, cajole, assist, and cordon where required. It is well known that although Tallahassee was the only Confederate capitol not to fall to the invader, Florida did not officially exist in the mind of the nation until 1971 when the Mouse reared his gargantuan ears over the sleepy Orlando skyline. Since then Yankees and other foreigners have swarmed and transformed the middle of the peninsula, officially annexing it for New Jersey just before the Mariel Boatlift stirred up the soup once again. The stirring continues, evidenced by tongues from peoples so varied that Epcot was almost a redundancy. The lines were long but full of ebullient, cheerful folks ready for the next bit of whimsy or thrill hiding around the corner. True, many of those waiting must have been foreign visitors here to take advantage of the weak dollar, but the bulk was still a great many Americans spending a great many weak dollars. There were stuffed animals, soft-serve treats, jumbo sodas, and enormous turkey legs aplenty, possibly explaining some of the stuffed, soft-serve, jumbo children, sleeping in enormous shaded strollers, being pushed through the crowds. Mark it down: pediatric diabetes is a growth industry.

The shows and rides were sparkling gems of technology and imagination far surpassing anything I expected from my last visit a quarter-century ago. From HI-DEF screens entwined with real actors, through a couple of teeth-splitting, belly-rupturing roller coasters, to the corny old robotic celebrities, it was just plain fun (it is especially fun mentioning to a six-year old that the upcoming roller coaster will be scarier than the last one, just to gauge the reaction, but then you have to bribe her with a present to coax her on). The entire park staff to a person was cheerful and genuinely happy to be there. I looked behind several bushes to see whether there were any aerosolized

Prozac sprayers, but found none. It must have been in the water. One night we were driven back to the hotel by a Haitian cabbie, as cheerful and happy as anyone we had met, tourist or resident. Yes he was concerned about the high gas prices, but he was making do. He has been here for fourteen years, and says that his family and friends back in Haiti think him quite wealthy. By his own reckoning he has not hit it big and gotten rich "yet." A uniquely American sentiment uttered at a ground zero of capitalism.

"Aren't you worried about the rising consumer price index?" I asked one little princess back on the bus. She ignored the point and wondered what sort of animals we would see on the safari ride. I made the point to her sister that the GOP is on the verge of total collapse this fall. The younger sister yawned and fell back asleep, dreaming of the mermaid Ariel. Apparently politics will not be disrupting anyone's summer."

It was a really fun time and the little princesses, bless their hearts, were fun and as good as gold, and therefore exceptional.

❖ ❖ ❖

An unfortunate but necessary fact of this awesome, freewheeling culture, whatever government nannies say or pursue, is the recognition of each individual's power to royally screw him- or herself up. Self-harm began back in The Garden, and has been a permanent facet of the human condition. History is replete with the monumental excesses of Nero, Vlad the Impaler, Kim Jong Il, as well as those who populate the ER's, clinics, talk shows, support groups of the nation. I have never met a solitary soul who has not on multiple occasions, either through booze, drugs, doughnuts and Cheetos, laziness, grouchy-ness, a combo of the above, or plain damn pitifulness pursued a course of self-harm. It is just who we are. Recognizing it helps to ameliorate the poor choice, or as the twelve-steppers will tell you, "recognizing that you have a problem" as the first step. Of course there are those who take their own self-destruction, like a TV preacher sneaking out of a sex club, to Olympic levels...

American Self-Destruction: We're Number 1!

"It is oft repeated that we lead the world in the production, distribution, and consumption of entertainment media, from movies to recorded sound (that way we can include rap). Thanks in great measure to a media which promotes, devours, and often originates such, the United States stands on the threshold of a new world championship, bypassing our competitors as we stride purposefully to the top of the heap: the Kings and Queens of Grandiose Personal Self-Destruction. The reader might wonder whether short shrift is given dubious marvels that arose from the dark monsters of Europe and Africa. But here we differ in scale and style, and therefore in entertainment value. Germany's self-destruction under Hitler has been a gold mine for filmmakers, novelists, and computer gaming; but the elements of personal disintegration were only a postscript, and not the big show. As grand a spectacle as national disintegration can be, it really doesn't catch the western public eye in the same fun way as celebrity dissolution. For all George Clooney's wailing, most Americans couldn't find Darfur or Haiti on a map, and wouldn't remember Somalia unless they had seen the movie, or had a relative get shot at over there. The cultural, shambling suicide of France is merely the slow poison of conceit undoing the cohesion of that country quicker than you can say "Louvre" and more thoroughly than the feared McDonald's infestation. Socialist economic policy and abased immigration will sadly destroy the once great nation, but it won't catch our entertainment eye. The final scenes for France won't have enough action sequences – let's hope – for Nicholas Cage to play Jacques Chirac. Self-exploding Muslims in the Middle East don't really meet our definition of entertaining personal destruction, as the moment is just too quick for us to really get to know them on an individual basis.

Our British cousins made a fair run at being Number 1 with all of their prostrations over the late Princess of Wails. All that Prince Charles has ever accomplished is to exist, sort of, so his follies really don't even warrant an entry fee. And Di's trysts, rows with Buckingham Palace, and final car chase scene were less self-destructive impulses than unwitting participation in a script. In the beatification of Saint Dianna, Britain totally embarrassed itself over one dead non-monarch, and waived all claim to the dignity of imperial legacy. The spectacle was not so much self-destruction as the death of an elderly demented relative that no one wanted to watch. Add in fabled eastern stoicism, and our general ignorance and/ or apathy regarding doings in Russia, India, and the Orient, and Americans are left to look inward.

Where to start? There is the booze-and-pills triumvirate of Kennedy-Gibson-Foley, leaders in America's apology industry, laying important groundwork for Michael Richards and Don Imus. Imus must be given special plaudits as taking the basics and reaching – really reaching – for a new level of sophisticated self-immolation. He not only engaged in broadcast racism from a perch within the elite media, but he located the perfect wood chipper of emotion, mass appeal, and technology, and stuck his whole arm in. And he did it by being less funny than his usual, which itself is a noteworthy achievement. Pick your poison America: We have enough Bonaduces, Spears, Hiltons, Lohans, Jacksons, and Simpsons to keep ETV, VH1, CNN, MSNBC, and all the illegitimate progeny of Jesse Jackson employed for generations. And don't get me started about the Clintons (please don't – we are near election season, when their detractors traditionally get "sad" and suffer some of their own self-destruction). We need to contract with Dr. 90210 to update the Statue of Liberty to fit the times: Anna Nicole holding a bottle of methadone aloft in her right hand, and a movie script in her left." *When this was written I suspected, but could not yet confirm how grandiose and pervasive this trend would become. Only the United States of the Jerry Springer 21ˢᵗ Century could become so eager for self-harm as to actually grant itself the Jell-O-meth-high indulgence of electing Barak Obama.*

Big herd movements are the reality of the shrinking individual in the interconnected, mass communication web of homogenizing that is also, a major facet of the culture. The popular culture as in other nations has shaped and has been shaped by its government, an active reflection writing its own biography in real time. Popular enthusiasms need not in themselves be bad or harmful, but the moment they take on a coercive nature, you can count me out. Producers and purveyors of popular entertainments, for reasons of self-aggrandizement from either dollars or adulation, will often times project on to the masses messages and opinions that are accepted by the mainstream. Think of the self-righteous garbage vomited out by the likes of a Keith Olberman, or the attitudes presumed by TIME *magazine or* The Washington Post. *Of course the herd thinks health care should be free! The mob will not tolerate the intolerant. Big corporations are evil, as is Fascism, because both (the Left will assure us) feature hate-spewing, white male Republicans who want to run over starving children on the way to feed pure gold to their polo ponies...*

Two Movies, One Lesson

"The last weekend before football season seemed a good time to rent a couple of movies, and I did just that. The flicks were quite different in plot, theme, and style. One was lauded by the critics; the other panned. Both should be loved by left-wing bleeding hearts, and both should be heeded by thoughtful conservatives. Movie No. 1 was "V for Vendetta", set in a dark Great Britain of the near future. The scenario postulates a ruined, fragmented United States that has succumbed to the consequences of the "American war" on terror. Britain has survived, even prospered, by simultaneously encouraging economic growth and shackling the civil rights of expression, religion, and freedom of association (the defining document for which a present-day U.S. high school student might be hard pressed to recall). A ruthless autocrat has risen, amidst Nazi-esque trappings to rant about godless lawbreakers, homosexuals, and any who would support terrorists by the simple act of disagreeing with their government. The movie is cartoonish, both in its wonderfully engaging visual style, the grinning Guy Fawkes mask forever hiding the face of the prime catalyst "V", and for its portrayal of conservatives. The overt message of the movie is "conservatives dress and behave like Nazi's, who are bad, therefore conservatives are bad. They are so bad that they destroyed America by pulling her into a world war, and they wish to wipe out all freedom wherever they take power. Liberals, represented by the artistic community, only want love and to be loved, and would manage everything quite well despite the world having gone mad, if only left alone. In the movie the conservative government murders, rapes, tortures, and uses biological warfare to stage a terrorist attack, as a pretext to expand their power. In the end the masses will wear it no longer, and overwhelm the powers that be in a mostly peaceful revolution.

"The Constant Gardener" should delight liberals who see corruption as the natural byproduct of wealth (and who interestingly, never see such corruption as the natural consequence of ravenous "compassionate" government). The movie weaves a truly thrilling tale of a big pharmaceutical company, sacrificing (presumably) dying AIDS patients in Africa by testing on them a possibly fatal new drug to combat multi-resistant tuberculosis. The corporation grotesquely rationalizes risking a few thousand Africans to claim for the rest of the world a way to combat a coming plague, asking: Is it really so bad that Big Drug makes a few billion along the way? In this picture, the very best in fascist rationalization is employed, as shadowy corporate hit men carry out the remote will of government ministers, intent on preserving British jobs and corporate soundness. The only thing to stop this evil is the pluck and heart of a selfless, self-described "bleeding heart" who is quickly rubbed out. The cinematography, casting, suspenseful directing, and thoughtful storyline make it well worth your time.

There is a central lesson here that liberals will not learn and "conservatives" cannot remember. In "V", the totalitarian government grasps power by promising freedom through security, both physical and economic. Liberals, who shriek that this is Nazism when applied to speech and assemblage, turn a blind eye when such protections appropriate a man's treasure or land. The real kernel of truth is that ANY government will by its very nature become a force of dehumanizing evil if allowed to grow too large. Witness the IRS or Medicare for examples of this. In "Gardner", the central truth is that the crime of dehumanizing occurs not at the hands of honest profit-seekers, but is committed by those whose corruption rationalizes its shadows and murders. In each movie, the individual is sacrificed for the greater good, always enjoyed disproportionately by the boys at the top. This is not a call for either stupid populism, or lunatic anarchy. The real lesson in both films is that freedom demands the constant re-assertion of the primacy of the individual, with no favorites played. When rationalization greases the skids for safety, compassion, or profit, the individual is the sacrifice. Two movies, one very important lesson."

America was set up, different from all other nations, as a land that put the individual before the collective. That is a simplified way of describing something that is not simplistic. The early colonial governments evolved, devolved, and revolved into a mishmash of conflicting interests including hereditary patronage and new-fangled mercantile riches. It was a strained, painful process to put it all together, crank up a revolution, and then get all the players to hold hands long enough to form a constitution. No we have not been perfect, as with the question of slavery, Mexican and Indian lands that we successfully coveted, and Prohibition. But in the context of our culture, the nation's people have been at their best, at their most "American" when they have been successful and having a damn good time, two mutually supporting states (of mind) bound more tightly than any of the original thirteen. A lot of the neo-Puritans in the ranks of the earnest and compassionate hate to see anyone enjoying themselves outside of the Oscars or the White House Correspondents' Dinner. Like the old line, a great many too many in this land live in constant fear that somebody, somewhere is having a good time. Is it envy, the pointy end of the battering ram of poor self-esteem that causes so many to actively expend their efforts in the service of making others as miserable as themselves? You can buy the sci-fi Star Trek silliness of an attainable utopia where money is no longer used if you like, but I'll stick to reality. As long as humans are human, some will do better and some not. Truth be told, I prefer it that way – how damn boring would it be, really, if everyone were automatically successful, just because...? Yes it is sad that there are those who starve, or suffer from cancers, or from being chronic business failures, or from senseless losses in their life, truly all very sad. But would we trade all the courage, innovations, revelations, and triumphs that spring from hardship? If everybody automatically gets a ticket to the big game, is it really worth going? Rather than feign contrived disdain at honestly earned excess, real Americans celebrate the good times of their fellow man. Which is not to say that pervasive stupidity won't stick its nose under the tent flap, as in the 2004 Superbowl...

A Moral Malfunction

"Admittedly this is a tough topic to get a handle on. In the wake of the momentous Janet Jackson faux-faux pas, the entire nation is now grappling with the issue of public nudity, specifically, the unfettered breast. Far from a touching moment of accidental innocence bared, all speculation is now that this was a cheap attempt to titillate the masses. I was at first distressed to have been outside working on a relative's electric scooter during what was likely to be another flat halftime show. Imagine my horror upon coming back inside to learn that I had missed what was likely the greatest moment in Super Bowl history.

Actually I think a funnier thing has been the shock and moral certitude with which the punditry and callers-in have addressed this point. Rushing to prove himself above sophomoric humor, FCC Chairman Michael Powell shrieked his outrage at the MTV-produced "classless, crass, and deplorable stunt. Our nation's children, parents, and citizens deserve better." Ignoring the difficulties of classifying citizens separately from either children or parents, one must wearily recall the Claude Raines "shocked" cliché from "Casablanca." The simple truth is that Super Bowl shows on average have been getting dumber, more boring, and less connected to music or genuine entertainment with each passing year. Where was Chairman Powell's outrage last year over the inflicting of Shania Twain's lip-synched talent vacuum on the rest of nation?? Or several years before, witnessing the coupling of rock legend Aerosmith with En Sync (or the Backstreet Boys, no one can tell the difference. Memo to Steven Tyler and Company: when you need to perform with no-talent pinups to justify your rock relevance, it's time to make sure your Social Security card is activated).

Back in the early 1980's, mankind's Greatest Decade, I was a huge fan of MTV. The videos, occasionally shaky in technical quality, were far more engaging as both story lines and art, primarily I suppose because they involved actual music. Acts such as The Stray Cats, The Motels, Cyndi Lauper, The Eurythmics, and even good old Fleetwood Mac produced memorable video outings based on solid musical talent that continues to wear well. To this day I would stand "Gypsy" by Fleetwood Mac against any video ever made, the very "Gone With the Wind" of the medium. Ironically much of the decline in music video quality is directly attributable to the Janet Jackson machine that began to wrest MTV's interest toward en masse synchronized dancing as a substitute for actual melody. Yes there is musical talent still available on the tube, but for every Gwen Stefani, Sheryl Crow, Moby, or Toby Keith, there are scores of talent-devoid Backstreet/En Syncs, Mariah Cary-clones fresh from the hatchery, or Dre-Dre-Phat-Dog-Snoops perpetrating unintelligible audible assaults. There is to be sure plenty of excellent music available from new artists trying not to have their efforts stolen by the free-download barbarians celebrated in the latest Pepsi ad. As I have remarked to Joe who runs the music desk at the local Barnes and Noble, I could easily blow a thousand bucks on great NEW music, none of which had ever been heard on radio or made into videos.

The great manufactured irony is the contradiction between celebrating the outrageous antics of the talentless famous, while sucking in our collective chins in a puritanical fit of piety over the intentional "accidental" breast baring. Is this not the culture that celebrates Victoria's Secret TV fashion shows, breast-feeding in public areas, and Hooters? We were being forced to contemplate Mike Ditka's admonition to "get in the game" during the three-dozen Levitra commercials followed by the use of the word "erection" in the lawyer-repellent voice-overs at commercials' end for crying out loud. Weren't JJ and the Boy just following suit?

America's schizophrenic culture continues to amaze, celebrating on the one hand entertainers which make the average automatic ice maker seem dynamic, while on the other sputtering in ostentatious self-righteousness over a pasty revelation. It is incredible, and incredibly tiresome that the talking media heads are goading America's parents into feigned disgust over a stunt disgusting only in its tired predictability. A culture which plugs millions of homes into HBO and Showtime, and celebrates a show about gay fashion designers, yet harrumphs at children's exposure to female topless sunbathing and Janet Jackson's pre-emptive launch is pretty doggone childlike itself. It's late, and the TV is going off. I think I'll go get on E-Bay and see if there are any takers for the electric scooter. Aerosmith may be on line."

But the title bout for our greatest sport, formulaic halftime displays notwithstanding, will rise above its producers' mendacity time and again...

Our Best

"The final notes from "Hey Jude" are wafting to the heavens, Sir Paul McCartney has left the stage and we're settling in for the second half of the 2005 Super Bowl. Some Super Bowls wow more than others, and the one in our very own Jacksonville in terms of sight, sound, and feel has been no slouch. The Super Bowl has gotten a little bigger, and a little more fun every year, which is pleasant knowledge for someone with absolutely no affinity for either team in this year's match. In the sports gloom that follows the end of college football, watching the pro play-offs helps to ease the pain, leading up to the Big Game. One co-celebrant is a serious pro fan who brooks no disturbance to her Sunday afternoons when the pigskin is flying, and she now stares intently at the tube, willing her chosen side to an unlikely comeback. All is well, and as it should be, which is the beauty of the Super Bowl.

I regularly follow a couple of sports columnists in Florida, one in Gainesville and one in Orlando, both of whom are quite talented and write a good deal about football. Yesterday, the day before the Super Bowl, the Gainesville columnist had a long human interest piece on a former local player who had a big career in the pros, and then went on to a bigger career as a sportscaster, and who would be calling this year's game on national television. It was an interesting piece full of insight and wit, and ended with a thud. Noting the sportscaster's grief over the recent loss of a brother to cancer, this otherwise excellent writer closed with "It is, after all, just a game." Okay, I thought, it was a human-interest bit whose author was just a little awash in his emotions. Then a couple of clicks later I'm reading the other columnist rail away at host city Jacksonville for their treatment of the homeless. This particular writer, a former Jacksonville resident, had only last week spewed laudatory bouquets over the little-city-that-could winning the big enchilada of hosting the greatest sports party of the year. Now in the most sanctimonious, sneering manner, this critic gave the entire city, her visitors, and the Super Bowl in general the biggest dressing-down he could muster for the crime of moving the homeless out of the downtown to different shelters two weeks prior to the game. Imagine that, a city that had fought for

426

decades to become a pro football presence finally gets the Super Bowl, and wants to put its best face forward. The column juxtaposed a homeless drug addict who wished he had a Super Bowl ticket to sell to "buy myself a good pair of waterproof boots" with a wealthy couple arriving on their yacht to watch the game, or people at a ritzy Sawgrass Country Club party complaining that the shrimp weren't peeled. The writer seemed not to notice that the wealthy yacht owners, fancy partygoers and anyone else paying the last minute scalpers' fee of $3,000 all earned the right to be there. No yachts were stolen from the folks in shelters nor were any winos elbowed out of the buffet line by the diamond bespangled. Most of all, the house-challenged of downtown Jacksonville have no right to sidewalks and shelters built and maintained by the dollars of residents and visitors if their presence gets in the way of those providers' good time. Of course the point wasn't to help the homeless. When all was said, the real point of the column was to demonstrate, without effort or expense, the incredible goodness of the writer by pointing out the thoughtless materialism of others. And now we come to the real crime scene.

This is not "just" a game. The Super Bowl is America's party, a spontaneous, shiny, hyper-commercialized, ritualized celebration of the best, and the best of our values. It is a gaudy display of consumption and competition, and achievement unrivaled by lesser nations. There are enough fireworks exploding, and there is more than enough imbibing and overindulging, end zone spiking, cheerleader jiggling, and overall cheerfulness to infuriate both feminists and mullahs alike. That fact alone makes the game as beautifully American as any public exercises this side of a presidential election. It is a spontaneous celebration, neither mandated by the drones in D.C. nor codified for government workers seeking yet another federal holiday.

The defender-in-the-abstract of the homeless might appreciate this irony. A lifetime Philadelphia fan who had long dreamed of seeing his team get to the top was featured in the news last week for borrowing against his home in order to afford Super Bowl tickets. Granted, when the Lord packed this fan's lunchbox, He may have left out the cookies. But it is admirable how the enthusiasm for excellence, for the chance at one great moment, can spur some to grasp for heights thought previously unattainable. A great impulse drove Columbus across the ocean, blasted Yeager through the sound barrier, and drove the captains of industry to wonder, "Can I build this and sell it?" That same impulse propels athletes both classy and obnoxious to strive for the pinnacle of excellence, and calls fans nationwide to road trip, party, cheer, gab, and gather together in front of millions of televisions the way no other endeavor can. That is because the set-piece plays, specialization, and minute drama, tailgating, whooping and hollering of American football make it simply better than any other sport in human history, and the Super Bowl proves it. The truckloads of chips and dip, mountains of ribs and hot wings, and oceans of beer, the crash of helmets, the taunting across the line of scrimmage, silly costumed and painted-face fans, the hilarious commercials making your mother wrinkle her nose in feigned disgust – all of this is a celebration of happiness, the happiness of living in the best damn country on the planet. If ever there was a howl of freedom in the winter night, a thumbs-up to Iraqi voters and the middle finger to terrorists, it is our Super Bowl. Shame on anyone trying to dilute this beauty with cheap sentiment. "

Cheap sentiment is easy to come by, it is free, plentiful, and takes no effort whatsoever. Like the attention-starved celebrities and reporters that swarm a disaster area to "raise awareness", any of us can beat our breast and publicly wail if we like, over the plight of our neighbors, starving kids across the ocean, or endangered pure strain freshwater snails too offended by a nearby dam to reproduce. No, no, no, now stop it! I hear you growling that I am being selfish and criticizing all charity, good feelings, fresh air, puppies, and sunshine, but that could not be further from the truth. Support what you value, nurture those causes about which you care, throw a twenty at the bum permanently ensconced at the interstate off-ramp if it makes you feel good. But please, be honest enough to recognize and admit what you are doing: Everybody does everything for himself or herself. When you sacrifice for a child or give to charity, you are serving your own sense of values by helping another, and that is a good thing! You are doing something that makes YOU feel good, which is as good and valid an incentive as hard cash money. While that certainly is not my original thought, history shows it to be a true, easily reproducible relationship that calls up the best in our weird and funny species.

But nagging and scolding your neighbor for his good time as a way to pump up your own sense of self-worth is sick, destructive, and the basis for the vast majority of federal legislation. If a Hollywood actress heads on down to help the Katrina victims in New Orleans then I say good for her; if she takes extra steps to see that you noticed her doing so, then I smell a waterlogged rat. In my professional medical experience it has been my daily observation that anyone may succumb to feeling bad deliberately, as a perverted secondary gain. Feeling good takes WORK, and it has to be for all of us, on occasion, a deliberate choice. As my friend with the two little daughters counsels: "Choose to be happy." Amidst the personal turmoil that we all get to enjoy once in awhile, the end of summer in 2007 found me in a foul mood, with a mission for better perspective ...

Lighten Up

"Will we withdraw from Iraq sooner, or later, based on Halliburton stock? Was Idaho Senator Larry Craig up to shenanigans in the Minneapolis-St. Paul airport restroom? Will the election of Hillary actually result in the earth splitting and frogs raining? Can Brittney and Lindsey ever find true happiness? These burning questions of the day can weigh on the mind, squash the soul, and dull the senses to no point at all. And that is no way to greet the fall.

The air is still late-summer humid, but the usual August oppressiveness has been interrupted by a shower here, and high pressure front there, and so far no hurri-... I didn't say it! It's still a beautiful afternoon to lounge in the Jacuzzi, fire up a cigar and peruse the latest insights from the current National Review. The cover story "Waiting on Fred" details the anticipation, and as yet unfulfilled intimations of the Thompson campaign. Lots of YouTube sound and fury, signifying...wait and see. But NR is an upbeat publication of varied topics and here, a more promising article, "The Bard of Optimism" by Kyle Smith, on the present and past of the legendary Paul McCartney. The piece declares up front that Sir Paul is THE definitive pop genius whose post-Beatle accomplishments were precisely due to his positive disposition, and not the other way 'round. The author does not shrink from the inevitable comparison with Lennon, but rather embraces it to make his point. John went in for the fussing, complaining, protesting, and marching from which sprang his solo work. This repertoire won the accolades of the professionally earnest, left no significant legacy, and sold not too many records. Though McCartney's work has sometimes dealt with the sadder inevitabilities of age and loss according to the author, his natural vocal styling and lyrical instinct have been such perfect mediums for an irrepressible outlook that silly critics have labeled him shallow.

The back page piece describes the $27,000 per month efforts of 41-year old Alexis Stewart – Martha's daughter – to artificially conceive. The author wonders whether the divorcee "domestic diva" with a barren, only child "has amputated the family from family life", a comment on the dichotomy of homey holiday rituals and test tube ankle biters. The column considers the changing Western demography that has more women opting for "wanted" pregnancies later in life, as opposed to the "oops" pro-creations right out of high school. The question raised is whether the progressive hyper-protectiveness of suburban mothers is the byproduct, leading to tight reins on a rising generation of clingy neuroses. Actually it's no question at all. Optimism is tougher to come by in this piece, a depiction of affluence consuming itself in an effort to fight off loneliness, a sort of fashionable catabolism. Author Mark Steyn is a funny writer, and even though he laments the "sad emblem" that is the younger Stewart, he still finds a smile in the whole topic, if only for the ridiculousness of it all: bombarding a dark shape with neutronic laughter, defining optimism by what it isn't. Ms. Stewart is an example of what happens when one takes herself too seriously, and McCartney shows what is possible when one does not.

The sun departed several hours ago, not yet leaving the fading gold on the Spanish moss that we shall see in October, but that is not far off. The trees are still, the evening a little cooler, and the bugs are quiet. The cigar has run its course and a nap beckons. Football and the fall start this week, leaving us all a bit more to smile about. Saturdays spent yelling at uncontrollable events on the TV, and Sundays spent breathing in cool breezes are great ways to take one's self less seriously. Life is grand. "

Damn right it is.

❖ ❖ ❖

Holiday Notes

To put not too fine a point on it, I absolutely love Christmas. I love the season and celebration so much that I hate, abhor, despise, and squint at lesser minds pushing "Christmas in July" sales (which mercifully have dropped off to nil). There is a time and place for all things, and there are no holiday tunes at my house until I start to wash the Thanksgiving dishes. The pre-holidays for most of us begin in those crisp late October evenings when the pumpkins are carved and the hot apple cider starts tasting really, really good. When I was a kid Thanksgiving was a great day to eat and an extra day off from school, but mom didn't allow the beginning of Christmas fun till December 1, good training and discipline to be sure, until my mind had grown able to absorb all the grandeur. Now Thanksgiving is more fun than ever before, and like a lot of folks, my favorite family get-together weekend of the year bar none. It is a distinctively American holiday, with all respect to our strange Canadian cousins, and it is with haughty glee that all southerners should remind the nation that the FIRST Thanksgiving was in Virginia, among English colonists, two years before Squanto and the boys learned the importance of a strict immigration policy. Thanksgiving generally does not inspire thoughts political or topical, apart from the now-annual cable news moaning over rising national obesity, between stories about the exploding federal budget and commercials for Taco Bell and Dominos Pizza…

Thanks All Around

"The turkey is mostly hacked off the bone for sandwiches now, and the long, sad, wonderful last weekend of regular season college football is underway. The cat is lying on the hearth showing her belly to the fire, and all the channel surfing will require a truly stoic thumb. There are wonderful moments of comfortable rituality throughout the year, and none gladder or more satisfying than Thanksgiving. As part of the calendar's pageant for op-ed columns is an annual recitation of a random "thankful for "list, let us consider this year's cornucopia of spewed abundance.

In the wake of the electoral blue-out, cable TV junkies should be thankful Nancy Pelosi doesn't use more teeth whitening than she does - permanent eye damage could become pandemic. Republicans in lieu of strategy can be publicly thankful for political as well as personal redemption - that way ex-judge Alcee Hastings can go from disgraced impeachee to distinguished intelligence committee chairman, undercutting the credibility of backslapping Dems who voted previously to nail him. And said donkeys can be thankful that the GOP senate caucus is considering Trent Lott as Minority Leader - he deserves it at least, since his leadership helped lay the groundwork for Republicans regaining the minority.

On the foreign policy front the radical egalitarians may thankfully regard Charlie Rangel's efforts to resurrect the draft on the grounds of necessity (but over the years he has repeatedly proposed such in the contexts of "fairness" and ethnic equality). We may be very thankful that the Iranians don't have the bomb, but that's a stance they will likely exchange after Christmas. And therefore, let us be thankful for Israel. In the final wheeze of a failed Bush foreign policy, we will have the Baker-Hamilton Commission, packed with preemption/invasion critics, whose prescription W. will be pushed to adopt. Embracing his father's administration at long last may not be Jimmy Carter-pitiful, but it does make one wonder what W. would look like in a sweater. Ideologues ought not be too thankful that McCain has used the Bush collapse to don a Reagan mask for '08. It's hard to square a guy who wants to grow democracy in the sandbox, yet limits political speech at home. One last question: for all the hoopla and falderal over foreign policy, what do will the Dems do when a terrorist dirty bomb goes off in a Cleveland parking garage? "It's the Republicans' fault" will ring a little hollow over the click of the Geiger counter. And we had all better be very thankful that we have so many men and women committed enough to their nation to guard the rest of us.

Here at home investors are thankful for the booming stock market, even though it only helps the "rich" (coincidentally, the only ones who also pay taxes). Wags will be thankful that we live in a country where former VP candidate John Edwards can blast Wal-Mart, then send an unpaid volunteer there to purchase the latest hi-tech video game. And socialists can be extremely thankful that nothing in the White House or on either side of the aisle has been done about entitlement spending – the squeal from Boomers lining up for their dwindling retirement and medical goodies will accelerate us into the more

European mindset of whipping a dwindling workforce to provide for all the legions of the deserving retired.

For my part I am thankful, truly, for the leftovers, friendships, cold weather, and football that decorate the weekend. And I'm thankful that the horrid do-gooder-ism so rampant in New York as to eliminate all trans-fat cooking is occurring far away in that cosmopolitan clime. Pass the Krispy Kremes and happy holidays."

Thanksgiving of 2008, just after the national exultation over Barak Obama, found a lot of folks twitchy around the dinner table. Most of my family, made up of more traditional tax-paying sorts, were pretty nervous about the all the hopey-changey convulsion waiting for us after the holidays. No matter, it in no way screwed up that Thanksgiving, my best ever. My mother's side of the family for longer than I can recall, has always gathered the night before The Turkey for the famed "Apalachicola Spaghetti", a distinctive dish local to the eccentric little gulf coast town most famous for its oysters. The actual pasta is pretty standard, but over it is poured a long and slow-simmered red sauce based in olive oil, garlic, and cubed beef that should only be really attempted by those to the manner born. The next morning the Almighty might have been mildly surprised to see my rare church appearance, but it was a wonderful service (even the sermon mentioned the wide-spread economic nervousness as context for thankfulness), and the fall blue sky of Augusta, Georgia outside was blazing and flawless. Off to a spectacular Thanksgiving feed, and then my cousin told me to get back and change, because now it was time to head off into the woods. Forty-five minutes down two-lane coun-try roads got us out to the leased hunting cabin my cousin's group occupies for such perfect occasions. On the way out, we passed a professionally-stenciled roadside sign with an arrow pointing up a side road, promising the simultaneous and co-located services of tax preparation, and barbecue. I knew we were in good country. From the cabin, we rode four-wheelers, the kind orthopedists love, along rutted dirt roads out to the deer stands. I walked a mile or so further on to my assigned spot, and ascended to watch the death of fall in quite solitary splendor. To my right was a long field, with shooting lanes bulldozed through tangled scrub almost too thick to traverse on foot. Behind my elevated deer stand and running forward to my right was a tree-lined creek, and a quarter mile further on, the line of trees was turned into a thick wall of golden leaves that blazed in the late afternoon sun. The air was cool and getting colder as the sun plunged, and the gray from the east moved with deceptive slowness to devour the sunny patches of the scrub immediately below. Years before, sitting on silent trails on cold winter mornings I had heard many deer, but had never seen one close enough for a shot, and always thought I had missed out on one of life's great achievements. The scrub to my front left and center had started to darken, and even the dying rays were fading rapidly off of the golden leaves in the distance. Well, thought I, nothing to complain about, not with such a wonderful Thanksgiving gathering, followed by this quite time in the woods. There was no stupid cell phone yapping, just a low breeze as the tendrils of a much colder night began reaching from the trees. I looked long off to the west, saw nothing, and started to fasten the shutters closed to make ready my resigned departure. I glanced back down the shooting lane at the muddy ruts in the green rye, barely visible, and then realized there had been no dark marks on that green earlier. The riflescope did not lie: there were three small does, legal and approved. I sighted, calmly inspired, blew half of it out in a slow, deliberate exhalation. The crosshair centered on the forward body of the future meal, I squeezed, slowly, the gun kicked... and I had missed the hell out of the first deer I had ever tried to shoot. Embarrassment gave way to thankfulness, as two of the three had bolted, leaving a solitary target, nonplussed and motionless. Hooray Darwinism. I repeated my process, pronounced my inner confidence, and dropped that sucker at over two hundred yards, no big deal for regular hunters, but a damn fine shot to make up for my miss. Cousin showed up and we loaded my very small – but still legal! – deer on to the four-wheeler, and rode like conquerors triumphant back to the cabin. Of course I offered to clean the deer, but no, I was told to man the grill and in less than ten minutes warm venison tenderloins were laid seasoned, and respectfully over the glowing coals. Despite the huge meal earlier that day, there were no leftovers. While the rest of the meat was being cleaned and packed in ice, the other members of the hunting club started wandering in with their bounty. The night had gotten cold and pitch black, the coals were dying, the weapons cleaned and put away, and the cold ones were coming out. Walking through the trees along the road, I enjoyed a delicious Honduran cigar while bragging to my girlfriend about my incredible hunting prowess. We spent the next several hours watching the annual Texas-Texas A&M showdown, sampling a bottle of limited batch, signature whiskey, damning liberals, and telling lies and ribald histories. Church, culinary opulence, hunting, alcohol, tobacco, football, male bonding, and proud criticism of damn Yankee intrusiveness ... I could not have scripted a happier, more politically unapproved Thanksgiving, for which I offered up true and heartfelt thanks before drifting off in my sleeping bag to the stark, crystalline notes of George Winston's "December."

The next Thanksgiving, a more subdued get-together with my sibling and her wild-humored boyfriend was preceded by assessing the big weekend against the more global context, in a happier world now that Hope & Change was in full cry ...

Warm the Planet and Chop that Gobbler

"The pre-Thanksgiving news is marked by reports that several major retailers have launched preemptive Black Friday sales to offset expected poor showings when the turkey meets the mayonnaise and white bread next week. For some reason the public is expected to be more frugal in their gift giving this year, certainly a source of bemusement if not downright amusement for our D.C. overlords who even now plot to steal down the chimneys of 2010 even before Cindy Lou Who's tree is up. It is as yet unconfirmed that poor sales in the wake of Obama's miracle stimulus will cause MSNBC and the New York Times to declare the term "Black Friday" racist.

Nonetheless it is just plain fun to see Thanksgiving upon us, as the roasting pans spring up in the supermarket aisles and "Planes, Trains, and Automobiles" is stuck into the DVD player for the 933rd time. It will take extra energy this year to keep the government and its legions of do-gooders from gumming up the feast but let us persevere. Airports will still be clogged this year, backed up just that much more by helpful TSA officials truly thankful that their jobs don't depend on productivity, but by keeping the skies safe from the bottled water and toenail clippers of law-abiding citizens. But when line-weary, rules-burdened, one-shoe a-hopping travelers make their destination, ah the banquet! Is there any red-blooded American (those whose ancestors didn't have their land swiped) immune to the tasty golden fragrance wafting from the nations' kitchens? (Random thought, but maybe in a wind spirit sort of way, eminent domain is the Indian's revenge). Granted we wish that vegetarians would just shut up and sit quietly at the kids' table, but now comes the UK's aptly named Lord Stern, puffing "Meat is a wasteful use of water and creates a lot of greenhouse gases. It puts enormous pressure on the world's resources. A vegetarian diet is better." This silly old fop and author of a 2006 review on the cost of tackling global warming will have our Chief Organizer's sympathetic ear at the Copenhagen Climate Change Conference in December. Combine this wretched veggie fanatic and a president perpetually embarrassed by his own nation's superior material blessings, and you have a recipe for soaring prices on food that actually tastes good. Enjoy your bird while you can, before General Motors acquires a poultry division.

A lot of us will use the coming weekend to string our Christmas lights in preparation for the start of the holidays, and there is no more magical moment in the year than seeing those babies twinkle on that very first night while waiting for our stomachs to settle sufficiently for the pie. One blogger from Celsias.com, doubtless in the throes of dyspepsia from a vegetarian diet, is worried that not enough of us will be using the energy-saving LED lights this year. He computes that 2,500 traditional incandescent lights on "one McMansion" (no class warfare here!) string will cause more than 10,000 pounds of deadly CO_2 to be spewed into the air, making your festive home a veritable volcano of death this joyous time of year. What he doesn't mention is that times are harder in the McMansions too, whose residents are increasingly jobless or expecting big tax increases in the New Year. Though the pricey LED's are much more energy efficient and can save money, folks might prefer to defer their lighting expenditures until January's power bill. Following this earth friendly advice might result in buying far fewer Chinese-produced lights, resulting in increased nervousness on the part of the folks who hold our debt, and who produce far more carbon emissions. On the other hand, a pro-American president would reassure our creditors by reversing the traditional pardon for the White House turkey, chop that gobbler's neck on live TV, and pardon the taxpayer instead. I'm not counting on it, but I will count my many blessings and hope you will too. Happy Thanksgiving." *In all fairness to President Obama, I had called on multiple occasions for Pres. Bush to seize the hatchet and chop the neck of the ceremonial turkeys he too pardoned. Foolishly and to his detriment, W. ignored me as well.   The picture of a U.S. president in suit-and-tie, with shocked advisors with mouths agape, chopping off the head of a prize turkey on live TV might have made the Iraq invasion unnecessary.*

And so much for Thanksgiving.   The last shreds of dried turkey have gone to sandwiches, the leftover stuffing thrown to the (happier) birds, and regular college football has given way the methadone of the NFL.   It may not be perfectly seasonal, looking at the twinkly lights in the tree through my open door, framed in larger Christmas lights, as a warm evening breeze meanders in from the gulf. Neither is the warmth unseasonable here, and I am not fooled; last week it was near freezing, and will so cold here later this week that, sailing on Port Saint Joe Bay, we will all need gloves and multiple layers.   The holiday week usually obliges, and it is always fun watching the Weather Channel, seeing the digitized snow fronts sweep across the Midwest, hoping that maybe just once we might get a Christmas dusting.

Politics are waived every year for the holiday column, because Christmas rises above such petty squabbles. Certainly I love it the way I do because no kid ever had it better than I for that pinnacle of holidays. We had the decorations, carols, and pretty lights; I started as a young ankle-biter helping my mom cut the cookies into shapes of stars, reindeer, and angels; in the earlier years the old man would come up with a goose, and in later years we went turkey or even "roast beast" for the big meal. When I was old enough, I was allowed to go to midnight mass, and later partici-pate. Two days before Christmas the youth would venture out with the priest and a helper or two to "gather the greens", cedar, pine, and the mountain crows feet which creeps green along even snow-laden ground. A couple truck beds full of greenery, and we would drive back to the parish hall where the moms had a big pancake breakfast waiting, after which we would all join in decorating the church for the big celebration. At night, the rows of pews would be outlined in candles, and every window like-wise had a burning flicker, all of it wreathed and entwined in evergreen beauty. The main hall, a Tudor sort of white plaster with dark wooden beams, framed beautiful sanctuary woodwork, glistening golden crosses, silver communion serving dishes, and tall ceremonial candles. To the left, unseen by the congregation was a tall stained glass window dedicated to Confederate Gen-eral Joseph E. Johnston, one-time defender of Atlanta. In those days this southwestern Virginia Episcopalian church enjoyed a sudden jump in the ranks every Christmas Eve, when goodly por-tions of Lutherans, Methodists, and even Baptists would strut in like they had been there all year. Everyone knew we had the coolest show in town, at least on Christmas Eve. Wherever the priest was in the service, usually in the sermon, we acolytes would slip out of the side doors a few minutes before midnight. Precision military operations had nothing on our attempts to yank the bell ropes at precisely 11:59:59, to try to hit the first second of Christmas Day with the bell notes. The service would stop as we rang for maybe a minute, and then the organ would strike up the first two verses of "Joy to the World" as the gathering sang. It was a special moment marking the birth of the Savior, and that would forever be my uncontested, favorite moment of Christmas against which all others would pale. More than once, as the worshippers would line up to approach the altar for communion, I would glance to the side windows to see the first few flakes of snow sneaking tentatively past the candlelight. By the time the doors were flung open with the choir belting out "God Rest You Merry Gentlemen", big wet Christmas flakes were falling so thick you could make a snowball in midair. Wonderful as they were, all the cool stuff later that morning took a back seat to this wonderful moment. Years later the church quit the practice of interrupting whichever reading or homily was underway, deferring the bells till the next scheduled break. The church is still decorated with greens every year, and still enjoys Christmas Eve snowfalls enough to make them expected, and the bells still ring, if less spontaneously than they should.

Years later my family moved to a large home right across the street from the church, and began their own custom of a yearly Christmas Eve open-house. My stepmother will annually fuss and wail for the week preceding in preparation for the annual party, to make ready a home on Main Street in a small town that Norman Rockwell could surely have used as a prototype. It's a large house, with spacious dining room and library that ultimately play second fiddles to the smallish and cozy den into which folks cram to enjoy the firelight and carols. The cleaning lady has to be called in early and given the same rundown on silver polish and dusting that she got last year. The caterers have to be visited and various helpers and associate family sent to retrieve the goodies in time to set out for the party. There is a mad dash in the last hours, just like the one at your house for your annual get together, as everyone is shooed off to the showers to scrub, brush, shave, and shine until all are ready to be received. When the first guest arrives the feeling of not being quite ready quickly gives way *to the beckoning food and drink, holiday tunes serenading, roaring flames in both downstairs fireplaces, and a revolving parade of laughter and good wishes.*

In those later years, the folks might still be up finishing the clean up, putting away leftover goodies for the morning. One year my two stepbrothers and I joined the old man, four older dogs in front of the dying fire in the living room late that night after the chores were finished. We had all gotten married, two of us had kids, and two of us had moved away. The years had knocked a little paint off all four of us, to the better, allowing us to gather laughing over this joke or that old story, an air of mutual congratulation hanging unspoken over us as it does in so many families, happy to have covered the miles and years to reunite at our best. Later that night when everyone else had gone to bed, I returned to a private ritual that I celebrate every year I can make it back to the little hometown for Christmas. When the rest of the world has gone to its rest, as Santa wings his way across the stars, I quietly go to the bar and pour a shot of whiskey into a pewter cup. Out of the front door to Main Street, and up the ancient brick sidewalk my steps lead to see an old friend. At the top of Courthouse Hill he stands, staring northward, watching, rifle held at the ready to meet the invader. I stop to look at him on his stone pedestal next to the courthouse, ever-vigilant even in the snow, raise my cup, and solemnly wish a Merry Christmas to the statue of the Confederate soldier. If I never have another Christmas, I will have had far more than my share of its joy...

Christmas the Illogical

"A couple years back, this column launched into a Christmas narrative that wound from the trenches of World War I, through the channels of Randian objectivism, onto the deck of a storm-tossed sailing vessel, all in a quest for the logic behind the holiday. Though lots of fun to write, the end result garnered mixed reviews, ranging from backslaps to pleas to resume my medication. And really from one perspective, Christmas makes no sense. The holiday is a funny time which inspires funny behavior, as seen in Seattle where the airport's response to a rabbinical request for a menorah has been to haul down all the holiday trees. The seasonal ire of some seems to grow in direct proportion to the joy of others, a now-perennial Yuletide conflict. The nut-job Cromwell puritans of 17th century England certainly would have understood this dichotomy; the outright bawdiness of the holiday revelry led the roundheads to criminalize most of the Christmas ritualizing, while their whacko cousins that made it to Plymouth Rock tried to take things a step further, and for a time Christmas was actually banned in New England. For decades the colonial American version of the holiday was seen only as a day of licentiousness with little redeeming theological worth. The traditional Christmas Day was in fact preserved by the Germans, and then launched throughout the British Empire as a byproduct of royal intermarriage between Albert and Victoria. Yet Christmas embraced commercialism in the 1820's with such success that it has wholly eclipsed all other holidays, and church leaders often feel pressed to deemphasize it in relation to Easter lest their flocks forget the point of it all.

Once my Hollywood movie producer uncle, aired typical elitist snobbery over dinner, looking down his nose at all the tacky, wasteful Christmas lights plastered all around by us less enlightened types. I pointed out that since not all of us possess Michelangelo-level talent, these more pedestrian displays were the means by which the meanest of us could express our joy over the Nativity. Through four decades and countless other debates, this is the only point I have ever known him to concede without qualification. Christmas seems to be the happy vibe that outshines every furrowed brow and leaches through all consternation. Last year CBS's "48 Hours: The Mystery of Christmas" underscored the nonsensical in one of the dumbest investigative pieces ever. It featured experts parading through ruins and running fingers over texts to make their points. The non-Christian scholars presented "evidence" that the Blessed Event could not possibly have happened (my favorite was that since a virgin birth was foretold, the event was likely adopted by New Testament authors as a nifty plot device). The featured Christian scholars presented "evidence" that apparently there was such an event, because it was written down. The whole thing boiled down to whether one believed the story or not, which they might have said an hour earlier, and I could have just put in my copy of "The Grinch."

The celebrations, lights, songs, and reverence of Christmas are one big festival of illogic. There is absolutely no reason for a rational mortal to believe that the Almighty would take the trouble to traverse the pain, grief, and messiness of childbirth - presuming of course that He subjects Himself to mortal reason. Over the centuries otherwise reasonable people have been pestered and harassed by the crazed minions of the Inquisition, and then the Puritans; even today screams of damnation from the fringe elements seem too often unbalanced by hope. Yet those who otherwise might be put off by this faith nonetheless smile at the thought of Christmas, drawn to it as a child is drawn to light and music. And confounding the mature inclinations of secular diversity, the Christmas message continues to benignly, even play-fully inspire people to ask "What if…?"

Naturally a sad minority is determined to keep Christmas a royal pain. From the pre-Black Friday hysterics of the media to the frantic sprint to get one more carton of eggnog before the store closes, too many Americans have become masters at developing a pointless angst that could only have sprung from true silliness. This woe and worry becomes a predictable part of the holiday pageant, without which we simply cannot do. Happily there are exceptions as I was pleased to note one year…

Christmas the Unpredictable

"After our Christmas Eve party we awoke to a cold, gray sky that teased all day but would yield no snow. With another fire blazing and Bing on the stereo, I was in the kitchen with the old man as he prepared ham biscuits and the second pot of good black coffee. We talked about what a wonder it was to have such blessings on such a fine day, and in the midst of our sincere thankfulness he turned toward me with an mischievous grin and asked "Say, do you know how to make a bomb?" Assuming I needed more coffee to clear my hearing, I answered in the negative. What I got was an immediate primer on the construction of an exothermic device, involving household cleaning products, aluminum foil, and a plastic soda bottle. He made his mixture, capped it, shook it, and hurled it into the yard where, for the next 10 minutes, the device lay inert. The old man finally shook his head in disappointment and headed back to the den where we resumed our gift opening. Minutes later the house shook as though from a grenade and the evil elf winked, adding "last week the cops actually showed up." The back yard was littered with the little shards of plastic under a veil of smoke and yuletide insanity.

One cannot plan the perfect holiday because by our very nature, it will never come off exactly as predicted. An aunt will get a migraine, a kid will stub his toe, the pot will boil over, a father will blow something up in the back yard for the sheer fun of it, or a new baby will arrive. The holidays are only a pain if we wish them to be, as there is no requirement for parties or bombs, and no wrong way to celebrate. Here's hoping you enjoy your own rituals, and your own share of unpredictable fun."

To be sure the story goes beyond fun, and I am not at all trying to be frivolous with such a magnificent topic. There is no doubt that fun and frivolity are important to a happy life, but we are well aware that light shines most brightly against the darkness. We can be amazed at the joy and happiness in the human heart that can rise above the darkest, hardest circumstances...

Not As the World Giveth

"An unknown Confederate soldier recorded: "Before breakfast the Doctor made some eggnog, a worthy luxury that is seldom enjoyed in the army. Had sausages for breakfast, quite a treat, the first within the last twelve months. Ralph Bailey and Willie Smith called at my cabin about eleven o'clock, when Bailey made the second eggnog. All went smoothly in the battery. Out in the open air some of the men were hopping to the notes of an old fiddle, trying to be merry." Another rebel recorded that he had paid 3$ for a dozen eggs for which to make an eggnog, a fortune in those days and tribute to a determined Christmas spirit.

Confederate Tally Simpson wrote to his sister on Christmas Day from camp near the killing field of Fredericksburg, Virginia: "This is Christmas Day. The sun shines feebly through a thin cloud, the air is mild and pleasant, [and] a gentle breeze is making music through the leaves of the lofty pines that stand near our bivouac. All is quiet and still, and that very stillness recalls some sad and painful thoughts." After confessing the horrors of war and wondering when it all might end, the reader can feel the brother step back, to comfort with happier descriptions his sister, trying recall his own small cheer by sharing it across the miles: "While we were there, [the Union Genl], with several of his aides-de-camp, came over under flag of truce. Papers were exchanged, and several of our men bought pipes, gloves, &c from the privates who rowed the boat across. They had plenty of liquor and laughed, drank, and conversed with our men as if they had been friends from boyhood."

Germany invented Christmas trees, and erected them on fronts flung over thousands of miles and three continents. Twenty-seven years removed from the 1914 Christmas Truce in the trenches of France, a Wermacht chaplain in front of Moscow saw his charges "awful, ragged, full of bed bug bites, entire bodies bloody, emaciated, dirty...Russian mortar shelling coming closer...I visit the men [and] read the Christmas story from the Bible to them. Later sang songs with the gentlemen from the battalion staff. The commander played the accordion..." A year later, the remnant of the German Sixth Army lay dying, freezing and starving, encircled by the Russians at Stalingrad. At midnight on Christmas Eve, thousands of flares lit up the sky over the dead city in celebration, by men whose death was all but certain. An unknown soldier wrote: "we have never been more grateful for the Christmas Gospel than in these hours of hardship." An infantry division quartermaster wrote from the death-trap a benediction to his wife and children: "Nothing can happen to me any longer. Today I have made my peace with God." Ammunition boxes draped with blood-spattered tunics served as altars, and "hard, black bread" was given as the holy sacrament. A year later, a German soldier on the Eastern Front survived a Christmas dawn attack, after which communion was jointly given by the unit chaplain and the Russian village's Orthodox priest. He recalled of his comrades: "Their sad and bitter hearts were soothed...the soldiers went back down with simple souls, pure as the great white steppe which glistened in the Christmas afternoon."

In a holiday broadcast on 12/21/44, the legendary Bing Crosby called out home front greetings to the fox-holes, ships, and airbases, describing for his audience Mass being held on a muddy French battlefield, and reminding them: "On our fighting fronts there are no silent nights, but there are plenty of holy nights." The coldest pre-ghost Ebenezer's heart would quake at the implications. On that same night his stage partners, The Charioteers sang a humorous warning to all in "A Slip of the Lip Can Sink a Ship." Three nights later, on Christmas Eve, a German U-boat sank the American troop ship U.S.S. Leopoldville, drowning 763 in the icy English Channel. The next day, with little news from beyond the horizon, American airman William Elliot marked his second Christmas in a German POW camp, remembering: "I would have given almost anything to be home, hovering around a hot stove or fireplace...I could almost smell Mother's cooking." Far to the south in Italy, enemy troops infiltrated forward positions on Christmas night, and launched a pre-dawn attack. Medal of Honor winner Lt. James Fox, never to return to a nation that would one day grant those of his hue equal rights, called in an artillery barrage on his own position to save the day, and died a hero. Lt. Col. Nurse Annie Ruth Graham, veteran of three wars, wrote her last Christmas note from Tuy Hoa, Vietnam, wishing her family a Christmas of joy, and hoping for prayers of peace. She died overseas the following August, never seeing again the land she loved. On Dec. 25, 2000, a group of old veterans radioed Christmas greetings to their families from the middle of the Atlantic, as they guided WWII veteran amphibious troopship LST-325 across the Atlantic to its final port in Mobile, AL. "The realization that we would not be together with our families for the holidays was truly painful. We hope that the joy of our forthcoming homecoming will in some way makeup for the disruption of the Christmas season."

This Christmas, good men and women are overseas in harms' way, on our behalf. Whatever their respective faiths, they too will dream and write of home and family, and long for the day they can return. It may be our tribute to them to enjoy the food, and music, and presents, and fun, and plenty that they defend for us. But take just a moment on Christmas, privately, or with your family, and say a prayer that they may each find the Star to guide them safely home. Another solider, never mind the nation or cause, knew that Light amidst his war: "Bright Merry Christmas is here again, and so am I, right in the breezy woods to enjoy it, unhampered by the restraints of custom, the fetters of fashion, and thralldom of etiquette, ready and willing to hide away a first-class Christmas dinner if I had it. I am glad I am alive and whole... At sunrise this morning we fired two rounds from our guns in commemoration of the birth of Him who said, "Peace I leave with you, my peace I give unto you, not as the world giveth." Merry Christmas."

❖ ❖ ❖

Part 5

Fall was definitely in the air out west when we awoke to the first cool morning of the season, jacket weather for at least a couple of hours, and it felt great. Western New Mexico heats up quickly enough and the rental's air conditioning was on well before lunch time as we rolled through crunchy, mountainous badlands with long streaks of black rocks turned up in the strata lining the roads, and countless mesas and gulches that could have hidden every desperado and Indian from the old days when it took some serious pioneer toughness to cross these wastes. It was a beautiful drive to and through Albuquerque, and around the mountains up to Santa Fe. Right into town we hit a conglomerate of Native American, folk art, and natural history museums, all of which were great fun. We also found a dead snake in the road leading up to the museums, but it was too mangled up to save for a decent belt.

The well-off and conspicuous consumers were definitely long established as we found after checking into the hotel downtown. Just walking distance from our lodgings, is the old downtown, old adobe and brick buildings built around a square, boasting shops that sell all the spices, overpriced jewelry, fancy leather ensembles, large bronze or marble statuary, paintings, food, boots, or hats an eager tourist with too much cash can covet. Out of the hot sun in the cool sidewalk shade were all sorts of tourists, and a noticeable portion of hair-and-nails trophy wives eager to help the local economy. Everything comes down to marketing, I thought.

A late lunch overlooking a side street from the balcony, over a mid-afternoon platter of blue corn nachos with spicy beef and black beans, washed down with local microbrews, absolutely hit the spot. I was getting a little edgy, the adrenalin not yet coursing, but mentally preparing myself: this was the last day before the Big Day. That evening I would begin a 24-hour fast to prepare myself for battle in Amarillo.

We headed up a side street to a store specializing in old-fashioned, custom-made western hats. The proprietor, son of the founder, introduced us to a fancy antique gizmo that had been used for a century to get the fittings right. The contraption is a ring of individually jointed mechanical arms, joined to a frame above the crown. Into the crown is inserted a file card, upon which the other ends of the mechanical arms describe a down-sized facsimile of the unique circumferential ellipse which is one's noggin. The cards are then kept on file so that should one decide to purchase, they need but go online, pick the style, and then give the credit card number. The Old West meets the New, and all in style.

The only disappointment was that evening, when we returned to one of the authentic appearing restaurants lining the central square. The place really cool, with saloon doors and a narrow adobe staircase leading to the upstairs dining room and bar. The tequila list was expansive, and such had been my mission, to sample a shot of the sort of excellence I might not find east of the Mississippi. We ordered some chips and a salsa *assortment that looked promising, and I asked the bartender for his recommendation among tequilas that went from $10 to $60 a shot. I wasn't out to blow money – Santa Fe clearly has other people to do that for her. And perhaps it was they who ruined the bartender; one hopes that he did not become a disinterested snot all on his own. "They're all pretty good" was all I got by way of recommendation, which reflected accurately the enthusiasm in the tip I didn't leave. The tequila was nothing unique, and I could have made better salsa at home. Precisely one shot into our visit we paid and left. The night was better saluted out by the pool, enjoying a couple of beers and some excellent cigars. Santa Fe is a beautiful town that I intend to visit again, in which resides a mediocre restaurant, overcharging on the basis of superficialities, and not delivering on the aesthetic promises made by its façade. It was a good preview of 2009 and the new administration.*

"Democracy means simply the bludgeoning of the people by the people for the people."
Oscar Wilde
"A man may be so much of everything that he is nothing of anything."
Samuel Johnson

Among the Obamites

*An Ominous Start * Mentoring the Less Fortunate * Great Band, Silly Idea * Nice Shot, Mr. President * Harley Refutes Finlandization * Another Select Justice * Mama Wants Back In Prison * Obama Just Cost me Millions * Deception Sounds Nicer * A Deadlier Contagion * Pining for Reason*

Two months after Santa Fe, what I remember the most about Election Night 2008, oddly yet comfortingly enough, was the guacamole. My pal Todd is married to a superlative lady who boasts not least among her many talents, great skill in the kitchen. I got away from work a bit late, so by the time I got to my friends' home they had already begun to eat, and greeted me with wan smiles appropriate to the evening. I was untroubled, having watched the polls and the utter ineptitude of the McCain effort with enough attention to know that the race was a foregone conclusion. The truly otherwise admirable concession speech that he gave was all that left me with bitterness that evening, disgust over an elegant piece of rhetoric that exhibited more effort than had his election strategy.

But the food was wonderful, including spicy oven roasted chicken wings, hummus from scratch (Tammy's is the best on the planet) with pita chips, excellent beer, and the first guacamole I've ever tasted that was blended with fresh, minced jalapenos. It was heavenly, and that evening was not the first time that I've made a pig of myself at their house. But even for all the good eats, we eventually had to turn our attention to the tube, the final calls for this state or that, and the gleeful, childlike faces of the news readers as they struggled not to burst into grateful tears at the ascent of their candidate. Eventually the president-elect and spouse took the stage, and the winner said his piece to the joyful crowd. Refusing to let an otherwise good evening go to waste, we went out back into the cold night air to sit around the fire ring, enjoying the roaring blaze, some fine cigars, and a little more beer.

We woke up in good spirits the next day, the world not yet ended, it was college football season, and there was more right with the world than wrong. We hit the Waffle House, where I had a chili omelette, grits, and at least a pot of black coffee. Considering the outcome, it was still one of the most enjoyable election nights I'd ever spent, and the least suspenseful of them all. I suppose for that at least, I can thank John McCain.

I did not enter into January 2009 full of gooey good wishes for the new president, any more than the W. haters had eight years earlier. Before Rush Limbaugh started his "I hope he fails" controversy, I already knew that I wanted Obama's efforts beaten back whenever, wherever possible. I wanted him stopped because like many of his supporters, I had listened intently to his stated policy pronouncements; and unlike the vast majority of Obama's supporters, I knew what they held in store for the nation. Of the two basic groups of liberals, bleeding hearts and bullies, community organizers fall into the latter category. Obama the organizer for all his smiles is a practiced and intent bully, unafraid to rough up the opposition and break some political kneecaps with a bat of demagoguery. The charm and the cool, and the condescending mannerism of lifting his chin toward an audience in order to speak down to them worked no charms on me. The man is a pushy know-it-all, who feels both obligated and entitled to get into everyone's business. This was confirmed early on, in one of his first policy statements…

An Ominous Start

"The nation is in serious trouble. Sure I know as much as the next schlub about the credit crunch, global warming so bad that polar bears are floating to Nassau, and the need to show friendliness to a Venezuelan weirdo styling himself as Fidel 2.0. These are the sorts of problems that will rise and flow with the level of affluence and education of a restive electorate more anxious to restore their self-esteem than their credit ratings. But now looms a threat more unsettling to the fabric of American life than any of these trivialities. On the eve of his ascension, Pres.-Elect Obama said "I think it is about time that we had playoffs in college football. I'm fed up with these computer rankings …Get eight teams – the top eight teams right at the end. You got a playoff. Decide on a national champion." If you were distracted by the joy of Hope & Change, Inc., mired in maudlin moroseness, preoccupied with preparing the gobbler, or just wondering how many boxes of China-made twinkle lights you would have to forgo to ease our trade deficit, then this tremor may have gotten by you: the next U.S. president expressed an opinion on fixing the heart of sport and one of the pillars of a dying American manhood already assailed by (no kidding) pomegranate-flavored beer.

All other sports pale in comparison to our beloved collegiate crashes. There is no season for golf or tennis, the sporting world's equivalent of info-mercials, baseball is only relevant in its last weeks, and the drama of NASCAR could be replicated merely by filling the washing machine with gas, selecting Hi-Spin, and putting a match to it. Come to think of it, that would be a LOT more exciting. To watch basketball, mercilessly crammed into our cortices by the 24-hour sports cycle, is at best to watch management, where the only critical decisions are reached at 4:30 pm on Fridays. Even the NFL, barring the occasional QB amnesia or accidental firearm discharge, is a subdued companion, methadone to the Saturday mainline of the college game. The rivalries are more intense, the cheerleaders prettier, and the last-second heroics more gripping than any contest since the Spartans were a 13-1/2 point dog to the Persians. That a U.S. president would take an interest is just plumb scary. A century or so ago Pres. Teddy Roosevelt took a similar interest, noting the unseemly number of fatal head injuries in the young sport, and nearly killed infant football in the crib. The return of Beltway Yes-We-Can-Fix-It foolishness might play for the UAW, but it could ruin football.

As we consider the specter of yet another illogical Bowl Championship Series coronation, the great majority of fans do indeed want a playoff. But loath we should be to accept such advocacy from our elected masters. The feminists will cheer to force more hesitant girls into jobs for which they by merit are not suited, whatever that female kicker at the junior college claims. Jesse Jackson complains yearly as it is about a dearth of black head coaches, and we certainly don't need a larger platform for his recoil racism in a sport so utterly un-segregated. Let Barney Frank and Chris Dodd start holding hearings on the need for "affordable" skyboxes, and the multi-billion alumni endowment industry will collapse into bailout status. Let the Pharisees of Fairness clutch the thrill of victory, and they will mandate low-fat, alcohol-free tailgating, and subdivide and dilute until every team is a winner, with losing schools receiving point handicaps, extra scholarships, and federally subsidized gift shops, paid for by increased taxes on the previous major bowl winners. The next president might be right about the need for a playoff in college football but Big Government will only give us a bland, dispirited replacement, more process than passion. Let Obama and His Immortals attempt to fix football and we will get ...soccer."

With that chill already up my spine, January was cold and busy, as the new president and his minions came into their own. It was tough watching the close-ups of the Inauguration Day crowd on the Mall and before the Capitol, beaming their earnestness into my living room, oblivious to what they had wrought. They saw the first black president and a symbol of hope; I saw,

correctly, another liberal whom free voters had loosed upon them-
selves, full of prescriptions and nostrums shown for decades to be
utter failures. So there we all were, America, bleeding from the
economic wounds inflicted by Bush, Frank, & Dodd, lacerations
to be staunched by Keynesian pigheadedness ...

Mentoring the Less-Fortunate

"What can be done, we considered, to stem this acid tide?
As a corrosive, leeching tsunami made of good intentions,
cult worship, bureaucratic entrenchment, class envy, and
plain old fashioned ignorance rises against the land, we
wondered: what can be done to slow this thing, before
heading to higher ground, crawling into the bunker, or
watching Oprah non-stop until voluntary lobotomization
occurs?

Amidst a lazy swirl of cigar smoke on the back porch
last weekend, we considered the stark assaults, not without
their hilarity, foisted upon us by the Obamites. The nation
is swooning in the paranoia and accelerated anxiety befitting a meth-head, well aware that he is dissolving himself
but daring not to criticize the victim in the mirror. A par-
ticipant at an Obama town meeting embraces the definition of village idiot, and is feted and lauded by the media
as though failure were somehow more authentic and representative of today's America. It may well be in due course.
The market crashes, and the Democrats rush to prop up
the failures. Strangled by entitlements, GM must bend on
subservient knee to Uncle Sam who demands reform. Yet
in this model the banks, housing, health care, energy, all vie
to become monuments to failure when forced to eschew
the cold numbers of the free market. What wonderful

irony that the Democrat victory machine now depends upon a dwindling number of viable producers to keep it fueled (not an original thought, I admit). Feelings can burn a building down or destroy an industry, but they cannot build or create anything absent useful work.

What of those left who have always believed that honest profit and freedom are one in the same, who have always sought to create and build for their own gain? How can they fight back and protest the monstrous doings in D.C.? How do capitalist Americans – and hey, don't we love minorities in this country? – make their voices heard? Dumping tea in Boston harbor makes a nice photo op, but the EPA would probably declare it a crime. Massive D.C. Mall gatherings a' la Rosie and Farrakhan haven't mattered since the Vietnam War, and that would be the day that the major networks all took a day off or shifted to 24/7 coverage of the Secretary of State's return to Tuzla to confront the snipers. And unlike many previous Mall marchers, wealth producers don't like to miss work. If we can get away with withholding taxes en masse then things are further gone than we would wish.

Capitalists love this nation and themselves, and wish to hurt neither. How then can they persuade and educate the lost and confused trying to drag them under? The answer is simple. Liberalism is of course a disease of low self-esteem wherein the practitioner seeks to profit from others' adulation, a condition that cries out for affirmation and good example. In this vein the media and government have for years celebrated murky mentoring and feel-good pageants like a day set aside to take one's daughter to work. Today the U.S. has a growing pool of laid-off, disillusioned, disoriented people who cannot comprehend what is happening to all of us. In this miasma they are joined by a swelling army of government workers, whose jobs are the only ones Obama is saving. In a spirit of compassionate persuasion, I propose that the remaining capitalists and freedom lovers hold a National Take an Obama Supporter to Work Day. It would certainly be a new experience for some, and would allow these decent Americans seeking real understanding to see for themselves how the nuts and bolts of wealth are made and assembled. Then they might understand how their guy's good intentions are tossing a bag of wrenches into the machine."

As with many, certain music resonates with me on a seasonal harmonic. In the winter I find Pink Floyd fits my mood especially, and gave me a further economic inspiration in the first quarter of the Obama years ...

Great Band, Silly Idea

"In the last clutch of winter - global warming notwithstanding - the cold and gray invites the complex multi-layered ennui and dreamy musings expressed so beautifully by the classic British group Pink Floyd. As most who do not watch American Idol know, the group grew from the psychedelic movement of the late 1960's riding beyond the drugged schizophrenia of their founder, to invent unique sounds and visions never before imagined much less heard. Their 1973 apex was a modern work of art worthy of The Louvre, the brooding "Dark Side of the Moon." The following years for the Floyd were some of incredible success and popularity, diverging interests, and personal squabbles, ending the band a decade later without ever regaining their highest mark. The band moved onto the stage of legend when their creative leader quit for solo, their remnants occasional touring little more than that of a tribute band.

The reunion of this legendary band was the centerpiece four years ago for the series of concerts styling themselves "Live 8", and you may be forgiven if you don't recall them. The effort was concocted by Bob Geldof, one-time rocker for the Boomtown Rats and professional global philanthropist responsible for such other wild successes as Band Aid and Live Aid (Band Aid featured a cool Christmas video, but set the stage for the execrable "We are the World" charity single. As for Live Aid, Ethiopia remained under Soviet control for another several years and by all accounts is still miserably poor). But since our society applauds loudest those whose failures in the service of good intentions are largest, Geldof had another go. He described Live 8 not as a simple charity concert but rather "the start point for The Long Walk To Justice, the one way we can all make our voices heard in unison." Wow. The big shindig happened on July 2, 2005 in various locales including Paris, London, Philadelphia, Rome, and South Africa. Luminaries included our very own Bill Gates, Nelson Mandela, former U.N. Secretary-General Kofi Annan (the cash from the oil-for-food Iraq heist must have been running out), and of course that ubiquitous Jimmy Carter of rock-n-roll, Bono. The shows were all reportedly good, and the crowd was suitably enthralled when the original Pink Floyd took the stage for the first time in 24 years. MTV and VH1 were carrying the shows fashionably live, while AOL covered the 'net side of the simulcast, and ABC carried two hours' worth of the highlights in prime time that evening. Famous Brit

Madonna somehow got onstage with the real musicians and screamed joyful curses in a fake American accent, and the Ecstasy-addled producer at MTV actually cut to a commercial during a Pink Floyd guitar solo, but overall the shows were pleasant and harmless enough.

What, the reader might wonder, does all this have to do with anything in the Age of Obama? The purpose of Live 8 was Geldof's move to "make poverty history" by pressuring the prosperous industrialized nations of the G8 to forgive the foreign debt of struggling third world countries, particularly those in Africa. To date there has been no appreciable change in the status of the underdeveloped world, although hilariously, the very nations held responsible for making it all right are now in the tumults of financial upheaval and credit freefall. Lamentably Pink Floyd keyboardist Richard Wright died in '08, leaving the Hyde Park show as the last ever for the famed group, which was all the whole silly exercise accomplished. As the United States prepares to throw a big charity party for itself by way of stimulus, maybe we can get Geldof to produce another disaster soundtrack. I can't say whether the Willie Nelson-John Mellencamp Farm Aid bunch will be available, but talent vacuums Britney Spears and the Simpson sisters will certainly want to do their part."

In August 1981 while working in the back of our hometown Kentucky Fried Chicken, I got an excited phone call from my dad, thrilled to cheer, "He shot 'em down." The old man was applauding Reagan's decision to allow U.S. Navy fighter jets to splash a couple unfriendly Libyan bogeys. Five years later I would be in the Gulf of Sidra the night we once again taught the Libyans about freedom of navigation. There is good reason to cheer when the U.S. commander-in-chief acts decisively to protect

Americans. For all of his ridiculous stimulus moves in early 2009, the president got one right and deserved credit, which I was glad to give ...

Nice Shot Mr. President

"When pressed on the legion of logical flaws in the positions of their guy, some of my, ahem, "moderate" pals (pssst...liberals) flail a bit shrill. They have often used as a fall-back the accusation that I would never give due credit to President Obama for any good idea or action based simply on my blood-spewing disdain for Himself as the guardian of all that is good and true. Read 'em and weep guys. It is a primary obligation of the U.S. president to ensure the safety of his fellow citizens, and the security of his national interests abroad. It is likewise an obligation of those citizens to give the president due credit when those duties are faithfully discharged. Americans should be proud and supportive of President Obama's decision to use deadly force in the rescue of fellow citizen Capt. Richard Phillips. U.S.S. Bainbridge skipper Cdr. Frank Castellano was the on-scene commander on whose shoulders weighed the final call. After long hours and repeated threats, an AK-47 was held up to the hostage and that call was made. Navy SEAL snipers fired three perfect shots and rescued the hostage. Like our commander-in-chief, the Navy deserves our gratitude.

A supplicant media, ever slavering at a chance to show their Chosen One adoration, have been thrilled over the decisiveness, the steely nerve of the chief executive. Well now, let's look at the bare bones of this deal: American citizens are held, our legitimate interests abroad are threatened, and the U.S. president acts according to constitutional mandate to correct the situation. Now say Sean Penn decided to go to medical school in order to study whatever parasite has infected his brain and influence him to consort with America-hating dictators. Great mind that he is, he might not do well enough to get into a U.S. school, and might be forced to go to one abroad. If his medical school's island is overrun by, say hypothetically, Cubans, and Obama sends in the military to rescue him, why he would again be applauded by the towel-holders of NBC et al. Of course when Reagan did just that in the 1983 Grenada invasion – rescuing American hostages, reasserting legitimate American interests abroad – he was scorned as a dangerous warmonger. Tell this to one of the Obamites and you will hear snorts of derision that the situation was utterly different, as though only their guy could be brilliant enough to work the alchemy necessary to conjure liberal goodness from the same right-wing lead of the outdated Constitution.

Bush '41 blundered us into Somalia, and Clinton made it worse. His pullout has been claimed by Osama bin-Laden to be the invitation for the current Islamofascist assault on the West. The Obama Administration has resumed a good standard by meting out death to pirates. When U.S. interests in the Caribbean are threatened by Chavez, will Obama build upon this posture? When the Iranians go nuclear will they be given pause by a resolute foreign policy? Moscow, Beijing, and Pyong Yang all took notice of the hostage rescue, but any honest observer should be skeptical that Obama will be as tough with these tougher customers. At least for now, he has taken one step down the proper road.

As for the pirates, I propose a national initiative: In a time of rising unemployment and military cutbacks, Federal stimulus money could be diverted to a massive ad buy in red states. Offer lawn chairs, free beer, and unlimited ammo to anyone willing to bring his or her own deer rifle. The only targets permitted must be located outside of the ships rails. Good ol' boys get a free cruise, merchant security is provided with a flare, and wimpy libs get to keep whining about the U.S. causing all the violence in the world. Pirate problem solved."

We're familiar with good 'ol boys down here on the "redneck Riviera" of the Florida panhandle, and God bless them. They come in all varieties, from the laconic cigarette dragging oystermen to the high-rolling lawyers tailgating in Tallahassee, pine forest moguls, blowhards competing with "Roll Tide" and "War Eagle", and cammo-clad bubbas hanging around convenience stores on lazy Sundays just hoping something will come into season. I love the South, and I'm glad that our northern cousins bypass this blessed land largely in favor of the Mouse and the condos below Ocala. We in flyover country often miss the attentions of the great and powerful when they venture forth from the Beltway to preen among the fawning northeastern elites and wannabes. Sometimes that access comes with a price, and ironically, they might want to look southward for their rescue...

Harley Refutes Finlandization

"Last week was marked by three significant events: the president's 747 flying with fighter jet escort, made a low pass over New York, the investors in Chrysler were targeted by the White House, and the annual Thunder Beach Motorcycle Rally went down in Panama City. Which got me to thinking about Finland. No, I don't want to move there.

"Finlandization" is a term from the Cold War describing the Soviet nullification of their tiny northern neighbor through sheer intimidation. In 1939 the Stalin régime sought to annex the better chunk of Finland, and got only a bloody nose from Finnish ski troops for its trouble. The Finns were allied to the Third Reich thereafter until the latter was annihilated on the steppes, after which the weaker nation became permanently cooperative with the USSR. The price of maintaining national sovereignty in the Cold War was to accede, and eventually emulate, the domestic practices of the USSR while agreeing with them on foreign policy. If not a vassal state in name, Finland was very near the definition.

Trevor Corson wrote for Yahoo News this week an article titled "What Finland can teach America about true Luxury." His lead in was to juxtapose U.S. tastes in fancy cars and flat screen TV's with Finland's "lack of …opulent homes, and an abundance of modest cars." After extolling a luxury that has little to do with cool toys or the need to acquire them, the author cites a U.S. expatriate who accepted the high taxes for free healthcare and free K-through-college education. Corson had to twist the toady's knife in his country, sneering that Finland "really does give its citizens a fair and equal chance in life in a way that the US just doesn't." He ends wondering if Americans should pause for their own "Finnish moment" to subdue their materialistic pursuits.

And so we have. As Caesar's Boeing air chariot glowered down at a terrified Manhattan last week, the nation got a visible if unintended look at what they have embraced. The tangible vision of federal power panicking the little people was consistent with the fear Obama seeks to sow on Wall Street, attacking hedge fund investors trying to protect their clients in the Chrysler takeover. The bully power could not tolerate the opposition in its drive to shower unearned wealth on its thug union muscle, and the White House attacked the cheated investors who dared complain with the swift brutality of an armored column in the middle of the night, forcing the subdued to accept a shared sacrifice of twenty cents on the dollar rather than the protections of a Chrysler bankruptcy they had rightfully demanded.

Our last hope might be, to the chagrin of purveyors of intimidation, precisely in our glorious consumption. This past week, the "Thunder Beach" motorcycle rally in Panama City, Fla. was a highway clog of chrome, smoke, noise, mirrors, denim, leather, shades, rubber, and smiles that would cheer the heart of the most pessimistic. The road last Saturday from Apalachicola to Destin was a mass of happy Americans, pursuing their interests on every bike imaginable, some quite expensive, in the land they love. This was a large bunch of people spending quite a lot of money, merely to have fun. When Mr. Corson's ilk sounds the trumpet for Caesar, will this crowd be ready to accept the more "modest", non-custom, eco-friendly, muted motorcycles and subdued vacations that their higher taxes will permit? One wonders if any of the riders who trailered their showpiece hogs to the gathering live in or aspire to "opulent" homes, which might be foregone in the spirit of shared sacrifice. How far will American business back down before a rampaging anti-freedom idealist and his amen media? When enough Americans see

469

mooching neighbors trying to steal their good times, a Harley's roar might sound like the new Liberty Bell."

Lest I sound too provincial, allow a regretful admission that Florida occasionally gums it up, like she tried to do in the 2000 election. The forces of inconsistency will seek to take hold wherever humans gather, in order to give motive to bad works. Would the ascension of Hope & Change finally do away with racism, and set forever the idea of equality for all individuals before the law? Yeah, right...

Another Select Justice

"Way back in '00, the U.S. Supreme Court took a hand in presidential politics when they ruled against the Florida Supreme Court's decision to elect Al Gore. The subsequent folklore for the feeble has it that the U.S. Supremes "picked a president" which is demonstrably false. The Democrat-majority Florida Supreme Court voted with their hearts, usurped the state law it was their task to enforce, and embraced an opprobrium that required the higher court to slap them down. The claims by the willfully ignorant that the election was "stolen" continue to redound with all the intellectual firepower of a Jesse Jackson rhyme. Judicial activism is a way for thugs to hide behind black robes.

We are told by a slavish Associated Press that the president's pick is a "Historic nomination: Hispanic Sotomayor as justice." In 1932 Benjamin Cardozo was nominated by President Hoover to the Supreme Court. Justice Cardozo's folks were Jewish and had come to America by way of England and Holland whence they had previously immigrated to escape the mercies of the Spanish Inquisition. I was confused by the AP, figuring that an Iberian descendant might have some 'street cred' in the media barrio, but I suppose not. Sotomayor is not breaking any gender barrier, unless Sandra Day O'Connor is not a woman the way Justice Thomas has been derided for not really being black (although somehow Thurgood Marshall was). No, the only real history made with the Sotomayor nomination is of the repeated sort, the perpetual assault by philosophical barbarians eager to seize power by any means necessary.

What exactly would happen to the nomination of anyone who stated that his "experiences as a man and Caucasian" should guide his decisions? What sort of outrage would the media whip up if a nominee stated that being a "wise white guy" would help him "reach a better conclusion than a Hispanic female"? Swap the ethnic adjectives around and you have the quotes and very real racism of Judge Sotomayor. This combination of judicial activism and ethnic prejudice allowed her to opine in favor of a New Haven, Connecticut racial spoils system against firefighters denied promotion for being too egregiously non-diverse.

Of course none of that will matter, anymore than the utter irrelevancy of being the first Hispanic female on the Court. The pageant over Supreme Court nominations has become a depressing cliché: the Right argues that judges are to be appointed to interpret, not legislate. The bleeding hearts of the Left cover the green baize tables with their tears and furor, egged on by an amen media, until the Right caves and pledges to work with the new justice. Cowed by the usual accusations of racism, the opposition to a judge hostile to what is quaintly referred to as constitution principle will wither quickly.

Over the past weeks the president and representatives have sparred sharply over the definitions of torture and the actions taken by the previous administration to combat terrorists. The president's position is that "we also cannot keep this country safe unless we enlist the power of our most fundamental values." From the carcass of Detroit, to health care, to taxes, to the nomination of a blatant ideologue masquerading as an impartial judge, the president continues to assault these same values and pit his countrymen against each other. As U.S. citizens, we schizophrenically demand the right to multiple abortions and subsidized fertility treatments, lavish private profits as well as government bailouts to negate risk, and a constitution with shifting boundaries and fungible standards. What exactly are we trying to defend?"

Just because the majority of U.S. citizens had elected a Dear Leader, I saw no reason to give in to the mass psychosis, turn the statue in the Orwellian square to point at the "real" enemy, and turn all facts on their heads. Economically things were bad, and in that summer's swelter, they were just plain weird ...

Mama Wants Back In Prison

"Well I was drunk the day my mom got out of prison." So begins the payoff verse of David Allen Coe's country standard "You Never Even Called Me By My Name," an ode to the hard path reality sometimes has to walk. Cued up on the iPod while cruising along the road, it was a more comforting way to ponder the radical contrast of our new, frightening dis-reality. We are a nation laudably trying to enjoy our summer while tiptoeing the cliff's edge of utter madness, lurking beneath thin ice of dull-witted apathy, or resignation.

Maybe it's the latter, listening to Coe lament over the credit his songs gained for others. He accurately jabs those who ignore the pedigree of facts and lineage of logic, apt criticism that should be tacked to the forehead of every smug Obamite assurance that we have to give the man a chance. And the singer "never minded standing in the rain", a sop to doleful Republicans who will still be rummaging for their umbrellas come 2010.

It is politics to spin the argument your way surely, but are there no limits? Can arguments be infinitely malleable, with no final fact or point put to a question? People rightly jeered at the stupid Bush stimulus thrown out last summer, adding to the debt and doing nothing to ease the pinch of higher oil prices. Now these same hecklers, transfixed through the tenuousness of their collective self-esteem, have cheered the same foolishness magnified many times when practiced by their anointed charlatan. The self-congratulatory suburbanites, who pronounced dissent as the highest form of patriotism since 2001, now sneer angrily at the ignorant rednecks attending anti-tax tea parties.

"Well I've heard my name a few times...and I've seen it on signs where I played" Coe wailed. We are seeing practiced with more audacity than witnessed since FDR, politicians wrapping themselves in the language of opportunity in order to steal from their bemused followers, and others. Sadly, it was no longer surprising to see Obama reverse every dishonest praise he ever uttered in defense of free democracy. For all his oratory about emerging democracies, the intellectual heir of Al Capone insulted the Honduran people by insisting that leftist dictator-hopeful Zelaya be returned to power; an office from whence he was legally removed when he tried to squat longer than his elected term, making Obama's support for him more troublesome still. Maureen Dowd or the Huffington Post will probably see some greater benefi-cence in his stance, if only it can be explained to the little people.

Maybe it was the sanctuary of a song famous for flip-ping a sarcastic finger to adversity, or maybe it has been the sheer weirdness of the past several days that makes the flaws of the standard honky-tonker so much more appeal-ing by comparison. As Kim Jong-Il launched his missiles to celebrate the 4th of July, the nation appeared to go into an Ecstasy-drool over the death of Michael Jackson and again, the standards shifted, the lines wavered, and we were left...where? I felt like the astronaut in 2001 staring into the void of the black obelisk as the stars swirled and the lines started streaking by, hurtling into another dimen-sion where it made sense to hear Rev. Al Sharpton say to Michael Jackson's kids at the funeral: "I want his children to know there was nothing strange about your daddy."

I just snapped, and wanted to listen to a song about "trains, trucks, prison, and gettin' drunk." For those unfamiliar with this tune, the singer's mama "got runned over by a damned old train." If the standards keep shift-ing, by the mid-term elections the song might have to be re-written. Mama might get hit after leaving her Ameri-Corps retraining class, but by a little two-seater running on green energy that leaves only a bruise, and her in line ahead of you at the local government hospital."

As the summer wore on the teapot began to simmer, and the Big O turned up his own heat as he hit the hustings to push his health care plan. And there the smartest-man-ever-just-ask-him shot his over-educated mouth off and let the cat out of the bag...

Obama Just Cost Me Millions

"It was bad enough having spent a goodly portion of the summer being referred to as a brown-shirted piece of Astroturf without Obama pulling this stunt. In the rambling dog days of health care, beginning with Michael Jackson's $100k monthly Propofol service, and tumbling through the president's scattershot attacks on Big Insurance, Big Drug, hospitals, and doctors, the proles are doubtless leery of any good coming from the medical industry. And now the Big O has to go and spill the beans.

The amputation industry began before antiquity, when the first surgeon probably fed target limbs to a restrained saber tooth and then prayed to the stars for some sort of universal care. In the modern age, amputations were all the rage in the days of fighting sail, where the clash of wooden ships and iron men tested the mettle of the latter with no shortage of work for the (hopefully) drunken sawbones. In 1786 an article in the London Medical Journal recommended delaying the amputation of limbs shattered by ball and splinter at least a few hours, in hopes of improving survival. Ignoring the cost to his colleagues in favor of a few crippled sailors, this early busybody must have been some sort of Admiralty plant designed to contain costs. A quick saw, a slap of hot pitch off a waiting brush, off to the hammock for some laudanum and rum, and God Save the King. Things got a bit more sophisticated by the American Civil War, when Dr. Samuel Cooper's text advised specifically how to cleave to the bone, which integuments to sever, and how to better preserve the remaining limb. A lower leg division would be closed "so as to make the line of their union not transverse, but obliquely perpendicular." Unlike this approach to preserve function, Obama has abandoned the oblique in favor of an approach directly transverse to the Union, and he has now begun the destruction of yet another industry.

At his 8/14 town hall audience in New Hampshire, Obama bemoaned the poor pay for primary care doctors who are paid not much to manage complex diabetic patients. Blowing the lid off of a sweet deal, this gifted orator obviously in command of his facts noted "but if that same diabetic ends up getting their foot amputated, that's $30k, $40k, $50k immediately that the surgeon is reimbursed". My heart sank.

With such a lucrative haul, how many foot amputation clinic chains must have been in the planning or construction stages, providing jobs to countless thousands in a nation whose rising glycemic index is so increasingly proportional to her unemployment rate? What about the brokers who, emulating our federal government, sought to tie their returns to these high-yield chop-property investments? Granted the ultra-snob kickback, I mean, reimbursement rate of $50k per flipper might be a bit excessive, but even thirty-a-foot could keep a diligent doc in beer and cigarettes. But now that the word is out, every family practitioner and pediatrician (those not busy doing pricey tonsillectomies, according to the prez) will beeline toward the nearest weekend foot removal seminar, eager to cash in. Soon the bills will come piling into Medicare/Medicaid, necessitating some sort of cost containment. As the doctors are paid less, they will drift on to other things and the J-1 visa exemptions will again be widened to meet the growing consumer demand to achieve power scooter status. Obama and his henchmen will rail against the amputators' junkets to Las Vegas, and a new round of convention depression will hit Sin City. Soon we will face the sort of shortages predicted for the other, apparently less-lucrative specialties. And they called Dan Quayle an idiot for misspelling potato."

(Note: a month after this miracle of a speech, I ran the numbers by a surgeon friend of mine, who was quite distressed. He assured me that he was only getting about $1,500 per amputated limb. It so unnerved me I suspended my application to enter a foot chopping residency, deciding to save on the application fees until the price went back up again)

The following month President Obama went big-time, and addressed a joint session of Congress on the need to reform health care. It was just a brief shining outburst, but it made me long for the parliamentary rancor of "Prime Minister's questions" in the House of Commons across the pond...

Deception Sounds Nicer

"You Lie!" So yelled Rep. Joe Wilson, R- South Carolina during Obama's address to Congress on his health care aspirations. What under the heavens could so prompt such a disruption of the most beloved orator General Electric has ever owned? Would the Democrat plan cover illegals? In July House Dems defeated an amendment by Rep. Dean Heller, R-Nev., that would have prevented illegal aliens from receiving government-subsidized health care under the bill in question. Why would they oppose such an amendment unless it would affect their plan? Federal law presently requires that anyone presenting to an emergency room receive a medical screening exam, and stabilization/treatment for any emergency condition without respect to cost, insurance, or identity. Sure an undocumented Canadian might be given a bill, but he'll be back in Windsor in front of a Labatt's long before the itemized charges are all printed. However you like, the donkey party wants to cover illegals and for their leader to claim that to be untrue is, well...

In some fairly amateurish flim-flamery Obama said, "My guiding principle is, and always has been, that consumers do better when there's choice and competition. That's how the market works." Then why doesn't the president favor allowing insurance companies to sell across state lines? Because then we would have no need for his miracle insurance exchange, the federal version of the Romney plan now gone way over budget in Massachusetts. Obama: "Now, I have no interest in putting insurance companies out of business... I just want to hold them accountable." Which is why the Dem plan levels a hefty surtax on to the insurance companies for the expected increase in business they are to enjoy, the cost of which will surely be passed on to the consumer. If your boss is the consumer, then consider a Kaiser Family Foundation study that found median health care costs as a percentage of payrolls equal to eleven percent. At your new Acme

GreenCorp factory retooling inner city Uzis into life-giving windmills, your boss will quickly discover that it is better to dump you on to ObamaCare, pay the 8% penalty, and increase his profits by the difference, which will no doubt be spent on midnight mentoring for disadvantaged puppies or SEIU volunteers. And once you are dumped on to the government rolls, the costs will further increase for those left behind under private insurance, until their bosses wise up and follow suit. Supporting a $900 billion plan, Obama swore not to "sign it if it adds one dime to the deficit now or in the future. Period." Really??

Obama reached out to the GOP by directing some applause to his usual prop, John McCain, and by using the words "malpractice" and "reform" in the same paragraph without any attached specific, to which he can never be tied and from which nothing will be allowed to blossom. Sprinkling his speech with the now tiresome whining of the problems he inherited, insulting characterizations of anyone who disagrees with his "reform", and a couple reflex "tax-cuts-for-the-wealthy" (was Pelosi pulling a string on his back?), he then reached for a clincher to please the seniors.

"In 1965, when some argued that Medicare represented a government takeover of health care, members of Congress, Democrats and Republicans, did not back down." At least tonight the GOP sat on their hands during the speech, their only significant accomplishment in the past five years.

Lost in all the post-speech hubbub over whether there will still be a "public option" is the reality that we have had one for forty years, providing cost inflation, shortages, and stoking the fear-fires of crisis thereby guaranteeing further government control. Hilarious that in the same month we marked the 40th anniversary of Woodstock, its participants were screaming at town halls for government to keep its hands off their Medicare. These same beneficiaries Obama praised for "a lifetime of hard work" may soon share the joys of willful self-deception."

The strangeness of the summer, when the CNBC talking heads were talking about a "zombie economy", continued on through the early fall. The nation had a sense that something was coming, big and lurking, but couldn't really put its collective finger on what it might be. As noted earlier, I believe in zombies, and know for a fact that they exist. Anyone working emergency room night shifts has seen, I promise, numerous examples. Anyone who witnessed otherwise sensible people vote for, and buy into insane anti-capitalist economic policies should have been convinced long before the first scratchings were heard on the front door ...

A Deadlier Contagion

"Flip the channels past the burning wrecks collectively known as the White House agenda, and things are starting to appear a tad pre-apocalyptic if not downright spooky. It's unnerving enough that Tom Delay was a contestant on "Dancing With the Stars", but now we have to wonder, was that really a stress fracture that knocked him out, or is he really preparing to make his way to a bunker with Sheila Jackson Lee somewhere south of the Alamo?

We are on the wrong sort of Disney "Small World" ride, where the happy little kidbots suddenly grow fangs, brandish guns, and prepare to pounce red-eyed upon well-fed, obtuse taxpayers. The revelations of schoolchildren reciting mass adulations to the Dear Leader (ours, not the one in Pyongyang) demonstrate convincingly that even while Obama ignores mullahs seeking to weaponize uranium, He Himself is weaponizing kids to further undo us into a new desolate equality. This administration is not un-American, but actively anti-American. The offensives into banking, housing, health care, and education exploit an environment where large impersonal, seemingly mindless forces appear to be at work across the land, abusing and fraying the ties that bind us together not as numbskull citizens of the world, but as the best of the red-blooded wretched refuse.

Into this gathering storm of angst and disruption one ventures, seeking the reality within this upheaval, questioning who we really are as citizens of a formerly rich, increasingly schizophrenic state. The movies are sometime a good place to start, so I loaded up with a large bag of buttered and settled back to learn the truth. Michael Moore in his latest infantile protest movie screams that our ship of state is headed toward the rocks because a drunken Captain Capitalism is at the wheel. But what is the basis of capitalism, if not the individual? Brainwashed kids and an insistence upon demonstrably unworkable ideas as vehicles for malignant government expansion encourage individuals to lose themselves while mindlessly tearing into one another, feeding as it were off of each other as assets are bled dry and the survivors hurled jobless onto a bleak road to scratch for subsistence.

Not that I wasted my time or cash on actually seeing Moore's garbage. The search for truth should be more fun than that, so I went to see "Zombieland", an authentic look at a desolated America in the Age of Obama. The narrator gives us certain rules for enhancing survival, such as "cardio" and "avoid bathrooms." The filmmaker has slyly inserted these as metaphors, obviously meant as warnings to pursue resume' flexibility, and avoid becoming locked in to speculative condo deals. When the survivors raid a grocery store for Twinkies, it might best be interpreted as advice to access as many dwindling tax loopholes as possible. Holing up in a deserted mansion for a few days off the road is actually advice to move offshore when the new health taxes hit, and to be ready for a long siege. Beyond the gates are the stumbling, drooling masses of Obamites in play-doctor white coats and SEIU t-shirts, no longer thinking but smelling money and lives that are not their own, lurching and snarling toward the non-infected to consume them in reflexive undead, never-to-be sated fury. HHS Secretary Sebelius can exhort us all she likes to take the H1N1 vaccine, but that is part of the charade. The virus has already hit, and may kill dreams and aspirations in the hundreds of millions if left unchecked. As plagues go, the Hope & Change virus outbreak last November has proven itself far deadlier to lives and property than anything that has come before. If "universal care" or a second stimulus package makes sense to a friend or family member, they are infected. Grab a bat and some Twinkies, and start running."

The list of incomprehensible, provably wrong and false assertions rolling out of the Obama Administration howled unabated into the first of December. What was good cause for derision a year earlier was now insightful and judged worthy of sober reflection. By now even the zany-left New York Times had admitted that yes, there probably were mass destruction weapons in Iraq that were moved just before the 2003 invasion, but by then of

*course, no one cared. The same newspaper features a regular lib-
eral columnist who will be taken seriously by the gang on "Morning Joe" and all of CNN no matter how silly is his latest line. I
was in need of a good laugh, and so turned to the masters...*

Pining For Reason

"While the frigid blasts of global warming sweep across
the nation, Obama's flying circus blew out of town for
a soiree in the fjords, a leftist prom date gala between
moneyed European morons and their favorite poster boy.
Watching Obama's Nobel speech over morning coffee
was, to be charitable, tedious for the most part. A number
of lines in his acceptance speech sounded like cut-and-
pastes from his West Point speech last week, a continued
self-congratulation for "closing" Gitmo and "ending torture". If he didn't sign the check in front of the crowd,
the prez at least gave enough rhetorical aid and comfort
to his fellow travelers in the room who believe that the
U.S. should pony up the cash to redress the wrongs of the
world. Maybe it was the falling thermometer, or maybe
it was the majesty of the Dear Leader jutting his jaw
toward his groupies so near the Arctic Circle, but something tugged at my desperate boredom. And it hit me –
where were the birds? We all heard about them in our
youth, the great azure-indigo plumed wonders that soar
the thermals, squawking and playing, and pining, always
pining for the fjords. Where, oh where were the great
Norwegian Blue parrots?

By now any properly educated reader will be rolling
his eyes at my naked attempt to rip off the greatest comedy act of all time, Monty Python, and their famous "Dead

Parrot" sketch. If you have not seen this incredible piece, run to YouTube immediately. To recap, an exasperated John Cleese bustles into a pet store wearing a mack and clutching an obviously dead bird, a "Norwegian Blue", demanding of pet store owner Michael Palin an explanation as to why the pet he had just purchased was "passed on." When western university students visited the old USSR to engage in publicized debates with their Commie counterparts, one of the debate techniques employed was for the Soviet players to flatly deny that which was provable and obvious. I don't know whether the Pythons were inspired by this tactic, but they elevated it to art. Cleese insists that the rigor mortised avian is dead, to which Palin responds "No he's not – he's restin'."

Our commander-commander-in-chief took great pains last week to explain to the West Point cadets why Afghanistan was NOT like Vietnam, then went on to outline a strategy that sounds remarkably similar in its unwillingness to seek victory. When the pet shop owner visibly nudges the bird carcass and exclaims that the bird just moved, the customer is incensed yet cannot sway the shopkeeper. Falsified data notwithstanding, Obama takes his science advice from experts like NYT columnist Tom Friedman, a lunatic ignoramus who last week declared that the carbon dioxide we put out today will remain in the atmosphere for "3,000 years."

The would-be parrot purchaser complains, "…when I bought it not half an hour ago, you assured me that its total lack of movement was due to it being tired and shagged out after a long squawk." At his "jobs summit" our anti-capitalist organizer said, "Many have figured out how to squeeze more productivity out of fewer workers…

That may result in good profits, but it's not translating into hiring and so that's the question that we have to ask ourselves today: How do we get businesses to start hiring again?" This level of willful stupidity recalls the pet shop owner explaining the parrot's state of death: "Well, he's... he's, ah... probably pining for the fjords." As Obama attempts to nail our economy's feet to the perch and prop us upright to simulate, sorry, stimulate life, let us hope that we will not soon describe our former prosperity as having "passed on, its metabolical processes of interest only to historians! It's hopped the twig! It's shuffled off this mortal coil! It's run down the curtain and joined the choir invisible!" And if you don't get this brilliant analogy, then clearly this sketch has gotten too silly."

Too silly was right. For the first few months of the Obama Joy, it was almost impossible to be interested in, much less write about politics. If a big-government Republican administration is necessary to prepare the way for a Carter, Clinton, or Obama, then Nixon/Ford, and da' Bushes certainly deserve their share of the blame for undercutting conservatism, and for not giving Americans a decent alternative to the smothering hugs to follow.

Squishy Republicans – that means YOU John McCain primary supporters! -should be scorned for throwing the gates of the nation open to the painfully earnest and the permanent failure i.e. "feelings" which they perceive to be a serious approach to big problems. Since Obama was inaugurated, my criticisms of him have been almost invariably, reflexively met with attacks on Bush, Dick Cheney, Big Business, the evil rich, V-8 engines, rednecks, and anyone desiring to be left alone. In the Age of O it is mandatory that everyone get in the pool no matter how many kids or seniors are turning the water yellow in the shallow end.

The Obamites were some of the most insufferable do-gooders seen since early Ralph Nader acid festivals. It is with no scant relish that I have watched their hopes fall flat on their collective childish faces. The propelling ideals of the Obamites, that "we are all in this together" always distills into component parts of tears and force as they try to force their will on their neighbors (even when they were often unaware of doing so!) I have been thrilled to see the stimulus-and-bailout approach to economic revitalization be shown to be the failure expected by any casual observer of the 20th century. The redistributionists may scream all they like about unfairness and greed, and how "trickle down" doesn't work. They might as well go down to the water's edge and yell at the wind for all the good it will do them. Human nature will not be fundamentally changed, certainly not by this herd. Individuals will always seek their own prosperity, however they choose to define it, within the bounds set by society. When those bounds become too tight, behaviors will change and humans will adapt. Take away a corporation's profit and SHAZAAM they will hire fewer workers. Make future hiring more expensive, and you can't be taken seriously whatever "laser-like" focus on jobs you claim to have.

It has been fun to watch the tricks and prevarications of the Obama team to defend the Democrat health care plan. As in 1994, they moved too quickly and overreached. The entire W. Bush error should have taught them that they are slowly eroding the average citizen's instinct for self-reliance. Buck up little campers, you're wining!

That depends, of course, on how you define victory. If a socializing health care and preventing more from getting better, all at a greater cost – if that constitutes a "win", then the Dem's should feel cheered. It won't really be a win in terms of jobs, GDP, consumer price index, or the average standard of living. It won't be a win in foreign policy terms as it becomes tougher to fund the military for legitimate roles, and our trading partners get antsy. It won't be a win for the Chinese, whose warehouses will swell with unsold, extra-leaded toys, but it sure will put them in the lead.

The Obamites will continue to fail and fail miserably, because the things they want to accomplish are impossible. We will never have cutting edge, perfect health care for all at low cost. Business owners large and small will always operate with their eye first on their bottom line; if we reach the point where the government starts to force businesses to hire, there will be fewer of them created in the first place as would-be entrepreneurs say to hell with it. Electric cars once profitable, will be sought by the public and until then no amount of GM bailout or tax subsidy will accomplish otherwise. Reason will always trump feelings if only in absentia, seen as credit collapses and the polar bears remain nonplussed. Let a conservative talk about the need to drill in Alaska and he is called a callous murderer of the environment. But during the BP oil spill in the Gulf of Mexico, Obama relayed how his daughter Malia asked one morning while he was shaving, "Did you plug the hole yet Daddy?" The story was greeted with "aww's" and serious respect from his supporters who waited for him to accomplish his daughter's wish a mile below the sea, oblivious that they were being played for chumps yet again.

Obama the man, "The One" (an Oprah quote), the President of these United States, has never and will never scare me. He's just one guy. But his supporters, the ones who uncritically bought his whole Greek faux-columned nothingness, who really believe in a Hope & Change based not on reason but feelings and forced love, scare the hell out of me. They are still out there, and ready to be herded up and duped again.

❖ ❖ ❖

Part 6

Showdown

I was well rested driving out of Santa Fe that Monday morn-
ing. We headed back down to an excellent French café in the
old town, and I hated passing on all the goodies I saw on other
peoples' tables. But today was the big day, Game Day, the event
for which I had planned, plotted, and schemed for almost a year,
and discipline was the key. I stuck to coffee for breakfast, and we
killed an hour wandering through an outdoor art gallery before
getting back to the car. Heading west toward the last line of the
Rockies, the news on the radio was of stock market crashes, wild
real estate fluctuations, and the first panicky news conferences
that would become the Troubled Asset Relief Program, a perverse
prophet ushering in the Messiah stimulus after the election of
H&C. It didn't sound too alarming at the time, and at any rate
it wasn't my priority.

   It was striking to look behind us after passing the last line
of mountains, to actually see the Rockies behind us, and a vast
plain spreading out before us. Cruising along the interstate the
change happens so fast that you could miss the dramatic break in

topography if you aren't paying attention. The onset of the plains announced that we were headed for Texas, and the final stop of the trip. I was really getting excited. Every so often we would stop to stretch and replenish, and I was pounding the water and coffee, chomping gum every so often in nervous expectation. As the land turned a little – just – greener, we approached the state line and began to see more farmland and more cattle. Somewhere after entering Texas we drove through a moderately large windmill farm, which looked really cool and space age against the mostly flat fields that stretched all the way to the horizon. A lot has been written about the big, futuristic windmills. Apparently the carbon emissions they avoid are more than produced by standby diesels that have to power up the grid when the wind slacks, and I read somewhere that Spain has lost a lot of money trying to save the planet with these things. Oh well, they looked cool, and it was not my purpose to tilt with these things on this day.

We pulled into Amarillo about on schedule, found The Big Texan, and checked into the adjoining motel resplendent in ticky-tack faux western motif. For the past several hours I had started to get phone calls and text messages from interested parties ready for the night's show. The table of honor for those attempting to tackle the 72-oz steak at the Big Texan is under permanent webcam surveillance, and I had spent a number of evenings observing aspirants, studying their habits, and judging their timing. Knowing that technology had brought big eating to the masses as a spectator sport, I invited certain friends and family to join me on my tribute to all that is great and good as I dove into this patriotic enterprise. And so the well wishes and the questions ("Are you getting nervous?") started rolling in.

Okay, now I was a little nervous, just a little bit. I needn't have been of course, because I had eaten this much on any number of occasions, liberally washed down with draft beer to boot. I had stuck to my game plan for a twenty-four hour fast, and lots of hydration. No sweat. I decided to shower up, wash the road grit off, and prepare myself with greatest respect to meet that part of the steer that had died in tribute to this great land.

For the event I had reserved my most comfortable jeans and one of my favorite Hawaiian shirts, black with strands of pink and white leis framing a half-naked surfer chick on the front. This went perfectly with my best pair of boots, custom Lucchese alligators stained in black cherry. This was a momentous day, and it was important to be donned as befitting the occasion. Ready, I nodded that it was time and we stepped out into the dusty parking lot.

The joint is a big western-styled building, lined with wooden rails and old timey leanin' posts, all in a garish yellow clearly meant to scream "tourist trap!" at every likely passerby. An enormous statue of a bull on a trailer guards the entrance, it's face feigning cow contempt for greenhorns and tenderfeet who even think they are good enough to enter. Huge blue letters screaming "The Big Texan" and "World Famous Steaks" at the highway are centered under fluttering Lone Star flags. To the side wait a couple of stretch limos, with roof-mounted signs offering free transport for diners. We were here, at the locus for my expectations for all these long months. It was a thrill to be here, too much so, as when one anticipates Christmas or a major football game for so long that it's hard to savor it through the excitement.

We walked right into the sun the short space to the front entrance of The Big Texan and stepped inside. Todd acting as my faithful second, made arrangements with the hostess as I walked over to the display case where the monster was housed. It sat benignly in the display case, its raw, bloody goodness wrapped in clear cellophane, framed by a foil-wrapped baked potato, a house salad, fried shrimp appetizer, and roll. The rules are simple and specific: all the contents in the display case must be consumed, and within one hour. Completion means the meal is free, and the victor receives a certificate, T-shirt, and his name is entered unto the roll of this Valhalla of gluttony. Losers get...I had not come all these long miles to lose. The main dining area is arranged about a wood plank floor like a huge dance hall with wooden booths and filled with wooden tables about half-filled this late afternoon with individual families and a bus full of retirees just arrived. The upper balcony is lined with deer and elk heads all solemnly staring down on aspirants and spectators alike. The far wall is open to the kitchen, a scurry of smoke, sizzle, and servers as the plates fly in and out. Diners may go up to the counter to peer in over the rows of grills to watch the meat turn, and wonder as to the real heft of 72 ounces, 4 ½ pounds of going-to-heaven cow. Between the general dining area and the grills sits a small raised platform, upon which the contest occurs.

Arrangements were made, the batteries in the video camera were checked, and it was time. Buddy that he is, Todd paid for the steak for which I wish to give due thanks. The waitress led me to the table, facing the crowd that had grown somewhat, and asked for a big hand as I took my seat. I hadn't really thought about being watched the entire time, but I've briefed portentous admirals and grouchy surgeons so I smiled and waved, then ignored them. I also waved at the video camera staring unblinkingly from the far balcony, well aware now that it was beaming my performance to my girlfriend, friends, and family in three states and two countries that were tuning in that night. The whole gang at the ER where I used to work was gathered 'round their computer screen, as was the night crew where I was presently working. My sister and her boyfriend ate their supper as they watched what she later told me was one of the most surreal things she had ever seen.

Todd would occasionally field phone messages for me during the performance and deliver a quick long-distance encouragement throughout the battle.

The steak was ordered and while waiting, the cowgirl-waitress cheerfully intoned the rules: all food must be consumed, and with in sixty minutes. A large digital timer mounted by the table would keep track for the audience, and the waitress would update me at thirty minutes, then every ten thereafter. The would-be champion was not allowed at any time to leave his seat, or forfeiture would result. Any regurgitation would end the attempt automatically. Fair enough I said, bring it on.

My strategy had been to order my steak cooked "medium." I prefer medium rare, but thought to have extra fat and water content cooked out to make more room. I would finish half at least within the first twenty minutes, figuring that would leave me a margin of error if I slowed too much. The steak arrived minutes later, sizzling, and not in the least bit intimidating. I was sticking with unsweetened tea for the affair, served in an authentic plastic miniature cowboy boot, to minimize the sugar load, and not fill up on beer. The waitress asked if I needed anything else and if I was ready. I said yes, she wished me luck, started the clock, and I began to cut.

Cutting rapidly and chewing furiously, it was a sprint right out of the gate. The steak, while not the sort of quality one might savor in a more upscale restaurant, was nonetheless flavorful and should have tasted great after a twenty-four hour fast. That was unexpected. During my initial assault, it was odd to realize that I was not even hungry. Whether it was the crowd, the webcam, the timeline, or the culmination of months of expectation, my sympathetic nervous system was revved and the adrenaline was flowing. I was not hungry. So what I told myself, it doesn't matter, no excuses. Cut, chew, a little tougher gristle there in the seam, wash that down, stuff down a shrimp, cut chew some more, and may I have some more ice tea please? It felt like only half the time when Todd came up to the table to tell me I had completed the first twenty minutes.

Hot damn, half the steak and part of the potato, and most of the salad was gone. I was on track. The knife and fork were in a steady rhythm now, working a practiced pace as I looked up occasionally to smile at everyone on the webcam, or acknowledge a well-wisher passing by the table to cheer me on. In the biggest state in the biggest, baddest nation on the planet, I was roaring in celebratory consumption, with a joyful heart. I needed more tea.

By the half hour mark I detected a tiny flaw, a burp if you will, in my strategy. If having the steak cooked "medium" did indeed reduce the weight, it dried it out to the point of needing so much tea to wash the bites down as to negate the intended benefit. My jaw was sore, and I was a little tired, but with a half hour to go and the whole world to gain, I was undismayed. Not really a half-hour as Todd warned, I was down to my last fifteen minutes. I know how to work under pressure, and I willed my hands to work faster, bent down now, chewing through the seconds with greater haste now. Damn, I felt full, but of course that was to be expected with more than three pounds of glorious American beef already put away. Once or twice I had to adjust my seat, and move back from the table just to take a breath, only for seconds, and then back to it. The crowd was calling out their support, and I looked up to give a working smile as I kept swallowing into an obvious pain building in my upper stomach. The cowboys and the pioneers and the captains of industry and the marines and the moms and the astronauts of this great land all played through the pain to create America, and so would I.

"Five minutes" called Todd from my peripheral left, and for some odd reason the practiced staff of The Big Texan placed a large trash can at my elbow, just in case...

Hell I thought, I couldn't look that bad, but I knew a deadly truth. Whatever the causative physiologic mishap, I was now fighting not only the clock, but also a solid column of packed steak extending upward from my stomach into the upper esophagus. It was a simple mechanical blockage at this point, not necessarily harmful, but one that would not budge. I sloshed more tea in, fought back the urge to lose it, swallowing hard to force just one more bite, come on now, at least one more... My eyes were tearing and my vision blurred, as the waves of nausea came at me again. (Todd's wife later told me that I on-camera looked really uncomfortable in those last few minutes). *"One minute left"* Todd called, and I stabbed at a last hunk, forcing it in. I had not tasted anything for the last ten minutes at least, and my digestive system now resembled the runner going on automatic through *"the wall"* in some insane marathon. Thirty seconds? Chew NOW, oh no, the nausea, fight back the urge, blink the watery eyes, chew, swallow... won't...budge...

Time. The waitress came to pat me on the back, and motioned to the trashcan, reminding me if I needed it. *"Let's give him a big hand y'all"* she called to the crowd and I rose painfully, a nod to the crowd, and walked unsteadily to the men's room. Standing inside the stall, waiting for the nausea to subside, which it did after several long minutes, I grimly reaffirmed that there was no way in hell I was going to hurl and humiliate myself in front of the crowd and my supporters out in cyberspace. Finally I felt safe enough to return to the dining hall and straightened, washed my face with a cold, wet paper towel, and returned to face that evening's part of my legacy.

I hate to lose, and I had lost. The routine is to weigh the portion remaining for those who fall short. I had been stopped just four small ounces short of eternity. There would be no certificate, and my name would not appear on the list of honor among better men and women that had won on earlier days. The waitresses were sweet and clucked over me, thanking me for being such a good sport, and presented me with the consolation Big Texan logo T-shirt that proclaims "The 72 oz. Steak - I Tried to Eat It All!!!" I had indeed, but had failed and will forever refer to my prize as the "loser shirt." Outwardly a good sport, I walked glumly back across the dusty parking lot in defeat to the motel, whereupon I went to the bathroom and made myself throw up. The quest was ended.

❖ ❖ ❖

Epilogue

An hour later, in less pain now, Todd suggested that we drive a round and kill some time while it was still light. We had an early morning flight the next morning back to work and new chapters. I felt physically beaten, and the several phone calls from my webcam fans weren't helping. I couldn't believe after years of eating ridiculous amounts of dead animal flesh and quaffing it with gallons of beer, I had blown it all four lousy ounces shy of the finish line. My friend who years before gave the brilliant speech about the "most expensive coat" called to cheer me, reminding me that now I knew exactly what I had to do next time to win the contest. But no, there would be no next time. The point of the exercise was one great (and futile) rocket's flight of glory, win or lose, and while I never in my worst fears considered defeat a possibility, there would be no magic in a repeat attempt. To go again would merely seem pitiful, proof to the cosmos and the next bus of retirees that a gaudy tourist gimmick was living rent-free in my future. I don't like the concept of "accepting defeat." We can recognize, or acknowledge, or admit the very real fact of a defeat without ever accepting it. This was no false pep talk I was giving myself: I HATE losing. But driving through the Amarillo streets, my poor sore abdomen not yet having resumed speaking terms with its owner, I started to take stock of the day and its place. We had ridden the stratosphere to Las Vegas, and the rental car through deserts, past craters and street corners, into and through the core of American freedom that has not and will not be beaten down by the little minds and lesser spirits. This land gave birth to a new version of human endeavor that had simmered in the civilization crock-pot for three millennia or so before being poured hot and bubbling all over this continent. But for all the critical importance of the frontier in the development of our crazy-ass national psyche, it could not contain what it nurtured. From America the Beautiful has risen America the Idea, loose upon an interconnected, internet-wired world where the best will never be quite good enough ever again. The idea of a free man has grown and evolved so from the ancients to a degree in the modern world that all the thugs, concerned talk show hosts, do-gooder collectivists and moderate Republicans will never again be able to beat it down. Whether or not it remains in bloom on the North American continent, America will continue to flourish wherever in the world men and women seek their own interests, and a really good time.

I was feeling a bit more sanguine as the streetlights came on, and we drove by a large western clothing store. It looked like a cool place, and we pulled in to check it out. It was huge inside, brightly lit, with every imaginable work, casual, or dress garment for both men and women. Displays of hats, cowboy boots, work clothes, and jewelry of turquoise and silver beckoned to the shoppers. There was thankfully nothing reminiscent of food in the entire store, and the air condition felt good now that my sweating had completely gone. Feeling more my old self, but not really paying attention to any display in particular, I wandered into the luggage section. There on an end-aisle display sat a brand new travel bag, of the hanging variety. It was light brown heavy canvas, with large cream-colored leather flaps stitched into it, and heavy double-stitched leather handle, whose straps were fastened with bright silver-plate buckles. While my origins are southern, *not western, something about the bag answered a question. The day was gone, but not lost. The zipper on my old trusty travel bag was shot, and it had seen travels and miles not to be forgotten, but like this trip now properly left behind. Over the years and miles leading to this spot I had seen and enjoyed enough to leave me as qualified as anyone to love the American dream for all it had afforded me. The fact that I had enjoyed a lot more breaks and advantages than the average bear in no way diminishes the fact that those breaks occurred in the country most likely to produce them. My American forbears were either smarter, harder working, more talented, or maybe just luckier than everyone else, but to be apologetic for my happiness and aspirations would be to betray the amazing legacy left to me. As most of us have to one degree or another, I had accomplished a few things, screwed up more than a few, knocked some paint off the hull, and survived it all. The bag cost $200, and that was about all I had left of my travel cash. It all fell into place as I plunked my cash down and left the store with the new bag and a grin. The quest was ended, the trip was over, and I was grateful to have taken it. It was time to start a new one, and I was looking forward to it.*